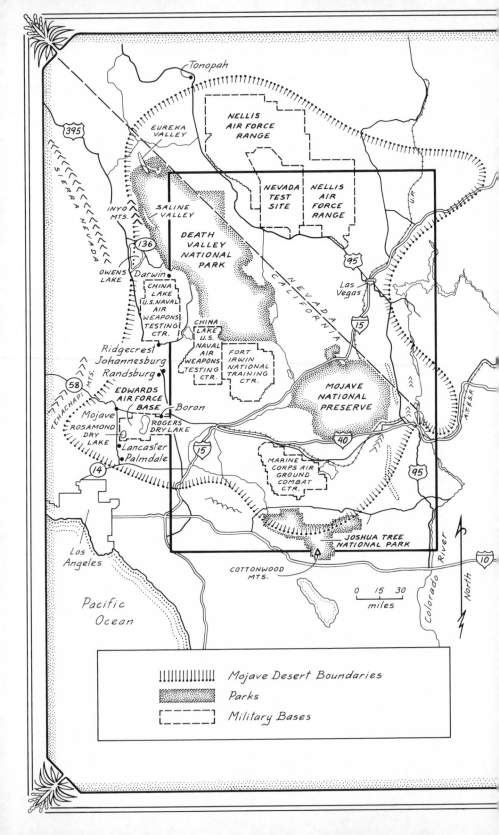

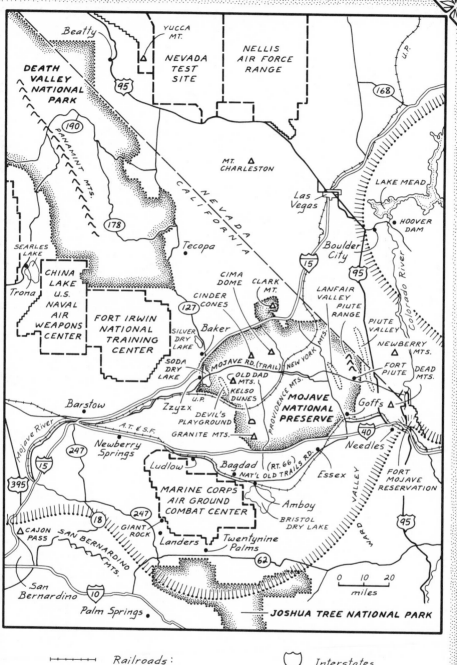

DEATH
VALLEY
NATIONAL
PARK

Beatty

YUCCA
MT.

NEVADA
TEST
SITE

NELLIS
AIR FORCE
RANGE

95

168

U.P.

190

PANAMINT MTS.

178

MT.
CHARLESTON

NEVADA

CALIFORNIA

LAKE MEAD

Las
Vegas

HOOVER
DAM

15

Boulder
City

95

Colorado River

SEARLES
LAKE

Trona

CHINA
LAKE
U.S.
NAVAL
AIR
WEAPONS
CENTER

FORT IRWIN
NATIONAL
TRAINING
CENTER

Tecopa

127

SILVER
DRY
LAKE

Baker

CIMA
DOME

CINDER
CONES

CLARK
MT.

LANFAIR
VALLEY

PIUTE
RANGE

PIUTE
VALLEY

NEWBERRY
MTS.

SODA
DRY
LAKE

MOJAVE RD. (TRAIL)

NEW YORK MTS.

FORT
PIUTE

DEAD
MTS.

Barstow

Mojave River

A.T. & S.F.

Zzyzx

U.P.

OLD DAD
MTS.

KELSO
DUNES

DEVIL'S
PLAYGROUND

GRANITE MTS.

PROVIDENCE MTS.

MOJAVE
NATIONAL
PRESERVE

Goffs

40

Needles

247

Newberry
Springs

Ludlow

Bagdad (RT. 66)

NAT'L OLD TRAILS RD.

Essex

FORT
MOJAVE
RESERVATION

15

395

247

18

GIANT
ROCK

MARINE CORPS
AIR GROUND
COMBAT CENTER

Amboy

BRISTOL
DRY
LAKE

WARD VALLEY

95

CAJON
PASS

SAN BERNARDINO MTS.

Landers

Twentynine
Palms

62

0   10   20
miles

San
Bernardino

10

Palm Springs

JOSHUA TREE NATIONAL PARK

Railroads:

A.T. & S.F. — Atchison Topeka
& Santa Fe

U.P. — Union Pacific

Interstates

U.S. Highways

State Roads

THE
MOJAVE

A Portrait of the
Definitive American Desert

DAVID
DARLINGTON

AN OWL BOOK
HENRY HOLT AND COMPANY
NEW YORK

Henry Holt and Company, Inc.
Publishers since 1866
115 West 18th Street
New York, New York 10011

Henry Holt® is a registered
trademark of Henry Holt and Company, Inc.

Library of Congress Cataloging-in-Publication Data
Darlington, David.
The Mojave: a portrait of the definitive American desert /
David Darlington.
p.   cm.
Includes bibliographical references and index.
1. Mojave Desert (Calif.)—Description and travel.   2. Darlington,
David—Journeys—California—Mojave Desert.   I. Title.
F865.M65D37   1996   95-42056
979.4'95—dc20   CIP

ISBN 0-8050-5594-0

Henry Holt books are available for special promotions and
premiums. For details contact: Director, Special Markets.

Portions of this book appeared, in somewhat
different form, in *Audubon* and *Outside*.

First published in hardcover in 1996
by Henry Holt and Company, Inc.

First Owl Book Edition—1997

Designed by Paula R. Szafranski
Map by Jackie Aher
Illustration by Leslie Evans

Printed in the United States of America
All first editions are printed on acid-free paper.∞

1   3   5   7   9   10   8   6   4   2

With gratitude, affection, and admiration, this book
is dedicated to the triple-S desert threat:

Russell Shay, Debbie Sease, and
Patty "Shortcut" Schifferle

CONTENTS

EXTRACTS

The desert, any desert, is indeed the valley of the shadow of death.

Joan Didion, *Slouching Towards Bethlehem*, 1965

I know what they tell you about the desert but you mustn't believe them. This is no deathbed.

Barry Lopez, *Desert Notes*, 1976

In the desert, there is all—and yet nothing. . . . God is there, and man is not.

Honoré de Balzac, *Passion in the Desert,* 1896

Desert is a loose term to indicate land that supports no man; whether the land can be bitted and broken to that purpose is not proven. Void of life it never is, however dry the air and villainous the soil. . . . If one is inclined to wonder at first how so many dwellers came to be in the loneliest land that ever came out of God's hands, what they do there and why stay, one does not wonder so much after having lived there. None other than this long brown land lays such a hold on the affections.

Mary Austin, *The Land of Little Rain*, 1903

Men and women who are at her mercy find it hard to see in Nature and her works any symbols but those of brute power at the best and, at the worst, of an obscure and mindless malice. The desert's emptiness and the desert's silence reveal what we may call their spiritual meaning only to those who enjoy some measure of physiological security.

Aldous Huxley, *Tomorrow and Tomorrow and Tomorrow*, 1956

It is easier to accept the message of the stars than the message of the salt desert. The stars speak of man's insignificance in the long eternity of time; the desert speaks of his insignificance right now.

Edwin Way Teale, *Autumn Across America*, 1956

The desert says nothing. Completely passive, acted upon but never acting, the desert lies there like the bare skeleton of Being, spare, sparse, austere, utterly worthless, inviting not love but contemplation. . . . There is something about the desert that the human sensibility cannot assimilate. . . . I am convinced now that the desert has no heart, that it presents a riddle which has no answer, and that the riddle itself is an illusion created by some limitation or exaggeration of the displaced human consciousness.

Edward Abbey, *Desert Solitaire*, 1968

To those who do listen, the desert speaks of things with an emphasis quite different from that of the shore, the mountains, the valleys or the plains. Whereas they invite action and suggest limitless opportunity, exhaustless resources, the implications and the mood of the desert are something different. For one thing the desert is conservative, not radical. It is more likely to provoke awe than to invite conquest. . . . In intimate details, as when its floor is covered after a spring rain with the delicate little ephemeral plants, it is pretty. But such embodiments of prettiness seem to be only tolerated with affectionate contempt by the region as a whole. As a whole the desert is, in the original sense of the word, "awful."

Joseph Wood Krutch, *The Voice of the Desert*, 1954

The weird solitude, the great silence, the grim desolation, are the very things with which every desert wanderer eventually falls in love. You think that very strange perhaps? Well, the beauty of the ugly was sometime a paradox, but to-day people admit its truth; and the grandeur of the desolate is just as paradoxical, yet the desert gives it proof.

John C. Van Dyke, *The Desert*, 1901

As interesting and provocative as the cultural geography might be, the desert may serve better as the backdrop for the problematic relationship between man and the environment. The human struggle, the successes and failures, the use and abuse, both noble and foolish, are readily apparent in the desert. Symbols and relationships seem to arise that stand for the human condition itself. It is a simple, if almost incomprehensible, equation: The world is as terrible as it is beautiful, but when you look more closely, it is as beautiful as it is terrible.

Richard Misrach, *Desert Cantos*, 1987

The geographical, geological, and other natural history features of our desert domains are so varied and with them are bound up so many entrancing problems that twenty years of intimate acquaintance and wide travel over the arid Southwest have not desiccated my ardor for continued study and wide wandering nor lessened my eagerness to lead others to the heart of my kingdom of joy.

Edmund C. Jaeger, *The California Deserts*, 1933

Most Americans who talk about the problems of "the desert" are talking about the Mojave. It is the best-known, most visited, and most studied of American deserts; but it is also, in an important historical sense, the most reliably typical of American deserts, the national standard. . . . No wonder it is the desert of definition for so many Americans—studied, loved, quarreled over.

Reyner Banham, *Scenes in America Deserta*, 1982

DESERT OF DEFINITION

The desert is evil. It is deadly and barren and lonely and foreboding and oppressive and godforsaken. Its silence and emptiness breed madness. Its plant forms are strangely twisted, as are its citizens, who live there because they can't get along anywhere else. Charlie Manson. Brigham Young. Bugsy Siegel. Carlos Castaneda and Don Juan's demons. Moses. In history and myth, the desert is the barrier to the Promised Land—our realm of trial and exile, the place where people go to be punished, seeking wisdom born of misery. Since modern transportation has compromised this relationship, reducing the desert's danger by abbreviating the time required to cross it, about the best thing you can say about the place is that it is boring. Aside from random deposits of minerals, it is valuable mainly as a zone in which to shed the shackles of civilization, race cars on infinitely straight highways, bask naked in unending sun, shoot guns at rocks and road signs, careen across sand hills on dirt bikes and dune buggies. In the desert, one is liberated from all restraint because nobody's around to notice. That's why we explode atom bombs there. Or dump things that might create problems elsewhere. They can't do any damage in the desert; there's nothing out there to damage.

Or so it was thought until rather recently, when the blinders were somehow removed and a new view was revealed to civilization: *the desert is beautiful!* It has limitless stretches of space, awesome landforms that loom up like monoliths, carpets of wildflowers that proliferate after rains. The crystalline air is inflamed twice daily, at dawn and dusk, when the landscape is washed in mauve and ocher and scarlet and vermilion. Far from oppressive, the desert is refreshingly free of clutter and contagion—"clean," in T. E. Lawrence's phrase—which is perhaps why Europeans in particular seem to be drawn to it (aside from the fact that they don't have anything like it at home). As for its supposed desolation, the desert is in fact full of life: hardy flora, resourceful fauna, a panoply of human artifacts no less stimulating than they are unsettling—dinosaur statues, opera houses in the middle of nowhere, buildings made entirely of bottles, rocks painted to resemble fish. The character of the place once considered so barren is now redefined as "austere." In the same way that Alaska has risen to an exalted place in the national consciousness after long being considered a wasteland fit only for polar bears and Eskimos, the desert—purportedly the exclusive province of rattlesnakes and prospectors—is now recognized as a fragile and fascinating environment. Indeed, in pristineness, population, precipitation, orneriness, and vulnerability to abuse, the desert has more in common with the Arctic than any other place on the North American continent. Deeply and utterly profound in its silence, it possesses inexhaustible mystery. Here, as nowhere else, one feels free.

This "new" view really isn't. The desert has always had its adherents—people who valued it for its beauty, its solitude, its science. The recent ascendancy of the New View of the desert owes its existence to the popular rise of environmental consciousness, to the American migration to the Sunbelt, and in no small measure to Madison Avenue's expedient embrace of "Santa Fe style." I don't suppose it would be honest to claim that I was converted to the New View by any influences other than these. I made my first trip through the desert soon after Earth Day in 1970, albeit for the same reason that most Americans did and do: to get from one coast to the other. Having spent my whole life up to that point within the humid purview of the Atlantic Ocean, I still recall how bleak Interstate 10 seemed east of Palm Springs, how alienating the dehydrated rockscape, how unnatural the absence of noise. The monumental emptiness of the place seemed a frightening weight to bear. The desert struck me as an enormous vacuum—a void, like outer space.

I later discussed these notions with a native Coloradan, who told me that she considered the East prettier than the West but found herself frustrated there because "you can't walk anywhere—there's *green* stuff all over the place." It took me several subsequent years of living on the West Coast, backpacking in the Sierra Nevada, skirting the edges of the Great Basin, and learning about arid-land ecology to develop the same sort of feeling. After a decade of such education, I finally acquired the wherewithal to mount an intentional fact-finding expedition into the California desert.

Not incidentally, I did it in the company of a friend with whom I had also spent time in the Arctic. Our destination, inevitably, was Death Valley—the place that has probably experienced the greatest reversal of reputation as a result of the New View. We arranged to meet at a trailer park near the town of Mojave, from which we made a classic drive along the northeasterly route commonly followed by people coming from the coast: Past the weird limestone pinnacles near Trona, where the Kerr-McGee Corporation mined chemicals from a dry lake bed, the air smelled putrid and stores were painted green, apparently to impart some impression of photosynthesis. Through the town of Ridgecrest, where we got lost inside the China Lake Naval Air Weapons Testing Center (I have no idea how we got in), and upon leaving saw a sign that said: WHAT YOU DO HERE, WHAT YOU SEE HERE, LET IT STAY HERE. Across the expanse of Panamint Valley, Death Valley's enormous sibling, where Manson & Company lived in an abandoned ranch house up an all but impassable canyon while awaiting Helter Skelter. Into storied Death Valley itself, where at midday we rested in the shade and swam in the pool but at dawn and dusk exposed great quantities of celluloid to the effects of light on a landscape devoid of cover, a veritable multiring circus of unexpurgated geology.

The most provocative place was a remote basin three hours by car from any telephones, utilities, or asphalt—an ancient lake bed strewn with greasewood and volcanic debris, ascending into alluvial fans that resembled earthen glaciers thousands of feet deep. The valley's western wall, a range of eleven-thousand-foot-high mountains, concealed astounding year-round streams that stay cool even when the air temperature reaches 120 degrees. Where these streams merged with the valley floor, they formed a salt marsh that serves as a haven for invertebrates and migrating birds. North of the marsh were sand dunes—the beach at the edge of the vanished Pleistocene lake—and beyond the dunes was the magnet that had drawn us, the pièce de résistance: a pair of hot springs that sat in the baking sand of the basin like imperturbable Arabian mullahs.

To reach this obscure and isolated place, my friend and I traversed two mountain ranges, guessing our way along an unsigned route, passing occasional water bottles set out to aid drivers in distress, winding through high passes of piñon and juniper, bouncing over washboarded dirt roads that destroyed our car's air conditioner. As we descended into the basin, the late sun threw the naked hills into sweeping relief, their brick- and chocolate-colored bands glowing a surreal orange. Gradually the granite mountainsides gave way to glimpses of the valley floor, its alkaline surface shining like a dream—and not necessarily a nice one. More than one person has disappeared without a trace in this area, prompting the *Los Angeles Times* to tag the place the Bermuda Triangle of California.

We turned off for the springs at a rock that was painted like a bat. After driving eight more miles up a sandy track, we made out some cars and trailers—even an airplane—arranged around a low stand of mesquite. We assumed we'd arrived when we saw a naked man walking down the road. As we passed the lower of the two springs, we encountered that indefatigable camel of the California desert—a Volkswagen bus—backing up while its driver, a guy with a gray beard and a headband, yelled something out his window at a Doberman loping alongside. A few minutes later, this bus pulled in behind us at the upper spring, unloading a half-dozen time travelers from the sixties. While we were walking around looking for a campsite, the group's dogs got into a fight. When I glanced over, I heard a fat guy comment: "I don't like the way that asshole's looking at me."

When the sun went down, we made our way to one of the hot pools, where somebody handed me a pair of binoculars and showed me Halley's comet. Bats swooped low over the tubs as we soaked in 105-degree water beneath a billion stars. Unfortunately the Doberman party proceeded to keep us awake all night, with one of their number yelling, "*I feel good!*" at regular intervals. At dawn he was accompanied by a wild burro braying off in the bush, which encouraged the dogs to join in.

Morning revealed our whereabouts: an oasis in the middle of an enormous saline bowl, surrounded by striated mountains, with creosote and burro brush dotting the desert as far as the eye could see. Mesquite, arrow weed, and fan palms grew around the spring; the hot water from the source, a natural well surrounded by grass, trickled down to two bathing pools—one a raised oval, the other a sunken hexagon. A pair of giant peace signs had been scraped onto nearby cinder cones, and an outhouse stood off in the scrub, wittily equipped with a seat belt and a sign that said: PATROLLED BY LOW-FLYING AIRCRAFT. Sure enough, as the sun began to climb, fighter jets appeared over the horizon, passing a hundred feet over the springs, well in advance of their engines' own roar.

While my friend and I were eating breakfast, the fat guy wandered over. He was wearing an olive-drab army jacket and a black wool watch cap. "Hi!" he said, staring at us intently.

"Hi."

"Real free country out here, huh?"

We nodded.

"We really love it out here," he said. "We're from Darwin [a mining town to the south]. My name's John."

Tentatively, we shook his hand. "What do you do in Darwin, John?"

"Whatever I want."

We chewed our granola; John kept staring. I wondered if maybe he wanted something to eat.

"I used to live here," he finally said. "People called me Dirty John because I never took a bath. We come out here to get away from the telephone poles and power lines. If we do anything that offends you, just let us know."

"Well," I volunteered, "I guess I thought you could have been a little quieter last night."

John shrugged. "We're working on it," he said. He started to turn away but then thought better of it. "You know," he said, "we come out here to be by ourselves and do what we want."

"With all these other people around?"

"Listen," he said. "I can show you lots of beautiful places where you can go to be by yourself. If you try to control people here, you're gonna get in trouble."

"Right," I said, and turned to my companion to ask if he thought it was all right to use soap in the dishwashing pool.

"You can do whatever you want," said Dirty John. "It's your place."

That afternoon, we hiked up a canyon in the nearby mountains. We found a rope at the top of a beautiful perennial waterfall that fed a fecund microenvironment of willows, ferns, and angel hair. At sunset we chased the light across the dunes, but it kept disappearing from the next ridge as we slogged doggedly along, barefoot. Finally we gave up, sat down, and listened to the quiet (the flyboys had called it a day) while the lowering sun turned the distant alluvial fans into giant root systems. A warm wind was blowing across the dunes, and as we sat there, we knew the intoxication—the giddy, unfettered freedom—of the desert.

We had no plans to revisit the hot spring—extended relations with Dirty John and the Dobermans weren't what we'd come here for—but those plans changed (as did our sense of freedom) when we returned to the car and heard a hiss coming from our left front tire. The infamous roads had taken their toll. We made our way back to the campground, which contained the only congregation of people within three hours' drive.

This time, however, we went to the lower spring. As we pulled in, we encountered a couple of septuagenarians wearing nothing but straw hats. When we announced our predicament, one of them said, "Bring the tire over by the pool; we'll spray some water on it and find the leak." The other one went and got his truck, which came equipped with a compressor. He used it to fill the tire after a third guy plugged it with rubber and glue. Pretty soon, we were relaxing in the pool with no worries.

The situation was completely different from that at the upper spring. There were several pools, a lot of shade, a dishwashing sink, a goldfish pond, a circle of couches, a lawn with a sign that said BERMUDA GRASS TRIANGLE, and a paperback library divided into sections ("Action," "Mystery," "Lust"). The person who'd plugged my tire turned out to be "Major Tom" Ganner, the official campground host. As an unpaid volunteer for the U.S. Bureau of Land Management (BLM), which controlled the property, Ganner lived at the spring year round—even in summer, when he said the main problem was sleeping on sheets that were hotter than the air. As we reclined in the tub, he told us that the upper spring tended to attract transient visitors; this one had a more committed clientele. Nevertheless, the BLM had a six-month limit on the length of any stay.

"There is no law here," Ganner proclaimed. "There are just varying degrees of common courtesy and consideration. For example, people have to put up with John, as long as he doesn't do anything too outrageous. We've had Manson people pass through here, but they're really more of a pain in the ass than anything else. People *have* been asked to leave; if somebody brandishes a gun, I get on the radio and the county sheriff comes over from Independence. But the percentage of problem people is real small. It seems to work out that the people we like to have around are the ones that come back."

It was a decidedly nonlinear universe, this terrestrial outer space. Though nowhere near as removed as the Arctic, which after all remains innocent of roads, it was still a largely anarchic kingdom where one was expected to get along without being ordered or nursed—a kind of lawless commons where people had to find their way with few directions of any kind. The hot springs were maintained solely by the people who visited them; the pools had been built by volunteers. The place was a free zone in the middle of nowhere, an antibureaucratic Eden. As such, it seemed the epitome of the American desert: a decidedly eccentric environment whose overarching quality is *openness*, established and encouraged by the landscape itself.

Which made the petition pretty interesting.

Next to the hot pool was a handbill condemning something called the California Desert Protection Act, a measure that had recently been introduced in Congress by Senator Alan Cranston. The act aimed to create eighty-two new desert wilderness areas totaling 4.5 million acres, plus a new Mojave National Park, while expanding the boundaries of Death Valley and Joshua Tree National Monuments and declaring them bona fide national parks as well. Under the proposed legislation, the area surrounding the hot spring would be designated as wilderness, and virtually the entire valley would become part of Death Valley National Park. According to the petition, the act intended to preserve the desert "for the enjoyment of future generations rather than for us." Attached was a pen for dissident visitors to sign their names.

I didn't sign, but I was vexed by the issue. As a rule, I'm all for wilderness; but it seemed that the area's ungoverned mystique would surely evaporate if it became part of a national park. From Yellowstone to Yosemite, our nation has no shortage of unique, trampled spots; while blank white areas on the map can catalyze the imagination, green ones are magnets for Winnebagos—and Ticketron reservations for the hot spring would be an obvious contradiction in its terms. On the other hand, owing to the absence of regulation, miners had defiled various sections of the valley, trees had been torn down in the canyon for firewood, and motorcycles crisscrossed the ancient basin floor as heedlessly as they might a supermarket parking lot. The bill was obviously designed to bring such problems under control.

Later I researched the Desert Protection Act and found that it had arisen in response to another federal arid-lands extravaganza: the California Desert Plan, which had been instituted in 1980 by the BLM. This plan—at the time, the largest regional planning effort ever attempted in the United States—directed the BLM to "manage, use, develop, and protect" the twelve million acres of California desert under its control. In so doing, it carved the area into a variety of zones. Two million acres were designated as wilderness study areas; the remainder was zoned for intensive, moderate, or limited development, including mining, grazing, off-road vehicle activity, and oil and gas exploration. While environmental groups were less than thrilled by it, they had initially gone along. After all, President Jimmy Carter and Interior Secretary Cecil Andrus were about to be replaced by Ronald Reagan and James Watt; and, indeed, the Desert Plan was considered so restrictive by developers that the BLM was taken to court by Inyo County, the California Mining Authority, and the American Motorcyclists Association. In an effort to mollify these plaintiffs, the BLM reduced its recommendations for wilderness and allowed, among other things, the resumption of the Barstow–Las Vegas motorcycle race, which had been outlawed since 1975. As a result, the Sierra Club abandoned its support of the plan and began assembling the sweeping conservationist components of the Desert Protection Act—which was in turn seen as a betrayal by the forces that had already compromised with environmentalists to create the BLM Desert Plan.

"If it weren't for national parks, the dickheads wouldn't know where to go," Ganner commented as we reclined in the hot tub. "It's weird in Death Valley—you pull over by the side of the road to make a pot of coffee, and a ranger shows up with a badge and a gun and an attitude on. There's a sense of freedom here that doesn't exist in many places anymore, and it doesn't cost one dime of taxpayers' money."

"They can have Death Valley," commented one of the elderly gents who'd fixed my tire. "They should let us have our place."

In the years immediately following that trip, I made several more sojourns in the desert—sometimes on journalistic assignment, other times simply for the sake of exploration. Wherever I went, two things never failed to occur. I was always asked to state my position on the Desert Protection Act, usually by people who lived in the desert and opposed it. Also, I found that people I met in the desert were never indifferent about it. The desert was an active force in their emotional lives, more like another person than a place. They might be viewed as misfits by people from outside, but they weren't in the desert by accident; they were there because they loved it.

Observing the controversy over the Desert Protection Act, I realized that something intrinsic was at work in the argument. The desert has historically occupied the most antiregulatory place in the American imagination: its residents and adherents have been people who wanted, in one way or another, to be left alone. In this sense, it has truly served (again, along with Alaska) as our last frontier. The modern fact of the matter, however, is that *this* frontier now lies within a day's drive of forty million people, greatly decreasing the possibility of being "left alone." As the swelling population of southern California, in particular, exhibits an ever-greater appetite for recreation and relief, this desert is increasingly a destination for many disparate groups and types: hikers, ranchers, photographers, miners, biologists, geologists, off-road-vehicle users. Like suitors vying for the same bride, each prizes the desert jealously and distrusts the intentions—indeed the very presence—of the others.

There was no small irony in this transformation of such a long-overlooked, if not outright maligned, region into a coveted object of ardor. The dissonance between the Old and New Views of the desert had, it seemed, grown to a fever pitch rather quickly. Practically overnight, this once obscure empire of emancipation had become an area of intense antipathy—a budding, and surprising, environmental battleground.

It shouldn't really have been surprising that the desert I visited on that first trip turned out to be pregnant with significance. It was, after all, the most visible, the most vulnerable, the most emblematic—i.e., the quintessential—American desert: the Mojave.

As the smallest North American desert, the Mojave seems to have exerted an outsized influence on the public imagination. This might be due to its geographic situation between the infamous urban poles of Los Angeles and Las Vegas, a location that has surely made it the most *filmed* desert in the world. In the heyday of the cinematic Western, the Mojave was the most prolific location, and today it's impossible to watch television for an hour without seeing a commercial that was shot there—on a dry lake bed, in a Joshua-tree forest, in front of a run-down gas station or café. The products advertised in this setting, I've noticed, run overwhelmingly toward cars, blue jeans, and beer. It's safe to say that, as far as popular American imagery is concerned, the sere visage of the Mojave Desert is considered somehow definitive.

The Mojave contains Death Valley—the lowest, hottest place in the Western Hemisphere and, excepting the Sahara, the world's most notorious picture of a desert. It is the site of Edwards Air Force Base, where Chuck Yeager broke the sound barrier and the space shuttle continues to land periodically on a Pleistocene lake. It contains the westernmost portion of fabled U.S. Route 66, Steinbeck's and the nation's "road of flight," lately eclipsed by the interstates but immortalized by Mssrs. Maharis and Milner and their Chevy Corvette. And, yes, it includes Las Vegas, America's homegrown Sodom and Gomorrah, whose love song to licentiousness has prompted Joan Didion to call it "the most extreme and allegorical of American settlements, bizarre and beautiful in its venality and its devotion to immediate gratification."

Among North America's deserts, the Mojave actually occupies a relatively narrow ecological niche. Located in southeastern California, southern Nevada, and a tiny corner of southwestern Utah, between the higher, cooler Great Basin Desert to the north and the lower, hotter Colorado Desert to the south, the Mojave is a transition zone combining elements of each. The northernmost section, where I first traveled, is an obvious extension of the Basin and Range Province, containing spectacular elevational contrasts over distances of only a few miles. The moister heights, though spartan, are sufficiently verdant with piñon and juniper that they hardly seem to qualify as "desert," while the lower, more southerly portions contain plants commonly associated with Mexico. The Mojave is hot in the summer (average daily maximum temperatures often exceed one hundred degrees Fahrenheit), but it also receives snow in the winter. Deserts are often defined as areas receiving less than ten inches of precipitation annually, with a rate of potential evaporation exceeding that of precipitation. The Mojave receives an average of one to five inches of precipitation per year, and its rate of potential evaporation is more than seventy. It gets most of its moisture during the winter from the remnants of Pacific storms, but the Sierra Nevada, Tehachapi, San Bernardino, and San Gabriel Mountains are an effective barrier to precipitation—the overriding reason for the dryness of the Mojave Desert.

Despite its archetypal status, the Mojave doesn't necessarily fit the classical picture of a desert. Only in limited areas, for example, does it contain sand dunes (as does only 2 percent of the arid United States); few of its surfaces are covered by sagebrush, that totemic shrub of the Great Basin; neither is it the home of the saguaro, the tall, upright-armed cactus that is wholly confined to the Sonoran Desert. The botanical symbol of the Mojave is, rather, the "grotesque" and spiny-armed Joshua tree, which occupies this desert exclusively. Most particularly, the Mojave isn't flat: it is everywhere characterized by mountains—etched, parched, naked mountains rising as abruptly as islands from a sea. In fact these mountains, their brown flanks strewn with flesh-colored sand, are burying themselves in their own debris. From their cleftlike canyons, storm-driven rocks and boulders have poured forth and spread out over millennia, building enormous, water-streaked alluvial slopes. Where several such fans join, they form bajadas—long sedimentary grades, dotted with cactus and creosote bush, descending gently to the desert floor. The basins at the bottom have no outlets (that is the geological definition of a basin, as opposed to a valley), so when rare rainfall collects and evaporates, it leaves behind alkaline deposits where almost nothing will grow. Seen from a distance, the white surfaces of these dry lakes—the only truly flat parts of the Mojave—gleam like lambent dreams among the duller desert browns. At the edges of selected basins, dunes collect like enormous piles of whipped cream. Interspersed randomly throughout the milieu is the checker-colored evidence of volcanic upheaval: burnt red cinder cones and charred black lava flows, laid bare by lack of rain.

The natural condition of humankind in this landscape is one of dauntedness. To define the scenery as "breathtaking" doesn't explain exactly how it takes away your breath: by sitting on your chest and pressing on your head. The Mojave is overwhelming, both physically and psychologically, partly because of the utter absence of moisture, but largely because of the sheer visual scale. Unobscured by vegetation, displayed to the eye for tremendous distances by huge elevations and depressions, it seems a world of crystal clarity and total exposure. In its enormity, it constantly challenges you to comprehend it, to come to terms with infinity. The curve of a bajada against the sky might be the edge of Earth itself. You drive toward distant points for hours without reaching them. Traveling in the Mojave, you feel adrift in space.

To understand this sensation—to fully grasp the psychic/spatial role of the twentieth-century desert—it might be necessary to spend time in the Los Angeles Basin. Crossing the passes, Cajon and San Gorgonio, that descend from the desert into the metropolitan area—especially at night—is to comprehend the attitude of space shuttle pilots as they enter the atmosphere of Earth. You descend from a noiseless, uncircumscribed realm to a conflagration of lights and radio stations, of civilized static and corporeal encumbrance. Traveling in the other direction—to the desert from L.A.—you go *out* and *up*. Clearing the passes, you feel cut loose from the urban milieu as surely as astronauts are released from gravity's restraint. In its undefined sprawl, negotiated over great distances in rapidly propelled capsules from one galaxy or asteroid to another, Los Angeles itself isn't *unlike* space; but it doesn't begin to approach, of course, the size, emptiness, or silence of the desert. If L.A. is space, the Mojave is truly outer space.

Owing to its freedom from confinement, the desert kindles a kind of epiphany as a matter of course—an almost physical sense of liberation, a sudden, sensual delight of being that is like nothing else. Whenever I arrive in the Mojave (even after repeated visits and considerable cumulative experience), it turns out to be emptier, more wide-open, than I remembered. Yet for every moment of freedom I've known there, I can recall an equivalent moment of despair—a time when the emptiness seemed excruciating, the dryness unforgiving, the vastness intimidating and incomprehensible. In the desert, my mood swings describe an especially wide arc. Each extreme of this emotional pendulum is probably a response to the shedding of civilization—both its comforts and its constraints. But the ready and absolute disclosure of such feelings is, I think, again attributable to the overall lack of obfuscation. Emotions here, like everything else, are completely exposed.

So you might ask: If everything in the desert is open for inspection, why does it exude such a palpable aspect of mystery?

One time, traveling with a group of people in the eastern Mojave, I remarked on the visual character of its mountain ranges, so concisely contained and defined. "They seem to hold all the secrets of the universe," mused one member of the group; and despite the Sierra Club–style hyperbole, she was right. In their innumerable folds and creases, their obvious role as refuges from their surroundings, the fortresslike ranges of the desert appear to hoard much information. Yet if you probe them—ascend the alluvial fans, enter the canyons, climb over the cliffs—secrets are not readily released. There will be lizards; there will be rocks; there will be sunbaked, uncomplaining plants. In some cases there might be springs, feeding fecund riparian environments of willows and ferns; if you're lucky, you might find an Indian petroglyph or glimpse a bighorn sheep. But usually there will just be more heat, more aridity, more infernal blinding emptiness. The desert seems simply a desert—a very dry place. Yet the aura of mystery persists.

This is the essential piquancy—the visceral, perceptual sting—of travel in the Mojave. Confronted by apparent openness, you find yourself unaccountably intrigued. Is the desert forthcoming or is it mysterious? Is it barren or full of life? Is it a realm of freedom or oppression? A place of peace or animosity? Of tranquillity or insecurity?

The answer, of course, is all of the above. The Mojave is an unceasing contradiction, a continual koan, a riddle designed to confound preconceptions. It's a wilderness defined by human ambition, an empty place full of activity, a blank slate brimming with meaning, an overflowing void. Confronting it, we return to something resembling our attitude when we first entered the world: vulnerable and defensive, excited and terrified, at ease and in danger of desolation. Exploring it, we investigate not merely our most misunderstood landscape but our own perplexing, profound hopes and fears.

A WEIRD AND REPULSIVE
COUNTENANCE

One morning in January 1991, I found myself at the Cottonwood visitor center in Joshua Tree National Monument—150 miles east of Los Angeles, 50 miles east of Palm Springs, and 5 miles north of Interstate 10, in the northernmost extremity of the Colorado Desert. I had left the Mojave the previous night, when I drove in from the north and dropped below the fifteen-hundred-foot contour into Pinto Basin. Owing to rules pertaining to national parks, I then committed one of my least favorite acts in the great outdoors: spent the night in a public campground, surrounded by other desert enthusiasts, all of whom had come to be blasted by a vicious wind that rocked my pickup truck all night long while I huddled in a sleeping bag inside the camper shell. Most of my fellow pilgrims were sheltered inside the walls of recreational vehicles the size of small houses, though the guy at the site next to mine, who had been traveling by motorcycle, had only a tent to protect him. Nevertheless, he grinned expansively at me when he fired up his hog and headed out in the morning, while I crouched in the lee of my truck, chewing a chilly mound of Grape-Nuts and waiting for water to boil.

A few minutes after eight, a gold Ford Bronco pulled up and disgorged a man with a reddish beard and blond hair covering the tops of his ears. Clad in boots, shorts, and a brown down jacket, he looked younger than his forty-two years, which I knew him to possess because I was there to meet him. His name was Jim Cornett, and he and I were about to go looking for the southernmost Joshua tree in the Mojave Desert.

I had met Cornett a couple of months earlier at the place where he works: the Palm Springs Desert Museum, to which I'd been directed by a friend well versed in desert ecology. Approaching the museum along the sidewalk on a hot November day, I'd passed a barefoot man in a long white robe who murmured, "Mercy . . . patience" as I went by. Inside the air-conditioned building, Cornett sat below a photograph of Joshua trees covered with snow. He told me he was engaged in a ten-year study of the species *Yucca brevifolia*—its range, growth, longevity, population, significance to other plants and animals, "anything that influences its numbers and distribution"—for a future exhibit at the museum. He had previously done the same thing with roadrunners and with *Washingtonia filifera*, the desert fan palm.

"I like being surrounded by indicator species," Cornett acknowledged, placing his hands behind his head and leaning back behind his desk. "When they're profound and grotesque in their distinction, it really sets the stage for me. Some scientists only study little tiny things, like seeds or insects. I like the biggest, most obvious ones. I think a palm oasis is the best thing to be surrounded by in the Colorado Desert, just as a Joshua-tree forest is in the Mojave. I say it's because it helps you unlock the keys to the ecology of the place—but that's really crap. The truth is, I just like it."

Cornett grew up in Los Angeles, where as a teenager he had been a surfer—a southern California avocation profound and grotesque in its distinction. "The crowds ruined it for me," he disclosed. "At the beach I went to, there was one place where the waves broke. With five or six people it was a ball, but with fifty or sixty it was a disaster. As a result, I stopped surfing. When I went to visit my relatives in Fullerton, there was always bumper-to-bumper traffic on the Santa Ana Freeway; the Artesia Freeway was being built to relieve the congestion, but the day it opened, it was bumper-to-bumper just as bad. At that point I realized it was impossible to keep up with the demands of the population.

"I didn't want to deal with hordes of people preventing me from doing what I wanted to do, so I started coming to the desert to escape the crowds and chase snakes. I fell in love with it because it was so peaceful and quiet. You could do your own thing. I began to associate that feeling with the vegetation—when I drove out from the city and saw the plants, I knew I was in the peaceful place. So I got interested in that and started taking pictures."

Still, Cornett majored in political science in college: "In the sixties, studying snakes in the desert seemed morally inappropriate. But I was turned down as a cop and an insurance adjuster, so I decided to be a teacher to change the world. I got a job at the junior high school in Twentynine Palms [on the northern boundary of Joshua Tree National Monument]. Part of the job was coaching the freshman football team, and I got upset because the local newspaper only covered the varsity— our kids worked just as hard, and unlike the varsity, we were winning all our games. The editor told me he didn't have the staff for it, but he'd pay *me* to write up the games.

"I ended up getting a lot of attention from it. I liked having a byline, so I did some wrestling stories that winter. Then I asked the editor if he'd be interested in a column about desert wildlife. It turned out to be very popular—people would write in and say they had a rattlesnake in their yard, and what about it? After a while I wrote to a paper in Yuma, Arizona, and they said they wanted it, too. When I had a total of eight papers, I wrote to Dear Abby for advice, and she said to try syndication by the news services. The first one I tried was Copley, and they said okay. They paid me two hundred dollars a month, and I traveled all over the United States researching plants and animals. Wherever I went, people always assumed that I had a biology degree, and eventually I became embarrassed that I didn't. So I went back to school and got one."

While he was at school, Cornett began working part-time at the Palm Springs Desert Museum, where he was now curator of natural science. "I'm just kind of an organized nature enthusiast," he explained. "I don't like *applied* science. I'm pleased if someone can do something practical with things I discover, but I'm not interested in applying my research to practical problems. People who put up bird boxes to save peregrine falcons bore me. I'm glad someone's saving endangered species, but I'd rather find out what made them endangered. My goal is to find out the secrets of nature. It's like playing chess—an intellectual exercise with no practical value."

To that end, Cornett wanted to locate the southernmost Joshua tree because, "in order to understand the ecology of a species, it's important to investigate its adaptation to environmental conditions at the limits of its range. You're more likely to see its physiological potential there. Think of a marathon: If you study the middle of the pack, you'll know the average speed. But it's more important to look at the extremes—who won and who finished last. That way you see what the possibilities are. Biologically, you're better able to speculate about the significance of the species in its environment. Let's say there's a severe drought. Some plants might die. But it may be that the Joshua tree produces more fruit than other plants do in a drought. Who knows? In a dry year, it might be the most important plant. If we study it in the most arid part of its range, we can better speculate how it'll do at the center of its range. Of course, I haven't drawn these conclusions yet; that's what the study is for."

For my own purposes, I wanted to find the southernmost Joshua tree because it represented the southern boundary of the Mojave Desert. The late dean of desert scientists, Edmund C. Jaeger, wrote that the Joshua tree is "the Mojave Desert's most distinctive plant. If a line were drawn around the outer limits of this strange tree's distribution, that line pretty well marks out the marginal confines of the Mojave Desert region."

Cornett agreed that the tree represents the Mojave better than any other single plant, but he didn't concur that the boundaries of the desert precisely follow its distribution. "There *are* some plants found nowhere except the Mojave Desert, but the Joshua tree isn't one of them," he told me. "You can find Joshua trees beyond the Mojave to the north, west, and east, mixed in with piñon pine, manzanita, scrub oak, and chaparral. I'd say about 85 percent of the range of the species is within the Mojave Desert."

Still, even Cornett admitted that the *southern* limit of that range corresponded to the southern boundary of the Mojave. Like him, then, I wanted to walk that ecological line "to see what the possibilities were"— not just for the tree but for the region that it signified. What exactly defines the spot where one desert ends and another begins? If there exists such a finite thing as a boundary between deserts, I wanted to see what it looked alike.

If the Joshua tree is the legitimate symbol of the Mojave, one can easily understand why the desert is viewed with ambivalence and foreboding.

Edmund C. Jaeger was far from alone in considering it "strange"; from the earliest European encounters, observers have searched for similar adjectives to describe it. Lieutenant John C. Frémont, who crossed the Mojave with Kit Carson in 1844, wrote in his diary on April 13 that he was "struck by the sudden appearance of tree yuccas which gave a strange and southern character to the country. . . . Their stiff and ungraceful form makes them to the traveler the most repulsive tree in the vegetable kingdom." Admittedly, as historian Patricia Nelson Limerick has pointed out, Frémont reserved especially for deserts "an arsenal of adjectival abuse: 'forbidding,' 'inhospitable,' 'desolate,' 'bleak,' 'sterile,' 'dreary,' 'savage,' 'barren,' 'dismal,' 'repulsive,' and 'revolting'"— but even botanists race to underscore the tree's unsettling visage. The esteemed Philip A. Munz wrote that "visitors to the deserts in four of our southwestern states have long been impressed by the weird appearance of the Joshua trees," while Peter Victor Peterson, in *Native Trees of Southern California*, termed *Y. brevifolia* "easily the most weird-looking denizen of the California deserts." No less objective an authority than Susan D. McKelvey, author of the definitive *Yuccas of the Southwestern United States*, found the Joshua tree "a curious looking plant, suggesting, in its oldest forms especially, another age; one would not be surprised to see a huge prehistoric monster standing by and feeding upon the fruit on its upper branches." The redoubtable C. Hart Merriam, in his account of a Death Valley biological survey in 1893, remarked: "Among the unusual and peculiar modifications of plant life of the desert region of the southwestern United States, none is more remarkable or striking than the tree yucca. . . . They branch in a very peculiar manner. . . . Looking northward over the Mojave Desert from the summit of Cajon Pass a continuous forest of tree yuccas stretches away in the distance until lost in the desert haze, adding a singularly weird element to the peculiar physiognomy of the region."

Merriam aptly described the bearing of the tree that so arrests observers. He noted that Joshua trees "are abundantly clothed with stiff, spiny leaves set so near together that their bases are in actual contact. As the tree grows the leaves die from below upward, and the dead ones at first point outward at right angles to the trunk, and then downward, their point surrounding the branch or trunk like a belt of bayonets, effectively preventing most animals from climbing up from below." "Clothed" is a fitting description: From a distance the trunk and branches of the tree appear to be coated with a kind of furry armor. It is easily the biggest plant in its habitat, reaching heights from fifteen to thirty—sometimes more than forty—feet. Its gnarled and twisted shape, silhouetted on the horizon at sunset, defined on all peripheries by countless barbs and spikes, presents to the paranoid eye a particularly tortured image, as if the tree had been bent to this shape by a lifetime of abuse.

The scientific name of the species, *Yucca brevifolia*, was conferred in 1871 by Georg Engelmann of the U.S. Geological Exploration of the Fortieth Parallel, led by Clarence King. The popular name derives from the notion that, to early Mormon emigrants in the desert, the tree's upraised arms resembled the prophet pointing the way to the Promised Land. McKelvey quotes a couple of sources named Bonker and Thornber, who in an obscure publication entitled *Sage of the Desert* wrote: "Not every traveller knows that Joshua, seeking the Holy Land, travel wearied, tired after a long dusty trek, looked forth to high Heaven for a sign which would tell him the right road to take. Guidance came instantly. 'Thou shalt follow the way pointed for Thee by the Trees. And Thou shalt enter in.' Be it noted that the Joshua Tree points its branches usually in one direction, its spears appearing almost like arrows poised for flight (One of the versions from which the name Joshua Tree has sprung)." Comments McKelvey: "No reference for the citation included in this quotation is given; unfortunately it does not seem to the author that the branchlets, even 'usually,' point in any one, but rather in all, directions." Still, as Cornett said, to Mormons en route from Salt Lake City to San Bernardino via the Old Spanish Trail in the nineteenth century, the Joshua tree "was the first plant even a novice would notice when coming out of the Great Basin into a hotter, more arid desert. It told them that they were nearer to California, that their journey was half over."

The Joshua tree is one of about thirty species of yuccas, all native to North America, most to the southwestern United States. The genus is divided into four sections, one of which—*Clistocarpa*, characterized by dry, spongy fruit that does not burst open at maturity—consists entirely of *Yucca brevifolia*. Munz noted that "because the Joshua tree's leaves are spine-tipped, these plants are 'cacti' in the popular mind, although there is nothing fleshy in their make-up and the whiteish flowers are lily-like." These flowers, which appear in large, upright clusters in the spring, are rubbery to the touch, musty and mushroomlike to the nose. The pale green fruit—about twice the size of a large walnut—is lightweight and blimp-shaped, enabling it to be tumbled by the wind, distributing seeds over the desert. New plants may sprout from these seeds or from rhizomes (underground branchlets emerging from the roots of the trees). Jaeger observed that the plant "has no tap roots but instead has numerous corky-barked fibrous rootlets fanning out in all directions to serve both as efficient anchors and for the absorption of water and soil nutriments." The roots are quite strong in relation to their diameter, which is only about that of a pencil; still, the sight of Joshua trees uprooted by the wind is a common one in the desert.

The trunk of *Yucca brevifolia* is made up of thousands of small fibers—one of the attributes that help to define it as a monocotyledon, the more primitive of the two types of flowering plants. Cornett enumerated the differences between monocotyledons and dicotyledons for me: "Monocots have a single leaf, or cotyledon, emerging from the seed," he said. "They have parallel veins in the leaves, no taproots, and only primary vascular cambium (no bark). Dicots have two seed leaves, branching veins in the leaves, a primary taproot with long branches coming off it, and both primary and secondary vascular cambium (bark). Grasses are the best example of monocots. Sometimes people say the Joshua tree isn't really a tree—it's a giant grass, like bamboo. In theory, once a monocot is fully formed, it shouldn't get bigger in width, but everybody knows that the Joshua tree does. Also, Joshua trees clearly have an outer growth like bark, even though monocots aren't supposed to have bark. One of the most hotly debated topics in plant anatomy is: Do Joshua trees have secondary vascular cambium? Ecologically, it's of little interest."

Many books about desert plants mention that the Joshua tree is actually a lily. I always attributed to my own lack of scientific background the fact that this notion mystifies me—as if a shark were classified as a crustacean, say, or a tiger as a dog. Cornett, however, told me that more recent sources have taken to categorizing *Yucca brevifolia* as neither a lily nor a grass but as an agave. When I asked him why any of this was true, I expected a pat answer regarding some specific aspect of the plant's biology; instead, Cornett fetched Munz's massive *Flora of Southern California* from a shelf and began poring over the criteria for the families Liliaceae and Agavaceae. After an hour, he still hadn't arrived at a sure explanation.

"Most agaves are desert plants that have rhizomes and thick, fibrous leaves," Cornett said, looking at his book. "In a lily, the perianth"—the external envelope formed by the flowers—"has six distinct parts, but in agaves, the perianth segments are united into a tube. Both agaves and lilies have six stamens and three sections to the ovary. In lilies, the ovary is vaguely superior (that is, above the petals). In agaves, it's clearly superior or inferior; in yuccas, it's always clearly superior. Some lilies have panacles (elongated and unbranched clusters of packed flowers), but yuccas always do. Agave fruit can be a capsule or a berry; the fruit of the Joshua tree is a capsule."

Cornett frowned and rubbed his chin, struggling with the criterial crosscurrents. Finally he said: "It appears that the flowers of the Joshua tree were not scrutinized very carefully at first. It was probably done by someone who was familiar with lilies but not with agaves, because it's actually more like an agave. The characteristics of lilies can vary quite a bit, but agaves' don't. It may be that the lily is sort of a hodgepodge family—a holding tank for monocots until we figure out more."

Several different records offer the Cottonwood Mountains, at the southern edge of Joshua Tree National Monument, as *Yucca brevifolia's* range of lowest latitude. The Cottonwoods, then, were the place where Cornett wanted to look. A four-wheel-drive road runs north-south through the range, so, true to desert tradition, we would be doing our survey by car. "I've driven the route before, but never looking for Joshua trees," Cornett said as I loaded my gear into the back of his Bronco. We pulled out onto the monument's main road and started driving south.

According to some geologists, the southwestern and northwestern boundaries of the Mojave are properly delineated by earthquake faults—respectively, the San Andreas and the Garlock. With regard to this view, one Hyrum B. Johnson has written:

> [These] boundaries setting off the . . . Mojave and Colorado deserts are particularly sharp on the western and southwestern interface. Toward the east, the boundaries become less distinct and every line drawn to demarcate the southeastern boundary of the Mojave and the northeastern boundary of the Colorado can only be arbitrary. . . . [However,] south of Twentynine Palms and the Little San Bernardino Mountains, the elevation of the Colorado Desert decreases rapidly, falling to sea level at Indio and well below sea level farther south. This zone of rapid eleva-

tion change constitutes a clear boundary which corresponds to changes in the climate and biota.

In illustration of this point, my ears popped as Cornett and I plunged toward the shining strip of Interstate 10, where luminescent dots moved slowly east and west in front of the Orocopia Mountains, slung across the great brown bajadas in the morning light. "Right along here is where some guys illegally harvested a bunch of ocotillos," Cornett pointed out. "They had a permit from the BLM, but did it in the national monument by mistake. I heard about another guy who got to harvest a square mile of yuccas for five dollars. A friend of mine discovered it because he was doing a bird study—he came back one weekend to check the nest cavities, and they were all gone."

This seemed to beg the question of why anyone other than the Chemehuevi Paiute Indians—who fried the flowers, ground the seeds into mush, wove the fibers into baskets and blankets, made paint from the roots and soap from the stems—would want to harvest yuccas. Apparently, at various times since European arrival, Joshua trees have served as firewood, paper pulp, surgeons' splints, and cooking oil. (The seeds contain twice as much oil—light, yellow, tasteless, and odorless—as do those of the soybean.) In the 1880s, the *London Daily Telegraph* invested in a yucca pulp mill on the Colorado River, but after being shipped off to England, the material—so unaccustomed to warm environments, after all—"heated on the way and was spoiled." John Milton Webber, in *Yuccas of the Southwest* (1953), reported the yucca fibers "are used in the manufacture of many novelties, such as post cards, scrapbooks, book bindings, napkin rings, window dressings, and lightweight clubs used in play and comedy." An 1898 publication entitled *Land of Sunshine*, related to McKelvey, explained that

> The peculiarity of the wood is that it does not split, and its pliability and lightness admit of the sheets being rolled and sent through the mail. Its durability and uniqueness make it of exceptional value for covers for booklets, while its beautiful grain renders it appropriate for art work in oil or water colors, pyrography, silk embroidery and for fancy work, such as photograph frames, glove and handkerchief boxes, screens, etc. . . . The evolution, in the hands of the Yucca Manufacturing Company, of this once

despised desert tree into so many useful and artistic purposes is eloquent of what ingenuity and enterprise may yet accomplish with other seemingly useless material in Nature's storehouse.

As McKelvey commented, "One can but hope that this tree, which contributes so much to the desert landscape, may be protected before it is entirely confined to 'useful and artistic' objects on a store shelf! The Joshua Tree National Monument is a fine step in the right direction."

In the early twentieth century, the major problem faced by Joshua trees was homesteaders who razed large tracts and later abandoned their clearings. More recently, the tree has succumbed to the aspirations of suburban housing developers—particularly in the western Mojave, which is now a full-fledged bedroom community of Los Angeles. "West of Gorman in the Tehachapi Mountains is the densest concentration of Joshua trees anywhere," said Cornett. "It's a precious natural environment, but it's being slowly bulldozed away."

Many accounts mention Cima Dome and Lanfair Valley in the eastern Mojave—not the Tehachapis or Joshua Tree National Monument—as the site of the world's largest, densest Joshua-tree forest. This area has been subject to widespread, long-term cattle grazing, and Cornett said that the density of Joshua trees may be ironically enhanced by the cattle.

"Normally, Joshua-tree seedlings are devoured quickly by herbivores," he said. "But when grass disappears *completely* from an area, as on Cima Dome, shrubs will spout. The shrubs are spiny and unpalatable to cattle, so they're an excellent protector for baby Joshua trees, which can sometimes grow inside them for three years without being disturbed. By that time they're pretty tough, and cattle don't want to eat them. Eventually, the Joshua tree kills the protecting shrub by taking up all the water. So it may be true that, except in areas that have been paved over, the symbol of the California desert is denser now than it's ever been. The *distribution*, though, is shrinking. That's bad; if you had to choose, you'd rather increase the distribution and decrease the concentration."

We departed the borders of the national monument and turned west onto a gravel road maintained by the Los Angeles Metropolitan Water District, following an underground pipeline that leads to Los Angeles from the Colorado River. We drove slowly past various Sonoran Desert plants: wispy, amorphous gray smoke trees and more brilliant shooting ocotillo, aflame with red flowers after some recent rains. "Generally speaking, I don't expect to find Joshua trees where there's ocotillo," Cornett said. "Not here, anyway. In Arizona you'll find them side by side. You'll even find Joshua trees next to saguaro cactus there. It's bizarre."

A word of orientation on the North American deserts. The Chihuahuan Desert is contained mostly in the highlands of north-central Mexico, with small extensions in southern New Mexico and southwestern Texas along the Rio Grande. The Sonoran is the large, hot, horseshoe-shaped desert that surrounds the Gulf of California and extends halfway into Arizona. The Colorado is a subset of the Sonoran—the portion west of the Colorado River, basically, distinguished from the Mojave by differences in drainage and elevation. All the rain that falls upon the Mojave stays there, trapped in the intermountain basins, while water in the Colorado Desert drains either to its namesake river or to the Salton Sea. Much of the Colorado Desert is actually below sea level, resulting in a hotter climate than that of the Mojave. Average temperatures in January and July are ten degrees higher and thus support a different flora. Primarily because of the heat, my limited experience in the Colorado Desert has defined it for me as somehow more *intense:* the first time I set foot in Indio, not far from where Cornett and I now drove, the summer wind was so hot at dusk that it hurt my eyeballs.

"This is a classic example of the Colorado Desert," Cornett said, looking at a group of small purple flowers blooming beside the road. "Here it is January, and the Arizona lupine is blooming because of the rain we had recently. It's our coldest month, but you still can't keep the plant life down. The Colorado is really a subtropical desert—it seldom experiences frost. By contrast, the Mojave *always* experiences frost—it has a distinct winter season. Every night in January, you can expect it to drop below freezing."

Southern California weather services are fond of referring to the Mojave as the "high" desert. (Conversely, to residents of the Mojave itself, anything south or west of the San Bernardinos and San Gabriels is "down below.") Cornett defined the Mojave as consisting of elevations higher than 2,000 feet, including the lower sinks surrounded by such elevations (with the exceptions of Saline and Death Valleys, whose floors lie at 1,000 and –282 feet respectively). The Great Basin Desert, which begins east of the Sierra Nevada and stretches throughout Nevada into Utah, Oregon, and Idaho, he assigned to 4,000 feet and above. "The Mojave is the transitional zone between this desert and that one," he said. "The Great Basin is too cold for Joshua trees. I've already found their northern limit—north of Goldfield, Nevada, almost to Tonopah, there are just a few. The Joshua tree has such a clean association with the transitional area that I often wonder what we'd call the Mojave if there *wasn't* a Joshua tree."

Actually, the Joshua tree is only the most conspicuous of the Mojave's characteristic plants. Fully one fourth of its species exist nowhere else, although most of these endemics—Parry saltbush, Panamint parsley, Telescope Peak buckwheat, et al.—are found only in the desert's driest pockets (the Death Valley area and the rain-blocked southwestern corner along the San Gabriels and San Bernardinos), plus isolated mountain ranges to the east. Otherwise, the Mojave is a melting pot for different, distinctive floras, as its north- and south-trending basins act as conduits of emigration—underground railroads, as it were, for fugitive foreign species. Owing to its transitional location, the Mojave is thus the northern or southern limit for many North American desert plants—the former, obviously, for many of those that we were seeing now.

We began winding up a rocky access road which, like many desert routes, followed a high-tension power line. The bare Cottonwood Mountains, just to the north, appeared to have been colored with a selective assortment of Crayolas: burnt umber, raw sienna, rust, flesh, and sepia. Cornett stopped the car and looked at them through his binoculars. "The southern slopes are very rocky," he said. "They don't seem to have enough moisture for Joshua trees—it appears to be too hot. But I wouldn't expect to see any Joshua trees in these real rocky areas. They like deeper soil."

Joshua trees are commonly found on desert bajadas, which by definition are composed of alluvial soils—sandy, loamy, and relatively deep (which, in the desert, means a couple of feet). They don't like clay, and therefore, as Merriam observed, "do not grow in the bottoms of arid basins or upon steep declivities of mountains, but thrive best on the higher gravel slopes that skirt the deserts." Such areas lie, for the most part, between two thousand and five thousand feet—the zone considered to contain the Mojave's most distinctive vegetation. While precipitation is important to the tree's distribution (it doesn't grow in areas receiving less than three or more than eleven inches per year), temperature is perhaps even more so, if only because of its influence on evaporation and the consequent amount of water available to the plant. In 1966, a student named Richard Gates found that the northern limit of *Yucca brevifolia* corresponded to the geographic line where the average minimum temperature in January is twenty degrees; the southern limit followed the line where the average maximum temperature in July is one hundred degrees. As to elevation, Gates posited that "the downslope limit of Joshua Trees may be related to a line where high temperatures reduce available moisture in the soil to the point where growth is no longer possible." Hence, a "high desert" tree.

Descending in elevation again, Cornett stopped the Bronco momentarily before driving over a berm and down into a wash. As he got out to check the car's clearance, I noticed a baby's highchair standing off in the sand. "This is Pinkham Wash," Cornett announced upon returning. "It drains into the Salton Sea—the lowest part of the Colorado Desert." Looking back to the south, I could see the shining surface of the "sea," created in 1905 when the flooding Colorado River burst the limits of an irrigation intake and flowed for a year and a half into an ancient geological basin. Ten-thousand-foot-tall San Jacinto Peak towered in the sky to the west, capped by snow and its own private cloud; immediately ahead, a sand-and-gravel track led through a grove of gray-green smoke trees. In other words, in every direction, landmarks continued to indicate our exclusion from the Mojave.

We soon came upon another: *Opuntia bigelovii*—Bigelow cholla (pronounced "choy-ya"), a.k.a. teddybear or jumping cholla, proclaimed by Jaeger "the most handsome of all our cacti" because of its brilliant golden-white crown above a dark brown underlayer composed of dying joints. The example we'd encountered didn't exactly fit the image that Jaeger admired: the plants had been spray-painted bright red and green. Nearby was a pile of green-and-white fence stakes—the federal government's paint scheme, Cornett observed, though we still remained outside the confines of the national monument.

"Teddybear cholla only grows where the dead segments fall, not where the seeds blow," Cornett said. "They form these little forests." Precisely because of the dead buds—which are said to "jump" when they pop off the plant—Bigelow cholla is one of the desert's most dangerous organisms. The fallen segments, which are full of spines, adhere tenaciously to passersby, to whom they can impart serious wounds. "My cat rolled in a pile of them once," Cornett said. "They got in her groin, up under her chin; she tried to lick the spines off and got a ball caught in her mouth. I thought she might have to be put to death. I didn't know how to get her to the vet, but when I opened the car door she jumped right in. She'd never done that before. The vet gave her gas, and we spent three hours picking out the spines. To my amazement, she completely recovered.

"Teddybear cholla is associated with the Sonoran Desert," Cornett acknowledged. "It gets up into the Mojave, but not into the Great Basin." Though by no means rare, cacti aren't what you'd call plentiful in the Mojave; like Joshua trees, they require a certain quotient of water and abound only on well-drained, salt-free alluvial slopes and lower mountain canyons. The two plants share the specialized water-conserving photosynthetic trait referred to as Crassulacean Acid Metabolism (CAM). While the pores of most plants are (like human eyelids and banks) closed at night and open during the day, collecting carbon dioxide and releasing water, the stomata of CAM plants are (like animal eyelids and bars) open at night and closed during the day, preventing the excessive—i.e., potentially fatal—loss of water that would occur under hot, dry conditions. Cacti are the predominant CAM plants of the Colorado Desert; the characteristic CAM plants of the Mojave are yuccas.

We ascended in elevation now as we headed north into the Cottonwoods. A kestrel darted back and forth before us on the wind. "It's a lousy hunting day when it's windy like this," Cornett commented. "The insects are moving around, too." We entered the mountains by way of a narrow canyon, but once we were in them, the terrain softened somewhat, and we found ourselves in a wide area with relatively gentle slopes. Barrel cactus like bright red balloons nestled on the hillsides. The daggerlike leaves of yucca plants were discernible among the rocks.

"Nope," said Cornett, looking through his binoculars. "Those are Mojave yuccas." In other words, *Yucca schidigera*, formerly *Yucca mohavensis*, or Spanish bayonet: a lower, shorter, stockier plant than *Y. brevifolia*. Jaeger wrote that this yucca "is scattered widely in the semi-arid coastal counties of southern California, attaining perfection only on the broad, gravelly benches of the southern Mohave and eastern Colorado deserts." Cornett explained that it has "much longer leaves than the Joshua tree does, and they're slightly yellowish, whereas the Joshua tree's are bluish. Mojave yuccas also have threads peeling off their leaves—you never see that on a Joshua tree—and the trunk of the yucca is thicker for its height. One difficult thing here is that Joshua trees are short and stunted in rocky areas; it makes it hard to distinguish between them and Mojave yuccas. In the northern part of the Joshua tree's range, there *are* no other yuccas—if you see anything that looks halfway like a Joshua tree, it *is* a Joshua tree, even though Joshua trees vary tremendously. They can be huge arborescent structures or dwarf shrubs; they can reproduce vegetatively or from seeds. Some branch after flowering, and some branch without flowering."

Where we were—or, rather, where we hoped to soon be (the southern Mojave)—all Joshua trees were of the first type, which branches only after the growing tip has been destroyed by flowering. This is the subspecies *Yucca brevifolia brevifolia*. The other variety—*Y. brevifolia jaegeriana*, which branches before flowering—is found farther to the east and north.

"*Jaegeriana* is smaller than *brevifolia*," Cornett said. "Its leaves and trunk are shorter and it's more densely branched, so it looks more compact and symmetrical." *Jaegeriana*'s lowest branches begin near the ground, whereas the trunk of *brevifolia* can travel upward for ten or more feet before dividing. Right beside the main road through Joshua Tree National Monument, a thirty-foot-tall *brevifolia* specimen exhibits no branches at all. (Nomenclature-enamored scientists have nicknamed it Slim.) Peter Rowlands, who wrote a thesis on Joshua trees while pursuing his doctorate in biology at the University of California at Riverside, found only one place in the Mojave (in southern Nevada) where the two subspecies overlap. He did note signs of hybridization there, which isn't surprising, considering that both varieties prefer the same latitudes and elevations. Where they seem to differ is in the matter of rainfall—not in its amount but in its timing. The taller, longer-leafed *brevifolia* grows in those parts of the Mojave that receive minimal rain during the summer, while the shorter, denser *jaegeriana* occurs in regions that garner at least one fifth of their annual precipitation between the months of May and September.

"It's almost like there are two Mojaves, represented by the two types of Joshua trees," said Cornett. "I've actually found examples of *jaegeriana* that flower before they branch, even though they're not supposed to. That must be the ancestral condition—the one shared by both subspecies. I think two populations of Joshua trees must have become separated at some point—probably during the Pleistocene, on either side of the Salton trough. After that, *brevifolia*, which is more cold-adapted, moved into the western Mojave. *Jaegeriana* moved into the east."

Modern scientists' understanding of past Mojave Desert vegetation—Joshua trees included—has been distinctly enhanced by two notable nonplants: ground sloths and wood rats. *Neotoma*, the pack rat, has aided the cause by being (in the words of Philip V. Wells, who did the first research) "avidly acquisitive and prodigiously excretory." The rats, which have been around since the Pleistocene epoch, build their nests, or "middens," from plant litter and other bits and pieces of their surroundings. In this they are not so different from muskrats or beavers; but muskrats and beavers locate their stick-houses near water, which reduces them to rot in relatively short order.

"In contrast," Wells wrote, "not only do wood rats collect an incredibly detailed inventory of the local flora and fauna in the form of twigs, leaves, fruits, seeds, even flowers, and bones, exoskeletons, shells, etc. but they also deposit them in dry caves, and often impregnate them with their possibly allelochemic, viscous urine"—a highly concentrated, amberlike syrup that is "so effective as a fossilizing agent that beautifully intact, delicate plant structures are preserved in their middens for time periods exceeding 40,000 radiocarbon years. Thus, records of Pleistocene and Holocene vegetation are accessible."

Of the many ancient middens that have now been uncovered, almost all contain twigs, seeds, leaves, and cones of piñon and juniper—plants now found only at the region's highest elevations. Many of the same nests also contain the tissues of Joshua trees. Such plants were apparently present in the (currently treeless) lower Mojave as recently as nine thousand years ago—in other words, at the end of the so-called pluvial period, when glaciers covered the continent to the north and the temperature of the Mojave was at least ten degrees cooler than it is today. At that time, the region experienced much more rainfall and less evaporation; Jaeger portrays the Mojave, circa 7,000 B.C., as "a land of meandering rivers and numerous lakes supporting a varied and abundant flora and fauna": mammoths, camels, mastodons, three-toed horses, saber-toothed tigers, and giant ground sloths.

Fossil remains of *Nothrotherium*, the sloth, were excavated in 1930 and 1931 at Gypsum Cave, eighteen miles east of Las Vegas, Nevada, by one J. D. Laudermilk, in concert with the ubiquitous Philip A. Munz.

The elevation of the site was fifteen hundred feet; the surrounding vegetation was "a typically sparse desert flora." Mixed in with the ten-thousand-year-old sloth remains were preserved layers of dung. The scientists felt that "identification of the plant tissues in the sloth dung seemed particularly desirable in order to answer two questions: (1) What was the flora of the region at the time the sloth inhabited the cave, and (2) does the identification of the flora cast any light on the climatic conditions at the time the ground-sloth lived?" Analyzing the tissues, they concluded that "fully 80 per cent of the material consisted of yucca"—notably *Yucca brevifolia*, which is totally absent from the area today.

"Joshua-tree fossils have also been found in the Sonoran Desert in southern Arizona near the Mexican border," said Cornett. In other words, before the warming that ended the Ice Age and the era of the woodsy Mojave, Joshua trees grew not only at lower elevations but at lower latitudes than they do today. Then, as Peter Rowlands puts it, "as the climate of the Southwest got progressively warmer, plant species more typical of the present warm desert invaded while the Pinyons and Junipers as well as other elements retreated upward in elevation. . . . The Joshua tree, though subjected to the same changing climatic conditions as the . . . conifer species, was evidently preadapted to the drier desert conditions." As evidence, Rowlands notes that since the pluvial period, the lower elevational limit of the Joshua tree has increased by only about seven hundred feet, while the lowest piñons and junipers have moved upward by a couple of thousand. "*Yucca brevifolia* remained in many areas while the new desert scrub communities formed around it. As a result, the present community relationships of *Yucca brevifolia* are far more complex than they were during pluvial time."

Floras for California and the Southwest usually make reference to a plant community called Joshua Tree Woodland, composed of buckwheat, boxthorn, and bladder sage in addition to piñon, juniper, and Joshua trees. Rowlands resoundingly debunks the idea that there exists any such coherent community dominated by *Yucca brevifolia*. As Cornett pointed out, Joshua trees can be found in surprising places, and their relatively wide range of altitude and latitude means that they grow in a wide variety of plant communities. On Cima Dome, in the eastern Mojave, they are accompanied mainly by grasses; near Hesperia, in the western Mojave, mostly by shrubs. In the northern part of their range, they mix comfortably with sagebrush; in the south, they coexist with creosote bush. What's more, Rowlands adds, Joshua trees "contribute very little . . . to total stand composition wherever they occur, and can be considered dominants only in terms of stature." (He sums up by declaring that the "community ecology of *Yucca brevifolia* is not well understood.")

"We're getting close now," Cornett said. "This is what I'd call the heart of the yucca belt of the Cottonwood Mountains. We're over three thousand feet, well within the elevational range of the tree. We're entering an area with north-facing drainages. And we're seeing yuccas on the flats. Joshua trees can establish themselves on open flats with only precipitation—that is, without access to the groundwater table." Mojave yuccas surrounded us on both sides of the road now: dark, spine-infested plants, backlit by the lowering winter sun, dotted the distant slopes. "This is the type of soil where you'd find them," Cornett added hopefully. "Fine-grained and not too rocky."

He stopped the Bronco and peered through the binoculars. "Nothing but Mojave yuccas," he reported. Not to mention creosote bush (*Larrea tridentata*)—the spreading, spindly, fragrant plant that covers three-quarters of the Mojave Desert floor, as well as those of the Sonoran and Chihuahuan Deserts to the south. Often erroneously referred to as greasewood (the popular name for *Sarcobatus vermiculatus*, a shrub found on the edges of alkali lakes), creosote bush is one of the few plants found in both North and South America; it adjusts to its diverse environments by adding genetic ammunition as it moves north. In the Chihuahuan Desert, each cell of every creosote bush contains two sets of chromosomes; in the Sonoran, four; in the Mojave, six. The Mojave is the coldest environment it can tolerate, and for that reason Cornett considered it a better indicator than the Joshua tree of the desert's northern boundary with the Great Basin. "You can see the very last creosote bush," he said. "It's a few miles south of Goldfield, Nevada." A few miles south, that is, of the northernmost Joshua tree.

The desert's *oldest* known creosote bush was growing sixty-five miles to our northwest, in Johnson Valley. This so-called King Clone—estimated to be 11,700 years old—apparently established itself at that critical time when the Ice Age was ending, the oaks and conifers were withdrawing, and the Mojave was receiving applications from more xeric flora. The résumé of the creosote bush was perhaps the most impressive of them all, owing to its unmatched ability to withstand heat and drought. The roots extend underground for forty or fifty feet (horizontally, if they run into a wall of clay), and because of competition for water, the bushes are distributed with perfect symmetry across the desert floor—in fact, they grow in rings as the plant reproduces vegetatively. (King Clone's ring is seventy-five feet across.) During especially dry times, the leaves fold themselves in half to minimize transpiration; in periods of extended drought they're shed altogether, with only the newest, smallest leaves remaining on the plant. These can survive a reduction in water content to less than half of their dry weight, but they respond immediately when rain arrives—expressing their gratitude, it seems, by dispensing perfume. During and after a rain, the pervasive, lovely smell of the desert is precisely the smell of *Larrea tridentata*.

The densely arranged branches of the creosote bush act as a net for sand and nutrients, so each windblown shrub is a veritable island of fertility. For that matter, so is each Joshua tree. Dead yucca leaves enrich the organic content and water-holding capacity of the soil, which itself is protected from erosion by the plant's roots and rhizomes. As Webber wrote in *Yuccas of the Southwest*, "Each yucca, like many other desert shrubs, gradually improves its immediate surroundings, until a small community of its own is established. This community, consisting of small plants, rodents, insects, and occasionally birds, could not exist without the protection of the yucca."

Occasionally birds, indeed: At least twenty-five different species nest in the branches of the Joshua tree. In the trunk, woodpeckers gouge holes that are later claimed by wrens, flycatchers, bluebirds, and owls; orioles weave their nests from yucca fibers and hang them from the lancelike leaves, which are cannily employed by loggerhead shrikes to impale their prey. The desert night lizard (*Xantusia vigilis*) lives underneath the fallen branches and in the rotting collapsed trunk, subsisting on ants, termites, beetles, flies, crickets, aphids, moths, caterpillars, ticks, and spiders, all of which live there too. The Navajo yucca borer lays its eggs on Joshua-tree rhizomes; the larvae burrow into the stem, feeding and pupating on the underground roots. The most celebrated relationship is between *Yucca brevifolia* and *Tegeticula yucasella*—the yucca moth. The Joshua tree's flowers, whose season coincides with the last few days of *Tegeticula*'s life, have evolved a scent that attracts the moth at night. Male and female mate inside the flower; the female then begins collecting pollen. When she has enough, she finds another vacant yucca flower and lays her eggs near its rudimentary seeds. After depositing each egg, she forces pollen grains onto the flower's stigmas, beginning the process of seed production. The emerging moth larvae eat the developing seeds but leave most of them to mature and germinate. In the fall, the larvae drop from the tree and pupate underground—emerging as adults during the flowering season. This cyclic relationship, upon which both species depend completely for survival, is considered one of the world's neatest examples of coevolution.

Out on the creosote flats, Cornett and I were joined by a pair of immature golden eagles. As one dipped and swooped right over the car, Cornett said, "You know you're really away from human disturbance when you see that." Gazing over the plains of creosote bush, he admitted: "I'm starting to become a doubter. I think somebody just made up the idea that Joshua trees are here. After all, we're looking at the highest peaks." Checking off other locations nearby, he said: "I know they're in the Hexie Mountains; I know they're at the southern end of Pleasant Valley; I know they're *not* in the Eagle Mountains or Farnum or Rockhouse Canyons. I really want to find them here, because if I don't, I'll have to investigate Arizona. I know that this latitude is lower than that one."

I looked out at the landscape to the south. In the foreground there was only creosote, taller than us, waving in the wind. In the distance the bajada stretched up and away, the olive green wash of *Larrea* merging with the milk chocolate tones of the mountains. From a north-facing canyon of the Cottonwoods, a small alluvial fan emerged—a perfect place for Joshua trees. "I'd say that's the last chance," said Cornett.

He stopped the car, raised his binoculars, and scanned the forest of yuccas on the brown slope.

"Nope."

We recrossed the boundary line of Joshua Tree National Monument. "Well, we struck out," Cornett announced. "I guess we'll have to redraw the boundaries of the Mojave Desert."

It was a curious pursuit, this business of ecological boundaries and scientific classification. A wholly empirical grasping at straws, it suddenly seemed—a desperate and finally dumbfounding attempt to make sense of a world that had been evolving and diverging and reshaping itself for millions of years before *Homo sapiens* ever entered into it. Even such an apparently straightforward and "young" place as the Mojave—an environment more recent than the human race—could, despite our vaunted curiosity and supposed sophistication, easily elude our fundamental efforts to define it. *Yucca brevifolia* is a lily; then again, maybe it's an agave. It's definitely a monocot, even though it has bark. The *jaegeriana* variety branches before flowering—most of the time. The Joshua tree's characteristic plant community doesn't exist, and the southern boundary of its habitat—the Mojave—isn't where it's supposed to be. In the face of scientific inquiry, the desert appeared to retain its mystery without much effort at all.

"One thing I've learned is that when you start looking into anything closely, you find out there are a lot of myths," Cornett said as we pulled up to the Cottonwood visitor center. He continued puzzling over our lack of results as I retrieved my gear from the back of the Bronco. By the time I returned to the driver's-side window, however, he had a hypothesis ready.

"You know," he said, looking pensively through the windshield, "with global warming, the Joshua tree might be retreating northward."

A ROAD RUNS
THROUGH IT

The Mojave is the realm of the Joshua tree, the desert tortoise, the high-speed jet fighter, and the car. The unofficial symbol of the desert is the abandoned automobile: overturned, covered with rust, riddled with holes made by bullets. In some places this sight is more common than cacti. The car has brought far more humans through the Mojave than did the early railroads; it has facilitated vastly more ambition than did the mule (whether singly or in teams of twenty). In most parts of the desert, as Reyner Banham observed in an essay entitled "Awheel in the Waste," "only modern road building techniques, and the modern automobile, could think of passing this way." Accordingly, 95 percent of the Mojave Desert today lies within three miles of some kind of road.

What kind? Banham went so far as to claim that an "American desert may be cynically described as an arid zone with a four-line highway slapped down in the middle of it." The Mojave has its share of such roads, but away from the interstates, the primary avenue of ingress is a dirt track following a high-voltage power line—long, straight, undulant, and washboarded by wind and rain. The primary agent of identification here—that distant disclosure of human presence—is a moving dust cloud. The characteristic desert vehicle is neither the terrain-conquering four-wheel-drive jeep nor the low-slung convertible of popular fable but rather the ancient, unwieldy station wagon—laden, often as not, with the driver's worldly possessions. Such cars have probed the length and breadth of the Mojave. (To be fair, extensive reconnaissance has also been performed in Volkswagens: for decades, the creature at the top of the etymological food chain in arid regions was the beetle.)

"Automobiles were introduced early into the desert country," writes historian Dennis Casebier. "Although they were unreliable in the beginning and fuel was at times difficult to obtain, they were no more expensive to keep than horses and mules." The reason cars loom so large in the Mojave can be explained, like almost everything else about the desert, by two letters and a number: H_2O (or the lack of it). Specifically, a car can carry it for you. So can a horse or a mule, of course; but since the car confined those animals to roles in ranching and recreation, the internal-combustion engine has notoriously held sway. Even where camping is concerned, while the desert has a determined coterie of hard-core pedestrians, the typical backpacker, who generally evinces a tendency to decry the influence of fossil fuel, whistles a different tune in these parts—not just because water weighs a lot but because the desert hiker, like everything around him or her, is completely exposed. Under conditions of such exertion, water grows more essential at the same rate that it grows scarce.

Tracing the social and historical effect of the automobile (and its superseding of the railroad) in the desert, Banham continues:

> The fact that the car is under our personal control also colors our perceptions. The mere fact that one could slow down, even stop at will—something that the train passenger cannot do without incurring legal penalties—in itself changes everything. The illusions of being in charge of one's own life as a desert traveller may be mere illusion, but they seem to bestow a freedom of observation and enhanced awareness. Purists like Edward Abbey may scream, "You've got to get out of that damned car and get down on your hands and knees," but the automobilist in fact sees and understands a very great deal about the desert.

Death Valley is a great example of a place that has gained devotees solely because of the automobile. Members of the Manly wagon party, which was stranded in the valley in 1849 after taking an ill-advised short-cut off the Old Spanish Trail, spent a whole month starving here. Today's traveler, after sampling cafeteria food in the lowest and hottest place in the Western Hemisphere, can quit it in an hour.

Unfortunately, for all the people it has exposed to the desert, the car has also served to expose many *in* it. As Banham noted, the idea of being in control here—that feeling so notably advanced by the automobile—is nothing but an illusion. The car is considered a life-support system—a survival capsule for outer space—but if it breaks or gets bogged down, life suddenly enjoys less support than it might with more primitive trans-portation. Sans auto, the modern traveler is quickly reduced to the level of the Manly party, albeit with fewer survival skills. In Death Valley in July, a carless person without water would live less than two days.

In the Mojave, if you leave the asphalt unprepared, you're risking your life. The San Bernardino County map is filled with roads that look like shortcuts between major highways; by virtue of their presence on the map, they seem to connote some element of civility (however remote). What they fail to communicate is the recent condition of the so-called road—or the uncompromising isolation of the country through which it passes. Hence, tourists take rental cars into raw desert. They maneuver Winnebagos down washes. They navigate sand dunes in pas-senger vans. They drive Troopers, Explorers, and Pathfinders onto dry lakes that, just beneath the sunbaked surface, turn out not to be so dry. Consequently, they find themselves doing something that they hadn't anticipated: walking for miles on end through the desert, looking for help.

According to a *Car and Driver* expedition that once traversed the Mojave Road, the town of Baker—south of Death Valley, north of Soda Dry Lake, near the sandswept waste of the Devil's Playground—exists solely "because people don't maintain their cars properly. The town's leading industry is dispensing radiator hoses and Prestone." In 1991, towing fees at Baker garages ran three dollars per mile, plus fifty dollars for a hookup and drop—one hundred dollars if off-road, where a winch must often be employed at a rate of forty dollars per hour. Every year, scores of chastened and dehydrated fun seekers contribute in such gen-erous manner to the local economy—*if* they're lucky enough to troop, explore, and find a path out of their predicament. Occasionally they aren't: Every few years, somebody gets stuck and tries to walk, without any water in the middle of the day, over what seemed a short distance in a car. Eventually somebody else finds the body.

The danger was even greater, of course, when cars themselves were less reliable. On April 28, 1927, a letter appeared in the *Barstow Printers* newspaper, penned by one Elmo Proctor, proprietor of a service station at a desert crossroads called Cronese. The letter told of a pedestrian who had come looking for his wife. The lady was supposed to have set out the previous day with a friend in a Ford coupe from Yermo for Crucero—a distance of about forty miles along the Mojave riverbed.

"The only road to Crucero [is] deep sand practically all the way," wrote Proctor, who was hired by the husband to go looking for the wife. "The women turned across the trackless desert sand drifts toward Crucero, going about two miles further. . . . There we found the car stuck in the sand and the ladies' tracks showing they had gone on afoot. Still driving by pushing, digging, and planking with wide rubber belting . . . we found the ladies completely all in from the heat, exertion and thirst. Turning back we dug the car . . . out and with the outfit complete once again we fought the sand back up the valley for several hours until I burned out my low gear band in my Ford."

The next day, Proctor returned with a tow truck, but a pin in his clutch twisted off. He went back for parts, repaired the truck, and eventually found the Ford. On the way home, however, he met a man who was "stuck in the sand but I helped him out and he went on his way rejoicing." Soon after that, he "found a Buick six touring car stuck in the sand and abandoned. Probably the driver had gone for help." Following this escapade, Proctor concluded that "driving through the Cronese-Baxter-King-Crucero route should never be attempted except in case of life or death and then with a light car, balloon tires, sand equipment and a good sand driver; also plenty of water."

In the early days, even if you drove a car instead of taking the train, the railroad was your lifeline. As Dennis Casebier writes: "If you were going to travel across the desert toward Arizona in the early part of this century by a means other than the railroad, likely you would follow the line of the railroad itself. The problem there was the sandy areas alongside the tracks. . . . It was not uncommon in those early days for 'autoists,' as they were called, to drive their 'machines' as far as Ludlow, load them on a train, and off-load them at Goffs to continue the journey.

Even in the earliest times, a few intrepid souls braved the roadless desert sands and drove on through."

The earliest such crossing recounted by Casebier—"one of the most daring and exciting automobile tours ever undertaken in the west," according to the *Searchlight Bulletin*—took place in 1907. C. A. Dundas and Ted Crossley departed Riverside, California, on Monday morning, March 11. Two and a half days later, they arrived at the town of Daggett, eighty miles away. At that point they spent several hours trying to find the road to Goffs:

> Failing to get information started to follow Santa Fe tracks. For four hours on the desert, lost direction but finally came to Santa Fe. At Ludlow, advised to take cars and ship machine. Populace insisted roads impassable and feared they would get lost on the desert. Run from Daggett to Bagdad in one day being eight-nine miles for the day, through sand, no roads, crossed Dry Lake, which in some places had a foot of water. Left Bagdad early in morning and struck lava bed, crumbling material and sharp as knife blades for twenty-five miles, also many boulders. Up hill all the way in a mixture of sand and lava. From Bagdad to objective point, Goffs, roads improved, and so on into Searchlight.

The following December, the first female is reported to have made the trip: Mrs. C. H. Bigelow, wife of the chief Reo auto dealer for southern California and Nevada. Not surprisingly, the couple—along with a companion named A. G. Pagett—"attempted the terrors of the Santa Fe and Goffs route" in a 20-22 Reo, their purpose being to collect information for the General Association of Automobile Dealers. The party described the 330-mile, thirty-six-hour journey from Los Angeles to Searchlight as "passable, but very heavy from [Bagdad] to Ludlow. Eight miles south of Ludlow and from there to Ash Hill it is almost impassable. Thence to Amboy it is very rocky but hard. From the last point to Essex it is up hill in sand but not very deep."

Little by little, as the years went on, more and more autoists braved the bleak terrain. Concomitant with this trend, according to Casebier, "was awareness in southern California that the automobile would change things so far as tourists and emigration travel was concerned." The fledgling Automobile Club of Southern California began to publish maps and promote cross-country travel; in 1914 it signposted the route east from L.A.—by then called the National Old Trails Road—all the way to Kansas City. Five years later, the *Barstow Printers* announced that "sign posts will be erected throughout the desert region in Death Valley and vicinity, making it impossible for an autoist to lose himself in the sandy wastes which have made the 'valley of lost souls' famous."

Moreover, the newspaper cautioned:

> Sign-shooters are going to get theirs if they persist in defacing the guide posts erected by the Automobile Club, according to a statement issued yesterday from the legal department of that organization. A nice little section has been found in the California Penal Code which not only makes it hot for the vandal who has no more sense than to destroy a road guide but which also provides for a fat reward for the party who catches him at it. One half of all fines imposed and collected against the nut who has nothing better to do than turn his pop-gun on an invaluable mile post will be paid to the person who causes a complaint to be filed against said nut.

In November of 1919, the *Printers* reported "over 1500 automobiles bound for Southern California over the transcontinental routes leading here. . . . Officials traveling toward the Grand Canyon counted 109 'out of the state' cars. . . . Garages and parking spaces along the route were filled to overflowing with those bound for the boulevards of Southern California. It is the greatest westward trek in history. The view from the top of a hill looking across the desert, according to the officers, was like looking down on the old-time caravans, so thick were the cars. . . . Cars representing 26 states were discovered between Barstow and Needles."

Casebier concurs that "by 1920, the trickle of adventurers that braved the unimproved, twisting, winding ruts of old wagon roads to reach California, turned into a young flood. Now, during peak periods, it would not be uncommon for a hundred vehicles to pass a given point on the road in a single day." The population of Los Angeles doubled during the 1920s; the city now had an automobile for every three of its citizens. Aiming for the increased business, local booster clubs along the National Old Trails Road began joining forces to promote the route.

Ever since the Civil War, a "good-roads" movement had been smoldering in the United States. Initially it had been stoked by the advent of the bicycle, but after the turn of the century, the automobile functioned as a bona fide bellows. America was still a rural nation, and with the coming of the car, all manner of difficult things suddenly became easy. Children could get to school. Letters could reach isolated mailboxes. Railroads could no longer monopolize the market for transporting farm products to the city. But all of this was contingent on the quality of the roads. Hence, grassroots "trail" organizations sprang up all over the country, and in 1916 President Woodrow Wilson responded by signing the Federal Aid Road Act, which called for a national network of highways funded by public dollars. By the twenties, though, the system was still pretty crude: many of the routes overlapped, and "signs" were often nothing more than color-coded fenceposts on corners. Finally, in 1924, the U.S. secretary of agriculture appointed a board of state and federal officials to develop a numbered, nationwide system of highways from existing thoroughfares. Eventually, more than seventy-five thousand miles were so designated—almost all of them on roads leading east-west or north-south along established, popular rights-of-way.

One of the few exceptions to the above was a proposed route leading southwest from Chicago through St. Louis, Tulsa, Amarillo, Tucumcari, Flagstaff, Needles, Barstow, San Bernardino, and Los Angeles, petering out at the Pacific Ocean on the Santa Monica pier. This was the dream of one Cyrus Avery, a Tulsa businessman and rabid road activist who had spent most of his adult life lobbying for better highways in Oklahoma. In light of the obvious commercial stakes, considerable politics were involved in decisions about the major routes; Avery desperately wanted one for the Sooner State, passing through his hometown of Tulsa and the capital at Oklahoma City. Moreover, as a member of the executive committee for the national highway board (not to mention his presidency of the insistently named Associated Highways Association of America), he had the clout to call some shots. He envisioned his pet highway as one of the "big" transcontinental routes, thereby deserving—as per the policy of the board—of a zero at the end of its name. He wanted to number it U.S. 60 but met with resistance from his colleagues in Kentucky and Virginia, who held that any national highway with one end at the Pacific should have its other at the Atlantic. This was consistent with the plans of the committee, which had already called for a cross-country route leading from Los Angeles to Newport News, Virginia.

In the end, Avery proved stubborn enough to force a kind of compromise. He didn't get his wish for number 60; that route would lead from Virginia to Springfield, Missouri. There, however, it would join Avery's road, which ran as he intended all the way from Chicago to L.A. by way of Oklahoma (and, in between, the Mojave). As it turned out, the numerology didn't much matter—or to the extent that it did, Avery ended up with a number apparently even better suited to attract attention. His road would, in relatively short order, assume an unassailable spot in the heart of the nation, entering the annals of American folklore as Route 66.

Even today, Route 66, as the nation's primary cross-country highway before the advent of the faceless interstate, enjoys a hallowed place in our pantheon alongside the likes of Will Rogers and Lucille Ball. Helped by a hit song, a TV show, and a great American novel, the so-called Main Street of America soon became—according to Susan Croce Kelly, author of *Route 66: The Highway and Its People*—nothing less than "a symbol for the American people's heritage of travel and their national legacy of bettering themselves by moving west." As Kelly goes on to explain:

> Route 66 came to be part of the uprootings and major changes in American life that took place during the first half of the twentieth century. . . . When it was born, traveling Route 66 was an adventure. Later, it was the mother road for destitute farmers and a haven for small businessmen fleeing the ravages of the Great Depression. Later still, it became the great military road to the army bases and airfields and armaments factories for World War II. After the war, Route 66 became the golden road west, carrying thousands more people than it had in the Depression on a great fortune-seeking migration to the infant industries on the West Coast or the glamour of Hollywood.

The first major celebration (if it can be called such in context of a book about the Great Depression) of the national psychosocial role of

Route 66 came with the publication of *The Grapes of Wrath* in 1939. "66 is the main migrant road," John Steinbeck declared, beginning his evocation of the highway and the journey of the Joads:

> 66—the long concrete path across the country, waving gently up and down on the map, from the Mississippi to Bakersfield—over the red lands and the gray lands, twisting up into the mountains, crossing the Divide and down into the bright and terrible desert. . . . 66 is the path of a people in flight, refugees from dust and shrinking land. . . . they come into 66 from the tributary side roads, from the wagon tracks and the rutted country roads. 66 is the mother road, the road of flight.

Actually, Route 66 wasn't fully paved until 1938. One of the first such civilized stretches was none other than that "bright and terrible desert," the Mojave. However, in its earliest years, this part of Route 66, like those in other sections of the country, ran directly through the dust, following the dirt tracks and wooden planks of the National Old Trails Road. Innocent of bridges, it also ran directly through dry washes, which brought flash floods down from the mountains, occasionally carrying away cars. On the other hand, when the sun was shining—especially in summer—the desert was unbearably hot. Hence many travelers, like Steinbeck's protagonists, chose to cross the Mojave at night. Even so, this was where Granma Joad expired, scant hours before reaching the harbor of the San Joaquin Valley.

Steinbeck referred to Route 66 as "a terror between towns," and even in its later years, the two-hundred-mile-wide breadth of the Mojave was considered the most grueling and dangerous stretch. Water bags were tied to radiators, and roadside proprietors enjoyed a booming business in ice—or, as the craftier ones demonstrated, in conjunction with *free* ice and other vital needs. For example, *The Filling Station* magazine reported as early as 1924 that "in many instances the restrooms draw trade. . . . More companies each month are adding this feature to their business." In fact, as Kelly observed, Route 66 was a godsend to small entrepreneurs, because "the first pioneering efforts at pumping gas, serving hamburgers, and offering souvenirs and overnight accommodations were the foundation for a whole new industry of highway service, one that did not seem to be affected by the vagaries of the economy the way similar businesses would have been in town." In fact, the cross-country corridor of Route 66 was practically a self-contained civilization, as even in the hardest times—in some ways even more so then—people needed to keep moving.

The zenith of this impulse—and the period universally considered the "golden age" of Route 66—came immediately after World War II, when middle-class Americans first began to enjoy the benefits of disposable income, paid vacations, and unlimited mobility. Not incidentally, Bobby Troup's "Get Your Kicks on Route 66" became a nationwide radio hit. Dennis Casebier recalls "an almost endless chain of gas stations, garages, and auto courts along 66 across the California desert." The sideshow in other parts of the country also reached an apogee: the Petrified Forest, the Buffalo Ranch, tepees and turquoise and silver vendors—every area of the nation had its own gimmick for hawking regional identity.

For people prone to sentimentality about such things, this vanished era still represents a boundless opportunity for shameless nostalgia. As Michael Wallis put it in *Route 66: The Mother Road:*

> Route 66 put Americans in touch with other Americans through its necklace of neon lights, Burma Shave signs, curio shops, motor courts, garages, and diners and cafes with big-boned waitresses. . . . Route 66 means a time before America became generic—when motels didn't take reservations, when there were genuine barber shops and drugstores, and doctors made house calls. Movie theaters weren't look-alike boxes in a shopping center. There were no diet soft drinks or imported waters. People drank straight from the tap and sipped iced tea brewed by the sun or Coca-Cola or Grape Nehi. America seemed more innocent. Billboards on the highway were legal; hitchhiking was safe. Nobody knew about cholesterol. Summers lasted longer because there were drive-in movies and miniature golf courses and slow-pitch softball games under the lights.

Actually, drive-in movies, miniature golf courses, and slow-pitch softball are all in considerably better shape than Route 66 today. In the early sixties, as Martin Milner and George Maharis tooled around on TV, Route 66 was dying a slow death in the real world. Only four decades after the Federal Aid Road Act literally paved the way for 66 and its ilk, the Federal Aid Highway Act of 1956 authorized forty-one thousand miles of high-speed interstate four-lane thruways free of traffic lights and turquoise dealers. One by one, 66 and its eccentric cousins were put to sleep, as I-80, I-95, I-70, I-5, and all manner of other numerals preceded by the first-person pronoun linked the nation in the trend toward stream-lined homogeneity.

Interstate 40 between Barstow and Needles opened in May 1973. It par-alleled Route 66 about ten miles to the north of the old highway; the results were predictable and immediate. Once-thriving motels, cafés, and service stations in the Mojave were abruptly deserted (so to speak). Scores of gas pumps still stand idle along extant sections of the National Old Trails Road. Some of the decaying motels now function as low-rent apartments. Mostly, however, the road is dotted with decaying store-fronts and empty service stations of interest mainly to incurable roman-tics. As Reyner Banham wrote, "You can still get your kicks on Route 66, though you may need to be a historian nowadays to do so."

Occasionally, enterprising establishments along the old right-of-way attempt to capitalize on the highway heritage. In 1991, for example, the El Rancho Diner in Barstow—located in the middle of town on old Route 66 and now flanked by the vinyl-covered likes of Denny's and Perko's—reopened with leather booths, red counter stools, a black-and-white checkerboard floor, a Wurlitzer jukebox with rainbow tubes, Coke bottles with plastic flowers on the tables, and a '57 Chevy coming through the wall. When I ordered a chocolate milkshake made with chocolate ice cream (not, in other words, with vanilla spiked by chocolate syrup), the waitress replied, to my vast approval, "That's the way I do 'em." While waiting for it to arrive, I looked up at the wall and mused on the time when, as a teenager upset over a girl, I ran my father's '57 Chevy head-on into a telephone pole. By the time my milkshake arrived, I was swollen with sentiment about vanished youth—both my own and the nation's. Apparently, however, the market for such nostalgia extends only so far: by the time I returned to the El Rancho a couple of months later, ready for another shake 'n' sob, the place had shut down.

One of the more recent, successful, and idiosyncratic treatments of near-necrology on 66 was the Percy Adlon movie *Bagdad Cafe*, in which an almost-defunct desert coffee shop is rejuvenated by the arrival of a unique waitress. This character, fittingly, is German (fitting in that, especially in summer, the Mojave seems to hold special allure for no nationality as much as the Teutonic). In fact, the movie wasn't filmed in Bagdad but in Newberry Springs—twenty miles east of Barstow on old Route 66, at a café/motel called the Sidewinder.

When I stopped by the Sidewinder one weekday, I noticed that the gloss of international cinema hadn't left behind much luster. The motel room doors were all standing open, and many of the windows were smashed. The café itself had a counter but no stools. There was a Mickey Mouse clock on the dining room wall, a bunch of baseball trophies on a shelf, and a boardwalk-style "Jumbo Skill" game in one corner, challenging the player to pick up stuffed animals with a hook.

I sat down at a table and ordered the special of the day: split-pea soup. The manager, whose name was Stephanie, was wearing jeans and a dark blue T-shirt that had a breast pocket. She said that the motel had never been open in the half-dozen years she'd worked there. As far as the film shoot was concerned, she allowed that she "wouldn't necessarily want to go through it again. This place was so depressing then. All the interiors were black and red. More than anything, it was a lot of work. We catered it, and we'd open at six, and they wouldn't start filming till nine. The crew had their wrap party at my house—they hired a country-western band and barbecued a pig in a pit. The director got real excited about it.

"Europeans still come in asking about it," she said, pouring me more coffee. "As soon as they hit the door, you can tell why they're here from the look on their face. A lot of 'em just take a picture and then turn around and leave."

As we talked, a middle-aged man in a white V-neck sweater came in and ordered a cup of coffee to go. Then he thought better of it and sat down. "I saw it by accident on HBO a year and a half ago," he volunteered. "It was so haunting—I don't know why." Now, on his way from Las Vegas to Los Angeles, he said he'd gotten off I-25 [*sic:* I-15] to pay the place a visit. "I'm from Hamlet, North Carolina," he said. "Dustin Hoffman's filming a movie there now—*Billy Bathgate*. North Carolina's number two in the country now in film locations. Florida's number three."

The telephone rang. Stephanie answered it. "Yes, it is," she said. A minute later, she called out to a friend at a table that it was somebody from Sydney, Australia, asking for directions to the café from L.A.

"Ask 'em if they want to buy it," the friend advised.

"We all have traumas in our personal lives that we can't deal with because we're working here," Stephanie explained to me after she hung up. I asked where she was from originally. She said that she'd been born in Chicago and had lived for a while in La Verne, west of San Bernardino. Later I realized that this meant Stephanie had spent her entire life on Route 66.

From Newberry Springs, I continued driving east across the desert, following the tracks of C. A. Dundas and Ted Crossley, reversing the journey of the Joads. Only in certain places today can you can still travel the National Old Trails Road; in many stretches there is no choice other than the interstate. The two do diverge, however, for a lengthy spell beginning at the town of Ludlow, from which 66 follows its original path for more than seventy miles through the Mojave.

In April 1922 the *Barstow Printers* related the fact that

> The town of Ludlow is surely an oasis on the desert. It is located 55 miles east of Barstow, and this time of the year, when driving to Ludlow, the traveler is greeted by a garden of wild flowers, their perfume scenting the country for miles.
>
> The first glimpse you get of the town as you go over the hill it is seen that all the buildings are painted, and as the traveler enters he observes how clean the yards and streets are kept. The absence of tin cans and rubbish piles along the approaches to the town are appreciated. The trees and shrubbery attract attention and show that the residents take an interest in making the place attractive. And then when the traveler learns that the water for irrigation and also for drinking purposes is hauled 30 miles, he certainly admires the pluck of the Ludlow residents.

Since Ludlow is still on the interstate, it continues to boast a functioning motel/coffee shop/gas station. Other than these less-than-charismatic establishments, though, only the shells of disintegrating buildings are scattered around the town. The ravaged storefront of the Ludlow

Mercantile Company, for example, had been spray-painted with the name L.A. GUNS. The shell of a former service station continued to advertise GENERATORS REGULATORS WATER PUMPS FUEL PUMPS. The sign in front of a dilapidated ex-restaurant read: L DL W CAFE. Meanwhile, carved onto a bare hill west of town in the American tradition of civic pride—notwithstanding the condition of its subject—was a giant letter *L*.

At one of the Chevron pumps in town, a squad of U.S. Marines in camouflage clothing was filling up a truck labeled EXPLOSIVES. Shortly thereafter, I was able to observe their handiwork. As I continued driving east, I began to notice flashes of light off to the right of the road. At first I thought I was hallucinating, but then I saw distant puffs of smoke and mini–mushroom clouds rising from the bajada. Suddenly I realized the reason for the explosions: just south of old 66 is the U.S. Marine Corps Air-Ground Combat Center, which annually trains fifty thousand soldiers on nine hundred square miles near Twentynine Palms.

Appropriately enough, along now came the actual—i.e., former— town of Bagdad, California. Prior to the release of the movie (filmed fifty miles away), and since the glory days of the Orange Blossom gold mine (nine miles to the north), Bagdad's primary distinction was having undergone the longest period without rainfall in the recorded history of North America: between February 1917 and January 1920, the place received one one-hundredth of an inch. Today the sole remains of the town are a single date palm and a sign announcing BAGDAD beside the Santa Fe railroad tracks. I got out of my truck and walked around, finding little of interest other than a lime green Volkswagen parked on a concrete loading ramp; its owners were wandering somewhere down along the train tracks. The car had running lights on its roof, a tow bar on its front end, raised fenders all around, an unhooded engine exposed to the air, extrawide rear tires, and an orange ball on the tip of its radio antenna. Its ancient black-and-yellow California license plates—obtained in the days before vanity plates were available—were nevertheless perfect for an early-model dune buggy: *OOF.*

A Santa Fe freight train was coming from the west—going my way. I got back in my truck and pulled out onto the highway. The train had a head start, but gradually I pulled even with it; we traveled parallel for some minutes, racing side by side from cinder cone to cinder cone, as, off to the right, the black outline of the Amboy crater intersected the sky. This was undoubtedly the model location for Steinbeck's "terrible desert, where the distance shimmers and the black center mountains hang unbearably in the distance." The Amboy crater, rising 250 feet from the desert floor, did offer ample evidence of anguish: it was surrounded for a square mile by the burnt rock of lava flows, some of which had occurred within the last few thousand years. Most of the Mojave's volcanic cones have been mined for their cinders; this, one of the few exceptions, remains relatively untouched.

The same can't be said of Bristol Dry Lake, located directly behind the crater. Once, as I approached this playa from the south, I thought I saw some banklike ridges shimmering at its edge. Mirages are common on dry lakes, but this turned out to be a different kind. As I drew close, I discovered that the surface had been bulldozed—what I'd seen from the distance was a ditch. The National Chloride flaking plant stood nearby, and the name of a road leading into the area aptly identified the task that civilization has assigned to the place: Saltus.

I walked out on the sprawling saline flats. My feet sank into the brown parts, but the white sections were solid. They almost seemed more frozen than dry; in fact, the surface was so hard that I couldn't chop through it with my hand. Ridges and fissures wove their way across the bleached crust. I broke off a piece and put it in my mouth; it was salt, all right.

Just beyond the point where the train crossed Route 66 to go around a town, I saw a sign that read:

FOR SALE
The Town of Amboy
Found 1858
Population 20

The town consisted of a school, a post office, and Roy's Motel/Café—a half-dozen white cottages with light blue doors, fronted by a garden of barrel and cholla cacti. To be honest, I already knew that Amboy was for sale; according to every article that had been written about it, the person to talk to was Buster Burris, proprietor of Roy's Café. As I entered, I noticed that the candy by the cash register was the kind I like: Mounds, Almond Joy, M & Ms, Hershey's, Snickers, Butterfingers, and Milky Way. The restaurant had a single counter backed by a plastic double-decker hamburger, pictures of Ronald Reagan and George Bush, and a sign that said, HIRE A COLLEGE STUDENT WHILE THEY STILL KNOW IT ALL. Behind the register, a white-haired man in a blue jumpsuit with a white T-shirt showing at the collar was peering closely at a handwritten receipt. Slowly he walked over to another man who was sitting at the counter.

The white-haired man handed the other one the bill. "What do you think that says?" he asked with a sly grin.

The other man held his head back and squinted at the piece of paper. "Dollar eighty?" he ventured.

"You're wrong."

"Dollar sixty?"

"You're wrong as can be."

"Dollar forty?"

"*Still* wrong."

"Dollar twenty?"

"*Still wrong!*" Finally the white-haired man called out to a woman working behind the counter: "What is it, Mary?"

"A dollar fifty," she said.

"I'll be damned!" said the man at the counter. "That don't look like a five-oh to me."

The white-haired man seemed tickled to death. Doesn't take much out here, I gathered.

"Excuse me," I said. "Do you know where I can find Buster?"

"Well," said the white-haired man, "he's pretty hard to find. Why did you want him?"

"I heard he was interested in selling the town."

"Well, he would be interested in selling it if somebody wanted to pay enough money for it."

"I don't suppose you'd be Buster," I said. The sly grin recrossed his face.

Taking a seat at the counter, I ordered an ice cream soda and a bowl of chili. The latter was good and spicy. "I bought fine-ground hamburger for it by accident," said Buster. "If I'd got coarse-ground, I guarantee you it'd be a hundred percent better."

I told him that I was writing a book about the Mojave Desert. "Number one," he said, "this is not the Mojave Desert. That starts on the other side of Ludlow. I have a map made in 1836 that gives everything here right to a tee—the Providence Mountains, the New York Mountains, all the creeks and washes—and it's all in the Colorado Desert. Bagdad used to be the county seat of San Bernardino County, and at that time *they* was known as the Colorado Desert."

"You might get some argument about that," I told him.

"Well, I'd just get out that map and settle the argument."

I asked him when he'd arrived in Amboy. "Nineteen thirty-seven," he said. "I was born in Bandera, Texas, in 1909. I stopped off in Arizona for a year before the government sent me to San Bernardino as a general inspector for the Air Force. I met my wife on the base, and she was from here. Her father owned this property, so we started coming out on the weekends with a few bags of cement at a time. We built every building here. There were two other complexes like this here then. One was owned by a Chinaman and the other one by a Greek. They said they was gonna run me out in six months. I never went to their places except for business; I didn't have time. I worked eighteen hours a day, sometimes twenty-four. We did more business in one day then than we do now in six months. We had ninety people working here—I used to fly help in from Oklahoma City, because people out here didn't want to work. We used to have over a hundred percent occupancy in the motel—we'd rent the rooms twice a day, daytime and nighttime. The traffic was bumper-to-bumper."

"You couldn't find a place to park out there," Buster's friend testified.

"I had three big wreckers," said Buster. "We had an average of three wrecks a day. The roads weren't marked, and all the bridges was blind, so there were head-on collisions all the time. The bridge rails were made with eight-by-eight redwood; they'd run right through the radiator, up the side of the motor, through the firewall, and through the driver—pin him right in his seat. We'd have to cut him out with a handsaw. The state engineer didn't want to paint lines in the road until this Navy boy ran head-on into a car that was passing a truck; he was arrested for manslaughter, but I said he's not at fault, the state engineer's at fault. So they sued and won three million dollars. After that, the state was out here working night and day painting stripes. They didn't even want to stop for lunch.

"When I-40 opened, it took away ninety percent of my business. That road is six miles shorter than this one is, but in a big car you need five more gallons of gas to take it—it winds around through the mountains. And it's a trucker's highway; a car ain't got much of a chance. You want to know why they didn't run it down through here? Because half the traffic would've cut down to Palm Springs and San Bernardino. As it is now, they go on to Barstow and down through Victorville. That's where all the money is. Movie stars live there."

When I finished my chili, I asked where the bathroom was. Buster directed me outside, toward what turned out to be a vast public chamber with three stalls, a defunct shower, and a trough-style urinal like those at ballparks, capable of accommodating crowds. When I returned to the restaurant, Buster was talking to a couple of male travelers—one German, one British. The Englishman had bare feet and a ponytail tied up high on his head. He wanted to know the condition of Kelbaker Road to the north. Buster said it was "paved all the way except for three miles."

When the pair departed, Buster told me: "We're on a direct route here from Palm Springs to Las Vegas. We've had an increase in traffic lately, from people going to gamble in Laughlin, Nevada. But I'm gettin' too old to take care of the place now. I haven't worked on cars since 1960—I can't get up or down. I'm asking two and a half million for the whole town—I own every building in it. I wouldn't take a penny less."

"Had any offers?"

"Two were willing to pay me cash, but they couldn't handle it. They were foreigners—they didn't have the skills for the services."

"What nationality?"

"Well," said Buster, "I won't say. But you know which ones are buying up all the motels and service stations, don't you?"

"Japanese?"

"No—Japanese are pretty clean people. But I have enough capital to keep on going. I can always draw on my savings. When you're as old as I am, it don't matter much."

Four customers at a nearby table were speaking French. I wondered idly what they thought of the food. A man approached the register and inquired as to how much the fluorescent Roy's Café keychains on the counter cost. Buster said, "Yours for the asking."

When he returned from the register, he was carrying a glossy pamphlet. "I'm hoping this will give us a shot in the arm," he said, handing it to me. It was a brochure for Rail Cycle, a company proposing to haul waste by train from L.A. and dump it in the desert near Amboy. Judging by news reports from more populated areas, one might have expected local opposition. But Buster was keeping his fingers crossed. "They say there'll be fifty-one families here full-time," he told me. "I'll get some of 'em; maybe I'll get all of 'em. Anyway, if it goes in, the town will be worth twice what I'm asking for it."

I thanked Buster and got up to go. As he shook my hand, he asked, "You know how this town got its name?"

"How?"

"The railroad crew was coming through, and one guy said to another, 'Sure is hot.' The other one said, 'Sure am, boy.'"

It had been an informative visit. Not only had I been ignorant of the fact that the East Mojave is actually part of the Colorado Desert; I'd also been totally unaware that Victorville had supplanted Palm Springs as a magnet for Hollywood glitterati. Buster had educated me on the characteristics of different races while simultaneously shedding light on a unique modern approach to environmental waste. Only on old 66, it seemed, was it possible to identify the existence of the PIMBY syndrome: Please, In My Back Yard.

As I continued east, the sun was low in my rearview mirror. I went by the deceased towns of Chambless and Danby and passed the Roadrunner Retreat, whose eye-catching sign, complete with roadrunner, still stood tall beside the highway while tumbleweeds overtook the gas station. The setting sun inflamed the vertical posts of its "Official Garage," which was, I noted, being circled for some reason by a helicopter.

Finally I came to Essex, the last town on old 66 (that is, after the highway was routed away from Fenner and Goffs) west of Needles and the Arizona border. Essex was also once distinguished as the last town in the United States to gain the benefit of television; as such, it had been featured on *The Tonight Show* with Johnny Carson. I was scheduled to meet someone there whom I'd met briefly once before: the local postmaster, Jack Howard, who had lived in Essex for forty years.

I found him at his ranch house beside the town's requisite extinct service station/café—this one with signs advertising GOOD FOOD and AIR CONDITIONING. As he came to the door to greet me, Howard—a big man wearing a mustache and cowboy boots—was moving pretty slow; he said he'd been up late the previous night, playing music with friends. "Sometime you go for a practice session, and it ends up being a full-fledged bang-a-roo party," he said. He had a soft, mellifluous voice tinged with an Oklahoma accent. As we sat down in his living room, I asked how he'd wound up in the Mojave.

"I came out with my brother in 1952," he said. "He told me there was jobs all over out here: working for the store, the school district, as a night watchman, at the courthouse in Danby. Back then, Amboy was the biggest town—they had National Chloride and Leslie Salt, and the same assessed value as the town of Needles. Route 66 wound around through Needles because they wanted to keep you in town. There were a lot of crooks on the highway then. If they caught a woman by herself, depending on how much money she had, they'd generally end up with all of it. A tow truck would come out and say, 'Can't fix your tire, lady, but I'll tow you to Needles for nine hundred and fifty dollars.' They'd puncture her tires, squirt oil on her shocks, put stuff on her alternator to make it smoke. Then they'd say, 'You better get that fixed—you're gonna have a wreck down the road.' They just rotated the parts over and over—no inventory, just pure profit. In those days there was very little communication, so you were at other people's mercy. The odd part of it is I never knew any of those fellas to prosper. There was one bunch that had to have a lawyer on retainer at all times.

"I managed the gas station here for a year or two. When I first came, I couldn't believe it; people were dying all over the place—it was just bloody. We probably had a good wreck about every two or three days, though it seemed to me it was *every* day. Most were multiple-car smashups—somebody'd go out to pass, get hit head-on, and take three or four other cars with them. It was a two-lane road with a sixty-five-mile-per-hour speed limit; people were fatigued and overheated. There weren't a lot of air-conditioned cars in those days, and most of the traveling was done in summer, which is the worst time. People'd strip down while they drove—take off their shirt, then take off their T-shirt, and then their skin got hot. Then they'd open the car door and fall out on the ground. Dehydration was common—it only takes three hours to make it happen. It happened to me once; the first year I got here, I went up

Sunflower Road to see the fireworks from Needles on the Fourth of July. When I got back in the car, it was dead. People never used the little roads in those days; if you left the highway, you didn't see *nobody*. If you get stuck, it doesn't take long to lose all your body fluid trying to get unstuck. My mother-in-law used to take a picnic lunch wherever we went, even if we were just going half a mile. If I see somebody walking by the road and I know there's nothing ahead for four or five miles, I'll stop and ask 'em if they want a ride. One time, I saw this movement up the road that looked like an adult with a kid running around in a red coat. I looked through my binoculars, and it was an old man waving a coat on the end of a two-by-four. I went out, and as I walked up to him, he fell down. He said, 'I can't go another step.' His truck had broken down, and he'd just walked ten miles. I brought him down to the station; he'd only been a couple hundred yards out of town, but he said I saved his life."

Jack paused for a minute and got up. He picked up a briefcase from beside the couch, opened it, and started searching through it for something. "A cigarette," he said. "I quit four years ago, but I told myself that if I ever feel like having one, I'll have one." He found a pack of Marlboros and lit one up. "These are really old," he said.

Settling back against the couch, he continued: "For a long time, I thought this was the best of all possible worlds here on this desert. Where else you gonna feel so free? After my wife and I got married in '69, we didn't have any kids till '76; in between, we had a ball—we just came and went as we pleased. There's so much to see out here. Even if you had every day to go out and explore, you could never see it all. I came on a spring one time, and this dove came up—then another and another, by the thousands. I'll never see that again. At another place, my wife and I found thirty or forty turtles. After that, we went up every day to check on 'em, and after a while I started noticing some of 'em were on their backs. Finally I realized what was happening: it was mating season, and the males were fighting, turning each other over so they'd dry up and die. One time I ran into a horned-owl convention in a wash where the freeway is now; another time, I came on hundreds of chukars when I was hunting with some friends. I said, We can get our limit right here, but I don't like to hunt that way. So we got two or three and scattered 'em. Right then, two jeeploads of guys came over the hill with automatic shotguns. I said, Boy, I'm glad I done that.

"I came to the conclusion some time ago that the desert is paradoxical—what's true one year might not be true the next. There's years where you won't see a tortoise, and others where you see a whole lot of 'em. Last winter it froze every night for a month or two; a few years in a row before that, it froze only two or three times each winter. Some people think the weather is harsh out here, but that's something you do to yourself. I *like* a little action in the weather—a thunderhead welling up, or seeing the dust coming. I've seen three tornadoes this year. Nobody really likes the wind, 'cause it's either cold or dusty; if it's dry, and a twenty- or thirty-mile-an-hour wind comes up, you can't see the highway, just the tops of the telephone poles. In 1970 we had no rain for a solid year. *That* gets on your nerves. You start getting obsessed with it. The bushes were as brown as the hills; it hurt your eyes to look at 'em. But in '64 we had monsoon rains, and six weeks later there was grass out there as far as you could see. A year or two after that we had so much game: foxes, coyotes, snakes, insects, just jillions of everything.

"Right now we're just coming out of another drought. The desert looks pretty good; there's a lot of green out there. We got some rain this summer that took seven bridges out between here and Danby. One time, the wash out there was running, and a guy tried to tow his trailer through it with a Thunderbird. If it was just the Thunderbird, it would've been okay, but the trailer started floating. The water turned it around and washed it down about a quarter of a mile. The next day the county was here trying to pull it out, but of course you can't; you gotta *dig* it out. It took two or three days, then another two or three cleaning the mud out of it."

I looked out the window. The distant mountains were still in sun, but the light was almost gone from the yard. I asked Jack if he felt up to taking a short walk. "Let's do it," he said.

We went out past the service station. "They filmed a Levi's commercial, and another one for Geo, in front of it a year ago," said Jack. "They were here for two weeks, and the commercial lasted about ten seconds."

A billboard beside the vacant station said, FOR INFORMATION STOP HERE. "When I-40 opened, it was just like shutting off the water," said Jack. "Everything dried right up. A month or two later our congressman, Jerry Pettis, made a trip through these towns; he told me, 'If you can survive without the highway, you'll be a better town.' And we *did* get rid of the crooks."

We strolled away from the setting sun, surrounded by bare brown mountains—the Clippers, the Paiutes, and the Old Womans, all now etched with black shadows. Essex's location amid these mountains was what had, until the late seventies, prevented it from getting TV signals.

"A guy came by from the Associated Press and wrote a story about it," Jack remembered. "It got the attention of somebody on Johnny Carson's staff, and they said, 'Well, let's bring *them* to TV!' They sent a secretary out here in a stretch limo and issued invitations; then they sent a couple of big Greyhounds, and everybody went on the show. I didn't, 'cause I had to keep the post office open—though before I got to work that day, somebody had put up a sign that said, CLOSED TODAY FOR THE JOHNNY CARSON SHOW. I hit the roof—if the higher-ups had heard about it, I would've been in hot water.

"After that, somebody who makes TV transmitters in Pennsylvania offered us one. We took a poll and the majority wanted it, so they put it over on Goffs Butte—the Santa Fe Railroad donated the land for it. They switched it on at noon one day; Jack Perkins of NBC News came, and the chief of communications for Santa Fe. They put an antenna on my house. The first picture we got was from the Middle East—all these camels with palm trees in the background. They were signing the Sadat-Begin treaty then.

"Well, this was just the start. The whole thing ballooned out of proportion—pretty soon CBS and ABC sent their top guys out, and the reporters and TV crews kept coming and kept coming, and the phone was ringing off the hook. They'd come to our square dances and show that on TV. One morning I woke up and heard a turkey gobbling—NBC had set up this fifty-pound turkey right out in front here, I mean it was a *monster*. This went on for I don't know how long—I was answering letters for two years. We should've hired a PR man, because I was out of things to say."

On the eastern edge of Essex were some old miners' cabins, plus the town water tank. I saw a house trailer and asked if anybody lived there. "That's a church," Jack said. Then he pointed out a small house where he and his wife had once lived, referring to it as "the teacherage." Turned out his wife was the Essex schoolteacher, kindergarten through eighth grade. In terms of acreage, this area is part of the largest school district in the United States—teenagers from Amboy and Essex commute several hours each day to the high school in Needles.

"Back in '66," Jack said, "because of some loose talk, a bunch of us got mad at each other. The upshot was that they closed the school, and the young kids had to go to Needles for a while. It's really quite different here from any other place I've ever known—we get to know each other real well. Probably too well. There's a certain amount I don't want to know about somebody. But I don't go to big towns much. I go to Needles once in a while. I go to Las Vegas if I have to, and I go to L.A. only if I'd lose my job otherwise. But things are getting heavier here now—we've got more problems than we used to have. Over in Ward Valley, twenty miles to the northeast, they want to put in a radioactive waste dump. They've done a lot of studies, and they said the water at seven hundred feet here was undrinkable, though as I recall, somebody over there had a well that was okay fifteen or twenty years ago. But there's not a lot you can do about things like that unless you wanna get up on your hind legs and fight it. We did have a local lady who was very outspoken against it, and guess what—they hired her. Fact is, they're gonna put it *some-where*."

Now the light was gone even from the mountains. The sky was turn-ing indigo in the east, above old 66 where it disappeared toward the interstate.

"The county's changed tremendously just in the years I've been here," Jack said. "We used to like it here because we could be independent, but we also used to help each other out. When I moved into my house, the neighbors started painting it before I even got there. But I'm seeing that feeling dissipate now. When I first came here, the desert wasn't really worth much. Nobody else was looking at it; most people just saw it as something you had to get through. We'd take care of things ourselves because nobody else did—but now, somebody's liable to shoot you. The desert used to belong only to us desert people, but now I guess it belongs to everybody."

FOUR-WHEELING
THE MIOCENE

Seven A.M. on a Thursday in March. Seventy miles below Hoover Dam and Lake Mead, sixty miles above Parker Dam and Lake Havasu, the Colorado River surges south toward the Sea of Cortez. Scores of swallows hunt along the surface of the gray-green water. Upstream, the smokestacks of the Mojave coal plant near Laughlin are visible in their own haze, which is slowly spreading downwind, obscuring an otherwise crystalline morning following a spring storm. Thanks to the rain, grass is actually growing in the desert dirt, and distant brown bajadas are faintly tinged with green.

On a gravel causeway lining the west bank, twenty-one vehicles are parked. Augmenting the Jeeps and Toyotas is a roll call of the rugged names favored by four-wheel-drive manufacturers: Bronco, Montero, Wagoneer, Comanche, Explorer, Pathfinder, and (warping the curve of the group's average value) Range Rover. Standing alongside the vehicles is a group of thirty-five people, ranging in age from twenty to seventy. Most are clothed in jeans or khakis. Some wear showily rugged hats: a camouflage army cap, a suede western hat with a feathered band. The youngest member of the group wears a black leather jacket that says METALLICA MEGADETH on the back. All are listening to a man dressed in a yellow polo shirt, pleated trousers, leather workboots, and a denim jacket. Nearing sixty, he wears wire-rimmed eyeglasses and combs his gray hair straight back from his forehead.

"Several people called last night and asked if we were going to cancel because of the rain," he says through a bullhorn. "Well, you never do that on the desert. If you said anything, chances are it would turn out different. What you *do* is come out and check how it is." This commonsense maxim is in keeping with the man's midwestern drawl, which he occasionally exaggerates for effect. As is the case with other mid-American raconteurs, his homespun delivery belies a carbon-honed intellect. By training, the man is a physicist and a mathematician; by passion and avocation, however, he is a historian. "You're standing on a very historic spot," he tells his audience. "This is Beale's Crossing of the Colorado, or 'Rio Colorado of the West,' as they called it then. There was a ferry here starting in 1859—the same year that fifteen hundred troops marched into this valley against the Mohave* Indians."

The man looks down the line of vehicles, many bearing blue FOMR pennants attached to CB radio antennas. "This is Mile Zero-point-zero of the Mojave Road," he tells the gathered throng. "Elevation four hundred and eighty feet. By early afternoon today, we'll be at five thousand."

The man, introduced in the previous chapter, is Dennis Casebier— the name pronounced precisely the same way as twenty-four cans of lager. Half a century ago, he grew up in Kansas. At the end of the Korean War, he joined the Marine Corps and thus found himself stationed in Twentynine Palms, California. He did not, however, react to the desert with the customary rancor of soldiers raised in more humid environs. Instead he began spending ninety-six-hour leaves in Joshua Tree National Monument. "It was a nice place then," he remembers. "If you pulled into a campground and saw somebody else, you'd go on to another one. Now it's wall-to-wall people."

Upon being discharged from the Marines, Casebier remained in southern California, working as an engineer for the Navy and exploring the Colorado Desert on weekends. In time, however, he realized that "the scenery in the East Mojave is more dramatic. The mountains are higher and moister; there are clearer blue skies because of the elevation.

---

*There is a sanctioned discrepancy in the spelling of this word. The rather arbitrary rule is that when the name Mojave is applied in Arizona, the *j* becomes an *h*.

There are a lot more people in the Colorado Desert, so the freedom to roam there is less. This is a big, empty country up here. The Colorado Desert just never grabbed me the way the East Mojave did from the first second I came here."

As part of his desert apprenticeship, Casebier collected every U.S. Geological Survey topographical map from Owens Valley to the Mexican border. Perusing the quadrangles for the so-called Lonesome Triangle— a sparsely settled section of desert between Interstates 15 and 40 that would soon become the East Mojave National Scenic Area—he noticed something called the Old Government Road running through them east and west. "I wondered what an 'Old Government Road' was," Casebier would later recall. "I didn't know the government had a road. And if I had known they had one, I would never have imagined they would keep it way out here in the desert."

A local rancher named Bob Ausmuss explained to him that this "road"—now nothing more than an intermittent patchwork of tracks— was a onetime emigrant trail that had connected a series of forts built at springs. Casebier began researching the vanished route at the University of California library in Riverside and, during his frequent work trips to Washington, D.C., at the National Archives and Library of Congress. He unearthed a mine of original sources—diaries, photographs, military records, old newspaper articles—and from it amassed a mound of material on the East Mojave. He explored sections of the old road, following its ephemeral path over playas, up washes, past cinder-cone fields, through Joshua-tree forests, across creosote-covered bajadas. He began to perceive it as "a unique artifact eight feet wide and a hundred and thirty miles long." By the midseventies, he'd pieced together the entire route from Fort Mohave, north of present-day Needles, to Camp Cady, east of present-day Barstow. He called it the Mojave Road.

One of Casebier's mentors had shrunk from publishing his own research because of the possibility that some other scholar might catch him in an error. As a result, his knowledge died with him. "I vowed not to commit that same mistake," Casebier declared. "I would write about the Mojave Road no matter how painful the experience might be in the beginning to a person trained in science and engineering." Casebier subsequently self-published five books: *Camp El Dorado, Arizona Territory; Carleton's Pah-Ute Campaign; The Battle at Camp Cady; Camp Rock Spring;* and *Fort Pah-Ute.* Meanwhile, "inspired by a public-spirited desire to bring the Mojave Road back to life," he puzzled over the best way to do so. Concluding that publicity was more salubrious than secrecy, he began giving lectures and slide shows and traveling over parts of the trail in the company of BLM officials, with whom he hypothesized about the introduction of horses, wagons, motorcycles, and four-wheel-drive vehicles. "At times," he recalled, "it seemed the only way to use [the trail] without damaging it was to hike it." Over a period of six days in October 1975, he hiked the entire trail himself. Later he led groups of U.S. Marines, complete with color guards and mounted cavalry, on one-day marches along the route.

Nineteen eighty was pivotal for Casebier's crusade. That was the year he led his first four-wheel trip over the Mojave Road. "At first I was reluctant to do it," he remembers. "I used to be suspicious of four-wheel-drive clubs because I thought they wanted to tear up the desert. But then I saw that they were interested in the flora and fauna, and brought bags out with them to pick up garbage." Each vehicle was equipped with a CB radio so that the drivers could converse as they rode—an arrangement that, to the communicative Casebier, came as a veritable epiphany. "*That* was the way to do it," he decided, and found that southern California four-wheel-drive clubs enthusiastically agreed.

Casebier soon formed his own organization, called Friends of the Mojave Road (FOMR). Its members received an irregular newsletter ("Mojave Road Reports") and removed rocks and vegetation from the trail on weekends; having concluded that the route should remain free of any signs, they used the collected stones to build cairns at crossroads. They convened a series of annual "Mojave Road Rendezvous," with field trips, lectures, catered dinners, guided tours, book releases, award cere-monies, and planning sessions. Over a period of several years, the group even put together a mile-by-mile guidebook filled with advice, pho-tographs, commentary by Casebier, and an odometer-calibrated, mapped log description of every turn, landmark, and point of interest on the Mojave Road. In order to furnish information for potential emergencies, Casebier and another driver named Spence Murray even made one full-length trip over the trail at night.

In a precise way, the final decade of the century saw the full consum-mation of Casebier's desert-rat status. On December 31, 1989, he retired from his job with the Navy and immediately moved to a house trailer in Goffs, an isolated intersection thirty miles northwest of Needles in the

East Mojave. There he bought property containing an old schoolhouse, which he set about transforming into a five-thousand-volume library and office. In time the site would also boast bunkbeds, a bathroom, a shower, a sink, a piano, a collection of western paintings, and a campground for Friends of the Mojave Road, whom Casebier continued to lead on excursions, dispensing wit and wisdom over the CB airwaves.

In the spring of 1991, I went along for the ride.

Three years later, another man—dark and swarthily bearded—stood on the shoulder of River Road, which runs north from the town of Needles. He was dressed in blue jeans, well-worn hiking boots, a striped workshirt open to the chest, a broad-brimmed khaki-colored hat, and a belt whose buckle said GEOLOGICAL SOCIETY OF AMERICA 1888. Perusing the line of pink cliffs that parallel the river a few miles from shore, he identified them as stream deposits left over from a time—not long vanished—when the Colorado was broad and meandering.

"The Colorado River is younger than four and a half million years," he said. "There's some fossil evidence that they started getting fish around then at Mesquite, Nevada, a hundred miles upstream from here. The river itself was preceded by the Colorado River Trough—an arm of a sea that didn't come quite this far north, and which would've been freshened by the river. Eventually the stream left these silts interfingered with gravels. They're probably very fertile. See those stands of cottonwoods? Several are a hundred feet higher than the river is today. Eventually the river breached somewhere downstream, and since then tributaries have been eating away at the drainage debris along here." The evidence was a stairstep succession of terraces, inset at right angles by stream courses, through which he passed as he left the road and made his way toward the river. Now thoroughly impounded and channelized, it extended only a hundred yards across to Arizona.

This man's name was Robert Reynolds. His position, earth science curator of the San Bernardino County Museum. On my first trip over the Mojave Road with Dennis Casebier, I learned that it adjoins some of the most dramatic and descriptive landforms in the Mojave Desert. Moreover, its course was dictated by such things as springs, riverbeds, fault lines, and lava flows. I realized that, while Casebier's specialty—human history—was compelling, it was only the last scene in the play; as geologists are fond of pointing out, if the entire history of Earth were a twenty-four-hour day, people would have appeared only in the last sixty seconds. Much of our history—whether or not we acknowledge it on a moment-by-moment basis—has been determined by millions of years of terrestrial evolution. As the imaginative Dr. Robert P. Sharp of the California Institute of Technology goes so far as to suggest in his field guide to southern California geology. "In subtle, psychological ways our youthful geology may be partly responsible for the high basal metabolism and mobility of our west-coast culture."

Viewed in this light, geologists are like detectives probing about with scrapers and microscopes, trying to piece together a picture of what happened before they arrived on the scene—and deserts are rooms full of fingerprints and discarded weapons, if not a dropped wallet with the perp's ID. "Most geologists love the desert since everything geological is so well exposed," writes Sharp. "No false eyelashes, no cosmetics, no fancy clothes—just pure plain naked geology with a good coat of tan (desert varnish)." Indeed, the desert commonly makes geology buffs out of laypeople, as its wealth of weird stripes and shapes kindles curiosity even among the scientifically blasé.

This is essentially the same sort of intrigue that seized Dennis Casebier when he first glimpsed the "Old Government Road": a need to find out what was responsible for its existence, what had gone on there before he arrived. It occurred to me that by traveling over the route with him—its preeminent scholar in human lore—as well as with one versed in the prehistory of the place, I might obtain something approaching the full story of the desert's past. Then, on the printed page, I could get both experts into the same jeep—or, failing that, at least engage them in a CB dialogue across time and space. So what if the two trips actually took place three years apart? On a geological timescale, that was barely a nanosecond.

Reynolds, for his part, is a desert veteran. Having grown up in Pasadena, he has been coming to the Mojave since he was a kid, and now, doing field research, he continues to camp out in the desert "about ten weeks a year." I first met him in 1990 at Thanksgiving, a holiday that he annually observes with his family and friends in the East Mojave. Reynolds showed up at the campsite for that event in his Land Cruiser, towing a trailerful of provisions that would have eased the mission of the early military expeditions. For our Mojave Road outing, he brought along a crate the size of a small wagon full of kitchen utensils.

The afternoon before the trip, Reynolds and I met Casebier at the Goffs schoolhouse, which is situated alongside the Santa Fe Railroad tracks on another historic emigrant trail: old U.S. Route 66. We signed in at the guest register, an iron replica of the schoolhouse with a hinged roof serving as a lid. As soon as we arrived, Casebier strode up to greet us; on every visit I've paid him, he has materialized in this same brisk way. Belying his scholarly output, he seems to be perpetually engaged in a foot patrol of his property.

We stood there chatting for a while, undisturbed by any noise other than that of a passing train. Casebier acknowledged the somnolence of the surroundings. "You kind of lose track of time here," he said. "There are two ways you can tell it's Sunday. First, you don't get any mail; that either means Jack forgot to send it up from Essex, or it's Sunday. So then you go out and watch for the chicken trucks. Tyson's Chickens has half a dozen that go by every Sunday afternoon."

That night Reynolds staged his first cooking demonstration: grilled chicken, steamed broccoli, and macaroni and cheese with tomatoes. I provided a homemade Sonoma Valley Cabernet, which didn't marry especially well with Reynold's favorite condiment—an orange liquid called "Mexi Pep." The sky had been overcast during the afternoon, and as I bedded down on the porch of the schoolhouse after dinner, there was a substantial rain. As is common under such conditions, the air immediately became infused with the aroma of creosote bush, which despite its industrial-chemical name is to the desert aficionado an intoxicating perfume.

Other parties arrived during the night. As our small caravan pulled out at 5:45 A.M., the sun was just clearing a low bank of clouds on the eastern horizon. Apart from the vanishing storm front, the dawn sky was perfectly clear. "Heading out onto the road from the schoolhouse, we're off on an adventure!" Casebier chimed over the CB. We stopped briefly for gas in Needles, where an inedible cinnamon roll revived my repressed memories of the local cuisine. (This, I soon learned, was no problem for Reynolds, who builds his appetite for dinner all day by consuming nothing but Diet Pepsi.) Then we drove north about fifteen miles on River Road, crossing the Nevada state line and turning right to reach the riverbank. In so doing, we entered the Fort Mohave Indian Reservation.

"Two thousand Indians used to live in this valley," Casebier told the group. "They were agriculturists; they planted in the overflow of the Colorado the same way the Egyptians did with the Nile. In June, when the snow was melting in the Rocky Mountains, the river here could get to be three miles wide. There used to be an almost impenetrable thicket of mesquite and vines through here, but the Indians had patches where they planted melons, squash, and corn."

The name Mohave originally referred to a trio of needlelike rocks for which the town downstream was named (and which we could now see, backlit by the rising sun, across the Colorado). The Mohaves lived in the lowlands along the river—and so, technically speaking, they inhabited the Colorado Desert. What we now call the Mojave Desert was the domain of the Pah-Utes, Paiutes, or Piutes—specifically (in the East Mojave) a subgroup called the Chemehuevis, who, unlike their agriculturally inclined enemies, were nomadic hunter-gatherers and hence had little in the way of a permanent culture. They wrested a rough existence from the open desert, living on lizards, tortoises, rabbits, seeds, pine nuts, mesquite beans, cactus joints, and Joshua-tree buds, moving about with the seasons (higher in summer, lower in winter), carrying everything they needed—bows, arrows, knives, scrapers, and bush beaters shaped like tennis rackets—on their backs. For this purpose, and for cooking, they created their most complex and beautiful artifacts: baskets sewn or woven from reeds and grasses into bowls, jars, trays, and cradles. These were coated with varnishlike pitch, which rendered them near-ceramic in toughness. They could hold water but couldn't be used over an open fire; hence, heated stones were dropped inside in order to make soup. The baskets were also used for parching and winnowing seeds and nuts, which were harvested from spring through fall. Famine sometimes encroached during winter, when the Chemehuevis donned their only clothing: cloaks and blankets of rabbit fur. The rest of the time, they went naked except for yucca sandals. To amuse themselves, they gambled and played a simple game involving a wooden pin attached with string to a dangling rabbit skull. Most of the Chemehuevis' energy, however, was occupied in getting a living; when it came to leisure (hence culture—particularly the civilized pursuits of art, travel, and war), the Chemehuevis were no match for the Mohaves, who slaughtered their neighbors on a regular basis, possessed as they were of not only arrows, clubs, spears, and shields, but imposing physical stature. Many Mohaves stood six feet tall, weighed three hundred pounds, and augmented their appearance by tattooing their faces with lines and dots.

The Mohaves belonged to the Yuman linguistic family, as opposed to the Shoshonean/Uto-Aztecan Paiutes. Besides being farmers, they made pottery, lived in log houses, and had a complex religion and clan system—all practices associated with staying in one place. But the Mohaves were also notorious travelers, embarking on regular three-hundred-mile journeys to the Pacific coast, where they traded pottery and pumpkins for seashells and beads. A relatively small volume of goods changed hands during those sojourns, suggesting that the Mohaves traveled mainly for the hell of it. And hellish it could be: their route to the coast traversed the entire width of the Mojave Desert—a distance that the tribe's legendary runners could cover in a few days, going by way of perennial springs and the at-best-intermittent Mojave River. "Being agriculturists, the Mohaves had time on their hands and knew where all the springs were," said Casebier. "When white men first came through here, they didn't figure their own way. The Indians guided them."

Such helpfulness was mixed up in the complex, unpredictable, sometimes fatal relationship between the Mohaves and European pioneers. When Lieutenant Edward Beale arrived at their villages on October 17, 1857, he found the Mohaves to be "fine-looking, comfortable, fat, and merry." Two days later, his young cohort M. H. Stacey declared himself "much astonished to wake up this morning and find my hair safe." This is a tidy encapsulation of Caucasians' conflicted attitude toward the Mohaves, who occupied both banks of the Colorado for a distance of some fifty miles, surrounded by rough and sun-scorched desert, from which they alternately aided and attacked travelers for the better part of a century. Although (unbeknownst to innocent victims or people in settlements far away) the seemingly random hostility was often inspired by unfriendly action on the part of previous passers-through, "all the white men knew," writes Casebier, "was that somewhere beyond the mountains and deserts in an inaccessible place there lived a powerful nation that they stood no chance of controlling." The situation was agitated by the so-called Mormon War of 1857–58, during which Brigham Young's followers fomented anti-American hostility among the Indians, suggesting (not inaccurately) that non-Mormon whites planned to steal their land.

Perhaps as a result, in August 1858 the Mohaves attacked the first
American emigrant train that tried to come through en route to
California, killing eight people and driving off the party's stock. The survivors barely made it back to New Mexico, prompting the U.S. government to take serious action.

The following December, Major William Hoffman set out for the
Colorado with a company of infantrymen and orders to establish an
Army post near the Mohave villages. He was turned back by the desert
and the Indians, convincing him only that a larger force should approach
upriver from the south. Thus, in February 1859, two infantry companies
marched east across the desert to Yuma, while five more made their way
by steamer to the mouth of the Colorado. Two months later—following
great logistic awkwardness and geographic hardship—a force of six hundred soldiers arrived at Beale's Crossing of the Colorado with animals,
arms, and provisions. The mere sight of this arriving army inspired the
Mohaves to surrender. The soldiers duly established a fort, christened
Camp Colorado by Hoffman; a few days after he left, however, its commanding officer, Lewis Armistead, renamed it Fort Mohave.

Ultimately the Mohave problem would not be settled quite so cleanly.
Within a few months, a handful of Indian hostages—having been held
beyond what they understood to be a temporary period of captivity,
imposed to guarantee the continued cooperation of the tribe—escaped,
and Armistead's troops began hunting down renegades, burning rancherias and destroying crops in the bargain. Employing a considerable firepower advantage, they crushed the Mohaves in a decisive dawn ambush
and thus succeeded in banishing them from their homelands around the
river crossing. "They wanted a good whipping, which they got," he wrote
to his commanding general. "They appear to be perfectly satisfied."
Casebier would later observe, "It was the end of the war, and perhaps
unknown to the Mohaves, the end of their nation."

Fort Mohave continued operating until 1890. Casebier told us that in
his history he had "a record of every soldier that ever served there—what
his name was, when he was born, how tall he was, what color his eyes
were. The fort had been established to subdue the Indians and 'ensure
peaceful status,' but later on it turned out that the soldiers' function was
more to protect the Indians from the white folks than to protect the
white folks from the Indians. When the Bureau of Indian Affairs ordered
the Mohaves down to the Colorado Indian Reservation, half of them

refused to go; the Army supported them, and the War Department allowed them to stay. Under the Interior Department, the fort became an Indian school and Mohave children were taken from their parents and whipped for speaking Mohave—all of which is consistent with my view that, throughout the West, Indians were treated better by soldiers than they were by Indian agents."

In an ironic turnabout in the 1970s, Casebier led a group of Mohave elders over the Mojave Road, showing them the way that their forebears had once shown the white explorers. Today the descendants of the Mohaves who stayed occupy a reservation around the site of the old fort across the river from where we now stood. As we got into our vehicles and filed out from the causeway, we passed several scrapers and caterpillars working in the floodplain: modern Mohave Indians bulldozing the site of their ancestral farms in order to build the new "Avi" casino.

"So—something new for the Mojave Road," Casebier commented over the CB. He had positioned his pickup—a beige Jeep Pioneer with a camper shell—in the middle of the caravan so as to broadcast with equal power fore and aft. "The rule of the road is to keep the car behind you in sight," he said. "If you don't, the guy behind you will do the wrong thing—guaranteed. We've had times when somebody didn't watch their rearview mirror, and after a while we realized that we only had a few vehicles. The others had taken a wrong turn and were off doing something somewhere else."

To our right and left, honey and screwbean mesquite were growing in the old river bottom. As we recrossed River Road and ascended, we passed through a grove of smoke trees with black trunks and yellow leaves—biological indicators of the Colorado Desert. Geologically, our location was even less clear.

"The southeastern portion of the Mojave Desert is poorly defined," Reynolds said. "It's generally bounded by the Garlock fault in the north, the San Andreas in the southwest, and the Pinto Mountain fault in the south. To the east is the East Mojave Shear Zone. The East Mojave has had most of its surface ripped apart by active faults."

Just as the Colorado Desert is a geographical "subset" of the Sonoran, the Mojave Desert is considered a subsection of the Basin and Range, which extends from the Sierra Nevada across Nevada to the western slope of the Rocky Mountains. This province is characterized by long, alternating, north-south–trending mountain ranges separated by broad valleys with no outlets to the sea—hence "Great Basin." The area of most dramatic relief is around Death Valley, where the elevation drops from 11,049 feet above sea level (at Telescope Peak) to 282 below (at Badwater) in only fourteen miles. The mountains throughout most of the Mojave proper—i.e., to the south—are lower and smaller; in its western portion, the landscape is relatively smooth, filled with erosional alluvium and strewn with isolated hills. In the east, where we now found ourselves, mountain ranges are much more numerous, trending northwest and southeast along scores of earthquake faults.

"The Mojave Desert is sort of an accommodation zone between all the provinces around it—the Peninsular Ranges, the Transverse Ranges, and the Sierra Nevada," explained Reynolds. "It's being crushed between them and the oblique attack of the Pacific plate from the southwest. That's why it's full of these northwest- and southeast-trending faults and mountain ranges. It's like one of those little toy blocks where you move the letters around to make words. Areas of it are sliding or rotating to accommodate the forces on all sides."

One such block loomed just to our north: the Newberry Range, "or Spirit Mountain, as the Mohaves called it," said Casebier. "It's a sacred place. The Mohaves won't go up in there—that's where you go when you die." Speaking of which, the Dead Mountains loomed dead ahead. According to Reynolds, their red-brown slopes were composed of "pre-Paleozoic granitic and metamorphic rocks more than six hundred million years old." Casebier identified a steep cut through them as Pictograph Canyon. "Jedediah Smith came through here in 1826, and he went right up that canyon," said Casebier. "But when Whipple brought the first wagon through here in 1854, the Mohaves showed him another way that wasn't quite so steep. The Indian route wasn't just one trail—it was a network, so they would show the white man what he needed for his requirements."

I noted that two of the people on this trip (Bob Reynolds being one) had named their own sons Jedediah. "People tend to get really inspired by Jedediah Strong Smith," Casebier acknowledged. Smith, the famous mountain man, was the first American citizen to reach California overland from the east, rather than sailing around Cape Horn. At the age of twenty-seven, after leading a group of sixteen trappers south from the Great Salt Lake in search of beaver, he passed two peaceful weeks along the Colorado River with the Mohaves, who subsequently escorted him west through the desert to the San Gabriel Mission. Smith returned the following year and traded with the Mohaves for several days without incident. However, upon departing, his party was ambushed while crossing the Colorado—half his nineteen men were killed and two women taken captive, while Smith and the others escaped after dark into the mountains we were now entering. Traveling mainly at night—and this time, obviously, without Indian guides—they somehow managed to retrace their previous path through the desert and reach the Mexican settlements in the west. Casebier surmised that the surprise massacre was a retaliation against a different group of trappers, who, between Smith's two visits, had killed several Mohaves in a dispute over beaver.

In our rubber-wheeled wagons, we followed a route more like Whipple's than Smith's, leaving a sandy wash that reportedly led to a dry waterfall in Pictograph Canyon. The road turned slightly rougher, but the ground was still relatively smooth. "This may be an early Miocene surface [i.e., twenty to thirty million years old]," said Reynolds. "It's erosional, not steep and craggy like the Dead Mountains." We went around a low rounded hill and eventually rejoined the wash, continuing on through creosote bush, ephedra, and catclaw acacia—a.k.a. wait-a-minute bush, a nickname attributable to its thorny twigs, which tug at the sleeves of passersby. Some of the branches were decorated with mistletoe spread by the phainopepla, a small bird from the waxwing family that lives in arid scrub. Although the species is considered rare, we saw one of its members flitting from bush to bush, resembling a small waxwing or cardinal except for its color, which was—oddly, it seemed, for a desert bird—black.

We passed under a high-voltage power line, the type of human development that has ironically benefited desert fauna: the arms of the steel tower harbored a hefty raptor nest. I soon noted the appearance of Mojave yucca, an indicator of increased elevation. "We've come eleven miles and gained two thousand feet," Reynolds remarked. "It's surprising to me that we still have patches of grusse—decomposed granite—here. It may indicate that the structural changes have happened recently; erosion hasn't had time to get rid of the grusse." To the right was a patch of chocolate-colored cactus—teddybear, or "jumping," cholla. "That's the only patch of it on the Mojave Road," Casebier said. "The Indians told the white men that if you get near it, it'll jump out and getcha." The desert, it seems, is full of such plants: another nickname for catclaw acacia is the gotcha bush.

We now found ourselves on a high plateau where the going was relatively level and easy. "This stretch of the road was as pleasant for wagonmasters as it is for us today," said Casebier. "They'd been down at the river and their animals were well rested and fed; they had Piute Creek to look forward to, where there was more plentiful water. As far as Indians were concerned, this was a sort of no-man's-land between the territory of the Mohaves and the Chemehuevis. In the 1870s, this road was a quarter of a mile wide—people brought seven thousand sheep through here at a time."

The Mojave Road functioned as a wagon trail for only two decades: 1860–80. In the 1830s and 1840s, the preferred route from New Mexico to California was the Old Spanish Trail, which ran northwest from Santa Fe into central Utah before turning southwest on the Mormon Trail for San Bernardino and Los Angeles—a total distance of some twelve hundred miles, circuitously followed (in Casebier's opinion) in order to avoid the Mohaves. When gold was discovered in California, however, pressure quickly mounted for a transcontinental railroad, and the government began sending official survey parties into the desert. "Those geologists, biologists, and draftsmen were the astronauts of their day," said Casebier.

One hypothetical right-of-way for the railroad followed the Thirty-fifth Parallel west from Albuquerque and the Zuñi Indian pueblos to the Mohave villages on the Colorado, then along the old Indian trail to Cajon Pass. The first person to explore this route was François-Xavier Aubry, a citizen of Santa Fe, who did it under his own auspices in 1853, fighting off Indians much of the way. As Casebier noted, the first wagon to make the trip was an instrument cart commanded by Lieutenant Amiel Weeks Whipple, who surveyed the route for the U.S. Army Corps of Topographical Engineers in 1854. The most celebrated expedition, however, was conducted by Edward Fitzgerald Beale—former Navy officer, Mexican War hero, owner of the Tejon Ranch, and superintendent of Indian affairs for the state of California. A noted frontiersman and "pioneer in the path of empire" who hobnobbed with the likes of Kit Carson and John Frémont, Beale was reputedly the person who carried the first gold from California to Washington, D.C.

In 1853, at the urging of Missouri senator Thomas Hart Benton—Frémont's father-in-law, who was eager for the train tracks to terminate in St. Louis—Beale explored the "central" route along the Salt Lake and

Old Spanish Trail. Four years later, he was appointed superintendent of the wagon road survey of the Thirty-fifth Parallel and directed to forge an avenue through northern Arizona. He subsequently pioneered the route of the Atlantic & Pacific Railroad past the present-day sites of Winslow, Flagstaff, and Kingman. This journey has been celebrated not so much for that achievement as for the fact that Beale made it in the company of two dozen camels, procured from the Middle East on the order of Jefferson Davis—soon to become president of the Confederate States, but then secretary of war under President Franklin Pierce—who believed that the animals might further the aims of the U.S. military in the Southwest. Judging from Beale's expressive journals, Davis was right:

> Certainly there was never anything so patient or enduring and so little troublesome as this noble animal. They pack their heavy load of corn, of which they never taste a grain; put up with any food offered them without complaint, and are always up with the wagons, and, withal, so perfectly docile and quiet that they are the admiration of the whole camp. . . . Without the aid of this noble and useful brute, many hardships which we have been spared, would have fallen to our lot; and our admiration for them has increased day by day, as some new hardship, endured patiently, more fully developed their entire adaptation and usefulness in the exploration of the wilderness. At times I have thought it impossible they could stand the test to which they have been put, but they seem to have risen equal to every trial and to have come off of every exploration with as much strength as before starting. . . . I have subjected them to trials which no other animal could possibly have endured; and yet I have arrived here . . . without the loss of a camel. . . . Leaving home with all the prejudice invariably attaching to untried experiments, and with many in our camp opposed to their use, and looking forward confidently to their failure, I believe at this time I may speak for every man in our party, when I say there is not one of them who would not prefer the most indifferent of our camels to four of our best mules.

In a sense, Beale got his wish. While trying to swim the Colorado, two of his horses and ten mules drowned—but every camel made it across with no problem. Though not everyone shared Beale's flattering opinion of these beasts, it was subsequently recommended that the government purchase a thousand of them. Unfortunately, the Civil War intervened, diverting not only money and attention, but the primary champion of camels in the capital, Jeff Davis.

After Beale completed his journey to Los Angeles, he returned to the Mohave villages in January 1858. As it happened, he arrived at precisely the moment when George Alonzo Johnson's steamship *General Jesup*, engaged in the first-ever navigation of the Colorado River, had stopped to take on wood. Beale reported his reaction with characteristic eloquence:

> Here, in a wild, almost unknown country, inhabited only by savages, the great river of the west, hitherto declared unnavigable, had, for the first time, borne upon its bosom that emblem of civilization, a steamer. The enterprise of a private citizen had been rewarded by success, for the future was to lend its aid in the settlement of our vast western territory. But alas! for the poor Indians living on its banks and rich meadow lands. The rapid current which washes its shores will hardly pass more rapidly away. The steam whistle of the General Jesup sounded the death knell of the river race. . . . I had brought the camels with me, and as they stood on the bank, surrounded by hundreds of wild unclad savages, and mixed with these the dragoons of my escort and the steamer slowly revolving her wheels preparatory to a start, it was a curious and interesting picture.

Within a little more than a year, Fort Mohave had been built at Beale's Crossing, and the river Indians were subdued for good. Their ancient trail through the desert to the coast subsequently became a supply road for the fort.

"Most of the traffic on the Mohave Road headed east," Casebier divulged. "The wagons went back empty. It never was much of an emigrant trail." It did, however, become a popular passageway for prospectors and mail, especially after the mining strikes at Prescott, Arizona, in the 1860s and Ivanpah, California, in the 1870s. Eventually, though, the long-awaited railroad—completed in 1883 and followed much later by U.S. Route 66—would pass twenty miles to the south. With that, the Mojave Road was effectively abandoned.

"Which, for our purposes, is fine," said Casebier, "because it's still in pristine condition today."

Our leader decided that it was time for a rest stop. Men were directed to the left of the road, women to the right. Some people continued conversing over the CB; away from the road, you could hear the collective radios resonating with *rogers* and *ten-fours*.

"Oh golly, look!" said Casebier. He touched my arm with excitement, pointing to a tiny round cactus blooming on a rock. "It's a fish-hook cactus with a little red flower. Look at the needles—each one is shaped like a hook. That's so pretty!" Nearby, infinitesimal purple flowers were spread over the ground. "Belly flowers," Casebier said. "You have to get down on your belly to look at them."

The day was sunny and slightly chilly—air temperature in the fifties, the atmosphere spectacularly clear in the wake of the previous night's storm. As we crested the pass between the Dead and Newberry Mountains (unceremoniously recrossing the California-Nevada state line), we gained our first sweeping view of the East Mojave: down into broad Piute Valley, and westward to the basalt-streaked Piute Range, with aptly named Table Mountain occupying the horizon beyond.

"Here we're surrounded by volcanic rocks," Reynolds noted. "Late Miocene basalt in the Piutes, early Miocene basalt in the Sacramento Mountains to the south. The Piutes sit on deeply eroded granitic rocks just like the ones we're on now, which makes me wonder how long this surface has been exposed. Something else has been stripped away from on top of it—something two hundred to five hundred million years old, and a mile or more in thickness. North of Las Vegas, there's a series of Paleozoic deposits two hundred to six hundred million years old, but here the rocks of that age have been eroded away. Granitic rocks pushed up the Paleozoic rocks, which began to be removed about seventy million years ago. By twenty-five million, they were mostly gone. Then the crust started thinning, which enabled volcanic activity to break through to the surface. Some other erosional surfaces similar to this one have Peach Springs Tuff on them, indicating that the surface is older than eighteen-point-five million years."

Peach Springs Tuff is the fused ash of an eruption known to have taken place eighteen and a half million years ago. Similar to the explosion of Mount St. Helens, magma shot out the sides of the volcano, forming a cloud that covered the earth between the present-day locations of Barstow, California, and Kingman, Arizona. The gorgeous mesas around Kingman owe their grandeur to Peach Springs Tuff. The caldera of the volcano is thought to be buried somewhere in the East Mojave—possibly in the Newberry Range, lending further mystique to the legend surrounding Spirit Mountain.

Fear of more modern explosions had created a newer feature in the landscape. Stretching away in the distance as we descended into Piute Valley was a long straight earthen line: the maintenance road for a cross-country telephone cable buried here in the early 1960s—around the time, in other words, of the Cuban missile crisis. The thinking, apparently, was that in the event of nuclear holocaust, an underground line would still enable people on the coasts to keep in touch.

Underscoring the point, a pair of fighter jets suddenly came streaking down the valley and—as is their custom—disappeared just as quickly. "We've had A-6's and A-4's so low over the Goffs schoolhouse that I could read the insignia on their helmets," Casebier commented. "I love it—I'm a D.O.D. man from way back. Maybe it's my imagination, but when the Iraq war started heating up, they kept getting lower and lower." Sort of a reverse thermal effect, I gathered.

We paralleled the cable road, bouncing over uneven terrain, accompanied now by buckhorn and silver cholla. To our right, a road leading into the creosote scrub culminated at a wood-frame structure intriguingly christened the Black Cat Saloon, but the convivial name was contradicted by a sign that said No Trespassing. A few minutes later, we crossed the blacktop of U.S. Highway 95, the main connection between Needles, Las Vegas, Searchlight, and Laughlin, Nevada—the latter a booming casino town that as recently as 1980 had only a hundred residents.

"This is category-one desert-tortoise habitat," Casebier commented. "One time, after a rain, I saw eighteen tortoises along the road here." As if to check the effusiveness of this observation, we soon came upon some old tank tracks left over from the Desert Training Center commanded by General George Patton during World War II. Casebier took the opportunity to launch an excoriation of the maneuvers' environmental effects.

"I had no idea of the extent of it until I moved out here and started interviewing the old-timers," he said. "They describe *dramatic* changes in the wildlife. People who were not well educated or sophisticated about what you and I would call ecological matters could still see that species were disappearing. The Army had policies to eliminate coyotes, and there haven't been any burrowing owls around Essex ever since the war. The desert to the south of us was totally devastated."

Coming as it did from the avowed "D.O.D. man," this modest jeremiad caught me by surprise. "I'm not saying we shouldn't have done it," Casebier quickly added. "You do what you have to do to win a war. But that was the effect. It's now a part of our heritage."

With that qualification, we drove on, crossing a number of sandy washes that ran south in Piute Valley. "Piute Valley is north-and-south-trending," Reynolds said. "To me that indicates that we're in the southern part of the Basin and Range Province—not the Mojave." Casebier, for his part, disputed the very notion that Piute Valley is a basin, if that term is used to mean a sink with no outlet. "Piute Wash drains to the south of the Dead Mountains and empties into the Colorado River," he said. "It's an exception to the rule."

Miles ahead, wedged in a canyon in the Piute Range, was Piute Spring—identifiable at a distance, like most desert springs, by its stand of bright green vegetation in the otherwise barren landscape. The terrain was very rocky now; we pitched to and fro on our seats, progressing at a tortoise's pace around a conical hill called Jedediah Smith Butte. Eventually we arrived at the remains of Fort Piute, first in the string of old army garrisons along the Mojave Road.

Casebier got out to direct traffic with his bullhorn, backing the vehicles one by one into a small circular turnout. Gradually the people assembled around him (excepting, I noticed, Master Metallica Megadeth, who stayed in the car). It had become a beautiful day. Countless shadows of cumulus clouds drifted across the yellow-brown landscape, upon which, far in the distance, was the pale, weaving trace of the wagon road we'd just followed from the east.

"Between 1866 and 1868, this was a mail route," Casebier said. "Carriers came through twice a week, but the Chemehuevi Indians were still hostile—they'd watch for slow wagons dropping back and ambush them. That was when the Army decided to build a series of forts. Eighteen men were stationed here in the late 1860s; the Army called it an outpost, not a fort. It had a really fine blockhouse engineered by Major Henry Robert, who also gave us a good map and a road log measured with an odometer. A few years later, he wrote a book called *Robert's Rules of Order*—he was the great parliamentarian."

The Chemehuevis' writings were right nearby. Pictographs had been scraped into the desert varnish—a dark coating that forms on rocks from manganese and iron oxide, providing the human inhabitants with a natural blackboard. Some of the art was sufficiently old that lichen had overgrown it. A few of the human-shaped forms appeared to be holding hands, a motif that one member of the group said could also be found near Moab, Utah, and Natural Bridges National Monument.

The sound of clicking cameras threatened to drown out the gurgling of Piute Creek, a mile-long perennial stream that disgorges a quarter of a million gallons of water per day, creating an astonishing riparian zone in the desert. The banks of the creek were cool, green, and grassy, and a pleasant breeze wafted a grove of willows and cottonwoods that marched up the slope behind the fort, gradually giving way to a profusion of red barrel cactus.

"The price the wagonmasters had to pay for water in Piute Creek was getting over the Piute Mountains," Casebier said. "The trail went right up this gorge, which was one of the steepest hills on the wagon roads of the West. They'd put sixteen mules on one wagon—or, when they were headed east, lock the wheels and let the wagons down by rope."

To Reynolds, the hill and the spring—like the figures scrawled on the rocks—went hand in hand. "Piute Spring is an underground river that drains Lanfair Valley to the west," he said. "The basalt slope behind Fort Piute forms a natural barrier that forces it to the surface. The Piute Mountains are an uplifted stack of lava flows, which must be fairly recent or they would've been stripped away by erosion. Faults have been active in the bottom of this valley within the last three hundred thousand years, which is really no time at all."

Casebier said that the old trail over Piute Hill was now too overgrown and eroded to accommodate our vehicles—our route over the range would follow the cable road. The caravan pulled out and continued south on a power-line road maintained by the Los Angeles Metropolitan Water

District. "This line comes from Hoover Dam to run the pumping stations on the Colorado River aqueduct," Casebier said. As we went through Piute Wash, Reynolds added: "I had a friend who drove through here in a VW one time; a flash flood came and carried him three miles downstream."

When we came to the cable road, we turned west, ascending sharply and hugging a hillside high above a wash. The plunging slopes were dotted with yucca, buckhorn cholla, and barrel cactus. Toward the top of the canyon, which was streaked with red igneous rock, were several cone-shaped hills. "These are metamorphic rocks topped with basalt flows," said Reynolds. "Things here are sloping, pinching, and alternating. To me it indicates that we're near the source of the flows."

As we cleared the crest, we beheld the next tableau: the broad flat plain of Lanfair Valley, elevation forty-five hundred feet. We could now see the jagged outline of the Providence Mountains, which led toward the granite-spired New York range in the northwest. Directly to the north were the white tailings cliffs of the Viceroy gold mine (recently reinvigorated by cyanide heap-leach technology), and beyond that were the Castle Peaks—plugs of hardened flows and ash from twelve- to sixteen-million-year-old volcanoes, the exterior slopes of which had since eroded away, leaving only picturesque crags. Straight ahead, the horizon was dominated by Table Mountain—"the point that the old wagonmasters used to head for," said the new wagonmaster. Accordingly, we rejoined the historic route, which skirted an ancient lakebed marked by scant vegetation.

"When the Piute Mountains blocked the drainage here, they created a playa," said Reynolds. "I'm guessing it was prior to three million years ago." We paused at the upper rim of Piute Gorge, a mini–Grand Canyon shot through with reddish silt. "After filling, the drainage broke through the basaltic layer and started eroding rapidly, creating the gorge. It looks like Bryce without the pinnacles. Hiking down Piute Canyon, you can see a cross section of the geology of the whole range."

Near the top, where the level surface of Lanfair Valley dropped into the canyon, the cross section revealed a stack of subterranean layers. "That calcium carbonate layer is the thickest one in southern California," said Reynolds. "When the playa stopped filling, the carbonates formed over a period of many thousand years." He began counting carbonate layers: "It looks like there were one . . . two . . . three . . . four events after the playa."

Driving out onto the floor of the valley, we passed a circular corral consisting entirely of close-set vertical posts. We were now unmistakably in the Mojave—a conclusion supported by the fact that we found ourselves surrounded by Joshua trees. Specifically the *jaegeriana* strain, which is shorter, with more branches, than its southwesterly cousin. Lanfair Valley boasts one of the thickest Joshua-tree forests in existence—a fact attributable to its elevated location among even higher mountains, whose cool air is constantly colliding with warmth from nearby basins. Averaging eight inches of precipitation annually, this is the best-watered area in the Mojave Desert; even in March, some of the trees were blooming with creamy, popcorn-ball-like flowers.

This climatic situation bestowed upon the East Mojave the "best" grazing land in the California desert. (The quotation marks are due to the fact that the entire region produces only 0.3 percent of the state's beef.) Cattle and sheep here date back to the 1860s, when miners and soldiers introduced herds for their own subsistence. "The commercial industry got going in the 1880s," said Casebier. "Livestock grazing has always been limited by distribution of water, so before the Taylor Grazing Act, the key to control of the range was control of the water sources. The Rock Springs Land and Cattle Company dominated this area till 1929—they had a million acres and ten thousand head. Their manager, Earle Greening, had exchanged some national-forest inholdings for a bunch of acreage over water holes in the East Mojave. With that and gunmen, he controlled this area for many years."

Casebier said that much of the original Rock Springs range was now grazed by Gary Overson, a rancher who owned the OX Cattle Company. Periodically, we passed Overson's isolated corrals and water tanks, holding water piped in from elsewhere. "It's always been a cow-and-calf operation," said Casebier. "They try to keep a static herd of desert-wise cattle, each of which produces one calf a year. The way cattle are managed and handled in the East Mojave hasn't changed for a century."

Here and there, foundations of vacated buildings crumbled into the desert—evidence of a vanished homesteading community called Lanfair. "Lanfair Valley, and Round Valley to the west, were thrown open to dry farming and homesteading in 1910," said Casebier. "You could get a hundred and sixty acres, forty of which had to be cleared and planted, whether the plants came up or not. At first they had a series of encouraging wet years, and a community of two or three hundred people with schools and a post office. But soon they started having trouble with the cattle company. Hardly any homesteaders could make a living off the land; most went off to work in mines or in Needles. If you woke up one morning and found your fences knocked down and cattle in your crops, well, you might feel justified in harvesting a beef. The result was a full-fledged range war."

Occasionally we passed through plots cleared by the homesteaders. The Joshua trees would disappear, giving way to scrub pasture, then come crowding around again. These denuded dry-farming spots were the only obvious scars in the surrounding range.

The road was now very rough. It almost qualified as a ditch, so deeply was it eroded. In places we were submerged to eye level. I watched the wheels of the truck in front of us as it negotiated the dips and bumps, the rear axle tilting from side to side under the chassis, enabling the vehicle to maintain equilibrium. At one place where the road leveled out, a Joshua tree extended its arms over the road; one limb was hung with a rusted can, into which each passing vehicle dropped a copper penny ("to appease the Mojave Road god," according to Casebier).

We continued crossing washes that ran north to south. "The underground flow from Lanfair Valley drains east to Piute Spring, but the *surface* flow goes south to Fenner Valley," Reynolds explained. "Woods and Watson Washes were very significant drainages in the Pleistocene—they freshened the water in Bristol Lake, and at Cadiz, there's still an abundance of fresh subsurface water. They have an agricultural project there—they're growing grapes and citrus with snowmelt from the New York Mountains."

Finally we intersected the Ivanpah-Goffs Road, a high-speed thoroughfare maintained by San Bernardino County. Near the intersection was a telephone box—the only such installation, it seemed, for many miles around. "There used to be an old-fashioned phone booth here," Reynolds recalled. "At night you could see the light from way off, go inside and change into your cape. But somebody blew it up with dynamite."

Had we turned south at this point, we would have returned to the Goffs schoolhouse. Instead, we crossed the graded road and continued west, approaching the low, rounded, shadow-mottled Grotto Hills.

"Those are fifteen million years old," said Reynolds. "They're the tops of mountains sticking up through the Pliocene surface. They're made of welded volcanic tuff—ash with pieces of rock in it formed by *nueé ardént*, which means 'glowing cloud.' During the eruption, it was so hot that it fused crystals and glass into a relatively flat layer that doesn't erode. But other *unfused* areas of broken rock, boulders, and tuff *aren't* hard, so they *do* erode, leaving holes—or a 'grotto.'" Right as Reynolds may have been, Casebier claimed that the name "Grotto" was a misnomer. He said that the hills were named for Mary Ann *Guirado*, an early homesteader in Lanfair Valley.

The surrounding terrain was thick with yucca, cholla, and Joshua trees. "This is very pretty through here," said Casebier. "I hate to use the word, but it's almost—parklike." His words were partially obscured by his tongue, which seemed to have gotten lodged in his cheek. He was alluding to the fact that Lanfair Valley had been proposed, under the terms of the pending California Desert Protection Act, to become part of a new Mojave National Park.

"Something about the national-park mentality wants to remove all human vestiges and make it the way it was before," Casebier said, gradually untangling his oral tissues. "They want to kick the people out and 'restore' it. Well, Long Island was wilderness at one time, too; why not restore that? Part of what I like about this area is that you can see the cultural heritage. The East Mojave *ain't* pristine; a society has functioned here for a hundred years."

After passing a luxuriant growth of pancake cactus, we intersected Cedar Canyon Road, a major east-west corridor of graded dirt—or, according to Reynolds, "deeply weathered clays. When it rains, they turn to real sticky mud—you fishtail even in four-wheel drive." We followed the road for half a mile, then angled off to the southwest, dropping down a steep hill into Watson Wash. This led us to Rock Spring, the next water source on the Mojave Road, and as such the site of Camp Rock Spring—a crucial stronghold in the pass between the Providence and New York Mountains, a piñon-and-juniper-covered region known as the Mid Hills.

We parked the vehicles and walked toward the spring, which seeped from a canyon full of boulders, gooseberry, and rabbit brush. Perhaps because of the previous night's rain, a trickle of water was just forging a path from the rocks into the sand, much of which had been transformed to muck by cattle hooves. "Rock Spring is granitic," Reynolds said. "The crystals here are dark—sort of salt-and-pepper-like. It's monzodiorite, whereas the New York Mountains are lighter-colored, beige adamellite."

In 1863, a notorious photograph was taken here, showing a party of travelers posed precisely where we now stood—against the granite cliff on the south side of the wash. In 1980, Casebier restaged this photo with some Friends of the Mojave Road. In the time that had passed between sessions, wagons had been replaced by automobiles, railroads by airplanes and trucks; all manner of human races and diseases had been conquered, while a vast, acquisitive civilization had grown up a few hours to our west. Judging from the two photos, however, the only thing that had changed—aside from the people's style of dress—was the height of sand in the wash. Any differences in positions, sizes, angles, fissures, creases, and attitudes of line in the rock are indistinguishable. For most of us, a century ranks as the ultimate benchmark in time—a method of marking momentous change. But in terms of Earth history, as these photos of the Mojave Road attest, a hundred years isn't even an instant.

We rejoined Cedar Canyon Road and entered the rolling terrain of Round Valley, elevation fifty-three hundred feet. Junipers accordingly appeared on the surrounding hillsides. We were now nearing the highest point on the Mojave Road, approaching Government Holes—site of a well whose metal walls had been repeatedly plugged with screws. Below each protruding screwhead, white stains left by water leaks descended in inverted V's.

"In trying to control the water sources in the East Mojave, the Rock Springs Land and Cattle Company sometimes pretended it owned a few water holes that it didn't," Casebier explained. "Government Holes became such a bone of contention that it was eventually designated a public water reserve. One time, a guy named Matt Burts was here with some fellas who were complaining about the heat. Burts said, 'I'll help you out,' and shot right over their shoulders into the tank. I don't think that's what those holes are from, though."

Casebier looked around the well, which was accompanied by a single cottonwood and a solitary windmill. "After the range wars got started here, most of the homesteaders left by the twenties. But some stayed around operating stills during Prohibition. One of those was Bob

Holliman, who was known as a good cook, a rustler, and a gunfighter. He was a sort of Robin Hood—he delivered beef to people who lived out here, and he could keep a can moving down the road by firing his guns with both hands. The Rock Springs Land and Cattle Company hired Matt Burts out of Arizona to come and get rid of this troublemaker, but when Matt found out it was Bob, he joined him and became part of their problem. So then the company hired another guy named Bill Robinson to do the job. By November 1925, there was quite a bit of talk in the valley about who had been hired to do exactly what.

"The cattle company stationed Bill Robinson here at Government Holes. One Sunday, Matt Burts pulled up in a Model T, accompanied by a local lady named Mrs. Riedell. Matt yelled into the cabin that they needed water for the car, and Bill invited Matt inside. A few seconds later, Mrs. Riedell heard gunshots. Turned out Matt and Bill had emptied their forty-fives into each other. Both of 'em died right here.

"Now, one version of the story says that a bullet in Bill Robinson came from a rifle. But Matt Burts didn't have a rifle. So there's a long-standing rumor that Mrs. Riedell went home, got her rifle, and came back to finish him off. She was taken into custody by the county sheriff for questioning but later released. Anyway, that ended the range wars—quite a bit after the time that most people thought the classic gunfights of the Old West were a thing of the past. As for Bob Holliman, he lived happily ever after. He died in the 1950s, a very old man."

As far as classic frontier scenes are concerned, one could hardly imagine a better backdrop than the one that was spread before us. Directly north across the valley was one of the most picturesque "Old West"–style landforms in the East Mojave: Pinto Mountain, streaked like a sprawling wedding cake with undulant stripes of strawberry and cream. It's safe to assume that this tableau, too, was little changed from the moment when the guns had gone off seventy years earlier. As a matter of fact, Casebier said, "I've got a picture of Government Holes that's fifty years old, and that cottonwood tree was just about the same size then."

On the other hand, said Reynolds, twenty *million* years ago, there weren't even any mountains around—forget about the tree. "The Miocene surface, which had developed on top of Mesozoic granitic rocks and Precambrian metamorphic, was planed flat by erosion. Cinder cones rose up, and Woods Mountain erupted to the south, sending ashes out in all directions. Some were laid down as crystals and glass shards raining from clouds—that's the light-colored material down low in Pinto Mountain. The top is welded tuff, which came out like a flamethrower along the ground, laying down a carpet of glass, crystals, and rock chips. The temperature of the gaseous cloud was so hot that it gave the rock a pinkish tinge and fused the pumice to porcelain. If it cools fairly rapidly, it forms columns at the top, like Devil's Postpile near Yosemite. There's another layer of it high up to the right; in between are layers of white unwelded ash, which erode more rapidly, leaving a series of benches, terraces, or steps. Each layer is like a book with its own chemical signature. Table Mountain, Pinto Mountain, and the New York Mountains all had more resistant rock than what was eroded away. Pinto has the least resistant, but erosion hasn't had time to remove it. Let's give it another million or two years and see what happens."

Now we headed west at forty miles per hour on the well-graded country road. I noticed patches of snow in the adjoining ditches and on the north slope of Table Mountain. As we crossed the pass through the Mid Hills, diving down through sunlit fields of waving yellow grass, a stunning panorama began to present itself.

To the north was the Ivanpah range, with snow-covered Clark Mountain—at 7,929 feet the highest point in the East Mojave—protruding from the rear horizon. To the south were the Granite Mountains, standing out like an albino in a family of suntanned siblings. At their base was a huge dish of frozen vanilla yogurt: the 600-foot-high Kelso Dunes. Presiding over everything were the jagged 7,000-foot Providence Mountains, looking utterly monumental in the late afternoon light.

Spread directly before us in the west was the cloud-mottled surface of Cima Dome. The first time someone tried to point out this notorious landmass to me, I had a hard time finding it—the invisibility due to its being simultaneously subtle and enormous. Cima Dome is rounded and symmetrical, twenty-five miles wide and fifteen hundred feet higher than the surrounding landscape. Casebier compares its shape to that of an inverted gold pan, though to me the almost imperceptible curve of its horizon suggests that of the planet itself. Its surface is strewn with compact mountains (the Beales, the Marls, Wildcat Butte, Teutonia Peak), covered with a coat of Joshua trees (the largest such forest in existence—larger than Lanfair Valley's, larger than those in Joshua Tree National

Monument), and cut by a complex of washes that drain south to Kelso Valley.

"Cima Dome and its broken flanks help describe thirty million years of history," Reynolds said as we crossed the Union Pacific railroad tracks and the Cima-Kelso Road. "It probably crystallized as rock a hundred million years ago. Prior to twenty million, it started shedding its gravels to the west; then it tilted east when faulting started, which began to stop about ten million years ago." On top, Teutonia Peak stood as a resistant remnant of rock that now formed the dome.

We made our way slowly across the southern slope, bouncing through innumerable washes, pausing by a quartz outcrop so Reynolds could go rock hunting. When he returned, he held a gray stone in each hand.

"Limestone," he grinned. "Probably shed by the nearest limestone peak to the east. Parts of the Ivanpah Mountains are also limestone— which is either an interesting coincidence, or it means something. I think it means they're structurally related. The down-tilted surface of Cima Dome was probably covered by gravels containing limestone boulders during crustal thinning ten million years ago. These limestone rocks are the same kind of gravel that I find farther north. It's very hard to keep rocks on top of Cima Dome—they just get washed downhill." We got back in the truck and continued bucking the channels that carried the rocks downhill. For such a smooth-looking piece of topography, Cima Dome was awfully rough.

After what seemed like a very long time clinging to the handgrips, we arrived at the next checkpoint—according to Casebier, the most crucial water source on the old Mojave Road. This was Marl Springs, elevation thirty-nine hundred feet, "the last good water for thirty-three miles of Indian-infested country." Unlike the other watering holes we'd visited, however, this one—situated at the base of the modest Marl Mountains— was almost indistinguishable from the surrounding desert. As Reyner Banham remarked of the place in *Scenes in American Deserta:*

> What is astonishing is how little difference this desperately nec-
> essary spring makes to the environment: apart from one or two
> smears of green moss by the tank, and a solitary tree (now dead)
> above the abandoned mine, there is rarely anything to be seen
> growing here that does not grow on unwatered parts of the
> desert. There is something joyless about the way Marl Springs

delivers its life-giving liquid, alienated, like the barmaid who serves you beer while obviously wishing she were doing something else.

Leaving aside the question of whether a bartender or desert spring, in satisfying the thirst of strangers, should also be required to make a show of enjoying itself, there could be scant argument that Marl Springs did little but what was required of it. Wrested from the sunbaked bajada was a humble corral (property, Casebier said, of the Kessler Springs Ranch, run by Gary Overson's son Clay) enclosing a single water tank and an old arrastra—a low stone structure surrounded by a circular footpath worn smooth by mules, once used for washing gold ore dug from shafts in the surrounding hillsides. Like the spring itself, a nearby mineshaft stood as evidence of subsurface faulting, which had brought precious minerals to the top along with the precious H_2O. "The fault-fractured rock acts as a reservoir and picks up water from both sides of the hill," Reynolds explained.

Other than these few earmarks, the place was characterized only by creosote bush and a bullet-riddled bronze plaque which read:

POZOS DE SAN JUAN DE DIOS:

On March 8, 1776, Fr. Francis Garces, OFM, on his most famous journey of over 2,000 miles from Mission San Xavier Del Bac, Tucson, Arizona, to Mission San Gabriel, California, rested here and named these waterholes "St. John of God Springs" (Marl Springs), and on the return journey passed through here, May 22, same year. Established by the Hospitaller Brothers of St. John of God, St. Mary Desert Valley Hospital, Apple Valley, California, 1972, in cooperation with the San Bernardino County Museum.

"All of us agree that it isn't," Casebier said (apparently in reference to St. John of God Springs). "We told 'em that before they put it up, and they did it anyway." In any case, the plaque commemorated the first Caucasian to thoroughly explore the Mojave Desert—a Spanish priest who, in the view of at least one historian (John Galvin), ranks as "one of the most attractive and respectable figures in all the early history of the southwest": Fray Francisco Tomás Hermenegildo Garcés.

Garcés was born in 1738 in the town of Morata del Conde in Aragon, Spain. He spent his youth in a convent at Ciudad Calatayud, where—according to one of his biographers, Father Juan Domingo Arricivita—he "began to scintillate the rays which divine love kindled in his heart of that zeal with which he was to announce in this new world and to every creature the Holy Evangel." He was ordained at the age of twenty-five and, five years later, assigned to the frontier mission at San Xavier del Bac in Arizona, where Tucson stands today. From there he embarked on a series of five *entradas*, or explorations of the desert, intended to ascertain which Indians were ready to receive the teachings of Christ and the rule of the king of Spain.

In 1768, Garcés journeyed up the Gila River to visit the Papagos; while he was away, his mission was plundered by the Apaches, apparently indicating their unreadiness. Two years later, Arricivita relates, "God"—in this case embodied by the white man—"sent an epidemic of diarrhea and measles to the rancherias of the Gila," so Garcés returned "to gratify the Indians who importuned him to baptize their little ones." The following year, he traveled west to the Colorado River, following it to its mouth on the Sea of Cortez. In 1774, he traced a southern route through the Sonoran Desert with Captain Juan Bautista de Anza to the Mission San Gabriel in California.

In September 1775, Garcés again embarked with Anza on a trek to San Francisco Bay. However, Garcés accompanied the expedition no farther than the Colorado, where he spent time among the Yumas and then, in February 1776, made his way upstream to the farms and villages of the Mohaves (whom he called the Jamajabs). From there he set off across the Mojave, avowedly to establish communications between the Hopi provinces in northern Arizona and the Spanish settlements on the coast.

"I laid before [the Mohaves] my desires to visit the Fathers living near the sea," he wrote in his diary. "They gave assent and offered to accompany me, for they had heard of them and knew the way." On these travels, writes Galvin, Garcés "generally had a few friendly Indians, but always different ones because tomorrow's might not be friendly with today's." For communication he relied on sign language and, in no small capacity, objects of religious art. "Since I saw that in no way could I explain things better to the Indians than with pictures of such sort that they could understand them at sight, I decided to take with me a canvas on one side of which was a painting of Mary Most Holy with the Divine Child in her arms, and on the other a painting of a damned man. I had noticed that on every occasion of my going into heathen territory the Holy Crucifix that hung at my breast excited devotion in the Indians and that they always adored it, acknowledging to me that it was a good thing."

Garcés noted that the Indians liked to listen to him sing and pray. He gave them tobacco and beads for food, which often consisted of mice and lizards. He hardly ever mentioned hardship in his travels. Father Pedro Font, who accompanied him on the Anza expedition, found that "Padre Garces is so fit to get along with the Indians, and go about them, that he seems like an Indian himself. He shows in everything the coolness of an Indian; he squats cross legged in a circle with them; or at night around the fire, for two or three hours together or even longer, all absorbed, forgetting aught else, discourses to them with great serenity and deliberation; and though the food of the Indians is as disgusting and as nasty as their dirty selves, the padre eats it with great gusto, and says that it is appetizing and very nice. In [summary], God has created him, I am sure, wholly on purpose to hunt up those unhappy, ignorant, and boorish people."

Garcés's success with the natives was also undoubtedly due to an attitude toward them that differed considerably from Font's. For example, when Garcés reached the Mission San Gabriel and learned that its commander had ordered the deportation of Mohaves who'd recently visited there on a trading trip, he entered this protest: "The law of nations permits free trade between one people and another. What reason, then, can there be to stop the harmless and long-established commerce of the river people with those of the sea, consisting as it does in some white shellbeads? If we preach to the heathen a law of peace and charity, how can we think of sowing discord?" Perhaps this explains why, as historian Dix Van Dyke has noted, "the Indians seem to have treated [Garcés] cordially everywhere, in marked contrast to the way their descendants treated later travelers."

As far as such later travelers were concerned, Garcés's route eventually became the Mojave Road. He described his journey in sufficient detail that it can be retraced today, though his observations are of interest mainly to historians—he was indifferent to flora and fauna, and seldom waxed poetic about the geography of the Southwest. (His only superlative regarding the Grand Canyon was a description of one pass as "hideous" and "horrifying.") He dutifully named important landmarks after saints whose birthdays fell on the dates when he discovered them—hence, Los Pozos de San Juan (Marl Springs, March 8) and La Sierra de San Marco (the Tehachapi Mountains, April 25). The Mojave River—backbone of both the Indian trail and the eventual wagon road, whose dry course Garcés followed for a hundred miles—obtained a more sweeping honorific: El Arroyo de los Martires.

Alas, this latter designation ultimately included Father Garcés himself, who—hardy, personable, and admirable though he may have been—was, along with three other priests, beaten to death by Yuma Indians in an uprising along the Colorado River in 1781.

The sun was lowering now, suffusing the yellow Kelso Dunes, and creasing the Providence Mountains with deep shadows. As we drove away from Marl Springs, Casebier mentioned that, prior to 1859, the original wagon trail had gone south over a tortuous hill called Rocky Ridge. Instead, we followed the later route north across "Cimacito," a small western flank of Cima Dome. Crossing this high plateau, we soon gained a 360-degree view of the surrounding Mojave, the cinder cones in the northwest glowing red and black like checkers in the last light, with endless ridges stacked beyond them in the west, growing successively dimmer in chiaroscuro as they receded toward the sunset. "If your soul is susceptible to the beguiling effects of wilderness, then you will be enraptured at the feelings you can experience at this spot," Casebier writes in his guidebook. "You can get the feeling that you are sitting on top of the world."

Down in the gathering gloom glowed the infamous white sink of Soda Lake. "At this point on the wagon road the easy ride was over," Casebier announced. "Ahead was the kind of terrain that separated the strong teams from the weak ones. The Indians were holed up in the cinder cones; then came the sandy Devil's Playground, where it was easy for them to attack the wagon trains. In the late 1860s, civilians along this route operated on a shoot-on-sight policy toward Indians." An unidentified voice on the radio added, "Now that the Indians are gone and tamed, all we have to worry about in the bushes are the Sierra Clubbers."

We passed an anomalous mailbox, inside of which was a visitors' register, placed there by Casebier's group and consulted occasionally by the BLM. Then we descended toward the volcanic cones, whose otherwordly aura was heightened by the oncoming dusk. More than thirty such mounds—some taller than five hundred feet—were scattered over the nearby desert, each one dark and solitary and changing color as we passed, dark brown turning bright orange from southeast to northwest, the burnt-brick slopes dotted with shining green shrubs that marched up the slopes from a black field of basalt. The primitive, elemental atmosphere was compromised by roads that encircled the flanks of the cones, enabling miners to probe for cinders. The top of at least one such ridge had been sliced clean through, revealing the sky through a square notch in an otherwise natural horizon. At the Aiken Mine a half-dozen miles to our east, an entire cinder cone was being dismantled and trucked away.

The lava flow came to an abrupt stop at the edge of Willow Wash. We drove slowly over the sand, past waving stands of green and beige rabbit brush, paralleling the basaltic cliff. "This probably isn't the edge of the original flow," Reynolds guessed. "This cliff may have been created by the wash, which is carrying away the basalt. Basically, it's fighting a battle against a wall."

To obtain a better view of the flow, we got out and climbed up the cliff. The rock was rough and treacherous, full of sharp edges and tiny holes. On top, it extended from our feet for miles across the landscape, supporting saltbush and concealing a maze of tunnels and caves—excellent hideouts, as Casebier had intimated, for natives engaged in guerrilla warfare.

"This surface we're standing on isn't the original flow," said Reynolds. "It has nonlocal debris from a quarter of a mile away, floating on top of sediment deposited here by wind and water. If you look at the bigger rocks down below, they have a crumbly texture, like coffee cake. That's probably the original flow surface. At one time, the whole surface was one flow, but expansive silts and clays have elevated blocks of basalt to form this surface we're standing on."

More than seventy volcanic vents have been counted in this field. Why so many are concentrated in such a small area is a question to which no one has an answer, given that volcanoes originate deep within the earth, beyond the range of scientists (though alkali basalts *are* thought to resemble materials comprising the mantle of the Earth). "We're very close to the East Mojave Shear Zone here, which might have something to do with it," Reynolds surmised. "The loose boundary between the mantle and the crust may have allowed these things to pop up." Of course, to him, "popping up" is a process that can span millions of years—though none of these cones took that long to form. "Comparable cinder cones in Hawaii have erupted in a few months or a year," he said. "Steve Wells at U.C. Riverside says these are polycyclic: each one erupted repeatedly over a period of a thousand years or more."

One time, on another visit, I climbed the side of a cinder cone here as a thunderstorm approached from the west. When lightning etched the charcoal sky above the scorched terrain, I felt as if were standing in some prehistoric forge. The place tends to conjure a picture of dozens of volcanoes exploding simultaneously, spewing sparks and magma skyward in some sort of holiday fireworks display. Reynolds corrected this picture for me.

"The lava flow from this kind of volcano doesn't come out from the top of the cone," he said. "The heavy liquid couldn't make it to the top of a loose stack of cinders, so it broke through at the base. The oldest flow here is about seven million years; the youngest is about fifteen thousand. The cones at this end of the field are very fresh-appearing—they still have a cone shape and a breached vent, as opposed to a perfect circle around the top. That is, they're higher on three-quarters of the perimeter, because they blasted ejecta out the side. The flow at the far end is still rough, and has very little vegetation, because it hasn't had time to collect silt or flatten out. Anyway, none of these eruptions was ever seen by man. It *would* be pretty wild, though; you could make a lot of money here with a hot-dog stand."

Casebier had now drawn his wagons into a circle on a bank above the wash (elevation thirty-six hundred feet). This would be our campsite for the night. "If it's not windy," he hinted, "we can have a Casebier fire."

"In case you're wondering," explained Carl Volkmar, the driver of the Range Rover, "a Casebier fire is one of sufficient magnitude that it can change weather patterns within a one-mile radius."

Casebier gave a crooked grin. "You know the difference between an Indian fire and a white-man fire?" he asked. "The Indian builds a little-bitty fire and sits close up; the white man builds a great big fire and stands far away." I still consider this the most cogent analysis of resource depletion by Western civilization that I've ever heard.

As soon as the sun went down, people began donning down jackets, mittens, and wool hats. Temperature conditions clearly called for a Casebier fire, but a strong accompanying wind dictated something between the preferences of our Caucasian leader and those of the departed natives. Reynolds's menu du soir featured Grilled Pork Marinated in Mexi Pep, a repast he dispatched with characteristic imperviousness to the cold and dark. Nobody stayed up long after dinner; by eight o'clock I was in my tent, and by one A.M. I was shivering hard inside my twenty-degree sleeping bag. Eventually I managed to cover myself with a reflecting space blanket, which soaked the bag with condensation but staved off cryogenesis till dawn—at which point I heard the sound of raindrops on the tent.

I peeked out through the flap. Someone had already revived the fire, apparently to Casebier's specifications, as another change in the weather soon took place. While we huddled around gulping coffee, trying to wake and warm up simultaneously, the rabbit brush and cinder cones slowly turned white. I rolled up my tent and tossed it, wet, into the back of the truck; everyone else did the same. Then we started our engines and filed out past the campfire, which was still blazing bright-orange in a pearl-colored world.

There would be no lingering over coffee on this spring morning. It was snowing in the Mojave in March.

The caravan fled down Willow Wash, its sand compacted and thus rendered negotiable by the dampening effects of precipitation (though not in sufficient volume to inspire the dreaded flash floods). We crossed the paved Kelbaker Road, which connects the towns of Kelso and Baker, and made for Seventeen-Mile Point—the northern tip of the Old Dad Mountains, seventeen miles in either direction from the nearest water source on the Mojave Road.

One time, passing through the Old Dads farther south, I glimpsed a khaki-colored animal, bigger than a rabbit but smaller than a horse, running through the desert off to my left. As I raised my binoculars, I realized that it was a bighorn sheep—six well-camouflaged bighorns, as it

turned out. Nothing but their divided white rumps betrayed their presence in the dun-toned landscape, but through my field glasses, I could
see the heavy horns racing backward as the sheep browsed their way
along Rocky Ridge.

"The Old Dad Mountains have been made into virtual paradise for
bighorn sheep by [artificial] watering," Casebier explained. "There are
sufficient numbers that they issue hunting permits for them. There are
only three or four permits a year, and they cost a lot of money, which goes
back to benefit the bighorns through some sort of ecological/financial
algebra that I don't understand. A lot of other people don't understand it,
either." However, enough people understood something well enough to
make this a decisive issue when Congress passed the California Desert
Protection Act in 1994. Since its inception, the bill had stipulated that
this area would become part of a new national park, but to preserve the
rights of hunters, it was downgraded to a "preserve" in the final legislation. Ironically, the following summer, when one of the artificial guzzlers
in the Old Dads went dry, thirteen bighorns in need of water broke
through the tank covering and drowned, poisoning the water with botu-
lism that killed another twenty-five bighorns.

The lava continued to parallel our route on the right, petering out just
before the point, leaving a convenient passageway between itself and the
Old Dad Mountains for wagons and four-wheel-drives. As we rounded a
corner of "Precambrian metasediments and conglomerate" (Reynolds),
we could see a thin white strip in the gray murk ahead: the playa of Soda
Lake. Far to the south, beyond the dark promontories of the Cowhole
Mountains, was the windswept waste of the Devil's Playground.

In November 1835, Lieutenant Robert S. Williamson, following the
bed of the Mojave River, led an Army survey party into Soda Basin from
the west. He described the area as follows:

> Upon emerging from the cañon, we entered a sandy plain, and at
> once lost all signs of the river-bed. After travelling 13 miles
> across this plain, we were fortunate enough to find a hole con-
> taining water, and here we made our camp late at night. The
> water was barely sufficient for our nearly exhausted animals, and
> a long time was occupied in giving them a scanty supply. This
> plain had an abundant growth of mezquite trees. We afterward

found some uninhabited Indian huts near here, and an abundance of old Indian tracks, but no Indians.

In the morning, upon taking a survey of our position, we found we were near the centre of an irregularly shaped plain, surrounded by hills. To the southeast appeared an opening, and here we concluded was the outlet through which the Mohave continued its course. We went in this direction about thirteen miles, the first seven or eight of which were over low sand-hills; but afterwards we travelled in the dry bed of a wash, which we found we were *ascending*. Being convinced that we had left the Mohave [River], and the men who had been sent in search of water having been able to find none, we returned to our camp of the morning. This was another very fatiguing day for the animals, and after reaching camp, there being so little water in the hole, which filled very slowly, it took till 2 A.M. to water them.

We observed to-day that to the north of our camp was a large lake-bed, and here we inferred the waters of the Mohave were collected. The question now was, whether this lake had an outlet, or whether it was a basin, and the terminus of the Mohave. To ascertain this point, Lieutenant [George] Stoneman and myself started to examine the lake, which was about fifteen miles long, and covered with an incrustation of salt, exceedingly bitter. We, however, returned to camp late, without any positive result. Not being willing to move the command upon an uncertainty, I resolved to devote one more day to examination.

To the east of our camp was a high range of barren mountains, its crest from fifteen to twenty miles distant. Lieutenant Stoneman and myself ascended to the summit of one of the nearest peaks, from which we had an extended view. To the eastward were to be seen nothing but mountains; we saw, however, that to the northward of the salt lake, and not far distant from it, were several other lake-beds. . . .

The results of these examinations was, that if the Mohave flowed beyond the salt lake, it could flow in no other than a northerly direction through these lake-beds, and the only thing to be done was to proceed in this direction, though directly contrary to the one we wished to go.

We had found at the base of the hills, on the edge of the salt lake, several fine springs, slightly brackish but not unpalatable. Around these was good grass. The camp was moved here, and the animals were refreshed by once more having as much to eat as they wanted.

On the morning of November 16, at 5 o'clock, we started by fine moonlight and travelled to the northern extremity of the salt lake, and thence on to the next one. We found the two connected by a ditch, cut by water in the clay soil, and about twenty feet wide, with banks two feet high. The two lakes were from three to four miles apart. The second one was six miles long and three broad. The character of the second lake was entirely different from that of the first. It was a dry, hard clay-bed, on which the shoes of the mules scarcely made an impression; while the other was covered with salt, and in many places too soft to travel over. The bases of the hills on the west, and the mountains on the east, were immediate on the lake bank, and as we crossed it we could see there was no outlet in either of these directions; but to the northward the hills were low, and we expected to find here a passage where water could flow. On arriving at the north end of the lake, we found a very low ridge, connecting the hills on either side. We searched for a passage through this ridge, but could find none; but everywhere saw, in the gullies, that the water from rains flowed toward the lake. I hence concluded that the true sink of the Mohave river was in the salt lake and that the second lake was formed principally from water flowing from the surrounding hills after heavy rains; but that in time of very high water in the salt lake, its surplus flowed through the ditch before mentioned into it.

We crossed this ridge, and at once descended into another valley some two hundred feet lower than the bed of the lake. After travelling four or five miles, we came suddenly upon a wagon-road. We knew it could be no other than the old Spanish trail, and this at once afforded proof that the Mohave river of the maps is a fiction. It was universally supposed by emigrants and others, that when the Spanish trail left the Mohave above the cañon, it never was on it again. The valley in which we struck the

> trail extended to the northward twenty or thirty miles, bounded
> on all sides by mountains.
>
> We were now, according to our estimates, over 100 miles in a
> direct line from the Colorado, with a mountainous country be-
> tween and neither wood, water, nor grass that we knew of. To
> attempt to reach the river could have been madness. Our only
> alternative was to turn back.

Williamson's depiction and conclusions proved remarkably accurate. The "low sand-hills" through which he passed were the Devil's Play-ground. The "high range of barren mountains" was the Old Dads. The "salt lake" was Soda Lake, which is—aided, very infrequently, by the "dry, hard clay-bed" of Silver Lake to the north—the terminus of the Mojave River, which flows northeast from the San Bernardino Moun-tains, past the present-day towns of Victorville and Barstow.

To say that the Mojave River "flows" is something of an exaggeration. It's dry for most of its sandy length, the water remaining underground except during periods of very wet weather. Jedediah Smith referred to it as the Inconstant River. Dennis Casebier—quoting the dean of desert naturalists, Edmund C. Jaeger—called it the Upside-Down River, seeing as how it (1) flows underground instead of above, (2) is larger at its source than at its mouth, (3) divides on its way downhill rather than col-lecting tributaries, and (4) flows inland, its waters never reaching the sea. Throughout history, its bed has offered ingress to travelers from the Mohave Indians to Father Garcés to the U.S. Army to Mormon emi-grants to the Union Pacific Railroad to U.S. Interstate 15. In the mid-nineteenth century, a hopeful rumor persisted that it might reach all the way to the Colorado River, presenting an unobstructed passageway through the entire Mojave Desert. But as Williamson showed, there was to be no such luck.

Some Christmases ago, an acquaintance of mine was sitting in his office in Los Angeles, listening to a downpour drumming against his win-dows. "It was really raining hard," he remembers. "And it was a warm rain, so I thought it might be reaching the desert. I called the KOA campground in Victorville and asked if the river was running; they said, 'Wait a minute,' then came back and said, 'Yeah, it is.' My son and brother-in-law and I put our canoe on top of the car and got to Hesperia by noon. We made it all the way to Helendale before the water ran out. We had to wait for it to catch up."

Over millennia, the Mojave River has carried alluvium toward Soda Basin in just this manner. "The river deposits a lot of sand where it turns toward Soda Lake," said Reynolds. "Then the wind picks it up and blows it east toward the Devil's Playground. In satellite photos it's real obvious—you can see the streaks." When this wind hits the Granite and Providence Mountains, it stops and goes up, dropping its airborne load to form the Kelso Dunes. Then, said Reynolds, "when it rains, the sand moves west again, and the wind picks it up and brings it back. It's a cycle."

At the end of the Ice Age—during the pluvial period, when glaciers were melting, rainfall was common, and most of Utah was covered by Lake Bonneville—the Mojave River was a bona fide stream, feeding several substantial bodies of water along its length. Cattails and cottonwoods grew on the shores of Soda Lake, as well as those of Silver Lake, Cronese Lake, and Lake Manix, which covered hundreds of square miles east of present-day Barstow. To the north was an even more extensive system: Owens Lake flowed into Searles Lake, which emptied into Panamint Lake, which drained to six-hundred-foot-deep Lake Manly, which extended ninety miles north and south within the confines of Death Valley (which was also fed, from the direction of Nevada, by the Amargosa River). As the rains subsided, the lakes dried up. Still remaining, however, was the alluvium in their beds—borates, carbonates, sulphates, and chlorides in such concentration that modern mining companies have profited for decades by digging them up. During times of heavy runoff, these playas still form ephemeral lakes, replaying scenes from the Pleistocene. Such lakebeds constitute some of the flattest natural landforms in the world: the bodies of water that materialize on top of them, during the brief time that they exist, might be miles long and only an inch deep; if a strong wind comes up, all the water blows to one end. Within a few days, weeks, or months, the liquid either is absorbed or evaporates, leaving—if drainage is good—a hard clay surface such as those of Rogers and Rosamond Lakes in Edwards Air Force Base, or the one described by Williamson at Silver Lake. However, if drainage is poor (and residual salt high), it becomes a damp, muddy "salina" such as Williamson described at Soda Lake—and which we now confronted on a decidedly drizzly day.

In traveling from the cinder cones to Soda Basin, we'd dropped more than two thousand feet in elevation. Consequently, the snow had turned to rain. In dry weather, Soda Lake's surface is firm and brown, mottled with a thin veneer of salt, scattered with forlorn atriplex shrubs, obscured at its edges by distant shimmering mirages, and bisected by a clear vehicle track marked at intervals by green steel fenceposts. The route dips and bumps through several shallow, hard-to-anticipate watercourses, which can become quite muddy when wet. Casebier—who, during his trans-Mojave hike, walked across Soda Lake at midday—was armed with tales of autos sinking down to their door handles in mud. Reportedly, the lake contains at least one army tank, in addition to God knows what else. For this reason, we elected to skirt the playa altogether—we took a hard right near the shoreline, abandoning the Mojave Road and heading north toward the town of Baker, visible at the end of the plain eight miles away.

Baker—population 390, elevation 923 feet—started out as a stop on the Tonopah and Tidewater Railroad (brainchild of the notorious Francis Marion "Borax" Smith), which ran between Ludlow, California, and Rhyolite, Nevada, during the first half of the twentieth century. Today—located as it is on Interstate 15 between Barstow and Las Vegas—it serves as gateway to both Death Valley and the East Mojave. It is, in fact, very near the geographical center of the Mojave Desert—and there have been times when, emerging from several days in the field, I have perceived Baker as the center of civilization itself. Many languages may be heard there on any given day; the town has a traffic light, a fire department, and a staggering selection of (i.e., at least three) motels, gas stations, restaurants, and trees. "Welcome to Bun Boy Country," crows a stirring billboard, referring to the town's flagship eatery—"Home of Fresh Strawberry Pie."

Not long ago, Baker was the literal hotbed of a movement to create a whole new county in the desert. The town is one of many unincorporated outposts in vast San Bernardino County, which with twenty thousand square miles is the largest county (in geographic area) in the United States, bigger than Vermont and New Hampshire combined. Most of the county's population, however, lies south of the San Bernardino Mountains on the edge of the Los Angeles basin, which suffers from the most notorious smog, traffic, crowding, and crime in the United States. Desert dwellers feel little affinity with this area; on the contrary, they tend to regard it with derision. Nonetheless, the bulk of the population dictates such countywide policies as surtaxes on building permits and restrictions on mobile homes, while receiving most of the county money, upon which remote communities like Baker nevertheless depend. Motel taxes in Baker amount to $100,000 per year, of which an average of only $5,000 is annually returned to the town. Baker has no local library, hospital, or clinic; the nearest medical facility is sixty-five miles away, the county seat and hospital twice that. A pair of local sheriff's deputies patrol a jurisdiction of four hundred square miles. Yet the same region harbors a wealth of revenue-producing pipelines, power lines, railroads, relay stations, and solar-power plants, which would—if only the degenerates "down below" could be cut loose—make it one of the richest counties in the world.

Alas, the proposition to create Mojave County was predictably defeated in a countywide election. And as fast-growing towns like Apple Valley and Hesperia became incorporated, giving them power over their own funds and statutes, the movement lost considerable steam. The Mojave Desert population boom hasn't yet reached Baker, but with the way things are going to the west and east, it may be only a matter of time.

Upon arriving in town, our caravan was crestfallen to find that the Bun Boy was being rebuilt after a fire. Thus, like so many others, we made our way resignedly to Denny's, whose digital sign reported the air temperature at forty-four degrees Fahrenheit.* Here we could fortify ourselves properly before rejoining the Mojave Road, which made its next stop at Soda Springs—the place where Lieutenant Williamson had found water and grass on the west side of Soda Lake.

To reach it, we went south down a washboarded gravel road that skirted the edge of the playa. The lake surface showed patches of water amid the salt-encrusted mud. After nine miles of slow driving, we came to a line of bedraggled, dead-looking date palms, their hanging fronds clipped at the bottom, resembling grass skirts. To the left was a vast stand of tamarisk trees, beyond which was a bunch of low stucco-covered buildings and a long pool with a dormant fountain. A street sign an-

---

*Baker has since erected a 130-foot-high thermometer visible from the freeway. Judging by every account of it I've ever seen, it perpetually reads 120.

nounced our arrival at the intersection of Zzyzx Road and the Boulevard of Dreams.

"Water used to gush from this spring in the wagon-road days," Casebier said. "The army established Fort Soda here in 1860; later, miners processed the lake minerals, and in the teens there was a German colony. Five years ago, a promoter with some high technology determined that the mud contained gold—he called it 'Soda Gold'—and tried to convince investors to buy mud by the cubic yard. Then he disappeared. The moral of the story is that there's more than one way to take a mudbath in Soda Lake."

Casebier paused and looked across the grounds toward "Lake Tuendae"—an artificial pond whose surface boasted several cormorants: seabirds sailing around in the middle of the desert. "The most interesting chapter in Soda Springs history began on September 13, 1944," Casebier said. "That was when Dr. Curtis Howe Springer established the Zzyzx Mineral Springs resort."

Curtis Howe Springer (the "doctor" designation was apparently self-conferred) was a radio evangelist and mail-order purveyor of health-food products who, sometime during World War II, learned about the "mineral water" at Soda Springs. Inquiring as to the status of the land, he found no record of active mining and hence filed a claim on 12,800 acres. He subsequently commenced setting up a resort called Zzyzx, "the last word in health." Now a desert-studies center operated by the California state universities, the place is closed to casual visits from tourists; but Casebier, who has lobbied tirelessly to open it to the public, had made arrangements for us to visit.

We ambled around inspecting the compound that Springer conjured from the desert: a church, a kitchen, a dining hall, and a mineral pool shaped like a cross, pointing at the North Star and divided into different compartments for temperature selection. Most of the living quarters were small, spartan rooms with double bunkbeds; Springer's residence, nicknamed the Castle, was two stories high with a long curved porch.

"Springer recruited winos from Los Angeles to come out and help him build the place," said Casebier. "He was a visionary architect and engineer. The buildings here are all steel-reinforced concrete. There were no telephones—they didn't use any public utilities. They generated their own power, including air-conditioning, and bladed an airstrip. They

dug a lake and got a good population of Mojave chub going—you could
go fishing here back then. Springer did all the construction without permits. The government couldn't stand that; they'd rather you did things
wrong *with* a permit than do them right without one."

Casebier was warming to his subject, becoming exceedingly animated
and impish. Later I would learn that he had a portrait of Springer hanging in his home. Clearly he revered this resourceful, antibureaucratic figure, whose story offered him a perfect platform to spin out his own
philosophy.

"Springer's innovative policy," Casebier said, pausing before the
placid pool of Lake Tuendae, "was that if you came to Zzyzx, ate good
food, thought pure thoughts, didn't drink or smoke or argue about religion or politics, *you'd feel better!* There was no charge to any of his
patients; he had a schedule of suggested values, but it was all done by
donation—you paid what you deemed appropriate. One judge in Los
Angeles sentenced skid-row people to his care; Springer paid them a
nominal wage, and they helped him maintain the property. He held religious services every day. He sold 'manna,' vitamins, crystals from the lake
surface, and a mild laxative called 'antidiluvian tea' through the mail.
Because of his business, the Baker post office got upgraded to first-class
status. He talked about Zzyzx on his radio show, and after a while people
started coming to Baker and staying in the motels while they were waiting to get into the resort.

"In the sixties, when Zzyzx was really booming, the *L.A. Times* published an article saying that Springer was squatting and not paying
income or county taxes. He brought in about a million dollars a year, but
he didn't keep any records. Furthermore, he eliminated the need for
medicine, so the American Medical Association got after him for calling
himself a doctor. In 1968, three things happened simultaneously: The
Internal Revenue Service charged Springer with evasion of income tax;
the State Food and Drug Commission said that information about his
line of health foods was false and misleading; and the Bureau of Land
Management began trying to evict him from the property, where he and
his wife, Helen, had been making improvements for twenty-four years.
They'd gone into the U.S. Lands Office once every three months or so to
keep the government informed about their progress, but now the BLM
said that their mining claims were invalid.

"Eventually the Springers were cleared of all the income-tax charges, and the state dropped most of the ones concerning the health foods. Springer tried to take the BLM eviction to the Supreme Court, but they wouldn't hear the case. He and Helen were escorted off the property by armed deputies on Good Friday in 1974. They were given thirty-six hours to collect all the things they'd been accumulating here for thirty years."

Casebier seemed to believe that the government's approach to Zzyzx epitomized everything that was wrong with society in general and its treatment of the desert in particular. "Once this land became 'public,' the public couldn't come here anymore," he pointed out. "Pretty soon the rats and the vandals took over, and for a while the BLM thought they might push the buildings into the lake and return Soda Springs to its original condition. Then a consortium of state universities expressed interest and offered to share the expenses of maintaining the place. So then the BLM decided that that was what they wanted all along. As soon as the universities took over, half the fish population died. They started to dig a new lake for 'em, but on the second day they ran into some Indian remains and had to stop. Turned out Soda Springs wasn't all that good a place for scientific research, because it's not a natural habitat. Mostly what it's used for now is classes; it *is* an excellent place for education, which we think can coexist side by side with recreational use by the public. Whenever people come here, they get fascinated with Zzyzx and the inspirational character of Dr. Springer. When he died at the age of ninety, his head was full of schemes and his heart was full of fight. He couldn't bring himself to abide by the rules when he knew better. He wasn't intolerant; he just didn't conform. That is a sin in our society. It's the greatest nation in the history of the Earth—no question about it—but the really exciting thing is how much better it could be."

The sun came out as we departed Zzyzx, heading southwest along the edge of Soda Lake. From here we had an expansive view of the low Mojavean moonscape: the Devil's Playground scattered with black magnetite, the Kelso Dunes peeking up behind, the tops of the Granite and Providence Mountains obscured by a distant storm. Beyond Soda Lake and Cowhole Mountain, in the cinder-cone area where we'd camped, the whole horizon was covered with snow. To our right, etched by numerous vertical watermarks, was Springer Mountain—christened by Casebier and described by Reynolds as "horribly brecciated [broken] limestone. It must be a gravity slide block—sort of a big hockey puck. The closest Paleozoic limestone is in Cowhole Mountain, or behind the Soda Mountains fifteen miles away. Soda Basin was probably formed by the pulling apart of a fault zone—the Soda-Avawatz fault on the east side, another one on the west."

We were now nearing the Rasor Open Area, where off-road vehicles of every description—dirt bikes, dune buggies, and three-wheeled ATVs—could go wherever they pleased. Hence, the southwestern surface of Soda Lake had been rutted and carved with tire tracks. "It was a poor management decision to locate it so close to Zzyzx," commented Casebier, "but one good thing about it is that it shows the difference between those people and us." After accelerating through some deep sand—a preview of things soon to come in quantity—we ascended a rocky alluvial fan topped by modest Shaw Pass. We then descended into the Mojave River floodplain proper—a five-mile-wide wash, the most treacherous part of the Mojave Road for travelers past and present.

"You are at a point of decision," Casebier's guidebook reads at this point. "The road ahead features blow sand, loose soil, and all kinds of hazards to vehicles. It is inadvisable to venture beyond here without more than one." Climatic conditions here can be the most deadly in the Mojave—a fact with which Dennis Casebier has some direct experience. In 1980, while first trying to publicize the Mojave Road, he set out on foot over the plain from Soda Springs with a detachment of marines. The time of year for the trek—mid-July—might have been better chosen, as the air temperature that day would reach 120 degrees. By midmorning, one civilian member of the party had begun to falter. Another soon developed heatstroke.

"The support vehicles were six miles ahead at Afton Canyon," Casebier remembers. "We put our guy in the shade with some damp towels on his face and waited there with three or four quarts of water. The marines went ahead, but they pushed too hard—one of them got heatstroke, too, and couldn't give instructions to the others. Finally two jeeps came back and immediately got stuck in the sand. We had to dig them out, which started giving *me* symptoms of heatstroke. It makes you weak, dizzy, and faint; you can't think straight.

"All my life I'd heard that if you get in trouble on the desert, you just wait for nightfall and your problems will go away. So we stopped and waited for dark in order to hike out. The afternoon got stifling—unbearably hot. But late in the day, a thundercloud came over and rained right on us, which was tremendously rejuvenating. Finally the marines were able to explain the correct route back, and a van came to get us. I remember sitting up there after the rain, watching the storms across the desert and feeling great."

The story didn't end as well for many earlier travelers. Shaw Pass, for example, had been named for Dr. Merrill Eugene Shaw, an army surgeon killed in an Indian attack here in 1867. With sand impeding the progress of the wagons and the largest stand of desert willows in the world making it hard to see far ahead, the Mojave River floodplain was one of the Chemehuevis's favorite sites for ambushes.

Throughout the floodplain, telephone poles and railroad ties stood as vertical road markers—a piece of wisdom left over from the wagonmasters, who found that blowing sand buried anything shorter. Casebier's guidebook offers tips on how to stay the confusing course: "Remember that you shouldn't drift so far south that you get close to the railroad until you're almost at [Afton] canyon. Another landmark to watch while crossing the floodplain is a strip of blow sand that stands out on the dark side of Cave Mountain about one-third of the way from the peak. . . . When you get down into the floodplain you can always see that streak of sand. Head a little to the left."

The sand streak in question resembled nothing in the world so much as a downhill ski slope. "You can drive down it in a car," Casebier corroborated. "You lock your wheels, and let me tell you, it's exciting."

Tiny pink flowers with rose-colored stripes and yellow stamens were blooming on the willows. "Everything other than willows must have been scoured away by the river," Reynolds surmised. "On the ground here I can see granite from Barstow, quartzite from Silver Peak near Victorville, and sidewinder metavolcanics from Stoddard Mountain." As we drove, fine alluvium (a.k.a. sand) rose from beneath the tires and blew east, demonstrating the natural patterns that created the Kelso Dunes.

The sun seemed to be out for good now, with big white cumulus clouds crossing the blue sky. As we neared the mouth of Afton Canyon, water appeared in the wash, running briskly over the surface, sparkling in the sun. We crossed and recrossed the stream as our path converged with that of the Union Pacific Railroad, which obliged us with some entertainment, sending a train over a trestle bridge beneath which we'd stopped for lunch. "The Union Pacific used to put observation cars on just for this area," said Casebier. We were nearing the home stretch—one of the most spectacular places in the Mojave Desert.

In the nineteenth century, Afton Canyon was called Cave Canyon—and as we made our way up the riverbed, it was easy to see why. The gorge, which had drained Lake Manix during the pluvial period, had been etched and winnowed into a kaleidoscope of cliffs, cutting and shaping the collected alluvium of the Mojave River. To my eye, the south wall contained approximately a zillion kinds of rock, eroded into red, white, black, and gray pinnacles, pedestals, footings, and ravines.

"In the Manix fault zone, gray Miocene gravels meet pink Pliocene gravels," Reynolds said. "Those are equivalent in age to the greenish playa sediments and interfingered gravels of the Mojave River formation. Over there on the south side, you can see black Miocene basalts and white volcanic ash." The north wall, on the other hand, consisted of beige gravels cut by alluvial fans pouring forth from side canyons, which—twenty feet wide and two hundred feet deep—carved their way back into the more elevated desert from the gorge. "Manix Lake used to overflow into these canyons," Reynolds said. "Two hundred thousand years ago, this place was like Niagara Falls."

As we approached the head of the canyon, we heard what sounded like a chain saw or lawn mower. Pretty soon, a couple of kids came along on motorcycles. Just ahead was the only BLM-maintained campground on the Mojave Road. "It really creates a problem," said Casebier. "It's the kind of place where people can bring in a trailer and tear down the canyon in ATVs." Sure enough, the surrounding slopes of the canyon had been ripped apart by tire tracks.

It was nearing three o'clock on Friday afternoon. The Mojave Road continued for another eighteen miles, at which point it once joined the Salt Lake Trail for the final leg over Cajon Pass. Our journey would go no farther, however. Casebier said that conditions in the riverbed ahead were hazardous, and scenically no more revealing than what we'd already witnessed. At the BLM campground, he thus collected the members of the caravan for a farewell. His voice was drowned out by the sound of revving dirt-bike engines.

As we drove north toward the freeway, Reynolds continued musing about Lake Manix, pointing out the ancient beach where Interstate 15 now flowed, pausing by a roadcut to look at layers of calcareous tufa. "At one time we could have water-skiied on Lake Manix," he said. "There were pink flamingos in the shallows and ground sloths frolicking in the cottonwoods on shore."

As he reconstructed the scene, I realized that both he and Casebier habitually beheld a landscape invisible to most. I suppose you could claim that they lived in the past, but it would be more accurate to say that the past lived in them. Gazing at things that hadn't changed in centuries, Reynolds saw nothing but evidence of alteration; confronted with landforms thrusting forcefully skyward, he perceived remnants of things worn away. It was a refractive view of reality, sort of like psychology-test pictures where some people see opposing faces instead of a vase. In any case, it was apparent that, like Curtis Howe Springer of Zzyzx, the Mojave served both historian and geologist the same tonic that it offered countless others, albeit in a more sophisticated form: an alternative to the everyday structures of modern civilized life.

As we abandoned dirt for freeway, the prescription ran out. Having spent two days traveling a hundred miles in the manner of nineteenth-century pioneers, we fought our way into weekend traffic, heading from Los Angeles toward Las Vegas at eighty miles per hour.

Free-Ranging Anxiety

After completing our trip over the Mojave Road, I returned to Goffs to do some research at Casebier's library. Along the way, I stopped by the OX Ranch in Lanfair Valley. I had met its owner, Gary Overson, the previous November when, driving into Carothers Canyon in the New York Mountains on a chilly autumn afternoon, I came upon two cowboys fixing a windmill. The first thing that impressed me about them was the way they were dressed. The younger of the two (the son, as it turned out) was wearing a mustache, a black hat, and a purple scarf, while the elder—Gary—had a white hat and neckerchief over his tan canvas shirt. Both had spurs on their boots, although there were no horses in sight. Such sartorial embellishment is not uncharacteristic of cowboys, who, despite their reputation for reserve and modern dependency on internal combustion, still display considerable romanticism about their equestrian calling.

I watched them puzzle over the mill pump until Gary finally declared it "a go-to-town case." When I asked if I might call him later, he said he was listed in Nevada information (despite the fact that he lives in California). He claimed that he didn't know his own telephone number since "I don't ever call myself."

When I visited Overson's ranch, I found that it didn't quite match the aesthetic in his attire. True to its desert location, it was a habitat devoid of adornment. Near the lime green house were a trailer, a galvanized steel shed, two low outbuildings made of stucco, a pile of white salt, and a tangle of orange and yellow rope that looked like lichen from a distance. A U-shaped pipe wrapped with fiberglass insulation protruded from the ground; a child's swing and a cook's triangle hung from a forlorn-looking tree. Completing the tableau were a windmill, a miniature cannon, a lone turkey vulture tipping on the breeze, and a solitary Joshua tree, beyond which a forest of thousands more stretched toward Castle Peaks, where the white scar of the Viceroy Mine was visible ten miles away.

The place was quiet except for a generator. A young, dirty-jeaned cowboy was filling a water truck from a well; when I approached and asked for Overson, he said, "I think he went to haul some salt." Even in these few syllables, the boy conveyed a certain patented sensibility: soft-spoken, unhurried, altogether timeless. Living and working as they do in such silent, austere space, desert ranchers exude a spirit that is literally otherworldly.

As Americans' relationship with wide open places has evolved over the last quarter century, our hallowed image of the cowboy has taken something of a beating. The Marlboro Man who once stood so prominently for masculine independence is, for example, now perceived as a disease-ridden despoiler of land. The seeds of this public-relations problem perhaps took root in 1934 with the Taylor Grazing Act, whose passage officially recognized that overgrazing and soil deterioration were threatening to ruin the American range. The legislation brought an end to the nomadic herding that, in the half century following the Civil War, had transformed seven hundred million acres of grassland into weedy scrub; the act tied the privilege of public-lands grazing to ownership of private land and charged a fee for it to boot. Unfortunately, this fee (which is uniform throughout the country and assessed according to "animal unit months" or AUMs—the amount that an animal can eat in one month) has remained so low—at one half to one tenth the fair market value for equivalent use of private land—that taxpayers ended up subsidizing federal range management to the tune of many millions of dollars per year, giving rise to the "welfare rancher" epithet for the once idealized rider of the range. Meanwhile, livestock continued to consume so much vegetation that, by the 1980s, the Bureau of Land Management found that four of every five acres of western rangeland it managed were in unsatisfactory condition—all for the purpose of producing 2 percent of the red meat raised in the United States.

Despite its aridity and consequent sparseness, the desert had been grazed with as much dispatch as any other place—if any forage was there to be eaten, livestock were let loose. Sheep overran the western Mojave, cattle took to the east, and feral burros mowed down everything in between, to the pronounced detriment of native plants and stabilizing soil. (Cryptogramic crusts, composed of lichens, algae, fungi, and mosses, stabilize desert soil by increasing plant productivity and retarding erosion.) Grazing also had a negative impact on pronghorn antelope, desert tortoises, and bighorn sheep. In 1980, however, the local terms of the Taylor Grazing Act were modified by the California Desert Plan—which, in calculating the amount of grazing that any public allotment could support, allowed only as much livestock as could (in the BLM's estimation) coexist with competing wildlife. The twenty-five-million-acre California Desert Conservation Conservation Area, created by the Desert Plan, produces only 0.3 percent of beef raised in the state; whereas the federal government assigns one cow to every acre of pastureland in Georgia (and every two in Texas), to find an equivalent amount of fodder, the average bovine between Los Angeles and Las Vegas must ransack a thousand acres.

Forage is twice that thick in the East Mojave, which contains the best grazing land in the California desert. Still, by any objective standard, a feeding range of five hundred acres per cow is slim pickings. Thus, when the California Desert Protection Act was introduced in Congress in 1986, its advocates aimed to banish cattle completely from the proposed Mojave National Park. The move would have affected only a handful of ranchers, but by far the largest—with close to two thousand cattle roaming over almost a million acres—was Gary Overson.

I finally hooked up with Overson by phone at six thirty in the morning. He told me that he was coming toward Goffs that day and I could ride along with him if I wanted to. When he picked me up at the schoolhouse, I noticed that he had his rifle on the seat beside him—not on a rack in the cab's rear window—and that, as he got out of the truck and walked bowlegged on his boots around the tailgate, he was still wearing his spurs.

He was small but sinewy, simultaneously sharp and blunt. "First of all," he said as I got into his truck, "I don't care about what you're doing at all. It don't mean nothing to me to be in a book." He spit some snuff juice into a bowl and, having thus established his independence, explained that he was out checking water lines and tank float valves. "I own sixteen of the main water rights in this area. Springs, windmills, over a hundred miles of pipeline—the land where the water is. That's the key to the desert; water is the whole thing." Indeed, if it weren't for such artificial developments, much of the Mojave would be naturally off-limits to livestock.

We pulled out from the schoolhouse and onto Goffs Road. As we drove south through the desert, Overson scanned the landscape for cows. "Cattle get fat on yucca blooms," he said, referring to the creamy-white blossoms I'd seen in Lanfair Valley. "Eating those, they might go two weeks without water. Then, when they get thirsty, they start a-walking down this way. I gotta watch 'em, or they'll go all the way to the Colorado River."

He told me he'd come to the East Mojave from St. John's, Arizona, fifty years earlier, when he was three years old. "I went to work for the OX Ranch when I was eleven," he said. "My father was a rancher till he went to work for the railroad. He was right across the road at that stockyard there. He got killed by a train when I was about fifteen. When I got married, all I had was a bedroll, a saddle, and a pickup payment. After a while, I managed to get a one-third interest in the Kessler Springs Ranch—a hundred cows, one bull, and two saddle horses. I kept on buying cattle, and later I bought my partners out. Bought the Sand Dunes Ranch at Kelso and sold it; bought the Valley Wells Ranch, sold it. Then I bought the OX Ranch. Now I got seven thousand acres of deeded land and close to nine hundred thousand of grazing land, not counting two ranches I take care of.* It's not all BLM land—I don't know how many sections of railroad land I lease—and it's not as big as it sounds. With this country here, cattle don't use a lot of it but once every three or four years."

The weather was overcast with occasional raindrops—not as chilly as

---

*In addition to his own, Overson manages the Valley Wells and Valley View Ranches, both of which are owned by Richard Blinko, an Idaho agriculturist.

it had been earlier in the week, but consistent with the recent pattern of repeated spring rains. "This is what you want," said Overson. "Warm rains out of Los Angeles, San Diego, and Mexico. March will make you or break you as far as feed conditions on the desert. It's unpredictable— with the wind blowing, it can freeze or dry the ground out. The secret is having moisture in the ground before it dries out. What you *don't* want is storms from the north; that just brings cold and snow and humps up your cattle. In most countries you have only one season, but here you have two: spring and summer. The spring of the year is your payday. We ship the cattle in June, and when we start work, we need seventeen or eighteen head of broke saddle horses and five or six of us riding 'em.

"The OX is the most productive ranch in this country," Overson went on. "It can carry as much as twenty-five hundred mother cows all year long. That black grama grass up at Carothers is as good a grass as there is anywhere; steers come off there in June weighing seven hundred pounds. A lot of ranches that people think are so great still have to feed hay in winter, and that stuff is getting expensive. But the OX Ranch has feed year-round."*

We turned east toward the Colorado River, where the country was characterized more by creosote bush than by Joshua trees. "This is a coarser grass in here," Overson observed. "You see that peanut cactus? When the ground gets so dry that cattle eat that, you gotta either sell 'em or move 'em. The needles foul their stomachs up. A lot of this country is only used three or four months out of the year. It's low, and in warm weather it's dry. The cattle would rather have green, so you move 'em up into the cooler country. I move cattle around all over. People from other places don't understand that. How the hell can you have all your cattle in one place in the desert country?"

When Overson expressed disdain—as he did with the last sentence— he dipped his head forward and wagged it from side to side as if imitating the posture of a prattling fool. "If a lot of the people who are against grazing came out here and lived a couple of years, they wouldn't be against it," he claimed. "*People* is what ruins the country—not cattle. And burros. That's a real bad deal, and a real serious deal.† Burros tramp down

---

*In 1994, local BLM officials reported that Overson fed his cattle mineral and protein supplements in winter, when natural forage consists primarily of carbohydrates.
†Wild burros are protected by the Wild Horse and Burro Act of 1971, which stipulates that their herds be monitored and maintained by the federal government.

everything. A cow can't bite, but a burro's got teeth on both the top and the bottom. We used to handle the burros ourselves—if you got too many, you got rid of 'em. But since they turned it over to the BLM, we've got burros all over this country—I've seen burros where they've never been before.

"A lot of people got the idea that grazing is government-subsidized," Overson said as he continued driving. "They call a grazing lease a privilege, but it's a right—you bought it and you're paying taxes on it. The OX outfit used to have five or six guys working, but I do it all now with one other guy; by the time I pay taxes, regulations and the rest, I can't pay extra men. In the last three years, I've paid two hundred thousand dollars in income tax. I pay the government thirty thousand dollars a year in grazing fees; I pay on a lease for railroad land, a lease for state land, a county use tax on my grazing permit, and property tax on my own land. In an average month, my operating expenses for wages, groceries, horseshoes, fuel, and salt are ten to twelve thousand dollars. This winter, it got so cold at my place that it cost me three thousand dollars just to fix broken pipe fittings and float valves along the waterlines. When the roads get too rough to use, I gotta maintain 'em myself—for who? Fish and Game uses 'em; the BLM uses 'em. But they don't put a nickel in the kitty. And they call us welfare ranchers?" He spit some more snuff juice into his bowl. "You'll make money in a good year, but when a drought comes, you have to sell your cattle. With the tax laws, you can't put money aside for bad years. Same as with any small business."

Overson stopped by an open gate. "Here's what people do for you, right here," he said. "They always got time to open a gate, but they never got time to shut it. I've had my fences cut, too—by Earth First, I think." (Fences are another impediment to antelope, which, unlike deer, are runners rather than jumpers.) "Them Mojave Roaders bring caravans out all over my land," Overson continued. "None of the people camping up there at Carothers know it, but I own that whole canyon. I told the BLM I'd sell it to 'em for a thousand dollars an acre."

He got out of his truck to close the gate. Then he paused and pointed into the distance at Goff's Butte, which was topped by the antenna that had brought television to the East Mojave. "See that road going up the mountain to that tower?" he asked. "To me that's an ugly eyesore, scarring up the country. I've said for years that the bulldozer's what made the United States, and the bulldozer's what's ruining it." He got his shovel out of the truck, thrust the blade into the ground, stepped on it with his boot, and turned over a spadeload of soil. It was dark a foot deep.

"That's good moisture, when it clumps up like that," he said. "We're gonna have a good spring—lots of feed and wildflowers. This filaree had to start from scratch; if it gets water in the fall, it takes root better. But you see all that green under the bushes? How long you think it'd take a turtle to eat that before it dries up and blows away? They can't even eat what's here now. As far back as I can remember, turtles, mountain sheep, and cattle have all run together. We know everything here can live with grazing, but we don't know if it can live without it. It was always grazed by *something*. I've made a forty-year study, and it hasn't cost the government a dime. But they ain't gonna ask *me* about it, 'cause they know I know the truth."

He got back into the truck. "I'm prejudiced," he admitted. "I like cattle. But I'm open-minded—and history is the best teacher in the world. Cattle have run over this country for a hundred years, and it looks better now than it did then. See what it looks like if *people* run over it for a hundred years."

Of course, nobody who's around today knows what the desert looked like before the arrival of Caucasians and their cattle. But in the Granite Mountains, forty miles to the southwest, there's a dramatic difference between BLM range and an adjacent ungrazed reserve operated by the University of California—a veritable garden spot, in good years, of blooming flowers and buzzing insects. In the other direction, in Ivanpah Valley to the northeast, BLM biologist Harold Avery found a "significantly" higher percentage of perennial vegetation, and lower soil compaction, within a ten-year-old ungrazed plot than without—all in an arid ecosystem, where recovery requires centuries as opposed to decades.

As far as wildlife is concerned, a Utah biologist named Frederic Wagner—extrapolating from pre-Columbian population estimates made by Ernest Thompson Seton in 1929—postulated that domestic livestock in the eleven western states account for half again as many grazing AUMs as did the twenty to thirty million large ungulates (bison, bighorns, elk, and antelope) that preceded them. Domestic sheep prevail over pronghorns in the quest for shrubs, cattle best bighorns for grass, and feral horses and burros outcompete everyone for everything. Meanwhile, quail and tortoises have been shown to suffer from loss of shrub cover and plant diversity attributable to livestock grazing, while cattle interfere with antelope birthing and domestic sheep are known to transmit diseases to wild bighorns. A 1994 review of scientific literature conducted by the National Wildlife Federation found that grazing was a significant factor in the decline of seventy-six species listed as threatened or endangered in the United States. Most such animals exist on arid and semiarid land managed by the BLM, as evidenced by the fact that the two most problematic states are Arizona and Nevada—which, as Overson acknowledged, are a lot more like the Mojave Desert than most of California is.

The plain fact of the matter is that ten years after establishment of the California Desert Conservation Area, range conditions in the East Mojave remained a mystery. No scientific studies or soil surveys had been completed, and although the BLM had collected information on fifteen different grazing allotments in the area (including Overson's), the data had yet to be evaluated. Such neglect goes back to the issue of grazing fees, which, if raised, might have enabled the BLM to assign more than two conservationists to the two and a half *million* acres of range that it oversaw in the area. Such thinness of BLM staff was another reason environmentalists sought to have the East Mojave transferred to the authority of the National Park Service.

"A representative's office called me the other day and told me this is gonna be a park in two years," Overson said. "They asked if I'd be satisfied with two or three more generations here. But it don't matter what I say—whatever it amounts to, they're gonna win and I'm gonna lose. The Indians tried to fight 'em, and that didn't work. I'm not too proud of our government, if you want to know the truth. It's gotten too big to operate efficiently; the BLM is all just damn paperwork. There are so many restrictions now—you can't do this or that because of turtles or Indian sites. There's a lot of things I'd like to do to improve the ranch—scatter the cattle out more or put a pipeline through. But it might take a year and a half to get a permit—and then when they talk about making it into a park, it just takes your heart out of it."

Overson started his truck and turned back toward Goffs. "When I was a kid," he mused as he drove, "people thought we was crazy to even live out here. Now they want to take it away from us. Why do people want the ranchers off? The cattle business has stayed here since the first cow. Everything else—mining, dry farming, real estate—has come and gone, because there's no water, electricity, or jobs. But grazing is a renewable resource. Grass grows back; nothing else does. If there ever was an environmentalist, it's the rancher, because your living depends on it. The difference between me and a lot of ranchers is that every penny I get comes out of the ranch—I built it up with my own two hands and no other source of income. I raised four kids here and got seven grandkids riding horses. I was to Idaho once, and Arkansas for a week when I was a kid; other than that, it's been right here—California, Nevada, and Arizona. I don't have time for no recreation. I get my recreation from riding a horse and gathering cattle. I love it—it's my whole life. I've never been to a park, and I never will go to one. I might be *living* in one, though."

For perhaps the first time since I'd met him, Overson grinned. In doing so, he revealed a pair of gold incisors that looked like ornamental fangs—yet another subtle flourish in his rough-and-ready wardrobe.

"Things can't be like they used to be," he finally admitted. "There's too many people; there's gotta be changes. But I don't think they should just come out and say, 'No more grazing.' That's not right."

A Convenient Place
for the Unwanted

The running joke among homicide detectives in the San Bernardino County Sheriff's Department is that if all the people they haven't found were to stand up simultaneously, the Mojave would resemble Manhattan Island. In 1993, Bureau of Land Management rangers found twelve abandoned corpses in the California Desert District; in one week of October 1994, three were discovered in the vicinity of Palm Springs alone. During the 1980s, San Bernardino County investigated 635 murders. Ninety-seven of the bodies had been dumped in the desert.

As a rule, the bodies aren't buried. Similar to more conventional refuse, they might be dropped down mine shafts or bagged and burned, but usually they're just unloaded from a car. Occasionally they give evidence of having been dispatched on the spot. Some are missing fingers, arms, legs, or heads. In a road turnout near Sheephole Pass in the East Mojave, a driver once found a human hand; a subsequent three-day search of the area produced two corpses, but between them they had four hands. Both turned out to be people who had been missing for some time. Some corpses have been found with hands cuffed behind their backs and bullets in their skulls, effectively eliminating the possibility of suicide—though this is another popular way to leave a body in the desert.

"You have to wonder why someone would drive all the way out here to kill himself," says Bob Moon, former resources chief at Joshua Tree National Monument. "But often they leave notes saying how they love this place where they've had so many moments of peace and solitude." Backpackers in Joshua Tree once came upon a suicide that had occurred seven years earlier. A corpse of a cowboy turned up recently in the shifting, wind-driven sands, which sing to us simultaneously of timelessness and transfiguration—especially so when you consider that the guy had been there for a hundred years.

The desert's dryness preserves dead tissue, but prolonged exposure to harsh elements will deteriorate a corpse as it will anything else. This makes body dumps "very difficult for detectives to investigate," says Lieutenant Dave Baker, chief of the San Bernardino County homicide detail. "The most critical times to solve a homicide are the twenty-four hours immediately before and after a victim's death. But if you can't identify them, you can't find out anything about them. You may not even find them for months or years—and as they decompose, you lose the fingerprints, the hair color, and the eye color. Clues and fingerprints get scattered to the winds. Animal activity makes it even harder."

Obviously, the reason the desert is popular as a dumpsite is its isolation. No one is likely to notice a corpse being ditched, nor is anyone likely to stumble across it for some time. According to Baker, most such finds are made, as in the case of the suicide mentioned above, by "recreationists—hikers or bikers." A typical scenario is the one described by a headline I saw one morning in the *Antelope Valley News:* BODY FOUND BY HUNTERS.

"A lot of the victims—most of them—come from outside the desert," says Baker. "They're from L.A., Anaheim, Fullerton, places like that. The further a killer can separate himself from his victim, both in terms of miles and alibi, the better off he is. Many people move *through* the desert, so it's a convenient place to leave the unwanted—corpses included. Lots of people who are into gambling have connections between L.A. and Las Vegas; the whole time they're traveling in between, they're in San Bernardino County. If they have a problem with somebody, this is the easiest place to get rid of them. We find lots of bodies within a few miles of Interstate 15. Depending on which side of the road they're on, you can tell whether they were going to or from Vegas. For a while there was a rumor that an organized crime syndicate was grinding bodies up in a talc plant on Afton Canyon Road and shipping them all over the country in baby powder. That turned out to be false."

In the five-year period that ended with 1993, the number of homicides in the San Bernardino County desert district increased by 66 percent. Assaults increased by 49 percent; robberies by 43 percent; rapes by 22 percent. "The *variety* of crimes has expanded," reports Jerry Bronson, a BLM ranger in the Barstow area. "Where we used to handle mainly off-highway-vehicle enforcement and resource violations, now there are more state criminal offenses. Where you have a problem in the desert is with a concentration of population nearby; the so-called L.A. frontier used to be the San Bernardino Mountains, but now it's been pushed farther out. With increasing population, people are more paranoid. More of them are carrying guns."

The rough consensus among cops and rangers is that four of every five people in the desert are armed. When weapons are confiscated—as they are hundreds of times per year—the average number on each person encountered is four. "I've seen people who had twenty-six or twenty-seven guns," says John Blashley, chief BLM ranger in the Palm Springs area. "They drive into the desert in a pickup loaded with seven hundred pounds of ammunition." The types of weapons range from concealed handguns to sawed-off shotguns, which are currently enjoying a renaissance—especially since passage of a law that banned assault weapons from public land. Nevertheless, rangers at Joshua Tree National Monument recently found three thousand spent rounds from AK-47s, which were perhaps related to the fact that paramilitary units have been found training in remote parts of the park. Farther north, a group called the Confederate Mexican Army (whose goal, in Jerry Bronson's words, is "to take back southern California by political means") conducts a boot camp near Barstow. According to *Outside* magazine, a group of Japanese-Americans reportedly affiliated with the Yakuza (Japanese Mafia) holds armed drills near Red Mountain, while Aryan skinheads stage armed rallies in southern Panamint Valley. Occasionally, in isolated canyons, rangers come upon city dwellers honing their drive-by shooting techniques: one person steers a car while another lies prone in the backseat, periodically popping up to fire out the window.

"I never used to worry about the people I'd meet while doing field-work in the desert," a biologist recently told me. "Now I do. It's overflow from L.A., mainly, and not necessarily the nicest." As it happens, she is based near an area that is, time and again, singled out as unsafe: the Panamint Mountains west of Death Valley. Its reputation is partly the legacy of the Manson family, who, after committing the Tate-LaBianca murders in 1969, lived at an abandoned ranch in Goler Wash while prac-ticing in dune buggies for a coming race war and searching for a fabled underground sanctuary where white people would be safe. The group was apprehended after setting fire to an earth-moving machine farther north in the Panamints, but after being released from jail, some of them continued to frequent the area, enhancing the perilous mystique of already-infamous Death Valley.

"I wouldn't go alone into the most remote parts of this park," says Paul Henry, formerly chief ranger at Joshua Tree. "There are too many crazy people. We're almost an urban park—we're surrounded by three hundred thousand people in the local communities [Twentynine Palms, Joshua Tree, Yucca Valley, and Palm Springs], and we're only two hours from a population of twelve million. There are parts of this park that we don't get into more than once a year." Jerry Bronson points out that "in a place like Yosemite, if you get into a fight, you just get on the radio and you'll have people backing you up. But in the desert, it's easy to get your-self in a world of hurt without any help. Back in some canyon, you might come on four or five people with assault weapons, under the influence of alcohol. We work alone and don't always have good radio communica-tion; even if help is available, you can't necessarily describe how you got there, so they might never find you. Sometimes the only hope is a Highway Patrol helicopter."

The kind of situation that rangers least want to come upon unawares has to do with drugs. Narcotics traffickers appreciate the desert for the same sorts of reasons that murderers and automobile advertisers do. "San Bernardino County has hundreds of dry lakes ringed by higher ground where people can keep watch for miles in any direction," ob-serves Lou Perry, a senior sheriff's deputy. "The entire desert is traversed by long straight roads—paved and unpaved—that make perfect landing strips. Smugglers set out landing patterns with two cars facing each other; the headlights illuminate some of the area in between, and the plane comes in on the taillights, knowing that the distance to the next headlights is free. It doesn't take very long to off-load the airplane after it lands; sometimes they'll fly forty or fifty loads into one place back to back. Probably a hundred planes come into the desert every month, and we catch one or two. We've tried using cameras tripped by sensors, but for the most part, the desert is pretty kind to these people. Sometimes they might land on a lake that isn't quite dry and break their landing gear; the wing is a gas tank, and the plane burns up. But then the prints and evidence are destroyed, so you can't trace who it belonged to. Mostly, it's marijuana—an airplane is still the easiest way to transport large quantities. The penalties are much greater for narcotics. And chemical powder can't be burned with the aircraft."

Chemical powder creates another kind of problem, however. On Memorial Day weekend of 1990, a ranger was on patrol in the remote southern part of Death Valley near the boundary of the U.S. Army's National Training Center at Fort Irwin. Following some off-road vehicle tracks up an isolated canyon, he came upon a collection of vehicles. Assuming that the owners were camping, the ranger approached to inform them that the area was off-limits, but partway through the conversation he noticed a peculiar smell. The people's clothing was covered with stains; the surrounding equipment—generators, burners, coolers, glass tubing—was uncommon for camping. Moreover, the subjects didn't quite seem to be in full possession of their faculties, which is probably why they didn't shoot him when he started running. As it turned out, their sentry was asleep. Ninety minutes later the Inyo County Sheriff's Department, backed by considerable firepower, collected fifteen pounds of methamphetamines along with an arsenal of handguns, shotguns, and rifles. Reportedly, this secret drug laboratory had been earning a million dollars a month for over a year. (The ranger was relocated to another part of the country, where he now works under an assumed name.)

Between 1985 and 1990, rangers in Joshua Tree National Monument found twenty-one such clandestine drug labs. Most were similarly situated on the remote boundaries of the park. East of Twentynine Palms, a plethora of "jackrabbit homesteads"—dilapidated shacks abandoned for decades—is likewise popular for the production of methamphetamines. "The houses are widely spaced, and nobody's around to notice the odors," says Lou Perry. "These people can go out in a motor home and have a batch ready in three days," says John Key, hazardous-materials coordinator for the BLM's California Desert District. "They mix it in garbage cans. When they're done, they leave the cans behind. It smells like urea. Once you've smelled it, you won't forget it."

Inhaling the atmosphere of a drug lab can be inconvenient in ways other than olfactory. Curt Gunn, a hazardous-waste specialist for the Ridgecrest BLM, has a catalog entitled *Chemicals Associated with Methamphetamine Manufacture:*

CHEMICAL	HARMFUL PROPERTIES	TARGET ORGANS
Acetic acid	Toxic, corrosive	Skin, eyes, and teeth
Acetone	Flammable, explosive	Respiratory system
Benzene	Flammable, explosive	Suspected carcinogen— blood, bone marrow
Benzyl chloride	Toxic, corrosive	Carcinogenic
Chloroform	Toxic	Suspected carcinogen— liver, kidneys, heart
Cyanide	Toxic	Cardiovascular system, liver, kidneys
Ethyl ether	Flammable, explosive, toxic	Central nervous system, skin, eyes
Formaldehyde	Flammable, toxic	Suspected carcinogen— eyes, skin, burns nose
Formic acid	Flammable, explosive, toxic, corrosive	Skin, kidneys, liver
Hydrochloric acid	Toxic, corrosive	
Hydroiodic acid	Toxic, corrosive	
Lead acetate	Toxic	Carcinogenic
Methanol	Flammable, explosive	
Methylene chloride	Toxic	Suspected carcinogen— central nervous and cardiovascular system
Nitrile acid	Flammable, explosive, toxic, corrosive	
Phenylacetic acid	Flammable, toxic	Burns lining off lungs
Propane	Flammable, explosive	Central nervous system
Pyridine	Flammable, explosive, toxic	Releases cyanide when heated—liver, kidney, GI tract

Red phosphorus	Flammable, toxic	
Sludge	Flammable, explosive, toxic, corrosive	Many unknowns
Sodium sulfate	Flammable, explosive, toxic	
Thorium dioxide	Flammable, explosive, radioactive	Dust ignites at room temperature
Ethyl acetate	Flammable, explosive	Eyes, skin
Phosphorus pentachloride	Toxic, corrosive	

"Often you don't know you're in it until it's too late," says Gunn. "The fumes can make your lungs close down or your heart stop."

Gunn subscribes to a magazine called *Pollution Engineering*. He showed me an article entitled "Illegal Drug Labs Pose Cleanup Problems":

> When planning a raid . . . shotguns, flashbangs (explosive devices that create a distracting noise and flash), and smoke or teargas should not be used since such weapons can ignite flammable vapors. Inside the laboratory, switches should not be turned on or off, heating or cooling equipment should not be unplugged, and refrigerators or freezers should not be opened. These may be booby-trapped or could cause sparks that could ignite flammable atmospheres. Also, containers should not be moved since they too could be booby-trapped. Matches or flames of any kind must not be used, and only explosion-proof flashlights are appropriate.

In his office, Key has many sunny snapshots of abandoned plastic containers backed by clean brown sands and pure blue skies. On his wall is a map of the Desert District, filled with blue and orange triangles and rectangles. The orange triangles, denoting sites of secret drug labs, are numerous in the Panamint Mountains—a fact that does little to lighten the reputation of the range. South of Barstow are a dozen orange rectangles signifying drug-lab "residues." In the East Mojave, often along railroads, are a dozen blue rectangles: "unauthorized landfills," or impromptu garbage dumps. "Some holes in the ground have been used as dumps in the desert for a hundred years," says Key. "The one near Nipton [in the East Mojave] has stuff from the state transportation department, Union Pacific, local restaurants, everything—it's the local dump. And more and more industrial polluters are dumping barrels of stuff at night."

"Sometimes these drums show up with no labels," says Curt Gunn. "It could be anything from anywhere. You need to treat it as the worst possible thing, so to clean it up you wear a foil-encapsulated suit with an independent breathing apparatus. Then it might turn out to be table salt."

In its celebrated pursuit of the good life, southern California generates eighty thousand tons of garbage every day. In addition, a million tons of hazardous waste—heavy metals, acids, asbestos, sulfates, nitrates, and phosphates, derived from such popular materials as plastic, petroleum, polyester, solvents, and detergents—are produced each year. Many of these chemicals possess the same dangerous properties as clandestine drug-lab residues. "Right now," says Key, "we've got battalions of consultants wandering the desert looking for sites for hazardous waste, solid waste, incinerators, and prisons. It's inevitable—25 percent of California is desert, and the rest of the state is taken up."

In the early 1990s, at least nine proposals were circulated for major dumps in the California desert. In the East Mojave National Scenic Area (now the Mojave National Preserve), an enterprising businessman espoused the idea of filling the old Vulcan iron mine—created and abandoned in the 1940s by Kaiser Steel—with shredded rubber tires. At another extinct Kaiser site—Eagle Mountain, just outside the southern border of Joshua Tree National Monument—Browning-Ferris, Inc., proposed to dispose of twenty thousand tons of municipal trash per day, hauling it two hundred miles by railroad from the urban parts of southern California. An almost identical plan was advanced for Bristol Dry Lake south of Amboy, where Waste Management, Inc. aimed to fashion a four-hundred-foot-high hill of garbage covering two thousand acres. Either of these "trash train" projects, in operating for sixty to one hundred years, would create the biggest garbage dump on Earth. Meanwhile, east of Barstow, at Hidden Valley in the Cady Mountains, hazardous waste was proposed to be buried in vertical steel and/or concrete silos within a wilderness study area, while at Broadwell Dry Lake near Ludlow the same sort of poisonous stuff was suggested for storage on a desiccated playa. And at Ward Valley west of Needles, the state of California—in conjunction with a beleaguered company called U.S. Ecology—aspired to bury five and a half million cubic feet of low-level radioactive waste nineteen miles from the Colorado River.

To conventional wisdom, the idea of using the desert as a dump makes perfect sense. After all, the place is a big, empty wasteland to begin with; and most of it is federal land, simplifying the problem of acquisition.* Best of all, it's notoriously dry—so not only will weather facilitate operations, but hazardous leachates are less likely to be mobilized by moisture. Groundwater, which usually lies several hundred feet below the surface, moves very slowly, minimizing the likelihood of traveling toxins. And desert basins are self-contained anyway, with all runoff collecting in their playas; the resulting concentration of minerals has rendered the subsurface water of many such places unpotable, effectively creating a prepoisoned environment. What better place to get rid of garbage?

But as Charles Reith observed in a 1992 book entitled *Deserts as Dumps? The Disposal of Hazardous Materials in Arid Ecosystems:*

> The deserts as dumps treatise is at least partly refuted by the equally simple observations that deserts are often well removed from the industrial sources of hazardous wastes, hence greater transportation distances are required; that deserts tend to have unstable landscapes with extreme weather, hence the risk of erosion and dispersal of waste is greater; and that the reduced quantity of water in deserts makes that water more valuable, hence the loss to society is greater if it becomes contaminated.

Desert thunderstorms are so intense that the danger of flash flooding (and consequent debris flows) can be even greater than it is in wet climates. Winds that overturn mobile homes can easily spread paper and plastic over the landscape. The erosive power of such elements—together with earthquake faulting—is known for sculpting the desert's surface: cutting channels, planing hills, tilting water tables. Vegetation, once

---

*In the interest of avoiding government liability, waste disposals aren't allowed on BLM land in the California desert. However, federal property sought for this purpose can be acquired by private parties through purchase or exchange.

disturbed, requires centuries to be reestablished. Desert soils and groundwater are sufficiently alkaline as to be capable of corroding metal waste containers. Surface cracks on dry lakes may descend all the way to the water table. The natural nonpotability of such places isn't prohibitive of other uses; calcium chloride, for example, has been mined from Bristol Lake since 1908, while at Cadiz Lake twenty-five miles away, grapes and citrus fruits are grown without pesticides, which are rendered unnecessary by the desert's dearth of insects. This situation could well change with the coming of the world's largest dump—as would the local population of ravens, with their documented depredatory effect on desert tortoises.

The apparent clarity of the "deserts as dumps treatise" is further clouded by the fact that few of the above prospects—whether nefarious or inconsequential—can be called certainties. "The farther you go out in the desert, the less we know, because the most remote areas haven't been studied," explains Howard Wilshire. "But that's exactly where they want to put all this stuff."

Wilshire was the senior geologist on a report that threw a wrench—temporarily—into California's plans to bury nuclear waste at Ward Valley. This scheme had been set in motion by the federal Low-Level Radioactive Waste Policy Act of 1980, a law that declared individual states responsible for their own nuclear refuse but suggested that they team up with others in order to share the burden. California subsequently entered into the so-called Southwest Compact with Arizona, North Dakota, and South Dakota, and, as the largest waste generator of the four, agreed to provide the first disposal site for the whole quartet. The operating contract was awarded to U.S. Ecology, a creatively named disposal company with a distressing résumé: Its Maxey Flats, Kentucky, facility became an EPA Superfund site after it leaked plutonium, and Illinois sued U.S. Ecology for $97 million when a lake near its Sheffield site was found to be radioactive. North Carolina and Nebraska rejected the company's bids to establish waste dumps within their borders. And Nevada shut down U.S. Ecology's low-level radioactive repository at Beatty after a series of unfortunate incidents, one of which resulted in the floors of several local structures—including a Nye County office building and the Sourdough Saloon—being poured with a radioactive cement mixer from the dumpsite. (This dumpsite was reportedly dubbed "the store" for distributing such tools among the local populace.)

After examining eighteen basins in the California desert, U.S. Ecology narrowed its prospective list to three. As it turned out, Panamint Valley had seismicity problems and—with vehicle access existing only on twisty mountain roads—was declared too remote. Silurian Valley, between Death Valley and the town of Baker, was finally designated the backup site to the winner: Ward Valley, a two-thousand-foot-high basin ringed by the Sacramento, Stepladder, Old Woman, and Turtle Mountains south of Interstate 40. The design called for a seventy-acre facility where trucks would annually unload 150,000 cubic feet of low-level radioactive refuse consisting mainly of medical material—rags, paper, tools, glassware, plastic gloves, and protective clothing. The waste would be buried in fifty-five-gallon drums in unlined trenches sixty feet deep; the dump would operate for thirty years, beyond which U.S. Ecology would continue to monitor it for five. After that, California would take over, keeping environmental watch on the place for one hundred years.

Ward Valley was considered ideal in almost every way. To begin with, it gets an average of only five inches of rain per year, with an evaporation rate twenty times that high. The water table is 650 feet deep in unsaturated alluvial fill; the nearest potentially active earthquake fault is twenty-eight miles away. The area *is* considered sacred by the lower Colorado River Indian tribes, but that was apparently deemed unimportant. The area *is* designated as critical habitat for the desert tortoise by the U.S. Fish and Wildlife Service, but U.S. Ecology promised to relocate all tortoises and build a fence along I-40 to keep them from getting run over. The site *is* only nineteen miles from the Colorado River, which supplies southern California with drinking water, but the basin was said to be hydrologically closed, with all drainage culminating in Danby Dry Lake forty-five miles to the south.

All *surface* drainage, that is. "The applicants stated unequivocally that Ward Valley is self-contained," says Wilshire. "But the more we study it, the more we see that mountain ranges aren't barriers to groundwater movement. If you need proof, look at any mine—a dry mine in the desert is very rare. Subsurface water can flow through fractures and move through cracks. The Ward Valley area was pulled apart twelve to twenty million years ago; in the process, the upper plate of a low-angle fault got shattered—it looks like a car windshield hit with a brick. It's broken up into a lot of small basins bounded by a myriad of faults. As these basins formed, they filled with sediments; meanwhile, the earlier sediments continued to deform by tilting and fracturing. It's really a mess, and together with the shattered bedrock above the fault, it could provide a subsurface pathway for groundwater out of the valley. Based on our understanding of the structural history of the area, we found five possible geohydrological connections to the Colorado River."

Wilshire and his colleagues were also concerned that traces of tritium—a by-product of atmospheric nuclear testing in the 1950s—were found one hundred feet below the surface of Ward Valley. If these were carried there by moisture, the depth would indicate that water moves through the unsaturated layer much more quickly than U.S. Ecology claimed.* Whereas the company posited that groundwater would take between 23,000 and 50,000 years to reach Danby Dry Lake, Wilshire's group argued that the time required would be only 500 to 5,000. That sounds like a long time until one considers that the government's definition of low-level radioactive waste includes such materials as carbon-14 (half-life: 5,730 years), plutonium-239 (24,400 years), nickel-59 (76,000 years), iodine-129 (16 million years), uranium-235 (710 million years), and uranium-238 (4.5 billion years).[†] The *bulk* of waste at Ward Valley was supposed to arise from the medical industry, but most of its *radioactivity* would come from nuclear power plants—in the form of contaminated hardware, control rods, curtains, filters, resins, even the structures of the plants themselves after they're dismantled. In the near future, twenty-five nuclear reactors in the United States are scheduled to be shut down, and as of this writing, thirty-one states have no place to dispose of low-level waste. According to its own bylaws, the Southwest Compact may accept radioactive refuse from other states, and in an "emergency," the federal Nuclear Regulatory Commission has the power to direct waste there from anyplace in the country. In this way, Ward Valley could become radioactive repository to the republic.

If that isn't enough to qualify it as the nation's premier nuclear dumpsite, the Mojave is leading a sluggish race to become the first repository for the country's entire stockpile of *high*-level radioactive waste—e.g., spent fuel, liquids, sludges, solids, and materials contaminated with radioactive elements heavier than uranium. (Considering that this stuff, which has been accumulating at the nation's nuclear power plants since

---

*In 1994 another U.S. Geological Survey scientist, David Prudic, found that tritium had percolated 357 feet below the surface of U.S. Ecology's Beatty dump, ten feet above the water table, in only thirty-five years.
[†]The hazardous period for radioactive material is ten times its half-life.

1957, consists of fuel too irradiated for further use, the term *spent* is as much a misnomer in this case as *low-level* is in the other.) The government has variously considered jettisoning such refuse—which will, for practical purposes, remain poisonous forever—onto remote islands, underneath seabeds, across polar icecaps, and into outer space; at this point, however, the plan is to bury it deep underground, specifically (for the first seventy-two years, anyway) in Yucca Mountain, on the northwestern border of the Nevada Test Site, where nuclear weapons have been exploded for half a century.

Yucca Mountain consists primarily of volcanic welded tuff, which is considered sufficiently stable and impermeable to safely contain radioactive garbage for the eons that it would remain dangerous. The rule imposed by the Environmental Protection Agency is that the security of any such site should be guaranteed for ten thousand years. This is, of course, merely a blip on the screen of geologic history, but—as the sociologist Kai Erikson illustrates in his book *A New Species of Trouble*—it represents a near-infinitude in the evolution of society:

> It is difficult to predict what human beings will do a year hence, hard even to guess what they will do a decade hence, but preposterous to think that one can even begin to know what they will do a century or a millennium hence. . . . Ten thousand years ago, the plains north of Nevada had only recently emerged from under a sheath of ice a mile thick. . . . Stone Age hunters elsewhere, speaking a language that no one now could make out, were learning for the first time to plant seeds in the ground and to harvest the result. . . . The distance we have come from the time of that tentative farmer, scratching the ground with a stick, is nothing compared with the distance—the potential at least—separating us from those who will follow.

The government has entertained the possibility that, in the distant future, people might unwittingly drill down into Yucca Mountain, tapping its reservoir of poison. Hence, the Energy Department has announced plans "to determine the anticipated drillhole density, borehole diameter, and depths of the drillholes over the next 10,000 years in the vicinity of Yucca Mountain." Further, "a warning system composed of surface markers and monuments will be placed at the site as a means of informing future generations of the risks associated with the repository and its contents." Considering, as Erikson does, that such ancient monuments to inscrutability as the Sphinx, Pyramids, and early Sumerian cuneiform tablets are only five thousand years old (and contemplating the huge changes wrought since development of such devices as the silicon chip and laser ray in only the last twenty-five years), such notions seem hysterical in every sense of the term.

The area surrounding Yucca Mountain contains more than thirty earthquake faults, which some scientists believe could be prompted to activity by the six-hundred-degree temperatures in the waste repository—to say nothing of the proximity of the Nevada Test Site itself, which effectively triggers an earthquake every time a bomb is detonated. Should radiation be released, or high-level waste "go critical" in an uncontrolled reaction, the nuclear fallout would remain poisonous for several centuries, wherever it came to earth.

The Nevada Test Site was established in December 1950, soon after the United States entered the Korean conflict and the Soviet Union detonated its first atomic bomb. With the advent of the Cold War, pressure was mounting to increase the nation's nuclear stockpile and to develop a hydrogen weapon whose power would ultimately dwarf the explosions that leveled Hiroshima and Nagasaki. Although it had contaminated the Marshall Islands to the point of uninhabitability, the government considered the postwar testing program in the Pacific a success. Still, it had a disadvantage in being carried out so far away—the tests were inordinately expensive, as well as complicated to bring off and difficult to keep secure. Hence, in 1947, a government project (code name: Nutmeg) was launched to locate a suitable spot for testing within the continental United States. The search was carried out in secret since, in the later words of Harry S. Truman, there was concern that American citizens might grow nervous if they learned that the government was going to be "shooting off bombs in their backyards."

The place that was ultimately chosen comprised 350 square miles of desert in Nye County, Nevada, an hour's drive northwest of Las Vegas. Conveniently, the area was already controlled by the federal government, enclosed as it was on three sides by the Las Vegas-Tonopah (now

Nellis Air Force) Bombing and Gunnery Range, and despite the fact that the Western Shoshone Nation had never ceded ownership of the land—the tribe has refused to accept payment from the U.S. government, which still keeps the amount of its small offer in a Department of the Interior bank account. Camp Mercury, a temporary installation at the site's southern end, and Indian Springs Air Force Base, a stone's throw down U.S. 95 toward Las Vegas, could easily be enlisted in support of the testing program. Most important, the place was isolated: the closest residents were in small communities twenty-five and forty miles to the southeast and north; otherwise, nobody lived any nearer than Las Vegas. Rainfall was rare and prevailing winds were expected to carry fallout toward what the government termed "virtually uninhabited" territory to the north and east.* Far from the coast, surrounded by desert, hidden from view by encircling mountains, the place seemed the very definition of "secure." In the traditional Old View of desert-as-dump, it was also considered worthless for anything else—in the words of a 1950s brochure entitled *Armed Forces Talk*, "a damn good place to dump used razor blades."

By the time of the first atomic test—January 27, 1951, a mere two weeks after plans for the site were revealed to the American public—the so-called Nevada Proving Ground had nearly doubled in size to 640 square miles. In later years (specifically 1958, 1961, 1964, and 1967), it would continue to expand, ultimately reaching its present allotment of 1,350 square miles, enclosed in a rectangle 28 miles east to west and 40 miles north to south, described in government literature as "a vast outdoor laboratory and research park, larger than the state of Rhode Island."

I'd driven past the Nevada Test Site (or NTS; the "Proving Ground" moniker was abandoned in 1955) entrance once or twice on U.S. 95. From the road, all I could see was a collection of low, fenced steel buildings in the midst of otherwise nondescript desert; the most provocative thing in sight was the unintentionally editorial Wrong Way signs by the highway. The U.S. Department of Energy (formerly the Atomic Energy Commission) does, however, offer group and individual tours of the NTS, as long as you provide your name, address, telephone

---

*This term resurfaced ironically years later when fallout victims downwind of the Test Site began to refer to themselves as "virtual uninhabitants."

number, driver's license, social security number, employer, and date and place of birth. I signed up and, early one weekday morning, met a man named Jim Boyer at the DOE office on South Highland Drive in Las Vegas.

Boyer was a portly, sixtyish guy in a khaki shirt, olive drab pants, black boots, and a black baseball cap with a patch showing a Casper-the-Ghost-type figure pushing a plunger on a detonation box bearing the letters NTS. In the embroidered background were a steer skull and some mountains below the word TENABO. "That was a weapons-related test we did about six months ago," Boyer said, turning over the ignition on a small white Chevy with government plates. "A guy made up a bunch of 'em and sold 'em for $5.50 or something like that."

At this writing, a moratorium has been declared on nuclear testing. When I met Boyer, though, an average of one blast per month had taken place for the previous five years. "Last year we only had eight tests," Boyer told me. "That was the fewest in the ten years I've been here." The most recent "event" (called "Coso") had, however, been conducted just four days earlier.

We left the parking lot and began making our way through the industrial back streets of Las Vegas. Before we reached the freeway, Boyer pulled over and donned a pair of black leather gloves. "I don't like the feel of steering wheels in government cars," he said—adding as he pulled back onto the road, "This thing ain't got that much pep to it."

We headed north on 95, passing the Cayman Bay Luxury Apartments. Despite the Caribbean imagery, once we escaped the city limits we found ourselves in the Mojave Desert: flat brown plains dotted with yuccas and burro and creosote bush, backed by stark, striped orange mountains. During the 1950s, the section of highway between the Test Site and Las Vegas was referred to as the "Widowmaker"—apparently due to a high fatality rate before the road was widened to four lanes. From what I'd read and heard, it seemed that the name might apply for other reasons as well.

As we passed a medium-security state prison, Boyer described the path that brought him to the NTS. After growing up in Louisiana and Texas, he'd worked for the *Houston Post*, the *New York Journal American*, and the *Albuquerque Tribune* before becoming the press secretary for U.S. Senator Joseph Montoya (D-NM) in the seventies. "I have a pilot's license, so I flew him around a lot," Boyer said. Apparently his experience on the government payroll pleased him: when Montoya left office, Boyer went to work for the armed-forces newspaper *Stars and Stripes* and later became southwest regional public affairs officer for the Civil Defense Preparedness Agency. From there, I guessed, it was a logical hop, skip, and jump to the NTS.

"This area's pretty similar to New Mexico," Boyer commented as he drove. "It's hotter in summer but not as cold in winter. The skiing's not as good. My wife and I used to be ski instructors." As he spoke, we were passing snow-capped Mount Charleston, southern Nevada's premier ski area. In fact, at eleven thousand feet, it was also a premier lookout spot for viewing atomic explosions in the fifties. The Las Vegas Chamber of Commerce promoted the tests as a tourist attraction, printing up maps and timetables for the blasts, suggesting that watchers take a picnic basket and wear dark glasses.

From some accounts, it seems that southern Nevada saw the advent of nuclear testing primarily as inspiration for a theme party. As one Las Vegas hotel manager put it: "Before the proving ground, people just heard this was a wide-open town. Now that we're next door to the atom bomb, they really believe it." As A. Costandina Titus observed in *Bombs in the Backyard*, a history of atmospheric testing,

> It was not long before the mushroom cloud was vying with the showgirl for top billing along the Las Vegas Strip. The "atomic hairdo," originally designed by GeeGee, hair stylist at the Flamingo Hotel, was a popular request for special occasions. The hair was pulled over a wire form shaped like a mushroom cloud and then sprinkled with silver glitter at a cost of only seventy-five dollars. The "atomic cocktail" was also a big seller in bars along the Strip. Made from equal parts of vodka, brandy, and champagne, with a dash of sherry, the potent drink was served at breakfast parties following the predawn shots. In the Desert Inn Sky Room, pianist Ted Mossman first played his boogie-woogie tune "Atomic Bomb Bounce," which soon had people swinging all over town. . . . a musical group known as the "Atom Bombers" boasted that they were the "Detonators of Devastating Rhythm." The Sands Hotel sponsored a Miss Atomic Bomb Contest which

featured beautiful young contestants wearing puffy white mushroom clouds pinned to their bathing suits.

From the beginning, the Test Site enjoyed great support in southern
Nevada, where it was a bona fide boon to the local economy. The NTS
provides about 8,000 local jobs—4,500 at the site itself and 3,500 in Las
Vegas. Clark County added the image of a mushroom cloud to its official
seal, and residents were encouraged to take pride in their proximity to
this vital component of national security. U.S. Senator Pat McCarran (D-
Nev.) had lobbied hard for it, as had Governor Charles Russell. "It's
exciting to think that the submarginal land of the proving ground is fur-
thering science and helping national defense," Russell declared in 1952.
"We had long ago written off that terrain as wasteland, and today it's
blooming with atoms." Joe McClain, a columnist for the *Las Vegas Review-
Journal*, went so far as to suggest that "it might be good for the town's
spirit if the scientists would send a few effects down Vegas way. Just to
keep people happy." Even the *New York Times* ran an article telling travelers that "there is virtually no danger from radioactive fallout" from the
"atomic cloud [that] may come over an observer's head."

"The Test Site has created a lot of jobs but never caused any problems," Boyer claimed as we approached the NTS entrance. "You don't
hear any complaints from people in Las Vegas about it; they want it to
stay just the way it is. Most objections to things nuclear come from areas
away from where people are actually connected with it." Near the
entrance were concrete—or, more accurately, chain-link—provisions for
those who begged to differ: two barbed-wire-crowned holding pens
(with portable toilets), one for men and one for women.

"They call us ahead of time and let us know when they're going to
demonstrate," Boyer said. "They tell us the number that are going to be
arrested. Usually it's for trespassing—the property line is a cattle guard a
hundred yards from the highway. They get out and do their dance, hold
hands, and go in circles. Sometimes they sing or beat on pie pans or
other musical instruments. Some of 'em dance around alone, or strip
down and rub mud all over themselves—even in their hair. I don't know
how that helps their cause. Every now and then, one'll let out a hoot and
take off for the boondocks. It's about five miles to Mercury, and you can
get winded or turn an ankle in this country real fast. We send somebody

down with a pickup truck or dirt bike to get 'em. A lot of times you don't even have to get out—they just climb in."

A collection of corrugated, quonset hut–like buildings was clustered around the entrance gate at Mercury. We parked and went into an office. The air inside had an antiseptic smell. All the officials seemed to be about the same age as Boyer; while issuing me a visitor's badge, one informed me that I couldn't take a gun, camera, or binoculars into the Test Site without a permit. The badge contained a dosimeter, which would record the amount of radiation I received during my visit. If I wanted to, I could then file Form NV-192 ("Request for Report of Radiation Exposure History") and, within three to five weeks, find out what level of infiltration had occurred upon my person.

Dosimeters are required of everyone who enters the NTS. According to DOE literature, "Of the more than 220,000 persons issued dosimeters between January 1974 and January 1987, 98 percent received no radiation exposure from test site activities." This is perhaps due to the fact that employees who record the exposures have been known to enter "zero" if they consider a dose insignificant—or too high. In any case, only external radiation—gamma, beta, or X rays—is registered on the dosimeter; internal exposure to alpha rays (the kind that can be ingested or inhaled) has never been recorded.

External environmental radiation is monitored constantly hereabouts, not only at the NTS but throughout southern Nevada and southwestern Utah. Originally, offsite radiation records were kept by the military and Los Alamos National Laboratory—an arrangement roughly analogous to a salesman doubling as an accountant for his clients. Nowadays, radiation monitoring is the task of the Environmental Protection Agency (EPA), which contracts with scientists and local residents to record radionuclides and reactive gases in 30 different locations. Noble gases and tritium are also collected in 18 places; radionuclides in milk in 29; tritium and other radionuclides in water in 51; gamma radiation in 28; *accumulated* gamma radiation in 157.* Radionuclides in beef cattle are checked twice a year, as are fifty human families. These desert residents sit gazing at pictures of pine trees and streams at a lab in Las Vegas while sensors

---

*These records have come under criticism because the collection instruments aren't calibrated to ensure their accuracy. In any event, owing to vagaries of the desert wind, radiation can bypass the instruments altogether without even being registered.

measure cesium 137 and other radionuclides in their bodies. The results, as of this writing, are classified.

We got back in the car and entered the Test Site proper, crossing a pass in the Spotted Range and descending into an enormous valley. About a third of the NTS consists of alluvial basins and playas—most notably Yucca and Frenchman Flats, where 126 atmospheric explosions occurred during the first dozen years of operation. On the northern edge of the "park" are the higher, piñon-and-juniper-dotted Pahute and Rainier Mesas, which conceal the underground tunnel blasts. The area's other topographical features—Rock Valley, Shoshone Mountain, Buckboard Mesa, the Spotted Range, Topopah Valley, Skull Mountain, Thirsty Canyon, the Belted Range, Mine Mountain, Calico Hill, Yucca Mountain, the Halfpint Range, Banded Mountain, White Rock Springs, Timber Mountain, the Specter Range—continue to embody the western landscape that predated twentieth-century technopolitics. Spread before us was a classic Basin and Range panorama: vast sloping plains strewn with cloud-mottled mountains, dirt roads running everywhere across the brown bajadas. Off to the east—i.e., our right—was a bald white lake bed at the bottom of the basin. "That's Frenchman Flat," said Boyer.

Upon the utterance of those words, I entered into a kind of reverie. This was the site of Operation Ranger, the first series of atomic explosions in Nevada. On January 27, 1951—the year, as it happens, that I was born—an Air Force B-50 bomber dropped a one-kiloton device from the predawn sky; the bomb was timed to go off in midair, and the flash startled ranchers in Utah. Seven minutes later, the shock wave awakened people in Las Vegas. Two days afterward, radioactivity in Rochester, New York, was found to be twenty-five times higher than normal. Four more bombs were dropped over the next nine days; eight-kiloton "Baker Two," the fourth in the series, shattered windows in Vegas and Arizona. Operation Ranger was a resounding success.

As we drove across Frenchman Flat, I tried to imagine the flash of white light, the roiling cloud, the multihued fireball hotter than the sun, the sound that one observer likened to "a thousand bullwhips in your ear"—a spectacle that prompted Robert Oppenheimer, the physicist who oversaw the development of the A-bomb, to quote the *Bhagavad Gita*:

> *If the radiance of a thousand suns*
> *Were to burst at once into the sky,*
> *That would be like the splendor of the Mighty One . . .*
> *I am become Death,*
> *The shatterer of Worlds.*

Over the years, bombs for atmospheric tests were not only dropped from planes but also suspended from balloons, positioned on top of towers, and placed directly in the ground. The latter type created surface blasts, as opposed to airbursts. "If you were trying to knock a runway out, you'd want a ground hit," Boyer explained. "The fallout would be greater because you'd be lifting more soil into the air, but the physical damage would be limited. An airburst can knock out a whole city, but it wouldn't have much effect on other areas, because there's less fallout. With an airburst, the heat spreads out—it's so tremendous that it would cause fires. The pressure goes out, creates a vacuum, and then comes back from suction. So it gets you going out and coming back—kind of a double whammy." With that, he flashed me a wicked grin.

Various ruins could be seen in the distance down on the flat: a railroad bridge; an airplane hanger; a (steel-reinforced) concrete building next to an irradiated combat tank. These were the remains of experiments done to determine the effects of explosions at different distances and angles from ground zero. In some cases, entire "doom towns" had been built, complete with motel, savings bank, parking garage, radio station—even a Ferris wheel. Model middle-class homes were stocked with cars in the garage, Cokes in the fridge, *Life* and *Redbook* on the coffee table. Male and female mannequins washed dishes or watched TV until it came time to—er—turn in. Dummy teenagers were, of course, totally blown away. But responsible investors were relieved: all that remained of the bank was its vault. As for the homes themselves, Boyer said: "All I can tell you is, don't live in a cinder-block house. Solid brick held up pretty well, though." This was good to know.

Inanimate objects weren't the only subjects of the experiments. Rabbits and sheep were sacrificed in pens at various distances from the blast; following one release of plutonium, dogs were dispatched at intervals of 4, 5, 16, 32, 64, 128, and 161 days. Curious about the effects of radiation on horses and cattle, the AEC hired cowboys to drive herds directly over ground zero. Less attention was paid to the effects on the cowboys. In one experiment—popularly known as the "Charge of the Swine Brigade," performed to test fabrics' response to a blast—111 Chester pigs were clothed in custom-tailored army suits with regulation seams and zippers; after a delay in the testing schedule arose, some of the pigs outgrew their uniforms and had to be refitted. When the explosion was finally detonated, seventy-two spit-polished porkers were microwaved in midsalute.

Experiments involving human beings began in October 1951 with the second test series, Operation Buster-Jangle (including shots "Dog," "Sugar," and "Uncle").* A bivouac called Camp Desert Rock was established alongside the Test Site so that troops could witness the blasts, engage in atomic field exercises, and undergo psychological tests. AEC policy prohibited anyone from coming within six miles of ground zero, but the Pentagon, desirous of more "realistic" training, demanded that troops be stationed a mere two miles away. (The military agreed to accept responsibility for "the possibility that exceeding the normal limits of exposure to radiation or pressure might endanger the participating personnel.") Sometimes the men crouched in trenches and foxholes, sometimes on open ground. Volunteers were positioned as close as two thousand yards to a forty-three-kiloton explosion. They'd been told it was twenty-three. When the bomb went off, soldiers were singed by furnace-like heat and whipped by hurricane-force winds laden with radioactive debris; having been warned to cover their eyes, they beheld their finger bones through their closed eyelids. Immediately afterward, troops were directed to advance on ground zero, where the earth had the look and feel of burned glass. As they marched, their footsteps raised columns of dust to their unmasked mouths and noses. Seldom was protective clothing provided; after the exercises, soldiers simply showered in their fatigues and threw them away. Some began vomiting soon after the blast. A few weeks later, when they combed their hair, it came loose in clumps; within a few years, many lost their teeth. Over the years of atmospheric testing, more than sixty thousand soldiers participated in such "games."

Similar effects were experienced by people who lived downwind of the test site. It has been estimated that, over the years of atmospheric

---

*Names for nuclear tests may be submitted for screening and selection to the DOE Office of Military Application. During the period of atmospheric testing, some of the memorable ones were How, Easy, Climax, Zucchini, Turk, Fox, Badger, Moth, Wasp, Bee, Dixie, Doppler, Galileo, Smoky, Lassen, Shasta, Whitney, Diablo, Encore, Sunbeam, Teapot, Plumbob, Hardtack, Nougat, Upshot-Knothole, Tumbler-Snapper, and Rio Arriba.

testing (1951–1963), twelve billion curies of radiation—150 times the amount released by the Soviet accident at Chernobyl—were introduced into the atmosphere by the NTS, from which fallout subsequently spread over North America and the rest of the world. In nearby parts of Nevada and Utah, ranches were enveloped by clouds that varied in color from pink to black. Children played in fallout that settled to earth like snow. Burns appeared on the backs of deer, horses, cattle, and sheep, many of which lost their wool and aborted their lambs. After Shot "Harry"—the notorious ninth detonation of Operation Upshot-Knothole, which spread high levels of radiation over southern Utah in 1953—more than four thousand sheep expired outright. AEC officials placed the blame on poor range conditions. The government insisted that radioactivity from the tests was minor—that the exposure was tantamount to a routine chest X ray. Hence, people with symptoms of radiation sickness were said to be suffering from sunburn or measles. Women who got headaches or lost their hair were diagnosed as hysterical or neurotic. Residents of the downwind areas were advised simply to stay indoors during tests, and later to wash their cars. "Fallout can be inconvenient," an AEC pamphlet acknowledged, "but your best action is not to be worried about [it]."

But it was both inconvenient and worrisome when "downwinders" began to develop cancer, birth defects, sterility, and nerve and muscle disorders. In 1957, Linus Pauling, the Nobel prize–winning chemist, estimated that ten thousand people had contracted leukemia from nuclear testing. In 1979, Dr. Joseph Lyons discovered that childhood leukemia rates in high fallout areas of Utah were two and half times the national average. In 1967, Dr. Edward Weiss of the U.S. Public Health Service found that thyroid cancer among Utah residents had increased fourfold between 1948 and 1962. Most* of the victims were patriotic Mormons who neither smoked nor drank alcohol, coffee, or tea. The AEC repeatedly denied that radiation was at fault. At the height of the Cold War, the government's greatest fear was not that nuclear testing might harm its citizens, but that something might occur to prevent it

---

*But not all: In 1954 the Hollywood production of *The Conqueror*—directed by Dick Powell and starring John Wayne, Susan Hayward, and Agnes Moorehead—was filmed in the dunes around Snow Canyon, Utah, an area hard hit by fallout from Shot Harry. Powell died of lung cancer in 1963, Moorehead of uterine cancer in 1974, Hayward of skin, heart, and uterine cancer in 1975, Wayne of lung cancer in 1979. At the time of Wayne's death, 95 of the 220 cast and crew members had contracted cancer.

from continuing. As Nathan Woodruff, director of the AEC's Division of Operational Safety, put it when confronted with a 1963 report (filed by AEC scientist Harold Knapp) that the government's safety standards for fallout were too low by a factor of one hundred to one thousand:

> The present guides have, in general, been adequate to permit the continuance of nuclear weapons testing and at the same time have been accepted by the public. . . . To change the guides would . . . raise questions in the public mind as to the validity of the past guides. . . . [Furthermore,] the world situation today is not the best climate in which to raise the issue.

In 1984 a federal judge in Salt Lake City found that some of the families of twelve hundred downwinders who died of Hodgkin's disease, leukemia, and cancers of the lung, thyroid, brain, stomach, skin, uterus, ovaries, breast, bladder, pancreas, prostate, colon, and kidney were entitled to $2.6 million in compensation from a negligent U.S. government. The decision was reversed, however, by the Tenth Circuit Court of Appeals in Denver, which cited the Federal Tort Claims Act of 1946—a law that renders the government immune to liability for injuries arising from policies carried out at its "discretion." In 1988, the U.S. Supreme Court let this ruling stand.

At the north end of Frenchman Flat, Joshua trees appeared by the road as we again ascended, crossing another low pass to reach the Test Site's primary test site: the broad, dry lakebed of Yucca Flat, scene of most atmospheric experiments in the fifties and, since the Limited Test Ban Treaty of 1963, most of the more than eight hundred underground explosions that have occurred at the NTS.

Most modern-day nuclear tests are detonated in vertical shafts to gauge the performance of missile warheads: the Trident 2, the Pershing 2, and the Cruise missile were all tested at the NTS. Upon detonation, the weapon* vaporizes a chamber of rock one or two thousand feet below ground, sending data to the surface through cables. Other tests assess the weapons' effects; eclipsing the doom towns of yesteryear, they

---

*Let the record show that NTS officials refer to a bomb not as a "weapon" but a "source."

take place in horizontal tunnels up to a mile long, drilled at a rate of eight feet per day into Rainier Mesa.

As opposed to buildings, mannequins, or motor vehicles, today's experimental targets tend to be satellites, nose cones, and communication equipment. They are placed at the end of a long pipe, and when the bomb goes off, radiation is recorded by instruments behind a set of doors that snap shut in time to block flying debris. Meanwhile, mirrors reflect an image of the explosion for high-speed cameras, which record the event at two hundred thousand frames per second, enabling scientists to replay it in agonizing detail. Earth vaporized by the blast eventually cools to a molten puddle; it and the instruments are later recovered for further study. Most of the explosives are developed at the nation's elite weapons labs—Los Alamos and Lawrence Livermore (both operated by the University of California) and Sandia (operated by Western Electric, a subsidiary of Bell)—at a cost that vaporizes the imagination: one and a half billion dollars in 1994.

I wasn't scheduled to visit any tunnels today—nor did I desire to. I'd heard too many tales about the health of Test Site workers who had entered "hot holes" to recover instruments and clean up muck. Hands were burned, feet swelled up, noses bled, heads ached. By some accounts, enormous jars of aspirin were constantly in demand, though they didn't help much with problems that developed later. Boyer reassured me, however, that "we've got radiological monitoring units down there; it's safe when it reaches background levels. I've been going there for ten years, and there's nothing wrong with *me*. Why, I've walked in those underground shafts wearing the clothes I've got on right now." I pressed closer to the passenger door.

"Background levels" are the amount of radiation that we encounter in everyday life. Boyer happened to have a fact sheet entitled "Radiation in Perspective"; it pointed out that "all life on the planet lives with natural radiation. . . . radioactive material, such as uranium and radium, is found in the earth and can be detected in buildings made of bricks, concrete, mortar. . . . Our bodies contained naturally occurring radioactive elements when we were born." For the general public, the Environmental Protection Agency puts the level of acceptable exposure at 100 millirems above the average background level—about 300 per year. Medical X rays might add 100. Smoking 30 cigarettes a day adds 8,000. The sheet also listed average background levels for eleven American cities: Las Vegas receives 69.5 millirems of "natural" radiation per year; Fort Worth, Texas, 88.7; Wheeling, West Virginia, 111.9; Denver, 164.6, apparently owing to the content of its underlying soil. "The radioactivity along this road wouldn't be much more than in Denver or New York City," Boyer said. "I don't think there's anything out here that would give you as much radiation in one shot as you'd get from your doctor or dentist."

Less than 1 percent of the Test Site is fenced off due to dangerous levels of radioactivity. Only about a fourth of the place has been used to test nuclear explosives; in the sixties and early seventies, experiments were also performed on nuclear engines, furnaces, and reactors, and the late eighties saw a number of exercises involving hazardous fuel spills. Much of the lingering radioactivity is the legacy of "safety" tests conducted during the fifties. The AEC wanted to be sure that an accidental bomb detonation wouldn't produce a nuclear blast, so it conducted a series of tests that ended up scattering plutonium (and in some cases uranium) over the surface of the desert. One such site on the Nellis Air Force Range, just off the northeastern boundary of the NTS, was subsequently used to study the effects of contaminated soil on grazing livestock. The hottest spot, popularly known as "Plutonium Valley," is in Area 11 east of Yucca Lake; in an effort to clean up the residue there, NTS workers have dug trenches and buried contaminated soil, but plutonium has been found several miles down a wash that drains from Plutonium Valley to Yucca Lake.

Plutonium—a manmade, alpha-emitting element that remains poisonous for two hundred thousand years—has been detected in many parts of Nevada off the NTS. One spot on State Highway 375—Queen City Summit, fifty miles north of Yucca Flat—was found to be seriously contaminated in 1970. Soil near the town of Ely, one hundred miles to the north, contains fifteen times as much plutonium as the amount correlated with high cancer rates near Rocky Flats, Colorado. Contamination isn't limited to Nevada; after the first eight years of atmospheric testing, concentrations of strontium-90—a radioisotope produced only by atomic explosions, capable of causing cancer in bones and blood—were found to be 50 percent higher in wheat grown in Minnesota and the Dakotas than the AEC considered safe. In 1959 the concentration of strontium-90 in the soil of New York City was five times higher than it had been in 1954. In October 1958 the NTS, cognizant of a looming moratorium on atmospheric testing, fired off twenty bombs in two weeks; weather guidelines for blasts were relaxed, so much of the radiation descended upon Los Angeles. Burdened further by fallout from some Soviet tests, the city received a year's worth of acceptable radiation in seven days.

The NTS command center—"Control Point One"—is hard by Yucca and Frenchman Flats. Boyer said I should go inside to look at the place and watch a movie. As we approached, I noticed a sign that said FALLOUT SHELTER. That was handy, I thought. When we stopped at the entrance gate, the guard demanded not only my visitor's badge but my driver's license. I wondered if she was checking to see if I was old enough for the movie.

Suffice to say that it wasn't *Dr. Strangelove*. I was, however, put in mind of that film when I entered the darkened control room, which contained several tiers of desks and telephones beneath an array of illuminated screens, upon which was projected a variety of multicolored maps and graphs. "You want to be the test controller?" Boyer said, pointing at one of the chairs. "That's where he sits." I took the bossman's place and, as my first official act, pushed a button that said HALT ALL NUCLEAR TESTING NOW.

Actually, I stared up at the screens. One said ENGINE RUNNING; another, ORBIT OVER YUCCA LAKE. Boyer said both referred to airplanes that would monitor an event whose countdown was currently being ticked off on a monitor. "Is there a test today?" I asked in alarm.

"No," said Boyer. "It's a dry run. If there was a test today, you wouldn't be here."

Not all nuclear tests are announced.* Government policy gives the NTS discretion—based on "technical criteria" and "public health and safety concerns"—whether to make a test public. "If a test is going to cause ground motion offsite in a populated area, we announce it two days in advance," Boyer said. "We wouldn't have even had to announce the Hiroshima blast here; it was too small."

One of the maps on the screen showed current wind conditions and predicted how far radiation would travel if it were accidentally released—a curving line indicated the reach of 170 millirems of exposure (per year). On another map was a similar line that didn't quite reach

---

*Recent disclosures by DOE Secretary Hazel O'Leary revealed more than two hundred previously classified explosions between 1951 and 1992.

Las Vegas, or Goldfield, or Tonopah, or Furnace Creek (in Death Valley). "That's the area we can evacuate," Boyer explained. He said the wind map was based on the 1964 "Pike" event, an underground test that vented unexpectedly through a crack in the earth. Its radioactive cloud drifted south over Las Vegas and was tracked as far as Mexico—violating, in all likelihood, the Limited Test Ban Treaty, which prohibits radioactive debris from crossing international boundaries. The AEC made no announcement of the incident; it issued a statement only after a reporter called to ask why radiation monitors had been seen on the streets of Las Vegas.

"If a strong wind was blowing toward Las Vegas or Los Angeles, we wouldn't conduct the test," said Boyer. "We wouldn't if it was absolutely calm, either—all [the radiation] would drop down over your head. A five- to fifteen-knot wind is ideal. The EPA sends teams into the downwind areas and notifies hunters and other people; miners get the day off and are reimbursed. We don't expect any releases, but if there is one, we want to be able to monitor it with aircraft and measure the radioactivity."

More than half of all underground tests at the NTS have leaked radiation into the atmosphere. Most notorious, albeit unannounced at the time, were the "Baneberry" event of 1970 and the "Mighty Oak" blast of 1986. In the former, a ten-kiloton bomb was exploded nine hundred feet underground; three minutes later, a black cloud emerged from a fissure as long as a football field, engulfing the Area 12 workers' compound, which contained nine hundred Test Site employees. The cloud took twenty-four hours to reach Salt Lake City; along the way, considerable quantities of iodine-131—which concentrates in the thyroid gland, where it can cause cancer—were administered to human beings and foraging animals. Under the circumstances, the time of year (December) was a blessing: had the fallout crossed Utah in spring, the concentration of radionuclides in green pasture could have been ten thousand times as high.

Mighty Oak was a tunnel test whose containment doors failed to close. As a result, the blast contaminated much of the Rainier Mesa tunnel complex, which resembles the root system of a tree. A month later, in order to decontaminate the tunnels, the radiation was intentionally released—thirty-six thousand curies' worth, or two thousand times the amount let loose by the accident at Three Mile Island. The Soviet nuclear accident at Chernobyl took place a few weeks after the Mighty Oak mistake—but *before* the release of Mighty Oak's radiation, which the U.S. government declined to make public. Mighty Oak came to light only when a Canadian researcher, analyzing radiation in that country's atmosphere after the incident in the former USSR, discovered that it differed from the type released at Chernobyl. Surmising that something unannounced might have happened in Nevada, she was borne out by some NTS employees, who applied for workers' compensation after being exposed to the radiation in the tunnels. Later, when it was determined that the accident was caused by the shock of the explosion itself, extra safety measures were added at a cost of nine million dollars per test.*

When we left Control Point One, the guard again demanded my driver's license. As we drove away, we saw a coyote standing in the middle of the road. "Look at that little ol' guy!" Boyer exclaimed as we drew close to the canine, who stood his ground and stared back. "Whaddya say there, buddy?" Boyer seemed overcome with affection and surprise. Turning to me, he asked: "You don't see anything on *him* that looks like radiation, did you? They thrive out here!"

The Test Site is home to 42 species of terrestrial mammals, as well as 14 lizards, 17 snakes, 94 spiders, and 190 birds (27 of which are year-round residents). Occasionally, deer, bighorn sheep, wild horses, raptorial birds, and migrating waterfowl are "detained" and measured for radionuclide deposits. The blood of some deer near the test site has thus been found to contain tritium levels thirty times higher than the acceptable standard for human drinking water.

This aquatic issue surfaced as we approached the Area 12 cafeteria, alongside the tabletop outline of Rainier Mesa. I had my doubts about eating lunch so close to such a contaminated place, but Boyer assured me that "the only danger is the food's so good, you might eat too much of it." I soon learned that this peril was heightened by subsidized government prices—I got fish, pasta, and carrots for a total of $1.30. I washed it all down with a can of juice, after Boyer informed me that the drinking water originated directly beneath the Test Site.

Radionuclides in NTS groundwater are sampled monthly in forty-eight places. Drinking water in at least four areas has been contaminated beyond safe standards; in some places, tritium levels exceed the limit by

---

*Underground shaft tests cost, on average, between $10 million and $20 million; tunnel tests, $50 million to $60 million. The total U.S. budget for nuclear weapons testing in 1990 was $314 million.

a factor of several thousand. Lying as it does in the desert, the Test Site had no permanent surface water—during storms, arroyos empty out onto the playas (Boyer told me he'd seen water a foot deep on Frenchman Flat), or, in the northern reaches, onto the Nellis Air Force Range, or, in the west and south, toward Death Valley. Groundwater is located six hundred feet below the basins and two thousand feet below the mesas; on the west side of the NTS, it discharges into the Amargosa Desert, again in the direction of Death Valley.

Fifteen percent of the nuclear tests occur at or below the water table. When an explosion goes off, groundwater is driven away from the spot and radionuclides are trapped in the rock. Gradually—that is, over a period of months or years—water returns to fill the cavity, delaying the transport of toxins to the underlying aquifer. The average speed of groundwater movement on the NTS is thought to be about ten feet per year; it's therefore assumed that thousands of years would be required for tritium to leave the test site, by which time it would no longer be radioactive. Recently, however, NTS geologists, drilling a hole for a shaft test, found that contaminated water had traveled at least half a mile (the distance to the nearest bomb cavity) in only two years—a rate that would transport it beyond Test Site boundaries in centuries rather than millennia. Groundwater movement can also accelerate under the pressure of forced pumping, which accompanies increasing population. As the fastest-growing area in the United States (and not least because it's situated in the Mojave Desert), Clark County is daily growing more and more desperate for water. Hence, in 1989 the Las Vegas Valley Water District laid claim to unallocated H_2O in more than two dozen drainage basins to the north. One of the targeted areas was none other than Nye County—home of the NTS.

Boyer ordered mashed potatoes, lima beans, cottage cheese, and a piece of cake. He declined any meat, explaining that he wanted to save room for the cake—which he proceeded to consume before anything else. "I 'most always do," he divulged. "Within twenty minutes after you eat sugar, it reacts with the chemistry in our body to form acid, which is what deteriorates your teeth. But if you eat it first, what happens? *The other food gets rid of the sugar!* If I want dessert, I'll go back and get another piece of cake—or bring two through on my tray."

I excused myself to make a telephone call. Upon doing so, I learned that a book I'd written about red wine had received a favorable review in an influential publication. When I returned to the cafeteria and related this news to Boyer, he said, "I used to prefer red wine, but now I only drink white." When I asked why, he answered, "Because red wine has too many contaminants in it."

We finished lunch and returned to the car. As we departed Area 12, picking up speed on the open road, an oncoming automobile flashed its headlights. Looking into the distance ahead, Boyer saw another vehicle parked on a hill. "That's the Nye County Sheriff's Department," he said. "They give speeding tickets here." It was nice to know that, in at least one instance, the law of the land was still in effect.

At the north end of Yucca Flat was a collection of what looked like sand dunes. In fact, it was "ejecta": alluvial debris blown out of the ground by the "Sedan" detonation of July 1962. Beyond the dunes, and invisible from the road, was a hole more than three hundred feet deep and almost a quarter of a mile wide. The Test Site is littered with such craters, which are created in two ways. Often, after a shot, the underground cavity collapses, followed—minutes, hours, days, or weeks later—by the ground above it. The movie at Control Point One consisted largely of aerial footage of spectacular cave-ins. Boyer said that the "Coso" test, conducted four days earlier, took thirty-eight minutes to create such a crater. Some of these holes are being used to bury Test Site detritus—for example, the towers used to detonate bombs during the fifties. Two craters have already been filled with eight million cubic feet of such debris.

The Sedan hollow is a memento of the "Plowshares" program of the sixties, when the government entertained the notion of using nuclear bombs for peaceful purposes—dredging harbors, building canals, excavating for oil and gas, or clearing rights-of-way for roads. The U.S. government was apparently imagining a new Panama Canal. The California Division of Highways, in association with the Atchison, Topeka, and Santa Fe Railroad, reportedly planned to use twenty-two nuclear explosions to gouge a route through the Bristol Mountains in the eastern Mojave above Amboy. To test out the idea, several bombs were buried and detonated at the NTS, giving rise to towering columns of radioactive dirt. "Buggy," a side-by-side explosion of five bombs that took place in March 1968, excavated a canal 855 feet long, 254 feet wide, and 65 feet deep; radiation from the blasts was detected off the NTS (in sites that were not disclosed). After the 30-kiloton "Schooner" shot nine months later, radioactivity was similarly discovered (though not announced by the AEC) in Canada and Finland—another possible violation of the Limited Test Ban Treaty. Sedan—a 104-kiloton thermonuclear blast (70 percent fusion and 30 percent fission) that blew twelve million tons of earth 12,000 feet into the air—was one of the most studied experiments in NTS history. No lizards survived within a mile. No vegetation remained within 3,000 feet. The following spring, however, annual vegetation in the area was the most vigorous on the Test Site, undoubtedly owing to the effects of ionizing radiation. Plants many miles away were found to have transmitted iodine-131 to grazing and browsing herbivores; even at a distance of one hundred miles, one study found, "it is an unavoidable conclusion that had milk been produced in this area during July of 1962, it would have contained radioiodine . . . far in excess of the limit." Five years later, tritium was still present in soil around the site. "We proved our point," Boyer asserted, which was true enough: the Plowshares program was abandoned in 1973.

Sedan Crater has a viewing stand on its western lip—a regular stop for tour buses and journalists. According to Boyer's booklet, the level of radioactivity there was only eighty-eight millirem per year—a claim that, upon close consideration, befuddled even my buoyant guide. "That don't sound right to me," Boyer said. "How could it be lower than the national average? I'm gonna check that with our radiological people when I get back." For my part, I decided that enough people had already seen the hole.

The DOE sheet asserted that "because we cannot see or feel radiation, people tend to magnify the perception of its risk." It was indeed an amorphous business, one that could never be assessed in reassuring terms. The poison was undoubtedly everywhere, but just how poisonous was it? Considering the vagaries of radiation and variety of its effects, it might or might not be killing things anywhere at any given time. Certainly the Test Site had increased the danger as well as the death—although during the Cold War, governmental "discretion" held that no matter what dangers testing entailed, it served to diminish the greatest menace of all (one that it had, of course, conspired to create). The NTS was located in the desert in order to keep the immediate hazard as small as possible; still, it had succeeded in strewing poison over the continent and around the globe, while giving rise to a local peril that would persist for hundreds of thousands of years. The Mojave Desert itself is only a fraction that old.

As we passed the doom-town ruins of Frenchman Flat on our way out of the NTS, Boyer said: "Some people who come here are just fascinated. They're thrilled to death—exhilarated. Especially the photographer types. They don't want to leave; they want to shoot it when the sun's coming up, when it's going down. . . . one guy said, 'Wouldn't it be fantastic to be here at *night?*' He was almost in a trance. The gal who was his assistant said she was leaving; finally he ran out of film.

"To be out here at night *is* a little bit different," Boyer allowed. "It's almost like being away from Earth on another planet."

Unfortunately, it's on this one. The real reason the Test Site is located in the desert is the raison d'être behind any dump. Especially since the explosions went underground, it boils down to the ostrich ethic: out of sight, out of mind. This approach is, of course, part and parcel of the Old View of the desert. Subjected to the New View, the Proving Ground hadn't proved out; its danger is invisible by definition, so out of sight is still in harm's way. Even with everything on display, as it seems to be in the desert, one still couldn't see what was really going on. In this fundamental paradox, the Test Site exposed its umbilical attachment to the environment in which it was conceived: the Mojave.

THE RHODE ISLAND
THAT GOD FORGOT

In the early days of continental nuclear testing, lip service was widely paid to the need for civilian control of the program. In fact, activities at the Nevada Test Site were always run by the Pentagon. This was not unusual in the desert, which has served the armed forces as a testing and training center for half a century. Some five million acres of the Mojave are overseen by the U.S. military, which goes a long way toward explaining the idiosyncratic atmosphere of the place. People and vehicles in camouflage are common, as are rumblings, vibrations, and explosions of unspecified origin.

The most notorious emblem of martial presence is both audible and visible—the latter condition usually occurring several seconds before the former. For example, a friend of mine, driving through Panamint Valley one day with no other cars in sight, suddenly noticed an object behind him approaching faster than any automobile he had ever seen. It rapidly grew larger in his rearview mirror until, at the last second, it rose and went over his roof; a second later, the din of jet engines threatened to burst his skull.

The Mojave is a playground for fighter pilots, who seem to enjoy buzzing motorists and pedestrians and (especially) naked women at isolated hot springs, which are overflown upside down. Planes are prohibited from airspace up to 3,000 feet above national parks, yet rumors persist of a "below sea level" aviation club whose military members have flown fewer than 282 feet above the floor of Death Valley. I myself was once ambushed by a low-flying jet at the Racetrack, the remote playa inside the park's northern boundary; another time, in the western Mojave, I chanced to look up and saw the Stealth bomber. Jets generally appear—as per design—without warning, startling terrestrial beings accustomed to total silence. Not to imply that suddenness is a prerequisite for disturbance. Once, on an otherwise quiet morning in the Kelso Dunes, my solitary meditations were interrupted by an olive-drab transport plane making its sluggish way through the desert like some airborne alligator. It seemed to take forever to cross the basin, during which time the entire desert was filled with throbbing roar.

Some years ago, the Mojave's militaristic milieu was enhanced by events in the Middle East. Israel provides a perennial model for martial displays in the desert, but in 1990 and 1991, the Persian Gulf War decidedly stole its thunder. Media images of that conflict—from the spectacular bombardment of Baghdad to the camouflage-clad troops advancing into Iraq—were hatched, honed, and mirrored in the Mojave. Sometimes the parallels are surprisingly complete. Departing Joshua Tree National Monument in January 1991, I turned on my car radio to learn that, following Saddam Hussein's failure to withdraw from Kuwait by the mandated deadline, the United States had begun bombing Baghdad, commencing Operation Desert Storm. As I proceeded through Twentynine Palms, listening to the sounds of explosions on the radio while watching Marines roll by in transport vehicles before the backdrop of the desert, I suddenly saw, just off the main drag, a sign that said BAGHDAD TRAILER PARK.

Even for a conscientious objector, there's something undeniably arresting about the Mojave's military atmosphere. To witness hypermodern jets against the bare brown mountains and pure blue sky is to glimpse something somehow archetypal, something evocative of evolution itself—even if, in social terms, it illustrates how far we've failed to come. For the armed forces themselves, the situation is unromantic: The thing that attracts the military to the Mojave is the same thing that makes the place popular as a dump. It's big, it's (relatively) empty, and its airspace is correspondingly free of intefering radio signals. The place hardly even has any clouds: good flying weather (ceilings above a thousand feet and visibility of more than three miles) exists on an average of 345 days per year. At the time of World War II—when, like so many other agencies and entities, the military began to focus its attention on the desert, and vast tracts were still available for the taking—every branch of the armed forces established a base of at least a million acres in the Mojave.

At first glance, Rhode Island might seem to have scant bearing on the Mojave Desert. But if its legislature were litigiously inclined, it might consider assessing royalties from the Pentagon, as every major military base in the Mojave describes its size by comparison with that state. According to their own publicity, the Nevada Test Site and the army's National Training Center at Fort Irwin are each "about the size of Rhode Island." The China Lake Naval Air Weapons Testing Center is "slightly larger than the state of Rhode Island." The Marines' Air-Ground Combat near Twentynine Palms—the fastest-growing base in the Marine Corps—is "three-quarters the size of Rhode Island." The Naval Weapons Testing Center, near Ridgecrest, represents a third of the Navy's total landholdings—1,700 square miles where bombs, rockets, missiles, warheads, projectiles, and propellants are dropped, launched, fired, and tested for speed, yaw, pitch, roll, accuracy, and stability. More than 80 percent of the base's six thousand employees are civilians—scientists and engineers who until recently bestowed upon the Ridgecrest population the highest average level of education of any town in the United States.*

In two weeks of May 1964, eighty-nine thousand Army troops fanned out over the desert west of Needles in something called Operation Desert Strike—a training exercise that laid environmental waste to sizable swaths of the East Mojave. The groundwork (so to speak) for such activity had been established during World War II at the so-called Desert Training Center, an area comprising some 17,500 square miles in southern California, Arizona, and Nevada—"the largest and best training ground in the United States," according to its commanding general, George S. Patton. The need for desert training had arisen within two months of the attack on Pearl Harbor, when Erwin Rommel arrived in Libya; fearing that German and Italian forces might seize the Suez Canal

---

*"They might have been well educated, but they sure couldn't make change," remembers Betty Hadley, who worked in the grocery store in nearby Red Mountain. "I could have robbed those eggheads blind."

and join forces in Persia (i.e., Iraq) with the Japanese—then making their way west through India—the War Department directed Patton to train American troops for armored-vehicle warfare in the "vast unoccupied area of the desert in Southern California." Setting up headquarters at the Hotel Indio, Patton began flying back and forth over the East Mojave, picking out a dozen suitable spots for camps, each capable of housing one division of fifteen thousand men. The sites were chosen for their proximity to water supplies or railroad tracks; each division required six hundred railroad Pullman cars to transport it, not including the freight cars that carried vehicles and artillery. The main receiving point was a railroad siding on State Highway 62 west of Rice, which, during the peak of activity, off-loaded fifty to eighty boxcars of supplies and material per night. When the resources of the Sante Fe and Southern Pacific Railroads proved inadequate to this task, the Army took over the job. Similarly, Southern California Telephone needed help from ten different companies in servicing the DTC, whose unpaid phone bill at one point amounted to sixty-five thousand dollars. Patton himself appeared before the Metropolitan Water District of southern California to declare his need for water. As the story goes, he was reportedly told by the board that he could expect action within months, at which point he informed the commissioners that no action was necessary—he'd already begun tapping into the aqueduct and was simply letting them know.

Within a year, the population of the DTC was 191,000. The East Mojave was transformed into a theater of military operations—and not entirely as an exercise in make-believe. A Japanese task force was at large in the Pacific, and Patton's forces were prepared to respond to an invasion of the West Coast. Meanwhile, they tested new equipment and training methods as well as tactics, transportation, supply, and communications systems under remote, arid conditions. The exercises, conducted jointly with the Army Air Forces, utilized close to twenty thousand tanks, trucks, jeeps, motorcycles, helicopters, and airplanes, which fanned out through almost every valley—Ward, Lanfair, Paiute, Kelso, Fenner, Ivanpah, Clipper, Cadiz, and Chemehuevi—in the East Mojave. Patton himself was ubiquitous, appearing everywhere in his jeep, alternately exhorting and insulting the troops, commanding thirteen major tactical operations in twenty-three days from the top of a hill called the King's Throne.

Among the soldiers, the DTC quickly became known as "the place that God forgot"—eighteen thousand square miles "of nothing in a desert designed for Hell." To young GIs who'd never before been west of the Mississippi, the place was not merely uncomfortable but unsettling and bizarre. Sand was a perennial condiment in K rations; sleeping on the ground at night, soldiers had to beware of rattlesnakes, and in the morning they were instructed to shake the scorpions out of their boots. Sometimes they awoke in the dark, drenched with water and mud, having bedded down in washes subject to sudden floods. Relief from the desert was difficult to obtain; the Army implemented USO shows and night baseball leagues, and local communities did their best to entertain the troops, but dances in places like Needles or Indio proved frustrating when four hundred men showed up to dance with fourteen women. Furloughs to Las Vegas were curtailed after three hundred soldiers rioted there on leave, killing one person and injuring three others. Social circumstances were especially trying for segregated black troops, one group of which, having apparently been pushed beyond some psychological limit, commandeered an arsenal and threatened to shoot up a café.

To simulate realistic battle conditions, Patton ordered exercises conducted without electric light, heat, or hot water. Supplies in North Africa were expected to be minimal, and so the general—prey to the common misconception that the human body can be weaned from the need for "excess" liquid—at first limited water intake to one canteenful per soldier per day. With marches lasting from dawn to dusk, it didn't take long for his error to be exposed. According to one soldier who arrived at the DTC in May 1942, when men became exhausted by dehydration or heatstroke, "large refrigerated boxes on wheels were brought in [and the stricken soldiers] were placed on racks in these boxes, much as in a morgue, for about 24 hours, or until their body temperature dropped to subnormal for a few hours, and most were then able to return to duty." Others weren't: of the million-odd men routed through the DTC during World War II, more than a thousand never left, expiring on American soil in the Mojave. The hardship allegedly aided the troops later on in Tunisia, where Patton gained fame by whipping the Army II Corps back into fighting shape in only ten days following its annihilation (sixty-five hundred casualties) at Kasserine Pass. As legend has it, Patton motivated the troops with the threat that if they didn't get their act together, he'd return them to the Mojave.

Patton spent only four months at the DTC before departing for

Morocco. After the campaign in North Africa ended, the place was renamed the "California-Arizona Maneuver Area," and troops trained there were assigned to duty in Europe and the Pacific. When the center was deactivated in 1944, fifteen hundred disabled vehicles were left behind in the desert. The buildings were dismantled by Italian prisoners, who were also reportedly enlisted to collect unexploded ordnance. The site of Camp Clipper, between the town of Essex and Interstate 40, is still marked by an old airfield, a water cistern, rows of rocks outlining tent areas, and a vanished main street lined by yuccas. Today, in typical historical fashion, these sites are imbued with nostalgia, despite the misery with which they were associated in their own time.

Nowhere is such selective recall more evident than at Chiriaco Summit on Interstate 10 west of Indio—site of the George S. Patton Museum. When Operation Desert Shield was in full swing, I visited the museum during a sunny Veterans' Day celebration at which a Patton impersonator was scheduled to make an appearance. As I approached from the parking lot, I heard "Chattanooga Choo-Choo" playing on some loudspeakers while a group of teenagers practiced the jitterbug on a stage; I soon learned that these were the Young Ambassadors, a song-and-dance troupe from Big Sandy, Texas. Folding chairs had been set up in rows marked with signs for different army divisions. Modern military personnel strolled about in conspicuous jungle camouflage, supported by three mounted cavalrymen and a couple of guys in Civil War suits. I saw one man wearing a T-shirt that said DON'T EVEN THINK ABOUT BURNING MY FLAG. Off to one side was a table where, for a dollar, you could send a postcard to a soldier in Saudi Arabia. The Stars and Stripes streamed in the wind as helicopters flew back and forth before a backdrop of naked mountains.

While waiting for things to get started, I went into the museum. Several books were being sold on a rack near the door: *Bill Mauldin's Army*, many on Patton, and one about Vietnam (entitled *Even God Is Against Us*) by an ex-Marine artist named Austin Deuel. On the back flap, the author was pictured wearing cowboy boots, a suede jacket, and a gray beard, standing before a fireplace with a stuffed pheasant, a set of antlers, and a Native American rug. There was a wide selection of war toys (of special interest: tiny army suits for toddlers) and various videos including *Sink the Bismarck, Von Ryan's Express, Guadalcanal Diary*, and *Sands of Iwo Jima*.

One of the books was entitled *Patton's Principles*. It was autographed by its author, Porter B. Williamson, who referred to Patton as "the king of all phrase makers." I wrote down some examples of the general's wit and wisdom:

> *An active mind cannot exist in an inactive body.*
> *If everyone is thinking alike, no one is thinking.*
> *The way to win is to never lose.*
> *Death can be more exciting than life.*
> *Fear kills more people than death.*
> *Success is how you bounce when you hit bottom.*
> *Always keep something in reserve.*
> *Keep moving and pain will never hit you.*
> *Never fight a battle when nothing will be gained by winning.*
> *Revenge belongs to God.*

The rest of the museum was filled with swords, rifles, canteens, helmets, handguns, gas masks, cannons, saddles, motorcycles, a jeep, and Japanese and German flags ("Trophies from a Defeated Enemy"). In one corner was a Rock-Ola jukebox; in another were some stuffed animals— a coyote, a gray fox, a javelina, a jackrabbit, a quail, and a rattlesnake. Hanging inexplicably amid the memorabilia of American military glory was a painting of Custer's Last Stand. The most striking thing in the place, taking up a good part of the floor, was an enormous plaster-of-paris relief model of the Desert Training Center itself, replete with all the mountains and valleys of the East Mojave.

Outside, the Ambassador College Dixieland Band finally struck itself up. The members worked their way through "I Got Rhythm," "South of the Border," "Deep in the Heart of Texas" (for which the audience instinctively knew to clap four times before the refrain), "Hot Hot Hot," and a few tunes by the Miami Sound Machine. I wasn't quite sure what most of these numbers had to do with Veteran's Day; ditto for "Waltzing Matilda," until I found out that the bandleader was Australian.

"At eleven o'clock we're gonna have a special surprise," he announced. "I don't know what it is, but that might be a foretaste of it up there." He pointed skyward, where a contrail was being traced by a distant jet. "He's pretty quiet, isn't he?" asked the Aussie. "We'll see if we can't make it a little bit noisier here soon."

At 10:59, everybody stood and sang "God Bless America." As the song ended, precisely at eleven, a jet appeared out of the distance, silent on approach but ear-splitting as it passed overhead. It took three minutes to make a huge circle in the north (where it was obviously overflying Joshua Tree National Monument), then came by again. The group sang the national anthem, followed by a gun salute. (Of the half-dozen riflemen in the Desert Hot Springs American Legion Color Guard and Firing Squad, two had beards and one had gray hair reaching to his shoulders.) An Army bugler played taps, echoed anemically by a member of the Dixieland band; then a minister began the invocation by summoning "O Mighty God, who has given us this good land for our favor"—an interesting way, I thought, to refer to the place that God forgot. A porcelain bust of Patton was unveiled by a sculptor who had reportedly just finished one of another great American, Steven Spielberg. The George S. Patton Award was presented posthumously to General Curtis LeMay, with the quote (Patton's or LeMay's, I'm not sure): "In our form of government, right will triumph in the end."

Finally the Patton impersonator came riding in, standing in a jeep and waving, a red sash draped diagonally over his brown uniform, a green helmet glinting on his head. He mounted the stage in knee-high leather boots and—in a booming, gravelly voice—said "Be seated" to the few remaining people, all of whom were already seated. He then proceeded to deliver what I took to be a famous Patton speech, updated for contemporary resonance.

"All true Americans love the sting of battle," the man declared. "We have never lost a war, and we will never lose a war because the thought of losing is repugnant. What you've heard about America not wanting to go to war is a lot of horse crap. We're going to bust that bastard Hussein's butt! I pity those Shiite sons of bitches we're going up against! The Iraqis are the enemy—we're going to spill their blood and put their asses out of business!"

It was shocking to hear these vulgar epithets in the midst of such a family-oriented event, but, I thought, maybe it was good. Patton was notoriously profane, and even if his World War II–era proclamations rang hollow to anyone who'd lived through Vietnam, this belligerent coda was undoubtedly closer to reality than the sanitized ode to death and dismemberment that had preceded it. As the saying goes, wars have no winners, only survivors. Many actual veterans had attended this "celebration," but by the time their reincarnated commander appeared to remind them of what they'd actually experienced a half century before, most of them had left.

The contemporary version of Patton's Desert Training Center is the army's National Training Center at Fort Irwin, north of Barstow. The NTC consists of roughly a thousand square miles—about the size of Rhode Island—parts of which bear such names as John Wayne Pass and the Valley of Death. Aside from barracks, schools, bowling alleys, and grocery stores, the place is devoted to ground maneuvers, tank and artillery live-fire exercises, and "force-on-force" infantry engagements—in other words, war games. The NTC processed most of the troops that took part in Operation Desert Storm but, similar to the DTC, isn't intended to prepare soldiers for desert warfare exclusively.

"It's for combat training," explained Will Bublitz, a mustachioed major from Colorado whom I met at the base's public-affairs office. "Troops prepared here for Panama [and the apprehension of General Manuel Noriega] too. To train for Saudi Arabia, they stayed in the lower, flatter areas—but sometimes, for other goals, they might be in the mountains. That's good light-infantry terrain."

According to American military doctrine, infantry troops are the basic "tool" in land warfare. Hence, fourteen times a year, a different unit containing between four and five thousand soldiers from somewhere in the United States rotates through Fort Irwin. "Beginning the day the rotational unit arrives they are in a tactical environment," says an NTC brochure. "They do not just go through the motions of war, they actually live it. . . . Long hours and little sleep follows [sic] them throughout. . . . They are attacked any time of the day or night. . . . The terrain and climate are harsh and serve to intensify the stress and fatigue. . . . [as do] dirt and dust, tear gas, smoke, simulated chemical agents and relentless sun." Air temperatures at Fort Irwin can reach 120 degrees in summer; at such times, the troops—in contrast with those commanded by Patton—are subjected to "command drink-ins," ensuring that each soldier consumes at least four gallons of water per day.

Fort Irwin has its own permanent unit, the 177th Armored Brigade. It consists of twenty-three hundred troops called the OPFOR ("Opposing Force"), which acts as the enemy for every visiting detachment. Bublitz explained that as of 1991, OPFOR soldiers "attend an academy to learn Soviet tactics—they're clothed, equipped, and trained as a Soviet force, and their army tanks are modified to look like the Soviets'.* The OPFOR is in the desert 270 to 360 days per year. They're considered the most proficient group in the U.S. Army. You might say that the finest Iraqi force in the world is right here."

Upon arriving at the public-affairs office, I noticed a group of men in black berets standing around its entrance. I soon learned that they were commanders of Fort Irwin's contingent of 650 "observer-controllers"— coaches and trainers steeped in army tactics, who spend twenty-four hours a day with the visiting units. "The whole purpose of the NTC is to learn from your mistakes," Bublitz said. "In fourteen days, you can die fourteen times." For two straight weeks, each visiting unit engages in a daily battle with the OPFOR. These are the so-called force-on-force exercises, in which "dying" is assiduously recorded and quantified. As the NTC brochure puckishly puts it, "Until now, Army training has been of the 'Bang, you're dead, no, I shot you first' variety." That, however, was in the era before Multiple Integrated Laser Equipment System, or MILES.

MILES is a training technology based on weapons that shoot lasers instead of bullets. "Each soldier wears a harness," Bublitz explained. "If you're hit [by an enemy laser], an alarm sounds. To turn it off, you have to pull a key out of your own weapon, which ceases to function. A card tells you what kind of casualty you are and how long you'll live without first aid. In the armored vehicles, a computer is able to discriminate between weapons that can kill it and those that can't—a rifle no, a tank yes. When a vehicle is disabled, a blinking light goes off on top of it. Tanks transmit a radio signal every five seconds, so we always know where they are."

As it's registered, all of this electronically encoded information— rounds fired, number of casualties, type of weapon, type of vehicle—is sent via radio signal from the battlefield to one of forty-four relay stations, then through a transmitting tower on top of Tiefort Mountain (the highest peak on the base) and thirteen miles of cable to a central computer, which decodes the data and compiles the stats. "All the radio communication is collected, and mobile vans videotape the exercise," said Bublitz. Within four hours of the end of the battle, the edited tapes and

---

*This policy has continued even in the wake of the Cold War.

computer graphics are microwaved back to the field for "after-action" review. The NTC brochure declares that "in order to beat [the OPFOR], Blue Forces [or visiting units] must do just about everything right." But Bublitz said that by the end of a stay, highly accomplished visiting units were sometimes able to prevail. "Lots of battles end when a unit loses fifteen or twenty percent," he told me. "But sometimes they fight to the last man."

With that, we went out to watch a battle.

The regiment visiting the NTC was the 155th Armored Brigade of the Mississippi National Guard. Its thirty-nine hundred members had been mobilized in December 1990 at the height of the Middle East buildup; for initial training they had been sent to Camp Shelby, Mississippi, and then to Fort Hood, Texas, before being transferred to Fort Irwin, where they had now passed one week of a three-week rotation. Bublitz told me that today's battle would be a "meeting engagement": "Two moving units bump into each other," he said, "as opposed to a hasty attack, relief, defense, et cetera."

When we tried to embark for the battlefield, we found that our Humvee wouldn't start. This was a major disappointment; I'd been looking forward to riding in one of those can-do convertible contraptions. Instead we made the trip in a dreary olive-drab "personnel carrier," whose rear tires spun out while attempting to ascend the hill that would serve as our observation post. When we started sliding backward on the loose gravel, I suddenly wondered if I was going to become part of the casualty list for Operation Desert Storm. Somehow, though, we made it to the top, where we found two young OPFOR scouts—one black and one white—watching for enemy movement in the north. Affixed to their armored vehicle was a long-range antitank weapon—specifically, a TOW (Tube-Launched Optically Tracked Wire-Guided) missile launcher.

Spread before us was a typical Mojave landscape. Directly to the west, the horizon consisted of unclothed mountains above a sprawling brown bajada; between it and us was a wide flat basin devoid of vegetation. In the south, the earth rose gradually in an alluvial plain toward another group of mountains drained by a large wash (*wadi* in the NTC/Arabic lexicon) which served to conceal an assortment of OPFOR tanks, visible from our elevated vantage point. The Blue Forces were reportedly somewhere to the north, although no movement or activity was at all evident. The 155th didn't seem to want to come out and play.

After a while, we heard on the radio that the OPFOR had located the 155th field headquarters. A group of jets from Nellis Air Force Base passed overhead, sending imaginary air strikes against it. Finally, a massive formation began to emerge from the northern hills: scores of tanks traveling in a wave across the middle of the basin, heading directly for the hidden OPFOR forces, dug in and waiting for them in the washes and depressions.

Abruptly the Blue Forces stopped advancing and began to back up. Apparently they'd discovered a minefield between themselves and the OPFOR. Discovered it, I should say, the hard way: lights soon began blinking on some of their tank turrets, which promptly turned around backward—dead. The whole formation proceeded to sit there like ducks on a pond, seemingly paralyzed, until some NTC observer-controllers came along in Humvees and tossed artillery flashes among them, simulating mortar fire in an effort to make them move.

Eventually most of the tanks came toward us, trying rather tardily to reach the cover of the hills. A group of 155th Bradley armored vehicles passed just below, attempting to outflank the OPFOR, but one of them suddenly halted as its light started flashing. The others disappeared behind a group of low hills to the south, where they apparently got into a fight—we could see smoke and dust rising in the distance. In time, the entire plain was littered with the disabled tanks of the 155th. Their occupants got out and stood around in the sun, waiting for the exercise to end, which it soon did in a massacre of the Mississippians.

"It just goes to show you can't roll straight across the flat," Bublitz said. "That's part of the arrogance of the armored vehicle—even if you're in a steel monster, a nice flat area is a perfect field of fire for an entrenched enemy. This was like the battle of Fredericksburg in the Civil War; the Union ran straight against a stone wall and got blown away. They should have come around behind this hill—then they could have gone up the wadi or sent dismounted infantry in to flush out the antitank weapons. But they didn't move quickly or decisively enough, and they didn't use any smoke to conceal their positions. You saw how the OPFOR used the terrain to their advantage: they put their tanks in the wadi, which is a natural trench. These guys from Mississippi are used to having natural cover—it's their first time in this open desert. The Forty-Eighth

Brigade from Georgia was the same way at first, but by the end of their rotation they whittled the OPFOR down to two percent on a regimental attack exercise."

A strong wind had now come up, blotting out visibility with suspended dust. We left our lookout and drove down toward the battlefield. Bublitz wouldn't let me attend the after-action review—he said it would be so "candid" that my presence would embarrass the troops—but he did allow me to visit the crew of a disabled Bradley. Its six soldiers (four white and two black), sitting in the shade of the vehicle, turned out to be quite friendly and forthcoming. When I asked what they thought of the desert, their comments offered a veritable checklist of associations with the Mojave:

"Too much sand."

"Too much wind."

"Not enough trees."

"All beach and no water."

"You can see further, but your damn ass is exposed."

"You can't stop or you're dead."

"It's hard to judge distances. That mountain range looks like it's two or three miles away, but it's probably eight or ten."

"When people found out we didn't have enough to drink, the tension got thick."

"It's cold at night—it even snows. I couldn't believe that!"

"It's real pretty, though. Especially early morning and evening."

When I returned to the public-affairs office, I encountered Major John Wagstaffe, with whom I proceeded to discuss the primary issue (other than Iraq) then facing Fort Irwin: its desire to expand its territory by more than a third. Since World War II, reportedly, the land requirements for infantry training have increased by 2,000 percent, owing largely to the kind of technological developments (e.g., increased mobility and firepower) in evidence at the NTC. Unfortunately for the army, during the same period, public environmental consciousness has increased by about the same amount, while available real estate in the desert has diminished.

Military control of land doesn't necessarily wreak ecological destruction. For example, the China Lake Naval Air Weapons Testing Center, most of whose activities take place off the ground, is known to harbor a considerable de facto wilderness and wildlife habitat. As I'd just witnessed, however, Fort Irwin is designed for heavy terrestrial use along the lines of Patton's Desert Training Center, whose tank tracks remain visible to this day. Four decades after World War II, heavily used areas of the DTC contained less than half the shrub cover of similar areas that had never been disturbed—a loss not only of plants but of the earth itself. Desert soil is held together by a thin veneer of gravel and lichens formed over hundreds or thousands of years; if this fossilized crust is broken, it's easily blown or washed away. (Fort Irwin seemed to me to consist mainly of bare sand, much of which became airborne as soon as the wind started blowing.) The base's lower bajadas are known to have lost two thirds of their original shrub cover, with a corresponding increase in erosion and decrease in wildlife; one 1989 study revealed that since the NTC's inception eight years earlier, desert-tortoise populations in the main valleys had declined by 62 percent. More than twice as many dead tortoises were found within the fort as live ones, and of forty-four carcasses, half were found in tank tracks.

Moreover, in 1990 the NTC was cited for forty-two toxic-waste violations by the Environmental Protection Agency. Its reputation in this department has never been good, which may have something to do with the difficulty it had encountered in expanding. Its latest aim—last resort, in fact—pointed east toward the Silurian Valley, bisected by California Highway 127. Explorations to the north, west, and south had been respectively foiled by Death Valley, China Lake, and the U.S. Fish and Wildlife Service, which found that expansion of the NTC would jeopardize the continued existence of the tortoise. Reptiles weren't the only problem in that direction, either; to cite only one other impediment, a Coptic monastery was situated just south of the fort.

"The Coptic Church has eight million members," Major Wagstaffe told me in amazement. "It had a schism with the Catholic Church in the first century A.D.; today it's mostly Egyptian. Its leader is Pope Shenouda III, who came here to consecrate the land for the monastery. I've been around [George] Bush and lots of other famous people, but I've only met two in my life who really had charisma: Colin Powell and Pope Shenouda."

Wagstaffe shook his head and laughed. Like the grunts who'd been blown away on the battlefield that day, the major's tour of duty in the Mojave seemed to have served him with an education in the complexities of the place.

"The geopolitics of this desert are incredible," he exclaimed. Then, citing the same preconception that had misled so many before him, he added: "And it looks like there's nobody there!"

The most prominent military site in the Mojave is Edwards Air Force Base—according to its own publicity, "the premier flight test facility in the world." Originally, the chief attraction of this place was a pair of playas named Rogers and Rosamond, which together constituted an unparalleled site for lengthy takeoffs and emergency landings—Rosamond Dry Lake contains a curvature of less than eighteen inches over a surface diameter of thirty thousand feet. Rogers, forty-four miles square, is a National Historic Landmark. In the early 1930s, the Army Air Corps used it for bombing and gunnery practice, which continued into World War II, when a life-size wooden replica of a 650-foot Japanese cruiser was installed on its surface. (The faux ship "startled many motorists driving along the northern edge of the base because it looked like an actual ship afloat in the shimmering heat waves radiating from the dry lakebed.") During the 1940s, Edwards—then called Muroc, a moniker which, despite its Native American ring, was actually a backward spelling of Corum, the name of a Scottish family that once operated a store and post office there—also served as a secret site for testing the country's first jet aircraft, which led to Chuck Yeager's breaking the sound barrier in 1947. The Air Force Flight Test Center was officially established in 1951, and ever since, Edwards has served as a development site for practically every model of airplane introduced into use by the USAF. It was the embarkation point from which aircraft first flew higher than 100,000, 200,000, and 300,000 feet, and from which people first surpassed speeds of Mach 1, 2, 3, 4, 5, and 6.

Over the last couple of decades, Edwards has gained even more notoriety from the space shuttle. The first aircraft to return from outer space for reuse, the shuttle made its inaugural landing at Edwards in April 1981—an event that derived considerable power from the desert itself, with the hosts of *Today* greeting the audience at dawn from a dramatically lit Pleistocene lake bed and the craft returning from orbit into our own version of outer space, gliding to the bare earth ("moonscape") under the power of nothing but gravity—a feat that had been tested and practiced at Edwards throughout the seventies. NASA's principal lab for aeronautical research, the Dryden Flight Research Center, had conducted the preliminary tests on the shuttle's computer software, thermal protection, solid booster recovery, and drag chutes at Edwards. Today the Kennedy Space Center in Florida, where the shuttle takes off, has supplanted Edwards as a landing site, but the desert remains the primary alternative, since Rogers and Rosamond Dry Lakes together contain ten runways to choose from.

Most shuttle landings are open to the public, so in May 1991 I drove to Edwards to witness the return of the space shuttle *Discovery*. It was a sunny, windy morning, which didn't bode well for the event, since wind is usually the one drawback to landing in the desert. Along Highway 58 there were lots of signs for the shuttle viewing site, although, at the indicated turnoff, another sign said NO PUBLIC ACCESS. An elderly couple had stopped their Blazer beside it, puzzling over this apparent contradiction. "Well," the man finally said, "we went this way last time"—alerting me to the fact that, for some, a shuttle landing isn't exactly a once-in-a-lifetime sight.

The approach was lined with Joshua trees and all manner of microwave equipment along the surrounding ridges. I came to a T, turned right on a lonely road called Mercury Boulevard, and lo and behold, beheld Rogers Dry Lake—a seemingly endless sand-colored expanse beneath the bright blue sky. On the near side of a fence that stretched across the playa, the lakebed had been demarcated like a drive-in theater, with permanent, parallel black stripes painted on the hard-packed clay, each one indicating a parking lane. At 8:30 A.M., about three hundred vehicles had already assembled: campers, trailers, and RVs with tents set up between them. One even had a portable satellite dish. Somebody was flying a kite; others were riding bicycles; one guy strolled along with a pit bull on a leash. As I pulled up, I heard someone say, "I've paid to camp in worse places than this."

In the distance across the lake, I could see the beige- and gray-colored hangars of Edwards and Dryden. Far to the south, landforms appeared to be hovering in midair. The arid heat had cracked the clay surface into innumerable geometric shapes, but only the top was hard; when I reached down and picked up one of the tiny, desiccated polygons, it was like cutting a fishing hole in pond ice: just below the surface I could dig into soft brown dirt.

Along the fence that separated the spectators from the runways, an army of vendors had set up a row of souvenir stands. I noted no shortage of T-shirts, baseball hats, pins, or patches. Some of the shirts advertised allegiance to the Mojave Desert Bikers, Mojave Beach Club, Mojave Golf Classic, and Mojave Ski Team—all of whose representatives were portrayed as grinning skeletons. Others proclaimed membership on Team Stealth or the Shuttle Landing Crew. A Desert Storm shirt showed a bunch of bombs raining on Saddam Hussein, who was taking refuge under an umbrella. There were also framed photographs of the doomed shuttle crew containing schoolteacher Christa McAuliffe. Then there were space shuttles: pictures of space shuttles, model space shuttles, blow-up plastic space shuttles, and moving toy space shuttles that turned around when they reached the edge of a table. The pertinence of much of the merchandise to the space shuttle was mysterious, though trick handcuffs and whoopee cushions might be just what the doctor ordered for a lengthy mission in space. Most of the vendors were wearing blue jump-suits, but at least one female entrepreneur was dressed in a black catsuit with black boots, a black cape, hoop earrings, and a silver belt buckle.

Suddenly a sonic boom sounded. Apparently, however, this did not signal the approach of the returning spacecraft. "For the shuttle, it's always a double," said one of the vendors.

"There are three little puffs when a sonic boom happens," added an elderly woman nearby.

"This is an unusual landing," commented a man next to her. "Usually it comes by the coast of San Francisco and down past Ventura. This one is going past the Oregon coast and over Owens Valley. It comes down at fifty-eight degrees, and levels off at ten or twelve thousand feet. The wind decision depends completely on the direction. In this orbit, if they decide not to land here, they can be at Kennedy six minutes later."*

A car came by carrying a couple of camouflage-clad MPs. Through a loudspeaker on the roof, they ordered all "personnel" to move their cars away from the fence and behind the motor homes.

Flags along the fence line stood out horizontally in the wind. "The first time we came here it was beautiful," said the elderly woman. "Then the wind came up, we went home, and it landed the next day. Now yesterday was beautiful and today here's the wind again."

---

*The shuttle travels around the Earth at a speed of 17,322 miles per hour; each orbit takes an hour and a half. The crew sees a sunrise or sunset every forty-five minutes.

"This is my sixth or seventh one," said the man. "There were fifty thousand people here for the first. I saw *Discovery* take off at Canaveral right after I had heart surgery. It was the most spectacular thing I ever saw. It was a night shot, and the light had an orange cast. Landings just last a couple of seconds, but boy, they get your adrenaline going, what with all the people screaming and hollering and whistling and shouting."

One of the vendors said he'd heard on his radio that NASA had decided to go to "Op Three." "That's Canaveral," he revealed. "We're Op One and Two. But nothing's ever set in concrete around here."

Clinging to this hope for sluggish cement was a family in a multiroom tent. One baby was in a playpen and two other kids were apparently in hot water. *"Get the fuck in here and shut your goddamn mouth!"* suggested their overstressed dad as he labored to secure his tent, which was threatening to become airborne. Lowering his voice, he said hopefully, "It might still land if the wind dies down."

Alas, there was to be no such luck. Soon the MPs returned, dispensing the bad news—*"The shuttle will be landing in Florida"*—over the loudspeaker. But, I quickly learned, shuttle watchers aren't the type to mope around after a setback. Before the announcement was even completed, a stream of cars and trailers was hightailing it across the lake bed for the exits, giving rise to a gigantic dust cloud. Shortly it became clear why these veterans had moved with such alacrity: a bottleneck immediately formed at the gates for Mercury Boulevard, creating a monstrous traffic jam.

Here in the military Mojave, the chasm between Heaven and Earth had become painfully apparent. As the shuttle continued its celestial journey, its earthbound worshipers found themselves in that most degrading of desert plights: having been misled by a mirage, they'd gotten stuck on a dry lake. Meanwhile, their heroes added insult to injury, hauling ass away from the Mojave at seventeen thousand miles per hour, opting for the humid succor of the Sunshine State.

George and
the Space People

Edwards Air Force Base isn't the only place in the Mojave that has served as a destination for travelers from outer space. North of Palm Springs and Joshua Tree National Monument, near the once (but no longer) tiny town of Yucca Valley, is a West Texas–type locale called Landers—epicenter, as it happens, of the 7.6-magnitude southern California earthquake of June 28, 1992. If you drive a couple of miles off Highway 247, away from the Country Gospel Church toward the large lone lump of Goat Mountain, on the boundary of the U.S. Marine Corps Air-Ground Combat Center, you will see—rising like a full moon from the surrounding arrangement of low-slung house trailers and chain-link-fenced ranch homes—a large, white, domed building. This is called the Integratron. A mile or so farther, beyond the pavement on a network of desert dirt roads, is a big rock. By "big," I mean that it covers fifty-eight hundred square feet of earth and is either three or seven stories high, depending on which of several accounts you believe.

It is, not surprisingly, called Giant Rock. Some sources maintain that it is the largest boulder in the world—heavier than Los Angeles City Hall. Some of these same sources also reveal that it was a sacred spot to the "Indians," who called it not Giant Rock but the "Great Stone," since

to them it symbolized the "Great Spirit." In any case, this oversized peb-
ble is said to have served as a magnet for nonnative races as well.
According to *Desert* magazine, for example, "close to the big rock are
mountains of smaller rocks piled one on top of the other which appear to
have been dropped from the sky by a lordly spaceship." But I'm getting
ahead of the story.

In the year 1930, a man named Frank Critzer arrived at Giant Rock in
a four-cylinder Essex automobile. Critzer had previously served in World
War I as a mess boy on a German submarine; he had also worked in the
Merchant Marine and the Santa Monica fishing fleet—and apparently in
connection with this maritime career, had (according to an unidentified
medical authority) acquired "too much moisture in his lungs." Hence
Critzer, by all indications an independent soul, decided to become a
prospector in the Mojave Desert.

First, though, he needed to get a rod knock repaired in his Essex.
Since he had no money, he had a hard time finding a mechanic who
would fix his car. But ultimately he managed to locate one Glenn Paine,
who—with the help of his nephew George Van Tassel—operated a
garage at Second and Broadway in Santa Monica. Years later, Van Tassel
would recall that "being interested in mining and having a period of lull
during the depression, we just happened to have a little time on our
hands." Not only did he and his uncle repair Critzer's engine for free,
they took him to lunch and let him spend the night in their garage. "We
discovered that he was a very intelligent person and that he did know
quite a bit about prospecting. . . . when [he] was ready to leave, we gave
him $30, which was a lot of money in those days. We also stocked his car
full of canned goods and headed him out. He told us that wherever he
would settle down then he'd write to us and also that we would be
included in any mining claims he should happen to declare."

As it turned out, the place where Critzer staked his claim was Giant
Rock. For shelter, he dug and blasted a cave under the north side of the
boulder, chiseling out a set of steps and a couple of rooms. In an environment whose air temperature annually varied between 25 and 115 degrees
Fahrenheit, Critzer's cave never fell below 55 in winter nor rose above 80
in summer. He had a wood-burning stove and a large kitchen table
where he made "German pancakes" for anyone who visited (or, according to another account, "was suspicious of every visitor, and would stand
in the doorway of his house with his hand on the trigger of his shotgun,

ready to shoot it out"). Critzer kept a couple of cases of dynamite under the table; he and his visitors liked to prop their feet on the sticks while they talked.

Giant Rock has never produced any valuable minerals in quantity. During the Depression, Critzer apparently occupied himself by figuring out formulas for plastics and penning a manuscript entitled *The Glass Age*. Dragging a rail behind his car, he graded several miles of straight roads around Landers, gaining the nickname among his neighbors of Straight Road Frank. He even established an impromptu airport, where he serviced planes lured to land by his unauthorized wind sock. He owned an Atwater Kent shortwave radio with a superheterodyne receiver, whose antenna was prominently displayed (or cunningly hidden) on top of the nearby mountain.

Of course, it didn't take long for local rumors about the hermit under the rock to arise. One held that, despite his subterranean abode, Critzer was "some sort of sun worshiper. . . . Just before dawn he would scale the barren hillside near his rock to greet the rising sun with stentorian bellows, at the same time beating his chest like a gorilla." Some suspected that he was smuggling dope (and/or aliens) from Mexico—"mysterious flares illuminating the night sky" had been seen in the vicinity of Giant Rock, and hangars for secret planes were undoubtedly camouflaged among the boulders. In 1942, the foremost theory was that Critzer was a spy, communicating nightly with Nazis on his three-dial radio. He was formally investigated and cleared of this charge by the FBI, but then it was claimed that the fifty-nine-year-old immigrant had failed to register for the draft. Moreover, there were reports that tools, dynamite, and gasoline had recently disappeared from the nearby towns of Banning, Garnet, and Palm Springs. The result was that, on July 25, 1942, three Riverside County sheriffs' deputies came to pay Critzer a call.

The reader won't be surprised to learn that there are several versions of what happened next.

> 1. Critzer informed the deputies that since Giant Rock is in San Bernardino County—not Riverside—they had no authority over him. They answered that they were arresting him anyway. Critzer said that he had to get his coat, but once inside his cave he barricaded the door. To get him out, the deputies lobbed a tear-gas grenade through a window.

2. The officers questioned Critzer in his house for thirty minutes. When they announced that they were taking him back to Banning, he made an excuse to go outside. Two deputies went with him; one stayed behind to look for a gun, since Critzer had been known to boast that he was a good shot. When Critzer returned, Deputy Claude F. McCracken asked him if he was ready to go.

"Do we all have to go together?" Critzer queried, which double meaning the officers missed.

"Yes, we have a car" was the reply.

"I do not mean that way," the recluse said . . .

3. As soon as Critzer saw the deputies approaching, he called out: "You ain't a-going to take me out of here alive! Dead men tell no tales!" and threw a detonating switch.

4. When McCracken told Critzer that the officers needed to search his cave, Critzer obligingly said, "Come—I'll show you" and took McCracken downstairs. Then: *"You're not taking me out alive. . . . I'm going, but you're going with me,"* etc.

In any case, the unargued upshot (so to speak) is that Critzer's dynamite blew up, killing him and injuring the three deputies, particularly McCracken, whose yogic experience was described in detail by one especially imaginative storyteller:

> The first wave of the explosion bent the deputy's body backward until his head and shoulders had almost touched the floor. But just before this could happen, the pressure wave, rebounding from the wall behind him, lifted McCracken up and bent him in the opposite direction until his face was but a few inches from the ground. Re-echoing from the wall in front of him, the wave lifted the officer's body and bent it over backward a second time, but not quite so far. Back and forth he vibrated, in a rapidly decreasing arc, like a horsewhip in the socket of an old buggy. After what was probably *less than a second* [italics mine], the deputy found himself standing on his feet, every shred of clothing, except his shoes, blown from his body which was bleeding from nearly 100 gashes.

❖

Since all the evidence vanished in the explosion, we'll never really know if Frank Critzer was a spy. We do know, however, that before Critzer's death, George Van Tassel had kept in touch with him.

"A year went by before we finally heard from him," Van Tassel later wrote, recalling the time when he and his uncle had fixed Critzer's car. "We had practically given up on him when we received a letter in which he had drawn a map showing how to get to Giant Rock." Van Tassel visited Critzer throughout the 1930s, during which he (Van Tassel) was employed as a flight-test engineer—first for Lockheed, later for Douglas Aircraft and Howard Hughes. "[Frank] had only squatter's rights and a mining claim on Giant Rock. He didn't own the property, for it was government land. By digging under the Rock he could have a place to live without having to purchase materials to amount to anything. . . .

"Frank had shrewdness and comprehension," Van Tassel observed. "In 1936 he had already in print all of the plastics we use today, and some of which we do not have yet. He was an advanced thinker in his own right with a brilliant mind."

A month after Critzer's death, Van Tassel went to Giant Rock and found that all of his friend's possessions, including the four-cylinder Essex, had been hauled away. He also discovered, however, that he had grown rather attached to the place, Critzer or no Critzer. He continued going there to camp out with his wife and daughters, and after the war ended, he applied for an airport permit from the BLM. When it was approved in 1947 Van Tassel moved his family from Santa Monica to the Mojave, leasing twenty-six hundred acres including Giant Rock, where he built a group of structures to support his airport, including a six-stool café called the Come On Inn.

As with the story of Frank Critzer, there are diverse legends as to how the next segment of Giant Rock history began. One of them holds that while standing in front of his restaurant one day, Van Tassel happened to notice an aircraft longer than a football field zipping over the mountains nearby. Although he was a flight engineer who lived next door to a military base, Van Tassel knew of no plane nearly so large or fast. In any case, soon thereafter—on January 6, 1952, to be exact—he began receiving psychic messages regarding the origin of the mysterious craft. The first contact reportedly came from "Lutbunn, senior in command first wave, planet patrol, realms of Schare"—a flying-saucer station eighty thousand feet above Giant Rock.

Soon to follow were alleged communications from many other extraterrestrial beings—among them Clatu, Clota, Elcar, Hulda, Kerrull, Latamarx, Lata, Leektow, Locktopar, Luu, Molca, Noma, Oblow, Singba, and Totalmon. The chief correspondent, apparently, was named Ashtar: As "commandant quadra sector, patrol station Schare, all projections, all waves," he would go on to contact many other earthlings. Van Tassel began holding Friday-night meditation meetings at Giant Rock, which he perceived to be a "natural cone of receptivity" for alien spacecraft. Going into a trance there himself, he was taken up to meet the "Council of Seven Lights"—reportedly a body of discarnate earthlings from the planet Shanchea. Moreover, according to his book *I Rode a Flying Saucer*, on August 24, 1952, while sleeping in the desert with his wife, Van Tassel was roused by a being named Solgonda and ushered into an actual spaceship waiting nearby.

From these contacts, Van Tassel learned that the human race was partly extraterrestrial in origin. The so-called space people, who turned out to be surpassingly wise and compassionate, wanted to raise earthlings' "vibratory attunement" for the sake of peace and harmony in the universe. Toward that end, Van Tassel himself formed something called the Ministry of Universal Wisdom, whose "proceedings" he printed and regularly mailed out. He also began work on the Integratron, whose design he said had been furnished by his otherworldly friends. Most notably, in 1954 Van Tassel held his first Giant Rock Space Convention—a gathering of speakers, listeners, and general testimony on evidence of extraterrestrial life. It was so successful that it became an annual event, attracting thousands of people to Landers over the next seventeen years, serving as it did as a focal point for the postwar UFO craze.

Van Tassel was only one of several "contactees" who came forward with stories of extraterrestrial relations during the 1950s. As fate would have it, a large percentage came from southern California and/or had their UFO experiences in the Mojave Desert. George Adamski (author, with Desmond Leslie, of *Flying Saucers Have Landed*) claimed that near the town of Desert Center on November 20, 1952, he met a man from Venus named Orthon. About 5′6″ with shoulder-length blond hair, attired in a belted bodysuit, Orthon admonished earthlings to live by the laws of the "Creator of All" (which, as it happened, Adamski had already been promoting). Later Adamski met a Mr. Firkon from Mars and a Mr. Ramu from Saturn, both of whom, like Orthon, expressed grave concern about nuclear radiation. Also in 1952, while driving home from his job at the Lockheed aircraft plant in Burbank, Orfeo Angelucci (*The Secret of the Saucers*) met an alien man and woman bathed in light; they assured him that Earth was being watched over by the Spirit of God, plus a hierarchy of angels and other highly evolved beings in a harmonious universe. They explained that, for various reasons, Angelucci had been chosen to be the first contactee.

Two decades before that, however, in 1932, one Howard Menger—as a child of ten playing in the woods near his home—had come upon a beautiful blond woman who told him that he had been reincarnated from the planet Venus. Menger related that Venusians liked health food, and that Venus itself was "young and healthy, with beautiful foliage, streams, forests, large bodies of water, mountains, and hills" similar to "some places in California today" (excluding, it seems, the desert—but then, Menger hailed from New Jersey).

On July 4, 1950, an electronics engineer named Daniel Fry met a being named A-Lan near White Sands, New Mexico, where Fry installed instruments on guided missiles. A-Lan told him that the space people were descended from a vanished supercivilization on Earth, specifically "Lemuria," which, as the archenemy of Atlantis, had been destroyed thirty thousand years earlier in an atomic war. A-Lan's people had escaped to Mars but later freed themselves from planetary commitment altogether, traveling about in large, independent ships. Fry reported that A-Lan took him to New York City and back in half an hour at an apparent speed of eight thousand miles per hour—consistent, as we shall soon see, with those calculated for other UFOs by the U.S. Air Force.

Fry founded a quasi-religious group called Understanding, Inc., but he flunked a lie-detector test with regard to his tales of extraterrestrial contact. That didn't dissuade Gabriel Green, however, from choosing him as a vice presidential running mate on the Universal Party ticket in 1972. Green—who, as a "vocal telepathic channel for the Space Masters and the Great White Brotherhood," founded the Amalgamated Flying Saucer Clubs of America—had, on the basis of an anti-nuclear-testing platform, received 171,000 votes in the Democratic primaries for the U.S. Senate in 1962. He claimed contact with beings from Venus, Mars, Saturn, Alpha Centauri, and Coma Berenices, who apparently instructed him in the principles of (nonmonetary) Universal Economics, offering unlimited aid to humankind "if we will but accept their friendly offers of help to our world."

The other major contactee of the fifties was Truman Bethurum. According to *The Encyclopedia of UFOs*:

> Bethurum became famous in 1954 with the publication of his book, *Aboard a Flying Saucer*. In it, Bethurum claimed that he encountered a landed flying saucer in the Mojave Desert, where he was laying asphalt for a construction company. Invited aboard the flying saucer, he said, he met the crew and its female captain Aura Rhanes. She explained to Bethurum that she had come from an idyllic society on the planet Clarion, where there was no war, divorce, or taxes. Clarion could not be seen from Earth because it was always behind the sun.

Bethurum claimed that he rendezvoused with Aura Rhanes ten times, usually at lunch counters. Eventually she invited him for a ride in her saucer, but she failed to show up at the appointed time and never appeared again. Bethurum died in 1969 in none other than the town of Landers, where he had apparently landed courtesy of George Van Tassel's Space Conventions, where he and his fellow contactees were made to feel quite welcome. As the *Encyclopedia of UFOs* describes it, "In the isolated, intense setting—in which people who usually find themselves a singular and often ridiculed minority were now the majority community—their messages had an unexpected ring of power":

> UFO contact enthusiasts would gather for two or three days during the convention in an atmosphere reminiscent of the camp meetings of old. Parking campers or pitching tents on the airport grounds under the desert sky, perhaps a thousand people (in the best years of the convention) would, during the day, hear a nonstop series of speakers and, during the cool evenings, enjoy campfire discussions of contacts and wait for signs of recognition by the Space People themselves. It was widely rumored in contact circles that the latter were aware of these meetings and their importance for their work toward Earth; they would, it was said,

acknowledge the assembly by flashing lights or flying in formation over the lonely airport. . . . During the day, numerous UFO
and cognate groups would have booths set up where literature
could be obtained, and pins, bumperstickers, pamphlets, and
books were on sale. Giant Rock was, then, a real axis of the contactee movement in its heyday.

Van Tassel himself was perhaps the most celebrated contactee of his
time. In addition to his books (*I Rode a Flying Saucer; Into This World
and Out Again; The Council of Seven Lights; Religion and Science
Merged; When Stars Look Down*), he gave 297 lectures and appeared on
409 radio and television shows. Even the anticontactee *Civilian Saucer
Intelligence of New York* described him as "a handsome, broad-faced,
fair-haired man . . . with a pleasant, deep voice and an easy-going manner of speech. It is impossible not to be struck at once by his evident
'sincerity.' . . . A person listening primarily to the *sound* of his discourse,
and applying little thought to its *sense*, would probably never have reason to suspect that this big, sincere, affable, humble man was anything
other than what he claims to be." The so-called Sage of Giant Rock
spent two hundred thousand dollars and twenty-five years building the
Integratron—a structure thirty-eight feet high and fifty-eight feet in
diameter, made entirely of wood with no nails or screws, which was
intended to rejuvenate human cells and preventing aging. Unfortunately,
it was still unfinished when Van Tassel died of a heart attack on February
9, 1978. The following year, in order to pay her taxes, his widow, Dorris,
sold the property to a San Diego developer, who announced plans to turn
the dome into a disco. Van Tassel's flabbergasted followers managed to
buy it back, but for years afterward his holdings around Giant Rock were
disputed, and much of the property was vandalized. After lengthy litigation, the BLM finally canceled the airport lease, filled in the rooms
under the rock, and dismantled many of the buildings. The Integratron,
however, still stands.

I visited Giant Rock one windy afternoon. I drove as far as I could on
ramrod-straight Linn Road toward Goat Mountain, then left the pavement and continued northwest on dirt. Near the point where the asphalt

ended, alongside the Integratron, was a prefab trailer house surrounded by a chain-link fence. A sign in front said:

```
PHYSICAL THERAPY AND X-RAY
DR. D. I. ANDRE, R.P.T., D.C.
```

As I rounded the corner of a granite-bouldered hill, Giant Rock loomed up in the distance. I parked near it and got out of my truck. The wind immediately blew my hat off, and I went running after it. Coming back, the gale was so strong that I could hardly walk.

Several campfire rings were arranged around the rock, whose walls had been predictably decorated with graffiti. Among the plethora of proper names were some garden-variety witchcraft symbols and words to the effect that "the planet Uranus spoke truth here." Under the north face of the rock were the remains of Critzer's cave; mostly filled in now with dirt, its residual hollow was littered with cans, bottles, and shotgun shells.

Another long, white car was parked nearby. Pretty soon I saw two people walking around. Both were male, sparsely bearded, and looked to be in their late twenties. They smiled when I raised my hand in greeting, so I walked over and asked if they knew anything about the place. "Yeah," one answered. "Quite a bit." He said he'd been there fifty or sixty times.

"It's a sacred Indian site, so whatever you do here, you should keep a pure attitude," he recommended. Then, regarding me quizzically, he asked: "You've never been out here before, and you're wandering around by yourself?" When I answered that this was correct, he shook his head. "Lots of people have died out here," he warned. "They don't tell you about that. I know somebody whose father is in the CIA, and after she came out here, her father told her not to anymore—he knew all about it. This place is under surveillance; we're being watched right now."

He went on to furnish me with a thumbnail outline of Giant Rock lore: how "a Japanese guy" had once lived under the rock; how Van Tassel had been "pulled into a ship" and given instructions for the Integratron; how the place is an "energy spot—a meridian runs through here, one of a network of lines that go around the Earth. Stonehenge is on one. Meridians are Earth energy. They're where dimensions overlap. UFOs ride on them. The ships might be from another dimension."

"It has to do with vibrations," the other guy chipped in. "Everybody has a vibratory rate. As you raise it, you change your energy state, and you can go into a different dimension."

"That's why there were miracles, and levitations in séances," said the first guy. "Where there's a lot of energy, supernatural things can happen. Read Buckminster Fuller."

"Well," said the other guy, "he's kind of crazy."

"He *is* crazy. But he knows what he's talking about."

As we walked around the rock, the wind was blowing so hard that I could hardly hear what my companions were saying. Still, despite the wintry conditions, the two were clad only in T-shirts.

"I've seen ships here," the first guy divulged. "A large, glowing, round one. Other bizarre things, too. Clouds and lights that suddenly appear—shifting landscapes, things like that. See that mountain? One time it was over *there*—not there."

"Tell him about that time," his friend suggested.

"Well," said the first guy. "I don't know . . ."

"Oh, go ahead."

"Yeah!" I said. "Go ahead!"

"Okay. One time I was out here with some friends, and a bunch of government trucks drove up. We hid, but came out later when they left. One of my friends said he heard footsteps, and I saw something about this high. It was fluorescent green, sort of half there and half not—I could hardly see it. Then my friend ran at it. I said, *Right*, dude, good move—*run* at it! He got struck in the hand by something, and he started screaming. We ran away up that hill there, and then he started having convulsions. He had a burn mark on his arm; it was starting to turn fluorescent green. I moved away from him, and then I heard footsteps again. I was freaking out—it was like *The Exorcist*. We had an Indian medicine woman with us, and she tried to take care of him, but she said there wasn't much she could do for him. We got back in our van and drove into town. By the time we got to Denny's, he mellowed out.

"That happened right here where we're standing. I don't do any drugs, either—I don't believe in stuff like that."

"Why do you keep coming out here?" I asked.

"I guess you could say we're thrill seekers," the other guy volunteered. "We're interested in all sorts of strange stuff."

We returned to our respective vehicles. They got into their car and drove a short distance away toward something called Quartz Hill. I went around Giant Rock a few hundred yards into the desert to survey the surroundings; by the time I got back, the two thrill seekers had disappeared.

I drove back toward the Integratron and stopped in front of Dr. D. I. Andre's place, which my new friends had told me was the home of Van Tassel's widow, Dorris. A sign on the fence said NO ADMITTANCE— EMPLOYEES ONLY. Then I saw someone walking from the house toward a trailer in the yard—a dark, fortyish man with a beard, wearing a plaid flannel shirt. I called out "Hello," and he came to the gate.

I told him I was interested in finding out about George Van Tassel and the Integratron. He said that he was taking care of Van Tassel's widow and didn't have time to talk. Then he proceeded to give me quite an earful.

"Van and his family used to live under the rock," the man said. "When he found that he had psychic abilities, he formed the Brotherhood of the Cosmic Christ. Their meetings led to thought contacts with interstellar beings and receptions from entities. Later they had physical contacts, and Van formed the Ministry of the Universal Wisdom.

"The space people looked like us. They spoke English until Van realized that they didn't need to speak. They would find an individual who they could communicate with and make predictions through him— things like earthquakes and political events. They told Van they were going to buzz Washington, D.C., and be collected on radar, and Van sent a certified letter to the air force about it. It happened, and it was on the front page of the *Washington Post.** That scared the shit out of the Air Force, because Van was getting more information than they were."

"Why did the extraterrestrials pick this spot to make contact?" I asked.

"Evidently," he said, "this area was an intersection point on a mag-

---

*On July 27, 1952, an account of seven "eerily glowing" objects, tracked at speeds of seven thousand miles an hour by twelve different radar installations, did appear in several prominent national newspapers including the *New York Times*, *Washington Post*, and *Los Angeles Times*.

netic grid on the planet, just like the Egyptian pyramids. You know how
there are certain places where balls roll uphill? The Bermuda Triangle is
one. Well, this grid was destroyed in the last two hundred thousand years
by a being called Lucifer, who operated between Venus and Mars. He
used thermonuclear energy to destroy Maldec, which is now an extinct
planet. Then he came here and destroyed the magnetic grid system so
that we couldn't communicate with other parts of the universe. Lucifer
has been notified by authorities over extraterrestrial things that he's
under quarantine. The space people are trying to put us back in touch
with the rest of the universe because Earth is an isolated planet. Their
problem is—well, if you had twenty-five thousand years of technology
behind you and could make yourself disappear, how would you introduce
yourself to people on Earth? These people are so far ahead scientifically—they can make something look like a restaurant on the side of the
road, and when you go inside, it's a spaceship.

"The space people are very concerned about the danger of slavery
through surveillance satellites and computer networks," he added.
"Right now, you can buy devices for thousands of dollars that can read
your mind and put thoughts in your head from half a mile away."

"I understand Van Tassel got the formula for the Integratron from the
space people?"

The man nodded. "A being gave him a seventeen-inch-long mathe-
matical equation for it. It's an electrostatic generator, built entirely of
wood—no metal. Van had done a lot of research on cells with George
Lakhovsky. Basically, the human cell is a battery—when you get old, it
runs down. They were finding that [the Integratron] reversed this. But
Van died before he could complete it.

"The Brotherhood of the Cosmic Christ was basically wholesome
Christian people," the man said. "Christianity came from outer space.
Read the Bible: Moses, Mount Sinai, the burning bush, the tablets of
stone, meetings with angels in the desert—Joshua, Jacob, Enoch. Where
were they getting their information? From *contacts with extraterrestrial
people* trying to aid humanity. Moses met two beings from outer space on
the plains of Mammary. What led him out of Egypt and parted the Red
Sea? The Bible says it was something that looked like a 'pillar of fire by
night and a cloud by day.' That exactly fits Van's description of a spacecraft. It was a corona—an *electrostatic generator* delivered the children
of Israel out of their difficulties. And it was the *Arc* of the Covenant, not

the Ark; it was misspelled by one of the scribes who couldn't translate very well. The best example I can think of is the Star of Bethlehem, which led the three wise men to the Son of God. What the hell, do stars always travel around like that? *Jesus Christ was an extraterrestrial!* The Bible is still happening today; God is still visiting the planet. God was a *person* in Van's meetings—not a faceless spirit. When I say God is powerful, I mean he has a spaceship."

Trying to bring the discussion down to Earth, I asked how he'd gotten involved with the place.

"My father was a regional FBI agent at China Lake in the fifties," he said. "I'd been coming here with friends from high school since '67, shooting 30-30s and drinking. The dome was a big secret. Later, when I was working at the Gemstone Mine, I saw that this property had a compressor on it just like the one we were using. I told Dorris I'd like to buy it, and she got to know me and trusted me. I lived here for six months, but I didn't involve myself with her personal life. Finally, though, I told her I was going to leave because she wasn't furnishing me with any information about the place or the things I was interested in. So then she brought out all this stuff.

"Two years before Van died, he transferred the lease for the Integratron to some other people. But they couldn't handle it—the taxes hadn't been paid by the corporation of the ministry, and the state tax assessor was trying to terminate it. So I helped Dorris with that, but then some other people claimed that she was senile and they got control of the Integratron. Priests from the Church of Satan occupied the property for seven years. They had open houses on weekends—people were invited into the dome and never seen again. I paid private investigators over ten thousand dollars to get background on those people; one guy who was working on missing children told me that I needed help—he said they were murderers. Dorris knew a guy who was a mining engineer in Nevada, and he came here to help; three days later he was chopped up in one-inch pieces. I got some FBI and CIA files through the Freedom of Information Act; one guy was a communist who'd been investigated by Senator Inouye and the House Committee on Un-American Activities, and others were possible KGB agents setting up a drug-dealing ring to the Marines."

"Why are *you* still all in one piece?"

"Because I'm smarter. I'm just not susceptible to fearfulness. I'm a miner—I've been held at gunpoint and told to get off people's land. I walk around with a loaded, high-powered weapon with a scope and full clip on my back. I finally got the court to get those people off; I occupied the property with seventeen [friends], including the vice president of the *Unsolved Mysteries* show on NBC-TV. The night before the eviction, a blue-and-gold star appeared on the horizon, and its center was full of heavenly colors. Two of my friends had just gotten here to help me—one guy in a schoolbus, the other on a Harley—and when they saw it they said, 'What the hell is *that?*' We got twenty-five cars with the eviction, and from the license plates we found that they belonged to twenty-five missing people."

"Who owns the Integratron now?"

"A wealthy guy from San Francisco. His name is Emile Canning."

Something in my face may have indicated that I was having trouble digesting all of this. "Listen," the man said. "I went to Bible college for ten years. I was gonna be a missionary. I'd never involve myself with these heresies if they weren't true! A lot of people who follow UFOs are gullible. I'm not like that—I'm a miner. I don't depart from facts. Van had *profound truth*. What I've found out here has changed my life."

He said that he had lots of printed material inside the house, so I gave him my mailing address and asked him to send me some. Then, on my way out of Landers, I picked up one of the leaflets that were in a box outside the Integratron. It listed several upcoming workshops and events on UFOs, time travel, and "rejuvenation," all facilitated by the aforementioned Emile Canning. It also included two telephone numbers, one in Los Angeles and one in San Francisco. When I got home, I tried them and reached a friendly, forthcoming guy named Gary Abraham—a kind of lieutenant, I gathered, for Mr. Canning, who (though he did return a call from his car phone) was much too busy to see me. In his stead, Gary agreed to give me a few minutes.

I met Gary at noon one day at the place where he worked—a new, galvanized-steel office building on the Sausalito waterfront. He turned out to be a boyish-looking fifty-one-year-old financial executive without a necktie. He described Emile Canning as a Silicon Valley entrepreneur and video producer with an "inquiring mind," someone who was into high technology, "especially if it benefits mankind." Still, he said, Canning maintained a "strong marketing focus," often lending a hand to people who were "growing a business."

"Lots of people are drawn to Emile," Gary explained. "He's an explorer—he's out there meeting people all the time." This, presumably, was what had prompted Canning to seek out George Van Tassel in 1978; the only problem was that the weekend he chose to go to Landers was the weekend that Van Tassel died. But Canning still managed to see the Integratron, and in the topsy-turvy decade following Van Tassel's death, rented it out periodically for workshops on meditation and healing.

In 1988, Canning and his wife took a trip to Machu Picchu and Bolivia. "When they came back," Gary said, "they went to the desert to cool out. It just happened to be the day the Integratron went on the market." Significant synchronicity on both ends, it seems.

Gary more or less reiterated what the others had told me—that the Integratron was built at the intersection of several lines of Earth energy. "Are you familiar with acupuncture?" he asked. "Your body is full of meridians with electric current flowing through them. The Earth has a system like that too—they're called 'ley' lines, or grid lines. Any vortex, where lots of lines intersect, is a very charged point, a center of energy. Machu Picchu is one; so are Stonehenge, the Pyramids, Mount Shasta, the Grand Tetons. They're all over the world. The Integratron sits on a point where several lines intersect. Giant Rock, being made of granite, is a very powerful crystal. Van Tassel had an antenna stuck in it—it was like a giant crystal radio."

To explain the function of the Integratron, Gary gave me a primer on one of Van Tassel's theories. "Within every one of our cells is a filament," he said. "If the cell is vibrating at its natural harmonic frequency, it's healthy; if it's not, it's diseased. Somebody named George Lakhovsky created a machine, called a multiple-wave oscillator, that vibrated every cell in the body at its natural harmonic rate. It was actually found to cure cancer. We used to have a small multiple-wave oscillator here; I could plug it in and"—he gestured toward the piles of paper and spreadsheets scattered around his office—"I mean, I'm the C.F.O. of a company, but I could just clear all of this stuff away.

"The Integratron is often referred to as a giant multiple-wave oscillator. It looks like a building, but it's really a machine. It had a giant circular copper coil in the ceiling of its lower floor, and an outer track that was supposed to rotate around the building—it was being tested at the time when Van Tassel died. Its purpose was to create a positive charge upstairs and a negative charge downstairs. You wouldn't have wanted to be upstairs when it was fully charged; it would be like a microwave. But it could create a strong negative-ion field downstairs, like the air at the beach, or in the mountains, or after a storm. It's physically, mentally, and spiritually rejuvenative—it facilitates the clearing out of disharmony. I've been going there once or twice a month for five years, and whenever I come back, I feel refreshed and recharged—healthier.

"If the Integratron were finished, it would create a very strong regenerating field downstairs. The purpose was to rejuvenate people on many levels. Van Tassel wanted to have thousands of people walking through it. The dome is also a sound chamber; musical groups use it occasionally for recording sessions. To refurbish the track, we'd have to pull it completely off—it's really worn. Today we could do other things to create the field, but it would cost millions of dollars."

He said he didn't know anything about the interim owners of the Integratron or the rumors of drugs, Satanism, communism, and kidnapping. Nor did he seem to be aware that Lucifer had destroyed Earth's magnetic grid. "All I know," he said, "is that Van Tassel's motives were completely altruistic—and that it's still a very nurturing, rejuvenating place."

Nothing ever arrived in the mail from the man outside the Integratron. He had, however, mentioned that Van Tassel's book *When Stars Look Down* was a good source for the information that he'd been summarizing for me. Needless to say, the book was out of print, but eventually I obtained a copy from the San Bernardino County library. I found it to be a rather overbearing tome—a compilation of Van Tassel's writings from the "Proceedings" of the Ministry of Universal Wisdom, including a string of chapters entitled "Life and Laws," "Pollution and Blood," "Motion and Time," "Principles and Proof," "Secrecy and Space," and "Lies and Facts." It's full of vociferous breast-beating about the sorry state of modern civilization, quotes from the Bible proving the historical influence of extraterrestrials, denunciations of the government's cover-up of the existence of UFOs, and declarations of the electromagnetic basis of reality. Among other things, Van Tassel claims that Native Americans got corn, tobacco, and potatoes from outer space and that the moon is a spacecraft that will eventually return Jesus to Earth. In one doomsday scenario, spaceships will rescue those who have been living right—that is, who have the correct "vibratory aura"—while a "cataclysm" will wipe out the rest of the "mammon lovers." Included are several diagrams explaining how the Earth rotates, plus blueprints for magnetic devices that enable the user to grow big garden crops and prevent citrus groves from freezing.

There's also a chapter on the Integratron, which, for want of the expertise required to interpret it, I've elected to reprint verbatim here.

THE INTEGRATRON

Since a number of our readers, and friends, have expressed a desire to know how the "Integratron" operates I am writing this article to try to explain it's purpose and function.

The purpose of the "Integratron" is to recharge energy into living cell structure, to bring about longer life with youthful energy. This has been the goal of many people, since Ponce De Leon started looking for the "fountain of youth."

Our effort here, in this giant machine, is not the first idea of it's kind. It is the first time that other research efforts have been brought together and applied simultaneously.

The work of George Lakhovsky, Dr. George Crile, Barnothy, Oneil, Tesla, Smith, and many others, is being combined, by us, in a basic research to make the principles work. The only new thing we have added to their research is to make the application of three principles occur instantly and simultaneously.

Lakhovsky's Multiple Wave Oscillator (U.S. Patent Number 1,962,565) was used by him, in association with many doctors, to correct cellular malfunctions, and accumulations, in many patients. His principle is opposite to control of radiation of radio and television transmission. He spread his radiations over a multiple wave, while television and radio confine it to channels and kilocycles to prevent overlap. Lakhovsky used a field in which every tissue, organ, cell, and nerve responded in resonance between 10 cms. and 400 meters. This corresponds to frequencies of 3 to 750,000 millards per second. The harmonics extended from 1 to 300 trillion vibrations per second. No harmful side effects or aftereffects were ever noted. In his book "The Secret of Life," first printed in 1939, Lakhovsky detailed the many cases, functions, and results. His Multiple Wave Oscillator took from one application to three weeks of daily applications to achieve its outstanding effects. Our frequency control makes these periods instant in a one shot application. Our basic research is Lakhovsky's *side* effect of rejuvenation.

Lakhovsky established that "every living cell is essentially dependent on it's nucleus which is the center of oscillations and gives off radiations." By the same token the sun is the center of our solar system, and life could not exist without it giving off radiations that set up oscillations in living matter. Everything on the earth has been proven to react to sun spots and solar prominences.

Energy principles work on the same basic universal laws; be they atoms, cells, or solar systems.

The wet battery in your car operates on an *acid* electrolite. The dry battery in your flashlight operates on an *alkaline* electrolite. The separators in your car battery are a *semi-permeable* matrix.

The D.N.A. structure is a caduceus winding coiled in opposite directions. The filaments in the nucleus of a cell exhibit coil and plate configurations. These are microscopic electric circuits that work with the cell electric capacity as oscillators. Cilia in the lungs and respiratory tract are antenna that extract radiations from the air and transmit their energy to the cells in the blood to be conveyed throughout the body.

We are electrical creatures using a biochemical body to exist in a electro-chemical environment. We know that in highly diluted solutions certain chemical compounds are disassociated with the result that electrical charges appear, equal, but of opposite polarities. Sodium chloride for an example is disassociated as sodium with a positive charge and chlorine with a negative charge. The body fluids are a saline electrolite with cells in suspension.

Every microscopic part of a cell emits radiations according to the atomic structure of its makeup.

Like batteries, cells run down, bodies run down, and the energy loss is manifested as ageing.

The Bible says Adam lived 930 years; Seth, 912; Enos 905; Cainan 910; Mahalaleel, 890; Jared, 962; and Methuselah, 969 years. Then after these people of the race of Man mated with "the daughters of men" the life span fell off to 120 years according to Genesis 5:5 to 6:3.

After years of Pyramid Generator energy research, there is no question in my mind that V.I.P.s were brought back from death in the sarcophagus of the Kings Chamber. The sarcophagus and the Kings Chamber were constructed of granite. Granite, because of it's matrix of feldspar, mica, and quartz crystals, exhibits a radiation caused by the pressure of the matrix on the quartz crystals known as the piezo-electric effect. Granite was called "spiritual rock" by the Egyptians because of this auric radiation. The energy generated by a pyramid in a vortex is neither electrical, or magnetic as such. It is composed of "this other energy" which radiates life property effects. This energy is everywhere in a static state, and serves in this respect as an insulator and separator while it remains static. When it is activated by thought, as in a prayer, or by resonance in electro-magnetic fields, it reverses it's insulating qualities and becomes an infinite conductor.

It is this energy that will respond to our control in the "Integratron" and integrate energy into the cell structure of the body.

There is no reason why people today cannot live as long as Methusaleh. I am convinced that he used the Great Pyramid to live so long without ageing.

The D.N.A. configuration, the caduceus coils, the Emerald Tablet principles, and the pyramid vortices all exhibit a method of life energy activity.

We have put in 18 years of endless effort to prolong life without further ageing. We are anchored here on dedicated property. We are not going to go anywhere. It is our intention to be able to regenerate our world leaders, our world humanity and defeat "the last enemy to be overcome—death." It is a thousand times simpler in research than the effort it took to put men on the moon, but we need an ingredient we cannot make and that depends on other humanitarians. We are approximately 90% finished, with new methods already being apparent from the associated researches being conducted by others verifying our earlier efforts.

Jeno M. and Madeleine F. Barnothy, of the Biomagnetic Research Foundation, in Evanston, Illinois, have contributed outstanding results in magnetic research with everything from enzymes to rabbits. They showed retardation of ageing and 30% increased activity in research conducted on mice, whose cell structure is like humans.

Nikola Tesla, and others, showed that high voltage static electricity caused ionization. This causes disassociation of structure and charging of particles in positive and negative polarity effects.

Dr. George Crile, in a fabulous research that he devoted his life to, established that every living cell was a battery, a transducer, and a condenser. In his book "The Phenomena of Life," printed in 1936, he states, "Electricity is the energy that drives the organism." He further states, "It is clear that in the second half of life the electrical potential of the elderly patient as a whole or of this or that organ, has been very much reduced and that by so much, the margin of safety has been dangerously diminished." Hugo Fricke, working with Dr. Crile in his laboratory, found that the film which surrounds red blood cells is on the order of 3/10,000,000 of a centimeter in thickness and that this lipoid structure has an electric capacity of high order, viz., 0.8 microfarad per square centimeter. Dr. Crile further stated, "The unit of structure and of function of the living organism is the cell. Plants and animals are disperse systems of cell suspension. The nucleus of the cell is comparatively *acid*. The cytoplasm of the cell is comparatively *alkaline*. The nucleus and the cytoplasm are separated by a *semipermeable membrane*. Therefore the cell is a bipolar mechanism or an electric battery, the nucleus being the positive element, the cytoplasm the negative element.

These cell batteries of the body are what we are planning to charge with the

"Integratron." Each cell has a capacity like the battery in your car. The human body is composed of over 100 trillion of these cells. Our principle of operation is as simple as applying Lakhovsky's multiple wave oscillation to Barnothy's magnetic fields saturated with Tesla's ionization to charge Dr. George Crile's cell batteries. Our method of control is through a time function of frequency from zero time to infinity. This is our contribution. The schematic circuitry is a hundred times simpler than in a television set.

Its a strange thing that George is involved in so many firsts. Maybe this is where the expression evolved of "let George do it." Here we have George Crile's research tied in with George Lakhovsky's principles, being extended by George Van Tassel. After all George Washington was our first President, and Nikola Tesla was financed by George Westinghouse. Nikola Tesla's discoveries made Westinghouse what it is today. Then there is the contrast of opposites because *Ge-or-ge* is ge twice with an "or" in between, and Westinghouse's largest competitor is General Electric or G.E., and further in the letter expression of meanings, G.E. means *generate energy*.

When I read this last paragraph, a previously overlooked piece of information hit me like a jolt from a positive-force-field generator. It cast a new, radiant light on the stranger in front of the Integratron—the guy who'd furnished me with so much confounding information. I don't know how I'd missed the significance of it before, but thanks to Van Tassel's astute observation, I suddenly recalled that this man had told me that his name was George Riddle.

Eventually I had an opportunity to go inside the Integratron. It was on the afternoon of a bitterly cold Easter Sunday marked by sporadic snow and hail. Gary's group had staged a workshop in the morning, after which a couple of people named Nan and Jack agreed to show me around.

The interior of the building was divided into two floors. Ceiling beams in the lower floor radiated from a central post, upon whose northwest side (the one facing Giant Rock) was painted a yellow triangle. This was referred to as the "healing zone"—the area through which Van Tassel had planned to usher thousands of pilgrims. The upstairs floor was topped by a domed ceiling, which was leaking in the rain. An American flag hung from a platform supporting a ladder leading to the ceiling; on a side table were some flowers and pictures of Jesus, Mary, Krishna, and Radha, the goddess of liberty. There was also a Bible, an amethyst crystal, and, near the wall, a metal structure in the shape of an obelisk with magnets attached to copper tubes. "They called that the ignition key when they first put it in here," said Jack.

"It brings floating, random energy to the center and lands it like a torch," said Nan. "We've seen energy move here in a way that is miraculous. We do a lot of healing work with sound."

Nan positioned me a few yards away from the central spot in the floor. Then she stood equidistant on the opposite side of the spot. "What does my voice sound like?" she asked me.

It sounded really loud.

"The ceiling is built like a tabernacle," she said. "Through chanting and toning, you can discover a deeper part of your own resonance. I've done healing work all over North America, and this is a particularly powerful spot with a lasting effect on one's well-being."

As it happened, waiting outside in my car was a friend who had hardly spoken to me all day. We'd just spent several days in the desert, and we were—well—having some problems. Nan said it would be okay if I brought my friend inside and exposed her to the energy of the Integratron.

When I positioned her in front of the yellow triangle, another couple watching asked if we'd like to see an example of their healing work. They led us upstairs, sat us down back-to-back, and chanted for a while; then they left us alone. By the time we went back downstairs, nobody was around. But for whatever reason, the energy between my friend and me had decidedly changed. As we drove away from the Integratron, she was finally able to discuss what had been bothering her, and our mutual defensiveness disappeared. We spent that night at a Motel 6, and suffice to say that, in the course of the evening, our difficulties evaporated more or less permanently.

The problem is, I don't know whether to attribute this miracle to the Integratron or Motel 6. But when I checked out of our room in the morning, I did notice that the manager's name tag said GEORGE.

Ordinary Prudence

When George Riddle, the caretaker in front of the Integratron, had wanted to convey the measure of his own courage, he did so with three words: "I'm a miner." In fact, most of the impetus for the exploration of the Mojave arose with just such people. No matter how far one ventures into the apparent middle of nowhere, he or she can be sure that some mosquitolike miner has already been there, probing for a vein. It's fair to say that miners are responsible for the existence of most of the roads in the desert, though a vehicle is hardly necessary to follow their traces. Climb to the top of any mountain—hand over hand up a tortuous canyon in dehydrated, sun-scorched terrain—and sooner or later you'll find a hole with a discolored perimeter and rotten four-by-fours framing the mouth: the onetime fancy of a stubborn loner hoping to strike it rich.

The Mojave is made of rock. From a distance it might look like dirt, but when you walk on it you realize that it's rock—rough, tough, sharp, and crunchy, represented in every order of magnitude from a granite monolith to a grain of sand. Similarly, where the landscape at first appears to be brown, on close inspection it is polychromatic: striped, spotted, streaked, and banded by multicolored *rock*.

In these lapideous foundations, the Mojave isn't so different from other places. But most of those receive more rainfall and are hence over-lain with plants and topsoil. In the desert there's no such organic distraction. The hard stuff is right there in plain sight on the surface. Botany cedes the spotlight to geology—big time.

The Mojave has powerful impetuses in the rock department. It is, for example, defined by two major geologic fault zones: the Garlock on the north and the San Andreas on the south. The latter is in the notorious process of pushing the Pacific continental plate underneath the North American, giving rise—literally—to all kinds of rock. "There are old-old rocks [early Precambrian gneiss], old rocks [late Precambrian carbonate, conglomerate, sandstone, and shale], medium-old rocks [Paleozoic lime-stone], not-so-old rocks [Mesozoic granite], and young rocks [Cenozoic sandstone, siltstone, shale, and volcanics]," writes the redoubtable Robert P. Sharp (that geologist who admired the desert for its lack of "false eyelashes" and "fancy clothes"). Moreover, as the crust of the Mojave has been stretched thin and pulled apart by faulting, molten rock inside the earth has been able to make its way upward, adding yet more ingredients to the mix. As the magma cools, some of the still-hot fluids find their way into myriad fractures in the shattered crust, transporting gases and metals and leaching others from the adjacent rock; where they cool and crystallize, they're deposited as agate, bloodstone, feldspar, garnet, obsidian, onyx, and quartz. "If someone asked which southern California province would supply the greatest variety of rocks for an avid collector," writes Sharp, "the answer would surely be 'Mojave Desert.' The menu offered equals that of a first-class cafeteria."

If we accept the idea of the desert as one big Hard Rock Cafe (hardly an original concept, judging by MTV), we can easily imagine the appetite of miners upon being presented with it. Their toothmarks and droppings pervade the Mojave in the form of pits and piles, scars and blotches, diggings and workings, all clearly visible on the verdureless hills. Under such circumstances, as Sharp observes, "most of the common metallic elements have been sought and discovered." Namely antimony, copper, gold, iron, lead, lithium, molybdenum, silver, thorium, tin, tungsten, uranium, and zinc.

Today the Mojave's most important minerals include none so sexy as these. Its premier products are sand and gravel, employed (along with limestone and gypsum from Lucerne and Antelope Valleys) in making plaster and cement. At Mountain Pass along I-15 between Las Vegas and

Barstow, a mine owned by the Molycorp Corporation offers up most of the world's rare-earth minerals (cerium, lanthanum, neodymium), which are used in fiber optics, gasoline refining, and color TVs. At Boron between Barstow and Mojave, the largest borax deposit on Earth is being removed (at the rate of ten thousand tons a day) from a mile-wide open pit. Fifty miles to the north, evaporate brines in 330,000-year-old Searles playa—the 400-foot-thick bed of a vanished six-hundred-fifty-foot-deep lake, part of the Pleistocene pluvial chain that originated with Owens Lake and ended in Death Valley—harbor 98 of the 105 known elements, which have congealed into commercial quantities of salt, soda ash, borax, tungsten, and potash. At its current rate of production (seven thousand pounds per minute), the North American Chemical Corporation expects it will take a couple of centuries for the reserves to peter out. Even in the 1800s, this type of sedimentary deposit—industriously dug and diligently hauled, year in and year out, from the forbidding region around Death Valley—was the most profitable enterprise in the desert.

Mining in the Mojave effectively began with the first forty-niners who found themselves in that infernal sink. All had been members of a hundred-plus wagon train that—having arrived too late in the year to cross the snowbound Sierra Nevada, which had taken its infamous toll on the Donner Party three years earlier—instead turned south from Salt Lake City along the Spanish Trail, led by a veteran of the Mormon Battalion named Jefferson Hunt. The antsy argonauts' enthusiasm for the alternative is indicated by the fact that they soon changed their name from the San Joaquin Company to the Sand Walking Company. Two weeks into this detour, they were overtaken by one O. K. Smith, a twenty-year-old New Yorker who announced that he was heading for California by way of the "Walker cutoff"—a supposed shortcut through the desert along an east-west mountain range. According to one member of Hunt's party, upon the hatching of this notion "a hearsay delusion seized the camp." More than a hundred wagons voted to follow Smith, with only seven choosing to stay on the proven Spanish Trail. "If you want to follow Captain Smith, I can't help it," Hunt is reported to have said as they departed in the first week of November. "But I believe you will get into the jaws of hell."

Within a week, three-quarters of the defectors had turned back. To begin with, there is no east-west escarpment in the Basin and Range. The party soon found itself stymied at a place they named Mount Misery, from which—vowing to die facing west if it came to that—O. K. Smith led his animals down a steep canyon impossible for the others to follow. Only about two dozen wagons chose to keep looking for a way around it; upon embarking, they split into a hodgepodge of groups, including the Jayhawkers of Illinois, the Bugsmashers of Georgia, and the families of John Arcan, Asabel Bennett, and Harry Wade. Eventually even their seducer would forgo his oath and turn back: having begun to eat his own horses somewhere north of the present-day Las Vegas, Smith was rescued on the brink of starvation by the last party to leave Salt Lake that year.

As the wagons persisted through the pitiless terrain, many were cut up and burned to make jerky from slaughtered oxen, refashioned into two-wheeled carts, or simply left behind. The groups continued to fracture as they guessed their way west, but by Christmas all found themselves in the lowest, hottest place in the Western Hemisphere. The Arcans, Bennetts, and Wades went directly across the salt flats near Badwater, repeatedly breaking through the crust and sinking in the mud, trying to reach the foot of the Panamint Mountains. From there the Wades struck out to the south and, unbeknownst to the others, escaped the valley by way of Wingate Wash. The Bennetts and Arcans, however, decided that two young men in their party, William Manly and John Rogers, should go ahead on foot and return with emergency provisions.

In a mission that Manly later described in his book *Death Valley in '49*, they made it to civilization and back in twenty-six days, by which time the Bennetts and Arcans had given up hope of salvation. Upon returning, Manly and Rogers—seeing no one stirring as they approached the camp, and having found the corpse of another argonaut while they were reentering the valley—fired a rifle shot from a distance, bringing the incredulous, emaciated families from beneath their stripped wagons shouting, "The boys have come!" Still another three weeks of hardship would pass before they reached civilization, bringing to four months (luckily for them, the four least meteorologically oppressive months of the year) their trip through an area that can now be crossed in a day.

As they were departing the basin on February 15, 1850, Manly gazed backward from the Panamints and, overcome with relief at deliverance, bid "goodbye to Death Valley." Within a few years, as Richard Lingenfelter observes in *Death Valley and the Amargosa*, "the cursed name they had left on the land and all of the sensational rumors of riches and horrors that had grown out of their ordeal had already transformed that lonely piece of desert into the deadliest, richest, and most mysterious spot in America."

The tales of riches around Death Valley originated with the Jayhawkers and Bugsmashers and those few forty-niners who had stayed with Jefferson Hunt. As to the latter, Lingenfelter observes: "It seems a whimsy of fate that with all the gold seekers trudging down the Spanish Trail in the fall of 1849, the discovery of gold [near Death Valley] was made by two Mormon missionaries bound for the South Seas." Namely James Brown and Addison Pratt, who, while scouting the trail for a spring on December 1, noticed a scattering of loose quartz in a rocky pass, which led them to look around for gold. Having found a few flakes, they blabbed about it unreservedly when they reached the settlements at Christmas, and within weeks, other parties were venturing out and returning with tales of a mountain of metal.

At that point the Jayhawkers and Bugsmashers were still trying to get out of Death Valley—a feat that they eventually accomplished by way of today's Towne Pass. Along the way, a Georgian named Jim Martin found a chunk of silver ore on a flank of Tucki Mountain; carrying it with him to California, where he had it made into a gunsight, he bucked the trend among his companions, who had been burying their own gold coins in the desert, trying to get rid of extra weight. (Some later came back looking for the cache without success.) Similarly, two young Jayhawkers—a German named John Goler and an unidentified companion—found some gold in a dry wash south of Searles Lake, but at that point Goler was interested only in finding water. The upshot was a pair of legends— the Lost Gunsight and Lost Goler Lodes—which spread like a virus among fortune hunters in the foothills of the Sierra Nevada.

Over the next few decades, hundreds of prospectors would scour the environs of Death Valley—including, oddly enough, Manly and Bennett who had almost expired there, but not Martin who had actually found silver. Leaving aside the working conditions, which were sufficiently barren of civilized comforts as to preclude even shade from the sun, those who found promising deposits soon learned the difference between striking ore and mining it at a profit. Chipping at hard rock with a hammer and steel, a typical miner could make about six inches of progress per day; in order to be refined into metal, the ore had to be smelted in a furnace or crushed in a steam-driven stamp mill, which required water or wood—two commodities notably absent from the area. Before the advent of railroads, shipping ore out by wagon was so expensive that the rock had to be rich indeed to realize any return. Still, in a tradition that continues to the present day, none of this precluded the mining of distant stockholders, more than one of whom lost investments in reportedly fabulous, decidedly remote, and ultimately unprofitable mines.

When the Comstock Lode was discovered on the heels of the gold rush, speculators both sober and silly began to imagine an underground river of minerals running all the way to Mexico. In the early 1860s, strikes in southern Nevada and northern Arizona seemed to bear this theory out, leading as they did to yet more silver and copper discoveries—Providence, Ivanpah, Rock Spring, and others—in the East Mojave. In the late 1860s, Cerro Gordo, an enormous deposit in the Inyo Mountains above Owens Lake, injected Los Angeles with silver capital in the same way that the Comstock had infused San Francisco. In 1872, the greatest bonanza yet was reported in the Panamints: recalling the specter of the Lost Gunsight, a trio of prospectors led by Richard Jacobs found a valley streaked with quartz at the crest of aptly named Surprise Canyon. Everyone in his group, including a half-dozen bandits who had been tailing the prospectors, staked out a claim, with Jacobs modestly calling his "the Wonder of the World."

The mineral belt turned out to be two and a half miles wide and five miles long. Believing that Jacobs & Company had found the "California Comstock," Nevada senators John Jones and William Stewart—both of whom had parlayed success at the real-life Comstock into great personal wealth, not to mention membership in the U.S. Congress—forked over a quarter of a million 1874 dollars for the Panamint mines, detonating the biggest boom yet in the vicinity of Death Valley. The senators quickly incorporated nine companies (with a total capital cost of $50 million), craftily retaining ownership of the one that milled ore for the others. Twelve miles up this claustrophobic cleft in parched and precipitous mountains, they built a complex of offices and warehouses, a reservoir, a store, a stamp mill, and a tramway. Just as Stewart and his business partner, Trenor Park, had done with a previous venture—the Emma Mine in Utah—they began shipping ore to England, where it could spur yet more excitement among foreign investors. Meanwhile, the Los Angeles and

Independence Railroad was incorporated for the sole purpose of connecting Surprise Canyon with Santa Monica. After the twenty-stamp mill went on line, silver bullion left the camp in the form of four-hundred-pound ingots, designed to be gravitationally impervious to swarms of outlaws hovering in the area.

By the winter of 1874–75, the town of Panamint City had two thousand people, two dozen saloons, two banks, a barber, a butcher, a baker, a triweekly newspaper, and one of the highest homicide rates in the history of the United States. Six hundred mining claims had been filed, which soon unearthed the fact that although the surface deposits in Surprise Canyon were inarguably rich, the underlying rock was really rather poor. Coexisting with antimonates of copper, lead, iron, and zinc, it was only a tenth as valuable as the quartz exposed in the cliffs. The senators consolidated their companies and reduced their stock prices; they continued to develop the site, but the population of Panamint City dwindled. Then, in August 1875, William Ralston's Bank of California went belly-up, exploding many a Comstock fortune and igniting general financial panic. Finally, the following February, the House Committee on Foreign Affairs convened an inquiry into the so-called Emma Mine Swindle, wherein Stewart and Park were accused of defrauding their foreign investors with the alleged aid of the U.S. ambassador to England.

The upshot among American speculators was a pronounced reticence when it came to putting money into Panamint. Thus—within two weeks of the hearings' adjournment, and less than two years since they'd acquired the mines—Jones, Stewart, and Park agreed that it was time to shut down the mill. They suffered a net loss of $100,000, which was merely a third of the amount in the bag held by their investors. Even the promised railroad reached only as far as Cajon Pass; it hadn't even penetrated the Mojave. On May 17, 1876—the day after the last shipment of silver from Surprise Canyon—William Workman, one of the two bankers who'd been financing the railroad, committed suicide, taking his place in eternity alongside the Wonder of the World.

The same year that the Panamint deposits were discovered, Congress had acted aggressively to encourage mining, which was contributing so much energy to the "settlement" of the West. Signed by President Ulysses S. Grant, the General Mining Law of 1872 essentially awarded ownership of minerals on federal land to anybody who found them; to be considered valid, a mining claim had to contain minerals "in a quantity and of a quality as would justify a person of ordinary prudence to expend further time and money with the reasonable prospect of success in developing a profitable mine." No royalties on minerals would be assessed by the government; the only financial requirement was that the claimant perform one hundred dollars' worth of work on his site each year. If he wanted to, a miner could also "patent" his claim—i.e., buy the land from the government for a maximum price of five dollars per acre. It was permissible to build a road through adjoining federal land to reach one's own claim site, and if somebody found evidence of unclaimed minerals beneath property owned by somebody else, the finder could tunnel below to remove them. At the time, such concepts as environmental restoration received about as much consideration as the rights of rattlesnakes. Minerals were seen as the one reward of an otherwise worthless, even hostile environment; the only conceivable reason for their existence was that God had put them there in order for Man to further himself and test his mettle (i.e., assay his metal).

Still, metals—hard as they were to retrieve and market at a profit—wouldn't prove the most valuable minerals in the desert. The same year that Congress passed the mining law and Jacobs announced his discovery of the Wonder of the World, a young man from Michigan named Francis Marion Smith was working as a woodchopper north of Death Valley. He had come to California looking for gold, but when he heard that ulexite (a.k.a. "cottonball" or crystalline borax) had been found in the Nevada desert, he went there to market the firewood that would be needed for processing. Until then, raw borax—a compound of sodium, boron, and water that had been used for millennia in ceramics and pharmaceuticals—had been practically unknown in North America, with most of the world's supply coming from Italy, Chile, and Tibet. It had been discovered in northern California in the 1850s, which served to drop the domestic price from fifty to thirty cents a pound; that still amounted to six hundred dollars per ton, but in the 1860s, total domestic production was only twelve tons per year.

Smith soon filed his own borax claim at a place called Teel's Marsh. Within a couple of decades, he had become known as Borax Smith—the biggest producer of the chemical in the country, and as such the holder of a $20-million fortune that included estates on San Francisco Bay and eastern Long Island. He couldn't have accomplished any of this, however, without one William Tell Coleman*—a tough-minded businessman and vigilante-committee leader from San Francisco who had already cornered the market on borax distribution in the western United States. Hawking the chemical's diverse household uses for washing, starching, dressing wounds, preserving milk, removing dandruff, treating epilepsy, and getting rid of moths and roaches (to name only a few), Smith and Coleman eventually controlled the entire U.S. borax industry, most of which emanated from the northern Mojave Desert.

The Death Valley Borax and Salt Mining District was created after the paysalt was found there by a prospector named Aaron Winters, who had previously been eking out a mean existence in the desert to the east. Another prospector had shown Winters how to identify borax: doused with sulfuric acid and alcohol and lit with a match, it gave rise to a green flame. As soon as this adviser disappeared over the horizon, Winters hotfooted down to Death Valley, where he'd seen some similar-looking stuff near Furnace Creek. As legend has it, he waited for nightfall, applied the chemicals, struck a match, and ejaculated with ecstasy at the emerald effects. Coleman subsequently bought his claim for twenty thousand dollars, which Winters spent on a ranch that he later lost to back taxes, living out his life as a hermit in the Shadow Mountains.

In the five years between 1883 and 1888, Coleman shipped ten thousand tons of borax out of Death Valley. The heart of his operation was the Harmony Borax Works in the middle of the basin—a literal salt mine where Coleman had sixty-seven processing tanks with a total capacity of 125,000 gallons. He paid his workers fifty dollars a month to run steam engines, stir brine, and collect mud and crystals separated from the salts that Chinese laborers scraped from the playa; in summer, when the air temperature hit 130, Coleman moved the operation uphill to Amargosa—not necessarily to spare the workers but because borax wouldn't crystallize in the heat. The nearest railroad junction was 165 miles away, so loads were carried by sixteen-foot-long wagons with iron-rimmed wheels six feet high. The wagons were dispatched in pairs, each trailing a twelve-hundred-gallon water tank—all of which, when fully loaded, weighed thirty-six tons.

---

*A requirement for success in the industry, apparently, was a folkloric combination of first and middle names.

The "horsepower" was, of course, provided by a team of twenty mules—or, to be precise, eighteen mules and two draft horses that could handle the tongue on turns. When the eighty-foot-long line of animals negotiated a bend, the chain connecting them would naturally remain straight, so to avoid sending the wagon into a wall or over a cliff, some of the mules were trained to jump the chain and pull it away from the turn. Such contingencies were common along the convoluted route, which led from the valley sink (initially over the Devil's Golf Course, a field of salt-encrusted hummocks that had to be graded flat with a sledgehammer) past Bennett's Well (where the forty-niner families had been rescued by Manly and Rogers), southwest through Wingate Pass (where the Wades, striking out alone, had escaped Death Valley), south along the Slate Range through present-day China Lake Naval Weapons Center past Pilot Knob to Mojave. The round-trip took three weeks; purportedly, there was never a breakdown or animal casualty, though one swamper did kill a driver with a shovel. (A San Bernardino jury ruled it self-defense.)

Economically, there was only one problem with such productivity: It dropped the price of borax to six cents a pound. To bring it back into line, Smith, Coleman, and other producers agreed to limit their output, but Coleman would later be undone by other pursuits. He lost a million dollars, for example, on a raisin venture in 1887, forcing him to put his borax operations up for sale. Unfortunately, just as a two-million-dollar deal was about to be closed with some Englishmen, a bill was introduced in Congress to remove the tariff that had protected the domestic borax industry throughout most of the 1880s. Coleman's short-lived empire collapsed, and in 1893 he was pronounced dead due to "a general breaking up of the vital forces."

In 1890, Smith had bought all of Coleman's holdings for half a million dollars. This assured the new Borax King a monopoly on both production and distribution, which he commandeered through his vast Pacific Coast Borax Company. At the suggestion of a young consultant, Stephen Mather—later to become the founding director of the National Park Service—Smith next decided to mine the legends of Death Valley, labeling his product "Twenty Mule Team Borax" and sending a wagon team on a promotional tour through the East. In reality, mules hadn't been used to haul borax in years; production was now centered in Calico, fifty miles south of Death Valley and only eight miles north of the Sante Fe Railroad.

Years earlier, after Aaron Winters had found borax, a neighbor of his named Phi Lee had tried the flame trick on some salts protruding from Furnace Creek Wash—rocks that everyone else had ignored, believing that borax existed only in dry lakebeds. As it turned out, Lee's flame also burned green. The rock was a previously unknown form of calcium borate, gradually lifted from the playa by a thrust fault in the wash. Ironically called colemanite, it was found in considerable quantity at Calico, where, in order to connect with a nearby railroad siding, Smith built a narrow-gauge track with two locomotives named Francis and Marion. He also established a $1.25-million refinery at Bayonne, New Jersey, to supplement the existing one at Alameda, California; not long thereafter he merged his operation with a British company to create Borax Consolidated, Ltd.—one of history's first multinational corporations, through which Smith gained a worldwide grip on borax production.

Still, the bulk of domestic product came from Calico. When that began to peter out—as it soon did in response to the Twenty Mule Team hype—Smith turned his gaze back to Death Valley. A silver rush was by then under way at Tonopah, Nevada, and he decided to capitalize on it by building a short-line railroad that would pass within a few miles of the Lila C., yet another mine that he'd inherited from Coleman. To smooth the way for the "Tonopah and Tidewater" (a poetic reference to its intended destination on the coast), Smith solicited the cooperation of Senator William Clark, the Montana copper magnate who had nearly completed the San Pedro, Los Angeles, and Salt Lake Railroad through the Mojave and Great Basin Deserts by way of a dusty little oasis called Las Vegas. In Smith's mind, he succeeded in winning Clark's approval of a short line from Las Vegas to Tonopah with a spur to Death Valley and the Lila C. Within a couple of months of their handshake, Smith's men had completed twelve miles' worth of grading and were ready to start laying track.

First, however, they needed to make a rail connection with the SP, LA, & SL. But when they asked for permission to do so, Clark's lawyers ordered them to cease and desist. Smith's men *had* noticed that one of Clark's companies was busy building an auto route alongside the railroad right-of-way; moreover, the SP, LA, & SL had been charging them exorbitant freight on redwood ties that were arriving to build the tracks. Wiring the absent senator for an explanation, Smith was informed that Clark was on vacation in Europe. As it happened, new mining strikes had recently been made at Bullfrog and Rhyolite, midway between Las Vegas and Tonopah; Smith deduced that the honorable senator had had second thoughts about who should take advantage of the opportunity. Upon returning from Europe, Clark confirmed these suspicions, announcing the formation of the Las Vegas and Tonopah Railroad and (ultimately) paying Smith thirty thousand dollars for work already completed. Clark insisted that this had been his plan all along—the only Tonopah and Tidewater Railroad he'd approved, he maintained, was the side spur to Death Valley.

Smith hadn't become the Borax King, however, by shrinking from cutthroat competition. In a flash, he made a deal to instead begin building the T & T from the Santa Fe siding at Ludlow, California. The route from there to the Nevada mines ran 167 miles north through the middle of the Mojave—straight across Broadwell, Soda, and Silver Lakes. With surveyors working just ahead of construction crews, 75 miles of track were thrown down between November 1905 and May 1906. But then the pace became literally too torrid. When summer struck, Smith's foreman (in Lingenfelter's words) "often had three crews in the field at the same time—one on the way home, having just quit, one just starting work; and one on the way out, to replace the second crew when they quit." Out of one group of a hundred laborers who started work in June, only seventeen were found to be working—and nine of those were spraying water on the other eight. When the line reached the tortuous Amargosa River canyon, requiring three trestles and massive rearrangement of eroded banks and cliffs, work came to a standstill. Even after it resumed in the fall with nine hundred men and eight hundred animals, six more months would be required to move the line twelve miles.

The T & T arrived in Tecopa in May 1907. Smith's first trainload of borate ore left the Lila C. that August, and the railroad reached the Rhyolite area on October 30—one week after the Knickerbocker Trust had fallen, and a full year since Clark's line had passed through on its way from Las Vegas to Tonopah. Meanwhile, a third railroad—the Bullfrog Goldfield—had begun serving the area in June. The local mining booms were over; the financial Panic of 1907 was under way. The T & T did fulfill its original purpose, ultimately carrying more than three hundred thousand tons of colemanite away from Death Valley, and even achieving some success at transporting local citizens (its Pullman service to Los Angeles was shorter, faster, and less expensive than Clark's). But periodically the "dry" lakes at Silver, Soda, and Broadwell flooded, forcing detours and disrupting service. The T & T never made a profit, and with the arrival of the Second World War, its tracks were torn up and abandoned.

In any case, within a half-dozen years of completing the line, Smith himself had been toppled from his throne. Drowning in debt from speculations in Oakland streetcars and real estate, the Borax King was stripped of his stock in Borax Consolidated and forced to resign in 1914. At almost exactly the same time, a doctor drilling a well for a homestead found borates in the desert midway between Mojave and Calico. A dozen years later, Borax Consolidated—sans Borax Smith—discovered that this deposit, a buried two-hundred-foot-thick, eighteen-million-year-old lakebed, extended underground for hundreds of acres. Now mined by U.S. Borax—a conglomerate consisting of Smith's old Pacific Coast Borax Company, its onetime competitor U.S. Potash, and the Rio Tinto-Zinc Corporation, Ltd.—it has been the United States' primary source of borax ever since.

After the Jayhawkers emerged from Death Valley, tales of the Lost Goler Lode slumbered through the 1870s and 1880s, overshadowed by the silver excitement at Panamint and Cerro Gordo. In 1893, however, placer gold was discovered in the El Paso Mountains midway between Mojave and Searles Lake, attracting a spate of prospectors to the quickly christened Goler Mining District. Two of them, Frederic Mooers and William Langdon, found a few gleaming traces in a range to the south, practically within sight of the twenty-mule-team haul route. Neither, however, was inspired to keep looking until the following year, when Mooers learned that miners at the nearby Summit dry diggings were planning to reinvestigate the site. This prompted him to recruit one John Singleton and another man from San Bernardino named Charles Burcham, who had a wagon team at his disposal, courtesy of his wife: Dr. Rose La Monte Burcham, a physician who had staked her husband to two years of prospecting that were just then approaching an end.

The spring of 1895 was a great one for wildflowers. The trio set out on an April morning, ostensibly for the water hole at Goler. As soon as they left sight of Summit, however, they turned south toward Mooers's former find. When they got there, the sandy washes didn't turn up anything, so Burcham and Singleton left their recruiter in camp and climbed a red-tinted peak. Along the way, Singleton—a carpenter by trade—hammered off a chunk of rock and, upon looking it over, called out to Burcham. As legend inevitably has it, the latter responded with the same four words that Aaron Winters had uttered to his wife (also named Rose) upon discovering borax in Death Valley: *"By God we're rich!"*

In this case, however, the pronouncement came true, helped along by considerable savvy on the part of the Burchams. After feverishly staking out claims, the three men were equally anxious to file them, knowing that the so-called sagebrush telegraph would immediately draw miners from miles around. Burcham, who had driven the wagon in their first diversionary maneuver, now hatched another scheme for throwing the competition off. He loaded some sacks with a worthless, iron-stained ore called bull quartz, threw them onto his wagon, and set off for Summit; when the miners there asked him what he'd found, he said only that he thought the place looked "pretty good." Then he wandered away from the wagon, counting on curiosity to carry the day. Sure enough, the loiterers peeked into the sacks, giving rise to general hilarity at the trio's foolishness—and affording them the time they needed to record the claim, which they named Rand after a distant discovery on the Dark Continent. This touched off a festival of Boer nomenclature in the area, even though—in homage to the spring flowers and the title of a pulp novel that Burcham was in the midst of reading—they later changed the name to the Yellow Aster.

After filing his claim, Burcham went to San Bernardino to give his wife the news. She warned him not to sell out in the way that Aaron Winters had done at the behest of William Coleman. As it turned out, the advice was well timed: as soon as Burcham got back to the desert, he learned that one O. B. Stanton had proposed to develop the Yellow Aster in return for a six-month option to buy it for half a million dollars. At the mere mention of such numbers, Mooers and Singleton had immediately agreed—but Burcham, heeding his wife, refused, bringing eventual lawsuits not only from Stanton but from William Langdon, who had been with Mooers when he found the first flakes. Such litigation was predictable in hindsight. Though the panhandling prospectors could hardly have comprehended it, their claim was located on an interstice between three geologic faults, in which were deposited millions of tons of severely fractured and highly oxidized Precambrian schists and Mesozoic intrusives. In its tectonically tortured soil, the place was lousy with precious metal. The Yellow Aster went on to reward its finders—at prices a fraction of today's—with $12 million in gold.

Within a month of finding out about her husband's strike, Dr. Burcham had closed her medical practice and moved to the Mojave. She became the bookkeeper and secretary of the Yellow Aster Mining and Milling Company, which she actually ran (despite the attachment of Singleton's name to the presidency) with an iron fist. A tent camp had sprung up almost immediately in Randsburg; in October the first frame building was built; by Christmas the Rand Mining District had been organized; by the following year several new mines—the Butte, the Baltic, the Sunshine, the King Solomon, the Hard Cash, the Big Dyke, the Dos Picannini, the Operator Divide—had been established, a post office was in place, a newspaper had begun publishing, and the first shooting had occurred over a crap game. A rival town (Johannesburg, naturally) took shape a mile away. Compared to the chaos of the mining camp, this latter place was purposefully laid out, to the point of having piped water and a municipal golf course (even if the latter consisted largely of sand). When the Randsburg Railway was completed in 1898 (connecting with the tracks at Mojave, forty miles to the southwest), it got only as far as Johannesburg—people and ore still had to travel the last mile by wagon or Model T.

Nevertheless, despite recurring fires and a smallpox epidemic, Randsburg—at the vortex of what would prove the most productive mineral region in the Mojave Desert—became one of the West's great boom towns. Stagecoaches disgorged travelers from the south five times per day, pumping the population to thirty-five hundred by 1899. Unlike Panamint City, it was a lively if not especially wild place, with a school, a theater, a dance hall, and an annual Fourth of July picnic supplementing the usual assortment of saloons and brothels (though at least one observer attributed the quality of life in the town to its high-grade whiskey). Legally, the place operated as a constabulary district, which meant that a typical troublemaker would simply be given a bottle of water and told to get out of town. In 1902 a one-hundred-stamp mill began operation, running around the clock and producing $100,000 a month; the Yellow Aster had 150 employees, but in 1903 they went on strike against Singleton's Desert Mine Operators Association for a pay raise of fifty cents per day. (Underground miners at the time were making three dollars a day, topsiders two and a half.) Two days later, a section of Randsburg burned down, partly because the town's fire-alarm bell rope had been severed and its water supply mysteriously shut off. Within three months, strikebreakers from Missouri had taken most of the jobs in the mine.

In 1905, just when it seemed that the Rand boom would go the way of so many others, tungsten was found at Atolia a couple of miles to the south. The resultant Papoose Mine—for a period the largest tungsten mine in the world—would keep things hopping for another dozen years, at which point a silver vein was uncovered next door at Red Mountain. The Yellow Aster continued operating until World War II; after 1905, most of its ore came from a large "Glory Hole" above Randsburg, but by the time the war arrived, workers found that they could make more money in aircraft and auto factories. When Limitation Order L-208 called a halt to mining of nonstrategic minerals in 1942, the Yellow Aster shut down for a period that turned out to last almost forty years. But in the 1980s, it sprang back to life on the back of the cyanide heap-leach revolution.

Throughout the first era of mining in the Mojave, minerals had been winnowed from the earth by digging up ore, pulverizing it in a stamp mill, and treating the resulting powder with a chemical in order to extract the precious metal. For example, sulfuric acid, when applied to copper ore, leaches out the copper in liquid solution. Mercury is capable of extracting 60 percent of the gold in crushed ore, but in 1879 Scottish scientists discovered that cyanide could recover fully 97 percent. It began to be used in the United States in 1895—the same year that gold was discovered in the Rand Mountains—and was employed at the Yellow Aster after the Glory Hole pit was dug.

It wasn't until 1969, however—as rising labor costs and "exhausted" deposits were threatening conventional mining with extinction—that the U.S. Bureau of Mines proposed using cyanide on large, open-air piles.

Ore was dumped into large heaps, which were soaked with cyanide in order to leach out the gold; the runoff collected downslope in a pond, whose pregnant solution was treated with carbon to retrieve the metal. In order to be mined this way, gold doesn't even have to be visible; in fact, the finer the dust, the more susceptible it is to leaching. Twenty tons of ore—uncovered by moving, say, four hundred tons of earth—might produce only a single ounce of gold, but the cost of obtaining it is much cheaper than digging, moving, and milling it the old labor-intensive way. Moreover, the improved recovery rate meant that "spent" or low-grade ore—containing yields of, say, less than .08 ounces per ton—could now be worked at a profit, sometimes at yields of .01 or lower. With modern earthmoving equipment, networks of veins extending over thousands of acres—which, like those around Randsburg, had formerly required miles and miles of underground tunnels—could be mined from one huge pit. Inconceivable to the likes of Mooers, Burcham, and Singleton, millions of dollars could now be made from a single, solitary hole.

As one might imagine, the process was not without environmental consequences. Cyanide breaks down quickly in nature, but if alkaline conditions persist, it can linger in heaps and tailings and affect the local groundwater—especially if the protective liners beneath the piles get torn, which is not unlikely under the weight of millions of tons of ore. More immediately, it was seen to have a directly fatal effect on wildlife; birds and bats, in particular, were drawn from the sky to what looked to them like ponds and lakes in the desert. Thousands of waterfowl died in cyanide heap-leach pools during the 1980s, including nine hundred at a single mine in Nevada. Moreover, heavy metals other than gold—iron, copper, mercury, zinc, cadmium, selenium—are solubilized by the leaching process, collecting and concentrating in tailings silt, creating what some envision as the toxic-cleanup sites of the twenty-first century. Nevertheless, when the price of gold was released from federal control in the 1970s and soared temporarily above eight hundred dollars per ounce, heap-leaching became a worldwide craze. In 1980 a million ounces of gold were mined in the United States; ten years later, that amount had octupled, most of it produced by the new technology. Whereas in 1975 the Mojave Desert had no heap-leach mines at all, in 1988 it had five on public land alone. Many, like the Yellow Aster, were historic mines that had been dormant for decades, awaiting some breakthrough in technology and/or economics in order to return to profitability; now they had both.

As it turned out, many of the new mining companies were incorporated in Canada, where securities laws were more relaxed than in the United States. By contrast, American-based firms, discouraged by the labyrinthian and costly permitting process decreed by the likes of the National Environmental Policy Act, were turning their attention to the Third World. In their absence, the Canadian firms, already accustomed to stiff environmental restrictions at home, were more than willing to mine free gold in the United States—which, under the 1872 law, demanded no more royalties from foreign corporations than it did from its own citizens. As the start-up cost of a heap-leach project ran upward of $50 million, gold mining had now become an international corporate enterprise. In the Mojave, the grizzled prospector with burro and pickax is as relevant to today's operations as stagecoaches are to commerce between Los Angeles and Randsburg.

True to the tradition that located the terminus of the Randsburg Railway in Johannesburg, U.S. Highway 395—the major north-south artery in the West Mojave—bypasses Randsburg a mile downhill. Driving up the connecting road, I assumed I'd arrived when I saw a hardscrabble collection of shacks, house trailers, tin-roofed houses, and junked cars amid the rocks and mesquite. An American flag flew over one house; the window of a stationary silver schoolbus read SMITTYBAGO. Pausing to survey the surroundings, I saw a middle-aged man in a World War I–vintage army suit—goggles, a visored cap, knee-high black boots, and (for personal flair) a black bandanna—mount an old rusted bicycle and coast downhill through the desert in the direction of Goler Wash.

Like Virginia City alongside the Comstock Lode, Randsburg is built on the side of a hill. I soon found myself on Butte Street, the town's main drag, featuring a post office, a general store, a gift shop, and several bars. Apparently the legacy of fires still persisted: one of the lots consisted solely of charred rubble. The mountain where John Singleton had hit the jackpot now looked rather like a volcano: terraced with horizontal dikes in some places, streaked with tailings gravel in others, it presented a convincing facsimile of a flat-topped cinder cone. Dust rose and engines

rumbled behind the high ridgeline beyond the town, which was decorated—inevitably—by a big white letter *R*.

Alongside the road, a sign announced that the Yellow Aster was now
being run by the Rand Mining Company:

> No Trespassing—Hard Hat Area
> Danger: Heavy Equipment Operating
> Cyanide Solutions—Blasting

At the far end of the street was a small public park with sunshades
above its steel picnic tables. Several people were engaging in civic fellowship there, aided by the contents of hand-held brown paper bags.
While eating lunch in the shade, I asked one of them how long he'd been
in Randsburg.

"Two years," he answered.

"What do you do here?"

"Nothing," he declared. "I dropped out."

Next to the park was the town museum, which contained the usual
display of picks, shovels, hammers, horseshoes, irons, arrowheads,
dishes, baby shoes, purple bottles, and faded photographs. One display
case was full of minerals and gemstones. Salt looked like a human brain;
agate was a marbled steak. An old picture displayed the shack of William
"Burro" Schmidt, whose nickname seemed to need a *w* at the end:
known as the "Human Mole," he had spent thirty-six years digging a
mile-long mining tunnel.

I had been advised to look up a guy named Karl Lindblom at the
Randsburg museum. Upon asking for him, however, I learned that he no
longer worked there; reportedly, he could be reached at an airplane
hangar in Trona, the company town (formerly Kerr-McGee, now North
American Chemical) next to Searles Lake, thirty miles away. The place
where I finally found him was a café in Inyokern (a town named for two
counties whose border it adjoins), sitting at a tableful of men considerably older than himself. Karl was a tall, portly, stoop-shouldered, mustachioed, bespectacled thirty-seven-year-old—rather young, it seemed to
me, for an ex-miner.

"I've worked at mines in the El Paso Mountains, in the Panamints, in the White Pines in Nevada, and at the Elephant Eagle—that was Governor Goodwin Knight's mine—at Soledad Mountain near Mojave," he told me. "I got disgusted with it when the government got heavy, but I still get involved at intervals. Every time I do, it's like taking a drink after being in A.A. for twenty years."

When Karl was growing up, his father—a mathematician at the China Lake Naval Weapons Center—had talked about miners so much that Karl became one while he was still a teenager. "I was probably the youngest stamp-mill operator in the world," he said. "My first employer went to jail for selling dynamite to an undercover agent, so then I went to the Butte Mine, where I did an old-fashioned apprenticeship with a guy named Bert Wegman. The Butte was the last old mine in Randsburg, meaning that it had the last stamp mill that wasn't a museum piece. We used a bar-and-arm drill, an old single-stage stationary jumbo compressor, and an 1896 Fairbanks and Morris hoist with wooden shoe brakes and a wooden cone clutch. It was stamp-mill amalgamation followed by vat cyanidization—the stamp mill crushed the ore, and then mercury was poured in with a spoon to adhere with the gold on the wall in an 'amalgam.' The fine particles of gold that the mercury didn't catch went into a dewatering plant; coarse sand went into a cyanide vat, finer stuff into a 'pachuka' tank that dissolved the gold into a solution but didn't alter the other rock in any way. The tailings came out. Most of the old piles you see in the desert are tailings dumps—that material is finer and lighter than the dirt around it.

"I worked full-time at the Butte for four years," Karl went on. "During one ten-month period, I made five hundred dollars. I walked to work, turned off everything in the house, cooked over a sagebrush fire, used a Dutch oven, and baked my own bread. Other times I made so much money that I bought an airplane. In the seventies I believed there would be another depression—droves of people would come up here, and I'd reopen the Butte Mine and put 'em to work. But the new environmental and safety laws make it inoperable. Dynamite used to be so cheap you wouldn't even count it in your budget; you could buy it from the hardware store. Then it became regulated to where it's now more expensive than labor. There's an FBI background check, fingerprints, a bond; the manufacturers have federal regulations, the sellers have insurance problems, and the transport drivers have these huge asinine restrictions. In 1976, the labor laws were a book six inches thick. The California Division of Mines and Geology used to be for helping miners, but now it's for reclaiming mines—it's packed with flower-throwing, tofu-eating wackos.

"The Butte was hammered by a lot of governmental agencies right when my partner and I hit one of the richest veins of gold in Randsburg history," Karl went on. "We had the mills loaded with ore, but we had a hundred-year-old unlined tailings pond and we didn't have the right permits. Under the new 'hot spot' law, you're supposed to quantify all the chemicals you use—cobalt, chloride, cyanide, et cetera. They found forty vials in an assaying kit I had, and there were eight pages of government paperwork for each one. So we finished milling what we had, and quit. After the revolution comes, and we've lined up every civil servant in America and decapitated them, we'll mine it again."

Karl eventually agreed to give me a tour of the area. The next day I met him at a trailer off 395, where he was employed by a local mine as an "environmental consultant." It was a windy day, and as we drove south toward Randsburg, visibility along the highway was obscured by dust from the Rand mining operation. Surveying the simulated volcanoes, Karl told me that they had only been there for the last four years. "Each one of those benches used to be a mountainside that's gone now," he said. "The Glory Hole has been absorbed into an open pit. Before the Anglo American Mining Company took over the Yellow Aster in 1930, a tunnel was drilled perpendicular to the vein and lined with dynamite; then the top was blown off the mountain—it went up and came down (as ore). They had thirty or forty tram tracks, one for each worker.

"The Butte was a classic mine capitalized by sale of stock in the 1890s. The owners bought it from H. C. Ramie in 1897; he got fourteen thousand dollars for it, blew all the money on girls and liquor, and had to go back to work for the mine as an employee—not even a supervisor, but a mucker. In the early days, a typical working stiff had a choice between a steady job herding cattle, or working in a gold mine on shares, where he'd have a chance of making some real money. Old-timers would go out and find somebody—usually a hardware-store owner—to grubstake them; they'd use the money to buy minimal supplies—coal for sharpening a drill steel, say—and eat bacon and beans and flapjacks. The grubstaker would keep funding them as long as they kept digging. In Randsburg, Judge Ed Maginnis—the youngest judge in California history—grubstaked a lot of the mines and thus ended up owning them. When he died, his sister got his holdings and willed them to the church; the current owner bought it from the church.

"The Butte is in an area that has one vein, as opposed to thousands of little ones like the Baltic. There are still a lot of tunnels under Randsburg. The Little Butte Mine goes down six hundred feet. In the 1906 earthquake, it filled up with water, which supplied the area for fifteen miles around. But in the fifties, the Tehachapi quake turned it off again."

Passing through Johannesburg, I noted the Afrikaaner motif on the local street signs. Karl said that Oompaul Street means "Uncle Paul," while Owego Street is named after a Boer general. "It was just a fad that caught on. They used to hook up with their sister city in South Africa by shortwave radio every year until apartheid put an end to it. Zillions of South Africans still come through here now, and I've never met one I didn't like."

We went uphill to Randsburg and drove slowly along Butte Street, repassing the row of bars: the Joint, the Hill, the White House Saloon. According to Karl, the latter was a watering hole for tourists. "When I first came here, this was truly a ghost town. The greatest tragedy in Randsburg history was when they formed a special district to administer the water. Before that, a spring owned by an old turn-of-the-century water company produced nine thousand gallons a day, and a well produced three thousand—all to feed a town of several hundred people. Each family was allotted three hundred gallons per month, at one cent per gallon. But in 1974 the voters formed a special district, which made it easy for lowlifers to move in—drug derelicts who needed a cheap place to live and retirees who didn't save money when they were young, so they can't live in Palm Springs. They don't care much for the mine—or for the dirt bikers, either. Then there are the L.A. yuppies who move up here and replace shiplapped siding and wood-frame windows with plywood mobile-home siding and aluminum window frames. I've seen trailers disguised to look like houses, but this was the first time I'd seen a house disguised to look like a trailer.

"When I came here, the [biggest bar] still had antlers on the wall and an old cash register on the bar, but the new owner was an L.A. interior designer who threw out the antiques and decorated it according to some 'old-fashioned' style he'd seen in pizza parlors. He said he didn't want any locals there—'rejects from the Joint,' as he put it. Except for Olga, who owns the Joint, the Randsburg Merchants Association is composed entirely of L.A. yuppies. Of course, you have to realize that around here, everything from Lancaster to Mexico is considered L.A."

I asked what he meant by the reference to dirt bikers.

"Off-road motorcycles are unlicensed," he said. "It's illegal to ride them on roads, but Randsburg is surrounded by private property and mining claims, so in '88 the merchants got together and proposed a dirt-bike trail to bring the bikers and their business into town. Not everybody liked the idea, so they held a public hearing, during which the county sheriff said that a dirt biker was lower than the lowest drug-dealing Harley rider, which prompted the president of the merchants to call him a Nazi. So when the next big holiday weekend came along, there were six sheriff's squad cars, two highway patrolmen, and some deputies up on a hill with binoculars, all coordinating with the local residents by cordless phone. They herded the dirt bikes up, impounded them on a flatbed Peterbilt with a ramp, and gave them the maximum fine. After that, no bikers came to Randsburg any more—which cut the soda-pop and ice-cream business by fifty percent. I, as the agent of the largest private property in town (the Butte), was considered the ringleader."

I'd heard some other talk about friction over private property and mining claims. Greg Thompson, resources staff chief for the Ridgecrest area BLM, told me that "historically, most of Randsburg was put under mining claims. Then people started building on them, but nothing was ever done about it, so now there are about thirty private structures on public land. There have been some congressional inquiries, but the residents aren't unified, and they're wary of the BLM. There's been a lot of feuding and hard feelings over it."

Karl had a different perspective. "Nobody ever gave a damn about that until recently," he said. "In the old days, they were gentlemen—they didn't care who owned the house and who owned the land; Randsburg was a *mining camp*. But the weekend warriors from L.A. don't understand that. Their greatest worry in the world is that somebody might live on somebody else's property."

We drove up a back street so Karl could show me an example. "In the 1890s," he said, "a guy had a good-sized claim here that became the Good Hope Mine. He filed for a patent, so he owned the surface and mineral rights. But meanwhile miners and families built shacks on the claim. Years later, as the mine became idle, its board of directors decided to subdivide; they went to the residents and offered to let them buy the lots underneath their houses. The deeds for the two were separate because the houses had been built before the lots existed. The houses had common-law, 'quit-claim' deeds—that is, the person who built the house gave the deed to the person who bought it from him. That might have happened fifteen or twenty times before the mining company decided to sell the lots.

"The county assessor drew up maps, but they didn't bother to survey or take into consideration where the cliffs and gullies were. The buyers had to guess which lots their houses were on, and a lot of times they guessed wrong. One lady named Winona, who lived right there"—he pointed at a small, wood-frame house—"realized eventually that she actually owned the lot next door, which had another house on it. So she offered to sell *that* lot to the guy who owned the house—Beatnik Bob, the town drunk. Well, Robert was belligerent, so she took him to court, but then Bob said, 'Here's my deed,' so the judge ruled in his favor. Winona then took the deed for her house and the deed for Bob's lot and convinced a guy in L.A. that it was for *both* lots. He bought her house thinking it was Bob's house. So then *he* went to evict Bob, whose defense was that he not only had the deed for the house but had been paying taxes on the property. He said, 'You can buy the house from me, or I'll remove it from your lot.' But since he was the town drunk, he ran out of money, his lawyer abandoned him, and the guy from L.A. won. Meanwhile, Winona sold her house a second time, took the money, and ran. The buyer died before he realized what had been done to him. I don't know who owns her place now."

We started the truck and drove farther up the hill, past the guard shack at the Rand Mining Company entrance, whose American flag flapped and snapped at half-mast, vigorously mourning a recently deceased Richard Nixon. We parked beyond it in a dirt turnout near the top of the mountain, where we could peer through a chain-link fence at earthmovers working the Baltic Mine—the project that the Rand Mining Company had tackled after the Yellow Aster. One-hundred-ton trucks were hauling ore up from a pit and dumping it into heaps, which graders were smoothing into level piles that would soon be doused with cyanide. "First they strip the overburden off," Karl explained. "Then they put down a layer of plastic and cover it with sand to protect it. Then comes coarse gravel with pipe embedded in it; the ore goes on top of the gravel, and the pipes collect the liquid as it seeps down, taking the gold out in solution."

I noticed that one of the workers was dusting the piles with lime, which blew about the site in clouds. "That's the worst job in the mine," Karl said. "Cyanide needs an alkaline environment to survive, and lime raises the pH to ten. This used to be a valley with a lot of little stringer veins—perfect for an open pit. The problem is that the Baltic channel was known for coarse gold, which isn't fine enough to cyanide. If they went to the trouble of milking it, they could do another flotation to catch the coarser gold. But they don't have any real intention of producing gold here. In order to borrow money, you put on a dog-and-pony show, sell stock and create a job for yourself; then, as soon as activity begins, unsophisticated investors buy more stock and the price goes up. The people who make money are the original investors who bought the virgin stock. If the company goes broke, the unsophisticated investors are left holding a piece of paper—but they still get a tax writeoff, so it's win-win for everybody. It's like wildcatting in the oil industry—raising capital through stock equity."

Karl fell silent for a minute as we watched the earth move. Suddenly he said: "In my opinion, historians a hundred years from now will consider heap-leach mining equivalent to hydraulic mining in the nineteenth century. They've taken a magical industry with highly skilled workers and replaced it with a dirt factory. With underground mining, there was never a dull moment—you could get killed at any time. But surface mining is just a job. It has no heart to it. When the federal government forced underground miners into open pits, it took the soul out of the industry. With all their regulations, they're harder on mining than environmentalists are. If there were no labor laws, I believe that the Yellow Aster would be an underground mine today. But I'm an underground miner, and I'm prejudiced."

We started the truck and drove back down Butte Street. At my request, we stopped at the Joint—reportedly the hangout for locals, as opposed to tourists. As soon as we entered its murky interior, a man in a plaid shirt rose from a barstool and captured Karl in a hug. Introducing himself to me as "Ordinary Tom," he sat back down across the bar from the proprietor of the place: a slight, elderly woman named Olga with a gravelly voice and dyed auburn hair, who almost seemed to be hiding in the dark behind the bar.

Karl and I took two stools alongside Ordinary Tom, who eventually asked me if I'd ever been in the service. I decided not to reveal my status as a conscientious objector; instead I commented on the wind outside.

"I'll never get used to it," Olga said suddenly from her place in the dark. "It's nerve-racking. But it goes with the desert."

Tom divulged that he'd just begun working at a recycling plant in Mojave. "It's the first time I haven't worked in a hard-rock metal mine," he claimed.

When I said something about that being a highly symbolic career change, he picked up the thread without hesitation. "I can't understand why we have such persecution from the government," he said. "If you don't farm it, you mine it—those are the only two things you can do. The next thing I want to see Greenpeace do is go to Iowa and stop all the corn growing because it's destroying the flora and fauna."

Karl said that the Baltic Mine project had been delayed by two things: desert-tortoise breeding and "piles of old tin cans that archaeologists call 'middens.' The Antiquities Act says they're archaeological artifacts if they're older than fifty years."

"You can go inside an Indian tipi and find things that are mined," Tom insisted. "Pigments for paints and stuff like that." He finished off a Bud Light; as soon as he did, Olga wordlessly provided him with another.

I mentioned to Karl that I perceived a less-than-sanguine attitude toward the Rand Mining Company on his part.

"I don't care too much for them," he admitted. "They're unprincipled about payments and resistant to the needs of workers, landowners, and the government. They took great pride in hiring a chemical engineer to be their manager—a guy who'd never worked in a mine before and paid his workers lower wages than any other company that does this kind of work."

"He has a bad temper," said Ordinary Tom. "He's the reason there's a union there now. When somebody asked him at a meeting why the wages were so low, he said, 'Nobody's holding a gun to your head to make you work here.'"

Later I telephoned this manager, who declined to furnish me a close-up look at the Rand mining project, despite the fact that it was on public land. When I subsequently mentioned this to Ahmed Mohsen, a BLM resource manager in the Ridgecrest office, he said: "Miners consider themselves to be above the law because they deal with adversity more than anyone else. Mining requires you to take a lot of risks up front: you have to put in sewers, water, power, and roads from scratch; trying to liberate or debond minerals, you're dealing with the whims of Mother Nature. And it doesn't matter what your costs are because you're competing on the international market with Indonesia. On the other hand, nobody asked them to get into this business.

"I'm skeptical about mining companies because I've dealt with them a lot," said Mohsen. "Some are excellent, but not many. They do a great job when they say, 'We aren't visitors here; we're part of this community, and we'll make it better after we leave with jobs, services, and education. One way they can educate people is to admit that mining is destructive by nature—that you can't make an omelette without breaking some eggs, that you can't restore but you can rehabilitate. We'd prefer to prepare for the worst and hope for the best, but the Rand Company doesn't have that philosophy. They're almost a renegade company. They don't want to play ball; they argue with us about everything we tell them to do."

Mohsen rummaged through his files, looking for an environmental impact statement. "The first thing that shows me a mining company is serious is when they hire an environmental specialist," he said. "Some mines have a plant nursery on the premises and a biologist on staff—but not Rand. Up there, it's the manager who makes those calls. They're mining a thousand acres, some of which is no longer in use and should be restored, but so far not one acre has been reclaimed. When we asked them to reshape their waste piles to conform with surrounding areas, we got a nasty letter back.

"From August to December of 1993, seven red-tailed hawks were found dead in their heap-leach ponds. We asked them to monitor the situation on a twenty-four-hour basis, and they said okay, but they thought it wasn't really a problem for seven birds to die. We believe it's a problem if *one* bird dies, because we said there would be no wildlife impact when we permitted the project. Still, all we have is a voluntary agreement for them to report any bird deaths. They've put nets over their cyanide ponds, but they still haven't put any over their heap-leach piles where the cyanide drips and pools up. Everything to them is cost, cost, cost. Rand is just a leech on the land—if the mining industry can be divided into lions and hyenas, they fit right in with the hyenas."

Later, looking over the company's annual reports and stock profile, I learned that Rand was a subsidiary of Glamis Gold, Ltd.—a Vancouver-based (but two-thirds American-held, in terms of numbers of shares) mining company that specialized in open-pit heap-leaching of low-grade ore. Its chairman, a British Columbian by the name of Chester Millar, had pioneered heap-leaching in California in 1981 at the Picacho Mine in Imperial County; during the 1980s, Glamis had owned mines in Spain, Chile, and Nevada, and was currently developing another in Chihuahua, Mexico, but all of its current operations were in the California desert. The company had begun life at fifty cents a share on the Vancouver Stock Exchange—a notorious breeding ground for scandals and swindlers—but had since joined the prestigious Toronto and New York exchanges, where its stock had gone as high as nine dollars in summer 1994.

Glamis formed the Rand Mining Company in 1986 in order to work the Yellow Aster, whose many private and patented claims it had acquired under lease in 1984. Since it had begun operating here—first by reworking old waste piles and a small pit called the Lamont—it had produced 168,000 ounces of gold through June 1994. In 1990, its first year of production from the Yellow Aster, Rand had also bought the adjacent, mostly unpatented Baltic claims for five million dollars. Having begun mining there in 1993, the company was now awaiting permits for another five-hundred-acre expansion, proposing to process sixty million more tons of ore.

While not necessarily characteristic of the king of beasts, neither did this sound exactly like the behavior of a scavenger. From a business standpoint, both parent and child mining companies appeared to be doing fine. Glamis had turned a profit in twelve of its fourteen years of existence; Rand was the fifth-largest gold producer in California, which had helped Glamis obtain revenues of more than $52 million in fiscal 1994. After expenses, that still left earnings of $8 million—a sixfold increase per share from the previous year. As a result, the company was being eyed on the market as a potential takeover target, with its efficient (i.e., low) cost of production ranking high among its attractive qualities. The average ore grade at the Baltic and Yellow Aster—.02 ounces of gold per ton—was one of the lowest in North America, but so was Rand's cost of extracting an ounce ($184). With gold selling for $375, this made it one of the most profitable such operations on the continent—despite the fact that it was recovering only 60 percent of the gold present in the ore, probably because of its coarseness. Such profitability was apparently achieved by means of Rand's noted tightfistedness, which in May 1994 had also inspired the mine's 150 hourly employees to organize themselves under Local #30 of the International Longshoremen's and Warehousemen's Union—reportedly because of low wages, arbitrary dismissals, and safety shortcuts. Having fought fiercely against unionization, management lost the election by only five votes (prompting Glamis to advise its stockholders that "the agreement will add at least $2.95 per ounce of gold to the cost of production").

As for the environment, Glamis boasted in its 10K report for 1994 that "during the past three years the Company has made no expenditures with respect to environmental compliance save and except as required by permits for construction at its mining operations." It further predicted that none would occur in fiscal 1995. Meanwhile, in 1994, former Rand employees alleged that its monitoring wells had been tampered with to conceal groundwater contamination, that the old Glory Hole was being used as a toxic dump, and that several species of animals including the federally listed, threatened desert tortoise were routinely being killed and secretly buried on the property—though a subsequent inspection by the BLM, the state regional water quality control board, and the state office of mining reclamation found no evidence to support the claims.

"I've never heard a positive thing about Rand from anyone," Mohsen concluded. "The word is that you won't get any cooperation from them unless you force them legally. Their goal is simply to maximize their profits to their stockholders—and why should they [act otherwise] when we haven't made it an urgency? Because of lack of staff time, we haven't enforced all the laws. The BLM is spending 98 percent of its time permitting new projects and putting conditions on operators, but not following up on them. It's like issuing visas to immigrants but never going back to see if they got a job.

"In the Multiple Use Act of 1955, Congress said that unpatented mining claims had to be shared for other purposes. But the nature of mining today doesn't fit the principle of multiple use. There are problems with dust, noise, and safety; open-pit mining creates different watercourses and drainages and leaves behind a big hole with a lake above a town. By law, you have to reclaim everything but the pit—but 15 to 20 percent of the disturbed land is the pit. The law was written to protect the small miner: one guy who dug a little hole and left a little pile. Today, though, it's mega-mining—an exclusive, long-term use of land that's being sold as a temporary one. And any company in the world can come here and do it without paying a dollar in royalties."

To get a look at the American land from which a Canadian company had excluded me, Karl suggested that we fly over the Rand mine. For the mission, we picked an April day so windy that he predicted the aircraft would function as a "vomit comet"; miraculously, though, conditions calmed down enough by afternoon that we could aviate the Mojave with nary a jiggle. We took off from the Inyokern airport, climbing parallel to the eastern face of the snow-capped Sierra Nevada; as we turned and banked south toward Randsburg, the creosote-dotted landscape stretched away below us, innumerable beige washes threading their way through the dun-toned desert—evidence of active hydrology in a seemingly waterless world. To the northeast were random placements of nondescript low buildings: research structures within the expanse of China Lake Naval Weapons Center. Just as on the April day exactly a hundred years earlier when Mooers, Burcham, and Singleton had found gold in the Rands, yellow wildflowers infused the slopes with the sheen of precious metal. It had been a wet winter, and far to the south, beyond the pale glow of Rogers Dry Lake and Edwards Air Force Base, the San Gabriels were covered with snow, posing a barrier between us and L.A. as formidable as that of the Alps (though today the most daunting obstacle for Hannibal, were he to descend on our modern Rome, would be the earthquake-damaged overpass on Interstate 5).

Up here in the Mojave proper, higher elevations were discernibly greener than the basins and bajadas. As we crossed the El Paso range, Karl pointed out various mines: "This was copper. This was a coal mine. A friend of mine owns the cabin on that ridge. Gold was down there in Last Chance Canyon—a lot of money got taken out of there." To the west was the broad, dark summit of Black Mountain, sacred to the Paiutes and Shoshones. "Strong powers," Karl said. "I've slept up there and had some really strange dreams."

It took about fifteen minutes to reach Randsburg. From the air you could easily see that the parts of the mining project visible from town were only the fringe of a sprawling complex of disfigurement. The disemboweled and sculpted mountain, once the site of countless small mines, now contained three huge cavities. The fabled Glory Hole was a tiny crater within an enormous pit. The area around the Yellow Aster looked less refined than the more recent Baltic, whose ore piles were as long and flat and right-angled as sheet cakes. Dark green and emerald cyanide ponds lay here and there like swimming pools; no wonder birds were drawn down to take a dip. Alongside the ponds were the factory-like towers of processing plants where gold got separated from cyanide by pumping the solution through columns of carbon, plating it onto steel wool, and dipping the wool in acid, leaving behind gold ingots.

I asked Karl what would happen when the company was finished with the pits. "They'll put a fence around them," he said.

Eventually we turned northeast toward the Panamints, where yet another heap-leach project, the incipient Briggs gold mine, was about to get under way. En route, we passed over the Spangler Hills off-highway-vehicle open area, crisscrossed everywhere by motorcycle tracks. ("I hate dirt bikers," Karl commented. "They tear everything to shreds.") After buzzing the Trona limestone pinnacles—a place where, early one morning, I'd given the finger to a helicopter that was scouting the area for a motorcycle commercial—we continued across Searles Dry Lake, whose far end was decorated by the smokestacks of the North American Chemical plant. As we approached, Karl, who hangared his plane in Trona, saw fit to share a quote he attributed, seemingly with admiration and delight, to the *Los Angeles Times*:

> The road to Trona winds like a hairline ribbon through the ugly scar of Poison Canyon and gently curves around the lifeless expanse of Searles Dry Lake. Nothing natural grows in Trona; the children play football in a field of sand. From time to time, a thirst-crazed animal wanders out of the hills, takes a drink of the alkali-fouled water, and drops dead.

Vivid as the description was, I wondered why it included nothing about the odor from the processing plant, which became pronounced as we crossed the playa. Below was a kind of chemical farm, red streams running through brown-and-white lake mud, holding ponds scraped from alkali crust, themselves held in place by walls of salt.

Finally we crossed the Slate Range and confronted the western face of the eleven-thousand-foot-high Panamints, topped by snow-covered

Telescope Peak. Afternoon light creased the massive range, outlining its north-south succession of canyons with deep black shadows. Here in the dark clefts of the burnt-umber edifice were the paths that the forty-niners had taken out of Death Valley, that the twenty-mule teams had negotiated with their loads, that the fortunes of stockholders had followed up to Panamint City and back down in the time it had taken the ink to dry on the 1872 mining law. True to the psychic terms of the Mojave, all of these venues were in plain sight though their reality remained concealed. Likewise hidden were the minerals that had brought people to this world without water or shelter—a realm still being probed and scraped and gouged and leached in pursuit of economic "security." Where prospectors had gone placer mining in places to which they were drawn by their eyes, companies now transformed whole landscapes if they panned out economically—if, in other words, they justified investment by a multinational corporation of ordinary prudence. Streaks of quartz were clearly evident in the rock walls of the range, but the stuff that would soon put a pit in the Panamints was nowhere to be seen. Like the legends that accompanied it, the presence of gold remained palpable but invisible, investing the desert with the bewitching allure of beauty and disaster.

THE TORTOISE AND
THE HARE-AND-HOUNDS

Perhaps the most meaningful of all the ways in which the desert hides its workings from sight is demonstrated by the desert tortoise, the Mojave's so-called indicator species—an animal that spends most of its time underground. At the end of the twentieth century, the tortoise is the premier performer of the desert's disappearing act, not merely in its subterranean habits but because its numbers have decreased so sharply that it is now listed as a threatened species by the U.S. Fish and Wildlife Service. Moreover, the thing that has most recently been killing tortoises is invisible: a respiratory disease that renders the animal too dehydrated and weak to forage for food. Yet even this specific ailment is more a symptom than a cause of the tortoise's decline. As has been seen in other species, individuals are made more susceptible to disease by stress. Most temperate creatures would agree that, owing to its heat and aridity, the Mojave is a stressful environment; but having evolved within it for many thousands of years, the tortoise is spectacularly adapted to living conditions there. The strain reflected by its plight is not the adversity inherent in the natural environment, but that imposed by the nature of modern civilization in the Mojave.

Sometime after the tortoise was declared a threatened species, it became fashionable to refer to the animal as "the spotted owl of the desert." The analogy arose in part from the fact that where the owl was blamed for bringing the logging industry of the Pacific Northwest to its knees, the tortoise managed to halt development in the fastest-growing city in the United States: a once obscure stop on the Old Spanish Trail called Las Vegas, Nevada. A more valid basis for congruency was the fact that both animals are indeed considered indicator species—creatures so dependent upon and inextricably linked with living conditions in their environments that a decline in their populations axiomatically reflects a deterioration of those environments, signifying dire straits for countless other species. In broader ways, the comparison can be carried even further. Dr. Kristin Berry—the controversial U.S. Bureau of Land Management biologist who is said to be single-handedly responsible for the listing of the desert tortoise as a threatened species—has observed that two of the most popular images sold in gift and jewelry stores are those of owls and tortoises, both of which have long and fertile mythological relationships with human beings. Each, for example, is considered a symbol of wisdom—the owl perhaps because of its ability to negotiate in the dark, the tortoise because of its longevity, patience, and persistence (as epitomized in the story of the tortoise and the hare).

That's as far as the analogy goes, though. In most ways, human attitudes toward owls and tortoises represent a marked contrast. The tortoise—quiet, plodding, self-protective, herbivorous—is the very model of harmlessness; it was ranked by the Chinese Book of Rites as one of four benevolent spiritual animals, and today it enjoys sufficient secular favor to have been named the official reptile of at least one of the United States (California). No owl, however, is about to be named any state's bird. Owls are universally agreed to be messengers of bad news; one of the world's most common superstitions is that something bad will happen if you see one. A British television survey found that while they're generally considered clever, fascinating, even beautiful, owls are also perceived as *cruel* rather than *kind*, *unapproachable* as opposed to *approachable*, and worst of all, *not cuddly* as opposed to *cuddly*. Our attitude toward them is fraught with foreboding and ambivalence, helping to explain the hostility that so quickly attached itself to the northern spotted species when its survival was perceived as competitive with our own. Signs bearing such messages as KILL A SPOTTED OWL—SAVE A LOGGER and I LIKE SPOTTED OWLS—FRIED proved quite popular in the

Northwest, whereas bumper stickers demeaning the tortoise are no-where evident in the desert.

This despite the fact that the tortoise's geographic range is far wider than that of the owl, thus containing much greater potential for frustration of "economic growth." Since it was granted emergency protection in August 1989 (almost a year before the spotted owl was listed), the desert tortoise has played havoc with all manner of human ambition. Not least impressively, it succeeded where two decades of environmental activism had failed to bring to a halt the Barstow-to-Las Vegas motorcycle race—the most prestigious "hare-and-hounds" event of its kind, annually run through the Mojave Desert on Thanksgiving weekend. But off-road-vehicle enthusiasts are only one of many "user groups" affected by the tortoise's listing. Others include cattle ranchers, gold miners, construction workers, and the U.S. armed forces—not to mention suburban civilians who simply want to build a house in a place where they can afford it.

As a practical matter, enmity fails to attend the tortoise partly because it doesn't threaten any one activity as directly as the owl does logging. "With the spotted owl, there's only one interested user group: the timber industry," explains Kristin Berry. "People are interested in [saving] that ecosystem who aren't interested in the owl—but you don't find people here who say, 'We're using the tortoise to save the desert.'" While she'd undoubtedly get some argument on that point from advocates of the Barstow-to-Vegas race, Berry is correct when she says that "the tortoise issue is much more complex [than the spotted-owl controversy]. It's about population growth—people spreading into the desert and behaving in an uncontrolled, uneducated way."

Unlike owls, tortoises are diurnal, terrestrial, and slow—therefore relatively easy to find and catch. Ever since Americans, native or otherwise, have been visiting the southwestern deserts, they've been coming across tortoises and taking them home (one of the causes, for reasons more complicated than the mere fact of removal, of the species' decline). Indeed, if the criterion were personal experience rather than popular legend, even unscientific travelers would probably identify the tortoise as the desert's indicator species, as opposed to such flagship denizens as rattlesnakes or roadrunners.

The fact that tortoises are such easy pickings, however, implies something intrinsic about their habitat to its "users." Whereas the domain of the spotted owl has always been considered valuable, both commercially and spiritually (the redwood forest, with its ancient, enormous architecture and beams of sunlight slanting down from Heaven, is, more than any other natural environment, commonly compared to a cathedral), the desert, aside from random placements of precious minerals, has always been considered worthless. Rather than suggesting a venue for Bible study, the desert is where the Bible is acted out—a realm of trial and exile, of barrenness and exposure. Yet while the old-growth forest conversely signifies shelter and solace, its amalgamated understory of hemlock, cedar, sugar pine, spruce, redwood, fir, and alder remains one of the least *penetrable* ecosystems in North America—hence a formidable obstacle to recreation and development. The chief attraction of the desert, by contrast, is its very openness: traditionally it has been a place where one is free to do and take whatever strikes one's fancy, eased by the utter absence of vegetative impediment. This laissez-faire status has been tacitly encouraged by the BLM, the federal agency that historically has "overseen" the desert by looking the other way, nurturing a tendency among its users to view the place as their own personal property.

As the New View of the desert has arisen, the ancestral home of the tortoise has shirked its mean and cheap reputation: it has come to be prized for its environmental values, not merely for its lack of restriction. In the process, the rules of the place have changed. When, in 1976, Congress passed the Federal Land Policy and Management Act, broadening the environmental authority of the BLM and directing it to "manage, use, develop, and protect" twelve million acres of arid California lands in imminent danger of despoilation, it marked the beginning of the end of the wide-open desert. When the tortoise was classified as a threatened species, requiring federal permission for any activity that might adversely affect it, that era—and with it, in a large sense, the western frontier—came to a close.

The protracted showdown that ensued between developers, environmentalists, the city of Las Vegas, and a group of radical off-road motorcycle racers led by someone calling himself the Phantom Duck of the Desert has, over the last twenty years, furnished a remarkable window on the changing relationship between North Americans and their environment. More than anything else, it shows how the paths of people and animals increasingly intersect in a no-longer-remote, archetypal American landscape once considered worthless and now considered priceless: the Mojave.

To many, a tortoise dwelling in the desert is an innately peculiar idea. Turtles are associated with water. *Tortoises*, however, live on land. The desert tortoise has claws, not flippers, with powerful forelegs adapted for digging. Its columnar rear limbs resemble those of an elephant; making its way across the desert floor, the tortoise looks like a walking table, piled high with provender. An immobile tortoise, however, bears a striking similarity to a stone. Its carapace, or shell, is dome shaped, more or less a foot long, covered with hard "scutes" that feel like fingernails, ranging in color from yellow to dark brown—the chromaticity of the desert itself. Its face is rounded, with a blunt, horny beak. The thin, leathery skin is covered with scaly plates that look like chain mail. As a matter of fancy, the tortoise—with its shieldlike shell and furrowed breastplate or "plastron"—resembles a knight in mottled armor. In overall aspect, though, it precedes even the medieval. It looks, in fact, like a little dinosaur. And it is genuinely prehistoric.

Remains of a giant Mojavean tortoise have been dated to the Pleistocene epoch, when today's desert was woody grassland. *Gopherus agassizii* remains the largest reptile of the North American desert, just as tortoises in general are the continent's heaviest terrestrial reptiles. The desert tortoise is one of only four North American species. The gopher tortoise *(Gopherus polyphemus)* lives in the southeastern United States; Berlandier's tortoise *(G. berlandieri)* dwells in northeastern Mexico and southern Texas; the Bolson tortoise *(G. flavomarginatus)* is found in the central highlands of Mexico. At one time, all may have constituted the same species, but the Ice Age fragmented their populations, pushing them south into the tropical peninsulas of Baja California and Florida. When the climate warmed and the ice retreated, tortoises again spread north, but by that time the various populations had become biologically differentiated and lost the capacity to interbreed. Nevertheless, all continue to exhibit a range of adaptations to high temperatures and scarcity of water.

There's some debate as to whether the Mojave, or the Sonoran Desert farther south, is the ancestral home of the desert tortoise. Today the species is found from southern Nevada and southwestern Utah into southern Sonora, from southern California to southern Arizona and the western slope of the Sierra Madre Occidental. In much of the Sonoran

Desert, it occupies densely vegetated and rocky hillsides, but tortoises north and west of the Colorado River and Grand Canyon—i.e., in the Mojave—are found in flatter realms: valleys, washes, and the creosote bush–covered lower flanks of alluvial fans and bajadas. A major predeterminant of their presence is the type of soil, which has to be stable and can't be too stony for the animal to excavate a burrow—its most vital shelter from the desert heat, and a habit that sets it apart from every other type of tortoise in the United States.

Temperatures in parts of the Mojave can vary by as much as 80 degrees Fahrenheit in a single day. A tortoise's burrow is cooler in summer and warmer in winter, with higher and more constant humidity, than the air aboveground (to say nothing of the surface ground temperature, which can exceed 200 degrees). As a result, desert tortoises spend about 98 percent of their time underground. In a year, a tortoise may use one or two dozen different subterranean sites. In summer these tend to be temporary, three or four feet long, and dug in banks or under bushes. Winter holes are more extensive; often built in the banks of washes (where they can sometimes be inundated by flash floods, drowning the inhabitants), they usually extend underground from eight to fifteen feet. The burrow travels horizontally or diagonally downward to a depth of about a yard. Occasionally, in the coldest (northernmost) parts of the range, it may go three times that deep. Mirroring the profile of the animal itself, the tunnel is shaped like a half-moon. A tortoise will often amplify on a hole inaugurated by a kangaroo rat, ultimately extending its hospitality to some thirty commensal species including snakes, lizards, owls, rats, mice, squirrels, rabbits, foxes, cats, spiders, and scorpions (not to mention its own kin: one burrow in Utah was found to harbor twenty tortoises).

With the onset of cold weather, the tortoise begins to hibernate. For six to nine months a year, it may not emerge from its den at all. It's active between March and September, prime time being spring, the period of peak plant growth. The animal's preferred temperature range is 65 to 105 degrees Fahrenheit (an average taken from animals afield is 86). In early spring, this thermal window brings a tortoise from its burrow between midmorning and midafternoon, but as the year progresses and the weather grows warmer, the schedule gets staggered: the animal emerges just after sunrise, vanishes by midmorning, and reappears in late afternoon. In summer it may surface only at night or during daytime thunderstorms. When the weather is warm and wet, desert highways are jammed to capacity with traveling tortoises.

Most of the tortoise's rounds are spent foraging for food. Its herbivorous diet is a complex and inconsistent affair, characterized by severe seasonal trade-offs and largely controlled—in an area that receives rainfall on an average of only a dozen days per year—by its need for water. The animal takes in most of its yearly food requirements in the spring, when it gorges itself on annual grasses, succulents, and wildflowers—the moisture-laden equivalent of a watermelon diet. During this time, it collects protein and produces urine, which it doesn't eliminate but stores in an enormous bladder. Months later, as the vegetation dries out, the tortoise continues to eat desiccated plants, drawing water from its stockpile of urine, which by now has grown dark and viscous. The shell and scaly skin limit body-surface evaporation to almost zero; nevertheless, in midsummer the tortoise enters a temporary burrow, where it passes the summer at an osmotic concentration that would kill most animals. Its blood chemistry, for example, is 50 percent saltier than normal at this time of year.

During this period of estivation, the tortoise loses considerable weight. When the summer rainstorms finally arrive (or often, mysteriously, just beforehand), it comes out and digs itself a little ditch. As the rain pours down, the tortoise wallows in the water, drinking and urinating simultaneously, flushing its system and increasing its weight by as much as 40 percent at a dip. New vegetation follows the rain, enabling the animal to resume the cycle and reopen the quasi-watermelon menu.

A single tortoise's home range is anywhere from 25 to 130 acres. The animal may sometimes be found a mile from its burrow, but doesn't usually roam more than a few hundred yards. When it decides to call it a day, no matter how haphazardly it has seemed to wander, it heads for home on a beeline. It knows the local landmarks, the locations of food sources, drinking sites, mineral licks, and other tortoises—particularly those of the opposite sex. As with human beings, in a lifetime estimated to last between sixty and one hundred years, mating commences around the time a tortoise turns twenty. Courtship—including competition among males—involves head bobbing and stretching of the limbs; an aggressive (i.e., successful) suitor bites the legs and lunges at the neck of his nemesis with his "gular horn," the forward-pointing extension of his plastron, which protects a tortoise's throat. Oddly enough, the amorous male behaves quite similarly toward the female of his affection. He approaches her with his shell held high, and if she turns away, he blocks her path and snaps at her. Should this somehow result in success at mounting her from the rear, his feet will frequently slip from the female's back as she tries to crawl away. If she stops, he flexes his hind legs, emits a hiss from his gaping mouth, and slams the rear of his shell into the ground. The rhythmic humping that follows is accompanied—again, as in *Homo sapiens*—by considerable grunting and drawn-out moaning, a sound that one observer (of tortoises) likened to that of baying hounds.

Eggs are laid in early summer. About the size of ping-pong balls, they come in clutches of two to fourteen. To deposit them, the mother digs an urn-shaped hole in sandy soil with her hind legs, often in open areas devoid of shrubs. Upon laying the eggs, she pushes them into the deepest, foremost part of the excavation, then covers them with earth and urinates on top. The nest proves all but invisible. Hatchlings appear about three months later; about the size of silver dollars, they are adorable miniatures of their parents, except that their eyes are more gold than green and their shells are slightly spongy. It takes fully five years for a baby tortoise's shell to harden sufficiently to protect it against predators.

Only one in ten hatchlings will live that long. Hawks, owls, eagles, ravens, roadrunners, snakes, and Gila monsters are all known to enjoy dining on baby tortoises. Even after the shell is mature, adults aren't immune to attack; while they prefer easier prey, badgers, bobcats, skunks, coyotes, and kit foxes can open a tortoise without too much effort. The latter two have even been known to dig tortoises out of their dens. A weapon the tortoise may employ in its own defense is its urine, which can pucker the mouth of a kit fox—though the loss of its precious bodily fluid may significantly weaken the sprayer, ultimately contributing to its demise.

This problem may also come into play when a tortoise encounters its most dangerous enemy of all. Of the various species that threaten the existence of *Gopherus agassizii*, the one that has exerted by far the biggest influence is *Homo sapiens*. Historically, the most common way that people have eliminated tortoises from the desert is by capturing them. The first such kidnappers were the Chemehuevi Paiutes, who not only kept tortoises as pets but made bowls, rattles, scrapers, and decorations from the animal's different parts. The Mohave Indians avoided eating it, but according to desert historian Dennis Casebier, a tortoise was "the closest thing to a microwave dinner the [Chemehuevi] ever had—all he had to do was turn it over on a campfire, and he had a meal." As recently as the 1920s and 1930s, tortoises were piled into crates, trucked to Los Angeles, and sold to restaurants. One collector reported shipping two thousand tortoises a year from California to Salt Lake City. Tortoises have been sold in pet shops, department stores, railroad terminals, and service stations along desert highways, from which they were transported all over the United States. Old U.S. Route 66, which ran through the heart of the Mojave, terminated in Chicago; perhaps not incidentally, one winter eight desert tortoises were found frozen in the woods of Cook County, Illinois.

In spring of 1973, the Mojave Desert had a spectacular wildflower bloom. Excited by media accounts, tourists rushed in. The following autumn, scores of desert tortoises were donated to museums hundreds of miles away. Estimates of *Gopherus agassizii* in captivity vary from a hundred thousand to half a million; as researcher Roger Luckenbach has pointed out, if one of every hundred families in Los Angeles County had a pet tortoise, there would be twenty thousand in L.A. alone. Tortoise population densities in some metropolitan counties probably approach the figures for the desert itself.

Since 1939, it has been illegal to purchase or sell desert tortoises in California. Yet even if this rule were obeyed, commercial traffic hardly constitutes the only disruptive kind. Military maneuvers, for example, affect tortoises in the same way that an automobile windshield affects bugs. General George Patton's Desert Training Center, in the early years of World War II, and Operation Desert Strike—a massive army ground exercise that took place in the eastern Mojave in the spring of 1964— were both known to have decimated local *agassizii* populations. Tortoise numbers have dramatically declined in the vicinity of Edwards Air Force Base, the Marine Corps Air-Ground Combat Center at Twentynine Palms, and the army's National Training Center at Fort Irwin, where two thirds of the shrub cover has been eliminated from valleys and bajadas. Of sixty-two tortoises found on survey transects at Fort Irwin in 1989, forty-four were dead, and half the carcasses were found in tank tracks.

Research shows tortoise densities to diminish within one mile to either side of a highway that sees moderate use. The most direct impact, of course, comes from cars crushing tortoises. But vehicular access also enables people to extinguish the animals in a number of other ways. Of six hundred tortoise carcasses found on eleven study plots in the Mojave Desert in 1986, one in seven had died by gunshot. Tortoises have been discovered beheaded; flattened tortoises have been found in car tracks that apparently swerved to hit them. People have been heard to brag about using baby tortoises for skeet-shooting practice, or running over adult tortoises to hear them pop. Occasionally such amusements acquire earmarks of mass efficiency. One person lined up forty-seven tortoises and dispatched them one by one with a shotgun. Another placed fourteen tortoises under a wooden plank and then drove his car along its length.

The most serious and widespread threats aren't so vindictive or direct. Human use has simply altered the landscape so intrinsically that the tortoise's environment today is much different from the one in which the species evolved. Ninety percent of desert-tortoise habitat in California has been grazed by cattle or sheep, which—being bigger and more mobile than tortoises—easily prevail in the competition for available forage, while their feet trample hatchlings, burrows, and nests. Even more pervasively, a whole new plant regime has been established under the influence of hooves and molars. Whereas the predominant plant cover once consisted of native annuals and perennials—bunchgrass, ricegrass, needle grass, fescue—most of the annuals in the western Mojave today are exotic Asian and Mediterranean weeds (brome, filaree, split grass, Schismus), which dry up earlier and are nutritionally less rich, weakening tortoises' overall health and strength. Some estimates put the totality of the takeover at around 90 percent. As Dr. Kristin Berry says: "We talk about [deforestation] in other countries like Brazil. But we're doing the same thing here—removing our standing crop."

Kristin (pronounced Christine) Berry is the doyenne of desert-tortoise politics. Pale and slight, prim and schoolmarmish, with thick-lensed eyeglasses and a bouffant hairdo, Berry looks more like a librarian than an activist or even a scientist. Her jaw, however, is strong and prominent—and one learns in short order that she has a no-nonsense personality and an iron will. Controlling almost all scientific research and lobbying every policy decision that affects the desert tortoise, Berry is inevitably behind schedule and constantly under fire. The first time I talked to her on the telephone, I felt a persistent temptation to rap the receiver with my knuckles; when conversing on the phone, I realized, one is accustomed to periodic sounds of reassurance from the other end: "Yes," "Uh-huh," "That's right," or even "That's wrong." Berry, however, seems to consider such interjections a waste of time and energy—she silently waits for a speaker to exhaust himself, then cuts directly to the chase with abrupt disclosures that are candid to the point of being inflammatory. Not infrequently in the past, her statements have contradicted the policies of her employer, the Bureau of Land Management.* As a result, in 1992, Berry was prohibited from talking to the press unless a BLM public-information officer was present.

For most of her adult life, Berry's existence has revolved around the species *Gopherus agassizii*. Born in 1943, she grew up in a house on the edge of the Mojave Desert (her father—a physicist, mathematician, and ballistics expert—was head of testing at the China Lake Naval Weapons Center), where she became fascinated by reptiles, lizards in particular. As a girl she won a science award for hatching fairy shrimp in earth collected from a dry lakebed; in 1961 she left to study biology at Occidental College in Los Angeles, and later received a master's degree from UCLA. She got her Ph.D. from the University of California at Berkeley in 1972.

At Berkeley—surrounded by bay and eucalyptus groves, watching the Pacific fog roll in every afternoon from the Golden Gate—Berry realized how attached she was to treeless, cloudless ecology. She did her doctoral dissertation on the chuckwalla, a large desert lizard, utilizing for her study sites the Naval Weapons Center itself. Unlike Fort Irwin, the army's ground-warfare base just to the east, China Lake tests aerial weaponry, and hence has relatively little effect on the landscape; the government does allow grazing there, and burros have occasionally overrun the place, but chuckwallas live among rocks in the mountains, where few domestic animals intrude. As a result, Berry was able to observe the lizards in areas free of human influence. She discovered that immature juvenile females flagrantly flirted with adult males, stroking their flanks and rubbing their chins, and that each chuckwalla had a "signature" head movement—a way of bobbing its skull that was utterly individualized, as Berry showed in graphs that resembled the recordings of a seismometer.

---

*In 1994, the federal government created a new Biological Survey department to house scientists like Berry.

While researching her dissertation, Berry worked part-time for the California Department of Transportation, removing tortoises from a stretch of state highway between the towns of Mojave and Boron; these relocations, which had previously been conducted by Boy Scouts, often proved unsuccessful. (Berry recommended a fence.)

As a result of this work, she found herself becoming obsessed with disturbance and change in arid landscapes. "The reason the tortoise is so interesting," she says, "is that it shows the range of what's gone wrong—it tells us about roads, grazing, visitation, collection, shooting, and off-road-vehicle use. It's a good indicator species for the lowland parts of the desert, and for small rodents and birds. The tortoise needs undisturbed soil in order to do well, so if its populations are healthy and stable, it means the fans and valleys are in good shape."

By way of illustration, Berry invokes the concept of ecological "guilds"—essentially, categories of animals that occupy particular habitats. Guilds can be classified in various ways: mammals, reptiles, herbivores, carnivores, canids, felines, scavengers, predators, seed eaters, shrub eaters, etc. Any one species is thus a member of several different guilds. A bobcat, for example, is simultaneously a mammal, a carnivore, and a feline. The predominant or "supreme" species in any guild achieves such status through size and numbers—in scientific terms, its biomass. Thus, the descending hierarchy for the carnivore guild on the valleys and alluvial fans of the Mojave Desert consists of (1) the coyote, (2) the kit fox, and (3) the leopard lizard. The herbivore guild for the same environment is (1) the antelope, (2) the tortoise, and (3) the iguana. (Per square mile, the tortoise possesses far greater biomass than the hare.) When the carrying capacity of a habitat is compromised, the biggest members of a guild are the first to disappear. As Berry explains of the overall North American guild: "The condor was the supreme scavenger. The grizzly was the supreme omnivore. The wolf was the supreme canid. The jaguar was the supreme felid. The antelope was the supreme herbivore. In other words, we've wiped off the top of the guild. And now the tortoise is going."

In terms of population ecology, the tortoise is classified as a "K-selected" species, a status arrived at through its lengthy life span, low annual birth rate, long reproductive maturity, and relatively large size. By contrast, so-called *r* strategists (for "intrinsic *rate* of natural increase") tend to be small in stature, highly reproductive, and not very competitive—their numbers explode and crash often and dramatically. K-selected populations (the K stands for "karrying kapacity," illustrating what appears to be a rare burst of biological humor), by comparison, are quite stable; they can survive considerable variation in their environments, and under natural conditions, their numbers take a long time to change. If a K-selected species is in decline, severe and fundamental degradation of its habitat is indicated.

Kristin Berry posits that during the century of European settlement that began in 1870, the desert tortoise population of the western Mojave declined by 60 to 90 percent. "Of all the areas of the Mojave, the western is the most devastated," she says. "Basically, it's now all creosote bush and Mediterranean weeds." Much of this has resulted from agriculture, specifically grazing by domestic livestock, which compacts the soil, promotes erosion, and eliminates native plant communities, which in turn eradicates animal habitat. However, as she began her career, Berry found that grazing's effects were being exacerbated and outstripped by an entirely new kind of land use—one that furthered the aims of humankind in a way that was sheerly psychological. It showed, in fact, how human attitudes toward the desert were fundamentally changing in the second half of the twentieth century—how the place was no longer regarded as an area to be shunned but as one to be embraced (even if the affection was aggressive to the point of violence—i.e., rape). In the decades following the Korean War, the western Mojave was perhaps America's primary magnet for off-road-vehicle recreation—a pastime that, as far as tortoises were concerned, Kristin Berry was inclined to call "a wave of death."

Concomitant with the formation of the modern character of the Mojave, off-road vehicles began to be popular in the desert soon after World War II. And as is true of most rhetoric surrounding off-road vehicles in southern California, some responsibility is inevitably laid at the doorstep of General George S. Patton and his Desert Training Center. More than a million men thus became acquainted not only with the desert but with machines designed to "conquer" it: four-wheel-drive jeeps and the formidable (if not very maneuverable) Harley-Davidson military motorcycle. Moreover, the war years, with their expansive influence on West Coast training bases, ports of call, and shipbuilding factories, furnished

California with its first major population boom since the gold rush—an explosion largely detonated by the internal-combustion engine. Hence, as the affluent postwar era got going, a claque of young, energetic veterans—recently awakened to the attractions of southern California as a place of residence and the desert as a place of refuge—began spilling out on weekends in the directions of Palm Springs, Lancaster, and Barstow, gunning the engines and grinding the gears of newly acquired jeeps and motorcycles.

The latter—usually made in England by companies like Triumph, Matchless, Norton, and BSA—were essentially street machines adapted for desert use. Tailpipes were raised, headlights removed, smooth-tread tires replaced by knobbies, and a massive skid plate installed to protect the low-slung engine. Since these "desert sleds" were clumsy to ride and complicated to maintain, eventually more specialized equipment began to trickle in from Europe, where rough-ground trials and motocross racing were already established traditions. These bona fide dirt bikes, whose brand names were more often Bultaco, Husqvarna, Maco, and Greeves, bore roughly the engineering relationship to their predecessors that a hummingbird does to a crow: what they gave up in stability, they more than made up for in agility and quickness. Engine ground clearance was as high as a foot; fenders were raised and shortened to avoid clogging with mud or branches; front forks traveled several inches to absorb impacts; fuel tanks were narrowed and indented to facilitate riding while standing on the footpegs, which themselves folded back on contact with rocks, roots, or ruts. Most important, compression was low and gearing wide, with five speeds rather than four, providing high torque and quick acceleration for power on hills and speed on flats. It all had to do with the fact that the engine was a two-stroke design instead of a four: on each cycle of the pistons, the spark plugs fired twice as often as they did on street bikes, enabling the engine to be smaller, lighter, and more responsive. Dirt bikes might weigh hundreds of pounds less than conventional motorcycles. None of these features removed the *challenge* from desert terrain; they simply made negotiation possible, and at considerable speed. To many, this combination of stimuli proved an irresistible elixir.

Aside from the use of four-wheel-drive for basic transportation, off-road-vehicle activity broke down into various categories. Dune travel was a barefaced way to get your yah-yahs out, careening through forgiving sand atop a peppy engine (often a converted Volkswagen bug) for the sake of sheer titillation—not that different from, say, jetboating or water-skiing on dry land. Trail riding, by contrast, was an individualistic biker's version of meditation—an intricate and demanding way to leave the beaten track. Then there was hill climbing—a full-speed assault on a dauntingly steep slope, a gutty challenge, and a way of proving oneness with the machine, since if you didn't make it to the summit, you might not be able to keep the bike from tumbling back downhill with you on top or underneath.

Any form of human transportation, it seems, soon culminates in crowds of people trying to transport themselves more quickly than all the others. It was inevitable, then, that the rise of off-road motorcycles would also lead to the racing of them. In southern California, especially, where the weather was favorable most of the year and vast tracts of essentially unmanaged land lay within a few hours' drive of major cities, off-road racing took hold with a vengeance. In the early 1950s, District 37 of the American Motorcyclists Association was formed to cover the entire area; by the 1960s the AMA was exclusively an off-road organization, dividing its members into skill classes and scoring the results of races throughout southern California. The Catalina, and later the Elsinore, Grand Prix—the latter staged in Riverside County north of San Diego, the former on an island off the coast—brought riders and spectators from all over the world. The Big Bear Run, which began in Lucerne Valley in the Mojave and culminated on a desert mountaintop, annually attracted a thousand contestants. In other parts of the country, woods trials and enduro races were increasingly popular and technically challenging, but desert racers were generally acknowledged to be a different breed. In the wide-open, unregulated West, off-road speeds could sometimes approach a hundred miles per hour. Sailing over ridges and washes, spending almost half his time airborne, touching down and flying forward before a constant column of dust, the hell-bent biker held on for his life as he unrelentingly gunned his machine. Trails were minimal, split-second decisions multitudinous: desert racing required a near-legendary level of skill.

Bob Perkins, a soft-spoken swimming-pool contractor who serves on the AMA's board of trustees, was attracted to motorcycles in the early fifties. But he had a job and a family and therefore found it hard to justify owning one. "Until I saw my first race," he says. "Then that all went out the window."

The first competition that Perkins witnessed took place near Bakersfield in 1957. "When the banner went down, it was like an explosion," he remembers. "The *noise* was exhilarating. There was a deeper sound to it then, not like the two-stroke screamers of today. Watching the front ten or twelve guys heading for the first turn—well, if you have a competitive soul, you just can't be unmoved by it. I said: This is for me.

"I learned by the seat of my pants. You just bought the motorcycle and the helmet, and you joined the AMA. Races were held every Sunday except the first one of the month. We'd start preparing days ahead of time and leave early Sunday morning—wake up at the crack of dawn and take off, three or four guys with bikes and an ice chest. Out of fifty-two weekends in the year, I'd be in the desert on forty-eight."

Aside from the racing, the atmosphere at desert events was invigorating. On one level, it was similar to that of any other hobbyists' convention: shoptalk and story swapping, the lore and lure of one's love. There was the initial excitement as scores of vans and cars pulled into the pit areas, hauling trailers decorated with dirt bikes, side panels painted with the names of teams and clubs. There was the Fellowship of the Barbecue, the burgers and the beer. There was the prepossessing, protective uniform of the sport: tough leather pants, boots, gloves, helmet—a getup that made its wearer look like some kind of modern medieval warrior. There was, to be sure, the powerful adrenal rush of racing itself: hurtling over bone-rattling ground at breakneck speed amid a cacophony of screaming engines, elbow-to-elbow with other riders, each one desperate to reach the front. But infusing everything was the spirit of the *place*—the rough proximity of sand and boulders, of Joshua tree and creosote bush, the vast sky unrestricted by any buildings or any rules. In its blue-jeaned, blue-skied, petrochemical version of liberation, dirt biking in the desert West—wide-open, aggressive, not introspective—was American through and through. It provided, in Richard Poirier's phrase, "a world elsewhere": a place where the mundane shackles of existence could be thrown off in pursuit of a richer, wilder life on the frontier. Its adherents even claimed that it exerted a positive influence on society: in a civilization whose social structure was roundly agreed to be breaking down, motorcycling gave families something to do together—offering kids, in particular, an alternative to juvenile delinquency.

The allure didn't stop at the boundaries of the Southwest. Rick Sieman had been making a living as a house- and signpainter in Youngs-

town, Ohio; a champion weightlifter, he'd been riding motorcycles since
he was nineteen. During the winter, Sieman recalls, "When I wasn't
freezing my butt off painting billboards along the Ohio Turnpike, I'd pick
up magazines and read about the desert races of the Great West. It
seemed unbelievably wild and untamed—the ultimate challenge."

At twenty-eight, Sieman abandoned Youngstown for Santa Monica,
where he got a job as an art restorer. But "the first thing I wanted to do
was find out what desert riding was about. I came out and saw the early
BSAs and Triumphs and Bultacos; I started riding in the desert right
about the time the big dirt-bike boom was happening. If you were a
back-East racer and came out here, you just got your doors blown off.

"My first race was down by Yucca Valley [near Joshua Tree National
Monument]. I took off from the starting line, and I saw this mountain off
in the distance. There was a little dust trail going up it. I stopped at a
checkpoint and said to the guy, 'Is that where the course goes?' He said,
'You got it buddy.' I went, 'Oh, *jeez*.' Coming from Ohio, my idea of a
long course was three-quarters of a mile. So I climbed up the mountain
on this long silty fire road. When I got to the top, I stopped and got off.
Then I went, 'God *damn!*' I could see about sixty miles—it just took my
breath away. When my buddies and I finished that race, all we did for a
month was talk about it.

"From then on, I rode in the desert almost nonstop. My friends and I
realized that we weren't good enough to compete properly, so we started
going out to the desert and training on weekends. We'd find a little section with beat-up fire roads and bumpy sand washes, and mark out a
course with ribbons on bushes and time ourselves. A club would have a
race in one area, and then the next year go to a different area; the winds
would blow and the rains would come, and when you went back to that
place three or four years later, you couldn't see a track—not a bit of evidence of its having been there. In other parts of the country, the only
areas where you could go, with the exception of certain parks where a
trail system was built, were on private property; but in the Great West,
we had this desert which was virtually wide-open. In the sixties, anybody
could go anywhere in the desert and do anything they wanted to do.
People write me letters now saying, 'We wish the new generation of people riding could experience what it was like back in the sixties and early
seventies—the joy, the pure innocence of people having their fun.' Man,
it was fantastic."

Bob Perkins concurs: "Back then, you could just unload your bike from your truck and go anywhere you wanted. There were no regulations—no Sierra Club. The terrain was virgin. We'd lay out a course with minimal markings, breaking up bags of lime in places where there'd never been any motorcycles. Then sometimes, after a weekend race, we'd stay over Monday—go for a ride and look at the view from on top of a mountain. That's when the desert gets serene. During the week—Monday through Thursday—there's nothing quieter than the desert."

"To most people, the desert is a foreboding, hot, desolate place where you don't want your radiator to blow up on your way to Vegas," says Sieman. "But to a desert racer, it was a place of beauty and joy where you could have thrills that most people only dream about. It was the E ticket ride."

By the 1960s, the postwar baby boom was approaching its apogee. In the two decades since 1940, the population of southern California had grown from three and a half to nearly nine million. There and elsewhere, American society was becoming oriented overwhelming toward youth—a fact that wasn't lost on the resurgent Japanese manufacturing industry. Hence, in June 1959, the twelve-year-old Honda Motor Company—the largest motorcycle manufacturer in the world—opened its first American office on Pico Boulevard in Los Angeles.

Eschewing, to some degree, traditional retail motorcycle outlets, Honda established dealerships in hobby shops and hardware and sporting-goods stores—where it began to sell, among other things, a lightweight "trail" motorcycle. The Honda 50 (named for its tiny engine's number of cubic centimeters) weighed 140 pounds, traveled two hundred miles on a gallon of gas, and went forty-five miles per hour—not exactly the sort of machine that Brando rode in *The Wild One*. But that was precisely the point. In the increasingly suburban, post-Eisenhower era, the outlaw image of the motorcycle was being retuned. As Honda saw the situation, its small, lightweight, easy-to-ride machines could appeal to the rising youth-and-leisure market without competing directly with the kind of large-displacement bikes that American motorcyclists had historically preferred. Fuel efficiency was underscored as an enticement to middle-class consumers; prime targets were the upwardly mobile, from college students to commuting stockbrokers. *"You meet the nicest people on a Honda,"* suggested the company's notorious American ads. Those of one of its competitors, Kawasaki, openly imitated the work of Norman Rockwell.

During the fifties, American motorcycle sales had fluctuated at around fifty thousand per year. In 1961, a few hundred Honda 50–type trail bikes were sold in the United States; three years later, the sales of similar lightweight machines reached three hundred thousand. Drawing on a worldwide volume base, the Japanese companies could mark up their products by 300 percent and still undersell American manufacturers by several hundred dollars. In 1964, Honda spent half its U.S. advertising budget on two television commercials broadcast during the Academy Awards ceremony; immediately thereafter, the company had requests for promotional tie-ins from such intrinsically American companies as Coke, Pepsi, RCA, Du Pont, and Westinghouse. The number of registered motorcycles nationwide went from five hundred thousand in 1960 to two million in 1966, with 85 percent of the market now belonging to the so-called Big Four: Honda, Yamaha, Kawasaki, and Suzuki. And of all the motorcycles now owned in the United States, one in five was found in California—with two thirds of those registered in the southern part of the state.

None of this had much direct bearing on the world of hard-core desert racers. If serious off-road motorcycles were hummingbirds, the Honda 50 was a gnat. It was typically seen strapped to the stern of an enormous recreational vehicle, steered by a driver only slightly less large, heading for the hinterlands on a Friday night. "Take-Along Trail Bikes Add Vacation Fun," observed an article published in 1966 in *Popular Science*, which, in describing the amusement to be had from this new toy, noted that "off-road riding is probably the safest, most enjoyable kind. Speeds seldom exceed 25 mph. There's no traffic to dodge, and terrain changes quickly. The bike need not be insured or registered; anyone can drive."

Indeed, this made it difficult to discern exactly how many lightweight trail machines were actually in use, though estimates put the number of unregistered bikes at around a half million nationwide. The biggest single share, again, was in southern California. Within a few years, the number of off-road motorcycles in the state would reach one million, supported by a task force of two hundred thousand dune buggies and five hundred thousand other types of four-wheel-drive vehicles. In 1968, recreational use of the California desert had constituted about five million "visitor days" (each representing one person staying for twelve hours); within five years it had nearly tripled, with 70 percent of the activity involving off-road vehicles.

According to Rick Sieman, this situation was a travesty to dedicated dirt bikers. "The Japanese figured out that they could take a cheap little proprietary engine and a cheap little chickenshit frame and give it a flashy name and a flashy paint job and a big manipulative ad campaign and flood the market with an unbelievable number of these toys and suck little Junior and his buddies into it and make everyone think they could go out and be Mister Racer," he says. "The Big Four made a fortune over a ten- or twelve-year period, but they never spent a dime on safety. Not one educational course was ever given on how to handle the new toys, and not one acre of land was ever set aside for them. They just told everyone to go out and have fun. So people were riding everywhere indiscriminately, and these idiots started flipping here and there, and they started getting these lawsuits. So then [what did the Japanese do]? They took an already bad situation and accelerated it. To take care of the pinheads who couldn't even ride a motorcycle properly, they brought out three-wheeled 'all-terrain vehicles.' A *chicken* could drive an ATV—you don't even have to balance the damn thing. So now, not only was the desert full of kids, but it was glutted with people who didn't even have enough coordination to ride a two-wheeler a hundred yards. They took a very dangerous sport—one that had been populated by a small group of enthusiasts who knew how to conduct themselves—and turned it into Everyman's Sport."

The elite still had their dangerous outlets, however. In 1967, the San Gabriel Valley Motorcycle Club—headquartered in an L.A. suburb adjacent to Pasadena—decided to hold a point-to-point "hare-and-hounds" race through the Mojave Desert. No permits were then required for such events on federal desert land, so the organizers had their choice of routes. They decided that the course would begin east of the town of Barstow—a railroad and highway hub, hence a modest desert business center, which had been incorporated as a city for only twenty years—and culminate in Las Vegas, Nevada.

At the time, Las Vegas had only recently completed its century-long transformation from remote desert trading stop into (in the words of at least one travel-guidebook writer) "the undisputed gambling, entertainment, convention, neon, and cash capital of the known universe." The attraction of this unlikely amusement area, in the eyes of both the southern Paiutes and the first European explorers, had been a group of four large springs that fed "the meadows" from which the place drew its Spanish name. As early as the 1830s, Las Vegas Valley was a crucial watering hole for traders on the Old Spanish Trail from Sante Fe, possessing as it did a perennial stream five feet wide and two feet deep. ("Oh! *Such* water!" exclaimed one Orson Pratt on arriving there in 1848 "at the termination of a 50 mile stretch without a drop of water or a spear of grass.") The springs lay almost halfway between Los Angeles and Salt Lake City, so after the followers of Joseph Smith founded San Bernardino in 1851, Las Vegas naturally became a rest stop on the Mormon Trail. A mission was soon set up, but the recently subdued Paiutes, while appearing to tolerate farmwork during the day, made off with the grain and cattle at night. Lead ore was ample at nearby Potosi Mountain, but it was so brittle and flaky—owing to high zinc and silver content, which the Mormons failed to notice—that attempts at smelting faltered. A few years later, in the Nevada silver boom that followed the California gold rush, Potosi became a going concern, but by then Brigham Young had ordered abandonment of the Las Vegas mission. In its ruins along Las Vegas Creek, one of the newly arrived silver miners—Octavius Decatur Gass—managed to establish a ranch that became a popular way station and the area's only successful settlement. Still, by the turn of the twentieth century, Las Vegas Valley had only thirty Caucasian residents.

What finally got the town going—as is true of so much of the West, and the desert in particular—was the railroad. As the San Pedro, Los Angeles, and Salt Lake line was laid along the Mormon Trail, Las Vegas's "inexhaustible supply of artesian water" (to use the words of then-current advertisements) became essential not only for the replenishment of travelers but for that of steam locomotives. As a distribution point for miners at Rhyolite and Bullfrog, the place was also a modest trading center: in 1905 it had six general stores, two blacksmith shops, three drugstores, two wholesale offices, three furniture stores, two assay offices, a bank, a hotel, fourteen lodging houses, a bottling works, and the only ice-making plant between Salt Lake City and L.A. All these buildings stood on property owned by one J. T. McWilliams, a surveyor eager to become sovereign of the official Las Vegas "townsite" once it was formally established. Unfortunately for McWilliams, however, a bona fide potentate—United States Senator William Clark, the copper kingpin who also happened to own the San Pedro, Los Angeles, and Salt Lake Railroad—had other plans.

Clark bought the eighteen-hundred-acre Las Vegas Ranch for $55,000. He proceeded to announce a townsite sale on the property for May 15, 1905—one month after the opening of commercial traffic on the railroad. He even went so far as to offer a discounted round-trip fare from L.A. for the day, with a full refund if the ticketholder purchased a parcel of land. As it turned out, on May 15 the thermometer, which until that spring day had been tranquil, vaulted to 115 degrees. The "sale" escalated into an auction, and by the time it was over, seven hundred lots had been sold for $265,000. The older McWilliams townsite ultimately had to settle for designation as West Las Vegas, while the spanking-new town of Las Vegas proper—site of the former ranch—beat out Searchlight to the south to become the official seat of Clark County, Nevada.

Nevertheless, over the next decade or two, Las Vegas remained little more than a remote railroad town—"one of the dustiest places in all creation," according to one disgruntled traveler, who seemed to concur with the *Los Angeles Times*'s advice that "to be happy in Las Vegas, one should not try to stay clean." In 1922, Clark sold his interest in the railroad to Union Pacific, which a year later closed the Las Vegas repair shops in the wake of a nationwide strike. To reach Reno or Carson City—the new state's commercial and political centers—one first had to take the train to Los Angeles or Salt Lake City. Telephone and telegraph service were equally sluggish. Never a terribly lively location, Las Vegas seemed to settle stolidly into the desert dust.

The keys to the city's future were held by the U.S. Congress, and by seven western states whose rainfall ran into the nearby Colorado River. In 1928, the Boulder Canyon Project Act authorized the building of a dam to provide water, power, and flood control for California, Nevada, Arizona, New Mexico, Colorado, Utah, and Wyoming. Several sites were proposed and surveyed, but the one finally chosen was Black Canyon: a narrow, precipitous gorge on the Nevada-Arizona border thirty miles east of Las Vegas. Work on the actual dam didn't begin until 1931, but its effect on the area was immediate. A half-dozen contractors—"Six Companies, Inc."—banded together to win the bidding (at $49 million) for the project, which ranked as the biggest construction job in the history of the world. Before the dam could go up, new road and rail systems had to be built, as well as machine shops, garages, warehouses, bridges, cableways, a transmission line to the construction site, and a camp to feed and house the workers. In summer, the air reflecting from the seven-hundred-foot-high walls in the canyon—technically located in a low strip of Colorado Desert along the river—reached 130 degrees Fahrenheit. Therefore the camp was situated eight miles away, where the elevation was two thousand feet higher and the air was ten degrees cooler (in other words, in the Mojave). Las Vegas's freight yards and storage facilities were rapidly expanded to accommodate the infusion of supplies, and before the local residents knew it, they also had a new post office, a federal building, long-distance telephones, regular air service, and a U.S. highway from Salt Lake City and L.A.

The first order of business in Black Canyon was the blasting of four tunnels—each one three-quarters of a mile long—to divert the river around the construction site. Then a couple of cofferdams were built to make sure that it didn't come back. Four hundred human daredevils were hired to hang hundreds of feet in the air, scouring the canyon walls of loose rock, and drilling and blasting niches for dam abutments. (Seven of the men died.) The empty riverbed between the cofferdams was excavated until bare rock was exposed, and then the forms for the dam went up: 230 vertical columns, to be filled with 66 million tons of concrete, mixed at a pair of cement plants built expressly for the purpose nearby. To guard against an epic flood, a pair of ten-story spillways skirted the flanks of the structure, *each* capable of carrying the highest river flow on record (two hundred thousand cubic feet per second). On the upstream side, four thirty-four-story intake towers were connected to penstocks by steel pipes manufactured a mile away, since each section weighed as much as two locomotives and thus couldn't be carried by a normal railroad. A twenty-story powerhouse provided a total generating capacity of 1,835,000 horsepower—ample electrical energy for the household needs of every inhabitant of the Colorado River Basin. More than a hundred tunnels and shafts extended for a total of seven miles. On completion, Boulder (later Hoover) Dam, 727 feet high, displaced the Great Pyramid as the bulkiest architectural structure on Earth. In so doing, it gave rise to the largest artificial reservoir in the world: Lake Mead, 115 miles long and 585 feet deep, would have covered the state of Connecticut to a depth of 10 feet.

Surveying such figures, it's easy to see why, in the vicinity of Las Vegas in the thirties, the Great Depression never materialized. In the dizzying half-dozen years required for its construction, Hoover Dam provided a living to more than forty thousand people, an eighth of whom, at any given time, were employed locally and simultaneously at a monthly payroll of half a million dollars, transforming the workers' camp, Boulder City, into a full-fledged town of six thousand—almost as many people as lived in Las Vegas, which itself had grown by 50 percent since work on the project began. The dam—generally hailed as the greatest engineering achievement of the era and billed, inevitably, as the "eighth wonder of the world"—attracted as many as forty thousand visitors per month. Mind-blowing metaphors for its capacities were breathlessly circulated: The total electricity generated in its powerhouse was capable of lighting a forty-watt bulb in every house in the United States. Lake Mead contained five thousand gallons of water for every person on the planet. Each of the spillways was big enough to float a battleship. If all the materials used in the dam's construction were placed on a railroad at the same time, the train would extend from the dam site to Kansas City.

As far as local citizens were concerned, most of these staggering statistics were indirect and transitory; in terms of permanent benefits, Las Vegas got water and power from the dam, but not much else. Unless, that is, you counted the people and what was in their pockets—at which point you realized what was perhaps the dam's most amazing result of all: the undisputed gambling, entertainment, convention, neon, and cash capital of the known universe. Maybe it was just a coincidence that the state of Nevada, which had outlawed gambling in 1911, decided to relegalize it the same year that work began on Boulder Dam; similarly, it may have been mere chance that, at the same time, the state reduced its three-month residency requirement for divorce to six weeks. In any case, these moves coincided quite profitably with the influx of millions of tourists and workers into southern Nevada. Boulder City had a thousand houses, a dozen dormitories, four churches, a school, a theater, shops, restaurants, recreation halls, and a campground, but even today, it remains the only town in Nevada where gambling is illegal. Hence its legions of young, single, able-bodied, adventurous, and financially flush male occupants were forced into Las Vegas for entertainment, which had now become available in copious amounts. In addition to the casinos, and despite Prohibition, there was no shortage of moonshine, or women for hire; there was even instant marriage to offset quick divorce. In the middle of the night of the Depression, Las Vegas functioned ironically as a searchlight, attracting restless insomniacs from around the nation.

Still, after the dam was finished—and despite the numbers of tourists that continued to visit it—the city needed some stimulus to replace the frenzy of construction. In 1939, Ria Gable provided some when she arrived to divorce her husband, Clark; during her six weeks of Las Vegas residency, newspapers around the world carried pictures of her playing roulette, boating on Lake Mead, and skiing on Mount Charleston. A year later, the Army Air Corps—attracted by the clear skies, remote location, and vast tracts of "public domain wasteland"—established the Las Vegas Aerial Gunnery School in the desert north of town. Inaugurated to train pilots for the B-17 Flying Fortress, it adopted the symbol of a maniacally grinning horned toad astride a flaming, flying machine gun. When the United States entered World War II, the facility was expanded; every six weeks brought a brand-new class of four thousand flyboys, an effective replacement for the troops that had built the dam. Just before the war, California had passed a law requiring a medical certificate for marriage on top of the normal three-day waiting period. So, as thousands of enlistees prepared to ship out, Las Vegas grew even more popular with sentimental servicemen: twenty thousand weddings were performed there in 1942. Meanwhile, a huge magnesium plant was built between Boulder City and Las Vegas, and to shelter ten thousand workers manufacturing ingredients for explosives, the Defense Housing Corporation followed the lead of the railroad and the Bureau of Reclamation: it carved a brand-new town—Henderson, Nevada (established 1942)—from the Mojave Desert.

After Las Vegas became such a focus of attention during a period of prosperous national stress, insightful entrepreneurs began thinking really big—in terms of large-scale hotels with ready-made recreation. Contrary to cinematic fable, the first prophet to pursue this vision wasn't Bugsy Siegel. In 1941, Thomas Hull, a Los Angeles hotelier who owned the El Rancho motor-inn chain, unveiled a sixty-five-room installation on Highway 91 south of town; with a casino, a showroom, a steakhouse, gift shops, and a swimming pool with palms, El Rancho Vegas was positioned directly in the path of incoming traffic from southern California in an unincorporated part of Clark County called Paradise. Out here along "the Strip"—as Las Vegas Boulevard/Highway 91 had been nicknamed by Guy McAfee, an L.A. vice cop who also operated a gambling club in Paradise called the Pair-o'-Dice—the demands of tax collectors, building inspectors, casino operators, and parking-lot attendants were considerably less confining than within the Las Vegas city limits. Predicated like Los Angeles on the nation's budding romance with cars and low-rise architecture, El Rancho Vegas was a smash. Hull promptly doubled its size, and the first of many hotel-building booms seized the city.

The next salvo on the Strip—fired even farther out of town—was the Last Frontier. The brainchild of R. E. Griffith, a Texas theater-chain magnate, it suffused the amenities of its predecessor with an Old West atmosphere that, in its thoroughness, suggested a theme park: the lobby, casino, and saloon featured big ceiling beams, mounted buffalo heads, Texas cattle horns, antique guns, saddle-shaped stools, a forty-niner bar and restaurant—even stagecoach rides and pack trips out of town. In time, an entire frontier village grew up on the premises. Meanwhile, back downtown, "Glitter Gulch"—so-called because of the neon it employed to attract attention—launched a feverish competition with the up-and-coming Strip, as the Monte Carlo Club, Rex Club, Las Vegas Club, Nevada Biltmore, El Cortez, and Golden Nugget all appeared in the forties. After the war, organized crime had begun taking a serious interest; out on the Strip, Siegel built the famous Flamingo (and was assassinated when it flopped), which was followed in the fifties by the Desert Inn, the Sahara, the Sands, the Riviera, the Dunes, the Hacienda, the Tropicana, and the Stardust, in the sixties by the Mint, the Aladdin, the Four Queens, the Las Vegas Hilton, Caesars Palace, and Circus Circus. From the beginning, the hotels and their stages were magnets for big-name show-biz stars, who, because of the casinos, could be paid in a style to which they were accustomed.

Taking into account all the associated activity, local development wisdom held that every new hotel room in Las Vegas created five jobs. As the postwar binge played itself out, the city and county exhibited predictable demographic effects. In 1947 the population of Las Vegas had been seventeen thousand; in 1950 it was twenty-five thousand; and in 1960, sixty-four thousand, with twice that many people residing in greater Clark County (Henderson, Boulder City, et al.) As it spread south into the desert, becoming a world-renowned spectacle of gaudy, uninhibited excess, Las Vegas seemed to be moving ever closer to L.A.—a route that led directly through the Mojave.

By 1967, the desert between Barstow and Las Vegas had become quite thoroughly trafficked—mostly along the corridor of Interstate Highway 15, which connected the casinos to San Bernardino and L.A. The Barstow-to-Vegas motorcycle race, however, eschewed the popular public thoroughfares. At some points it paralleled or passed under the highway, but its course consisted predominantly of dirt tracks, trails, washes, and cross-country routes through the desert. At 150 miles, it would be the longest one-day off-road motorcycle race in the world.

Held the Saturday after Thanksgiving, the first Barstow-to-Vegas race attracted five hundred entrants. The event had a mass start: all the riders lined up shoulder-to-shoulder and, at the drop of a banner, took off at the same instant, making for a smoke bomb—a pile of tires that had been set on fire, sending a black column skyward—a couple of miles away. Succumbing to dust, mechanical breakdown, or rough treatment from surrounding motorcycles, 10 percent of the racers wouldn't even make it that far. Those who did still faced four to six hours of tissue trauma and organ agitation. But in the gathering dusk, those who finished—roughly half of those who'd started at the crack of dawn—found themselves on the Strip, surrounded by crowds of tourists, cavernous casinos, and brilliant flashing lights.

"It was an unbelievable thrill," recalls Rick Sieman, who, unwittingly alluding to the origins of Las Vegas itself, compares B-to-V to "a great land rush. Experts went in the first wave, novices in the second. In the beginning, there was this wall of guys banging into each other and stalling, but once the race was under way, you were riding by yourself. A half hour or forty-five minutes into the race, a lot of people were very tired and settled into a pace. The rocky mining roads in the Clark Mountains were really rough to ride over. Colosseum Gorge had steps— it was very narrow and slippery, with little trickles of water. Even in cold weather you could see green moss there.

"Once you were over the Clark Mountains, it was fantastic, because you could see Stateline, Nevada, at the bottom. Know what it feels like to start out in California, crest a rise, and see Nevada a couple of miles away? Then you'd ride down another fifty or sixty miles, and you could see the pot of gold at the end of the rainbow: Vegas. So when you got done with this long, grueling race, you ended up in Glitter Gulch—the Fun Capital, Sin City of the West. And it was a long weekend, so you could take your family and friends and have a party afterwards. You checked into a motel, got cleaned up, went and had a couple of hundred thousand beers, lost a few dollars in the slot machines, relaxed for a day, and went home. It was *great*."

Others seemed to agree. By the early seventies, Barstow-to-Vegas had grown to three thousand participants, with three to four times that many spectators—the largest, most prestigious off-road motorcycle race in the world. Dirt bikers came from everywhere to take part, having trained as for a marathon, gorging on carbohydrates for days before the event. All of the above, from the travel time to the carbo-loading, was facilitated by the fact that the race took place on Thanksgiving weekend. Some crews and families began pulling in on Wednesday, prepared to camp out for three days and nights as they got ready for the race. Engines were tuned, tires checked, cables and chains adjusted, and all manner of off-road vehicles ridden around the starting area as the hour of the event approached.

The start was what truly set Barstow-to-Vegas apart from other such events. *Los Angeles Times* reporter Shav Glick called it "one of the most awesome spectacles in motorized racing":

> Three thousand cycles, three, four and five deep, extend in a crooked line across the sand, their riders wedged elbow to elbow. . . . As the time for the start approaches, a huge banner is raised several hundred yards down course. At its appearance, engines which have been started, restarted and revived since dawn, are turned off.
>
> The desert becomes so silent it is ghostly.
>
> The banner drops . . . and the desert is alive with shrieking screams of a thousand engines, a thousand knobby tires fighting for traction, spitting sand and silt behind them. A fortunate few riders get off the line first, their throttle hands and left feet fighting through the gears in a desperate bid for top speed.
>
> Everyone else is enveloped in an enormous cloud of dust. Those who took two kicks to start, or are too timid with the throt-

tle, are hopelessly blinded, but must grope ahead, hoping to survive the first few hundred yards. They can't stop because they might get hit from behind.

Gradually the dust from the first wave settles, and another group of several thousand other riders lines up, the second wave. A sweep crew checks the first mile for injured riders or broken bikes. After the course is clear, the banner is raised again, silence reigns for a moment, the banner drops and the cacophony is repeated.

The race, through creosote bush–dotted flatlands, dry lakes, alluvial fans, mountain passes, yucca highlands and patches of cactus, is anticlimactic. It is much like a hundred other races across the wrinkled desert, a bit longer perhaps, but nothing unusual for the competitors unless it is the finishing point—glittering Las Vegas.

As a matter of fact, to many participants it was much more than that. "Barstow-to-Vegas was a focal point for a desert rider," says Rick Sieman. "It was like Mecca to a Muslim—something you just had to do. If you considered yourself a desert racer and didn't have one or two of them under your belt, well, it was like saying you were a football fan but hadn't ever watched the Super Bowl. You just hadn't participated in the granddaddy of 'em all."

Which made it somewhat disappointing for Sieman and his friends when, in 1975, the Bureau of Land Management canceled the Barstow-to-Vegas race.

In 1975, the BLM was assuming a new role in environmental stewardship. For most of the thirty years of its existence, the agency had been notorious for its rubber-stamp "management" of the land under its control, an approach that had gotten it sarcastically branded as the Bureau of Livestock and Mining. The BLM oversees some 60 percent of the public land in the United States—a total of more than three hundred million acres, half of which are located in the western continental states. Most of this territory is literally land that nobody wanted when the federal government tried to give it away (through measures like the Homestead Act) in the nineteenth century. "What do we want of that vast and worthless area," asked Daniel Webster (on behalf of the nation) in 1861, "that region of savages and wild beasts, of wind, of dust, of cactus and prairie dogs?"

Had Webster included grass and hard-rock minerals in his list, he might have understood what was there for people to want. However, these things had been made generally available—without the responsibility of owning the land that produced them—through the government's policy of offering them to the public practically for free. The General Mining Law of 1872 awarded ownership of minerals to anyone who claimed them; the Taylor Grazing Act of 1934 established royalties for the use of public pastureland, but ranchers succeeded in keeping the fees infinitesimal. After all, when the BLM was formed in 1946, ranchers and their offspring comprised the bulk of its personnel. Under such circumstances, the agency operated as little other than a self- (or dis-) interested caretaker of land under its control.

In the 1960s, Congress began—through a series of legislative acts—to encourage the agency to take more of an interest in its job. The Classification and Multiple Use Act of 1964 directed the BLM to determine which public lands should be disposed of (i.e., sold for a song to ranchers) and which should be retained and managed for the purposes of multiple use and sustained yield. The BLM decided that almost all of the land should be retained—a finding borne out in 1970 by the newly created Public Land Law Review Commission. Still, as interior secretary Rogers C. B. Morton observed, "the enormous responsibilities of the BLM, the definition of its mission and authority to accomplish it have never been comprehensively enunciated by Congress." *Et voila*: the Federal Land Policy and Management Act (FLPMA) of 1976.

In theory, "Flipma"—as the act was and is referred to by environmental bureaucrats—gave the BLM supervisory status equal to that of the twin giants of federal land management: the National Park Service and U.S. Forest Service. At the most basic level, it authorized a force of badge-and-gun-carrying rangers to enforce the law on BLM land. More comprehensively, it directed the agency to classify and manage its property according to a policy combining "balanced and diverse resource uses that takes into account the long-term need of future generations for renewable and nonrenewable resources." In other words, the BLM was no longer supposed to function as a blasé caretaker; it was ordered to be an active steward of the public domain. To that end, flora, fauna, wilderness preservation, and recreation were now deemed to carry as much weight as mining and grazing. FLPMA thus served as a barometer of changes in American society since the days of the frontier—not only with respect to activities pursued on public land, but also reflecting the public's attitude toward that land itself.

As far as the California desert was concerned, the most important element of FLPMA was Section 601. That was the part that created a twenty-five-million-acre "California Desert Conservation Area," for which a long-term management plan had to be completed within four years.

Primarily because of population growth, the need for a special approach to the California desert had been pressing since the 1960s. That was when Russ Penny, the state director for the BLM, noted that the character of public-land use in southern California was different from that of any other area managed by the agency. Specifically, it had more people than cattle ranging over it. Ranchers and miners were part of the picture, to be sure, but so were cities, railroads, water projects, power plants, military bases, national parks, jackrabbit homesteaders, and thousands of miles of roads—to say nothing of the hordes of fun seekers now spilling over the passes from the Los Angeles Basin. Recreation was, in fact, fast becoming the predominant use of the California desert. Dirt bikers and dune-buggy drivers were hardly the only such refugees; the desert also attracted geologists, botanists, zoologists, hikers, photographers, rock collectors, and others who simply enjoyed going there for peace and quiet. To such people, the chain-saw whine of a two-stroke engine was worse than the sound of a mosquito in the dark; the noise of a single motorcycle, after all, was calculated to be ten million times greater than the ambient sound of the suburbs—ranking somewhere, decibel-wise, between jet transports and bomb blasts. In a place where silence was thought by many to be the most valuable resource, noise was considered the foulest pollutant of all.

Meanwhile, longtime residents of the desert found themselves increasingly beleaguered by pestiferous machines and drivers. Ranchers discovered that their fences had been cut in order to clear paths for racing. Pipelines were run over and ruptured, dispensing precious stockwater into the ground. New roads were extemporaneously formed, rendering remote landmarks accessible to people who spray-painted them with their names—or with shotguns. Shells, bottles, and cans collected at points where, previously, only animals and determined desert dwellers had gone. Well-intentioned ORV users claimed that "skilled," "courteous," law-abiding behavior would go far to eliminate problems, but as David Sheridan pointed out (in a report entitled *Off-Road Vehicles on Public Land*), even Saint Francis of Assisi would find ire unavoidable if he were performing his acts of kindness on an ORV.

These were merely the social conflicts. The environmental ones were more subtle and pervasive. Aside from its ability to transport people into places that had previously excluded them, the two-stroke motorcycle engine "created a different impulse on the rear wheel," according to Bob Perkins. "It's very explosive. You could go from low rpm's to high rpm's—from dead throttle to wide-open—in a very short time, so the style of riding became more aggressive. The four-stroke is more gentle; it allows you to slip and slide around corners, so the ground remains more level and flat. The two-stroke lets you square off around corners. The bike catapults and makes holes and grooves where it lands; it creates whoop-de-doos [bumps] from its pulsations. It changes the terrain."

Indeed, terrestrial changes were becoming evident wherever ORVs went. The most obvious initial effect was a decrease in vegetation: Knobby tires and spinning wheels could destroy small desert plants the way they sometimes did tortoises—by running over them. But more widespread vegetative impacts were fostered by the machines' compaction of the soil, which damaged seeds and root systems and rendered the earth unreceptive to rain. Less moisture thus became available to plants, so eventually even large and deep-rooted desert bushes like creosote were weakened by ORV activity. In places subjected to heavy use, plant cover was shown by one study to decrease by an average of 60 percent—sometimes by as much as 80 or 90 percent. Even areas that were used infrequently—with several years allowed for recovery, as bikers boasted—averaged a 40 percent reduction in vegetation. A single hare-and-hounds motorcycle race staged near Barstow in 1973, on a course consisting of two loops totaling one hundred miles, was estimated to have damaged 143,201 creosote bushes, 64,360 burro bushes, and 1,609 yuccas.

The effects didn't stop with the plants. Animal habitat disappeared along with vegetative cover; exerting an influence like that of livestock, plant reduction by ORVs got rid of native fauna at rates paralleling those of vegetative loss itself. ORV noise was found to disrupt desert animals' feeding, resting, reproducing, and rearing of young—even to damage their hearing, rendering them more vulnerable to predation and other threats. Tortoises were eliminated largely through the destruction of forage and of places where the animals liked to den: in the shelter of large perennial shrubs, whose roots stabilized the soil sufficiently for a burrow to be built. Moreover, in the absence of such roots, the ground itself was vulnerable to erosion. Even seemingly barren desert soil is protected by a delicate mantle of clay, salt, carbonates, algae, lichens, and/or fungi, which act to seal and stabilize it, allowing topsoil to slowly form. ORVs easily destroy this protective crust, drying out the soil and subjecting it to erosion by wind—which, in the desert, is notoriously strong and nearly constant—and by rain, which, while rare, often takes the form of pulverizing downpours whose runoff and erosive power are extremely high. Especially on steep slopes where soil is shallow, regular ORV activity eliminates the entire soil mantle, exposing infertile bedrock and creating a profusion of ruts that eventually prevents even motorcycles from using the place. In Red Rock Canyon in the northwestern Mojave (a onetime location for cowboy movies), it was estimated that a mile-long hillside lost twelve thousand tons of topsoil in five years. Relatively lush sites nearby like Dove Springs and Jawbone Canyon—formerly the scenes of spectacular wildflower displays and substantial populations of dove, quail, chukar, and cottontail—were effectively sacrificed to ORVs.

In an article entitled "Soil Formation in Arid Regions," Harold E. Dregne explained the situation:

> Soil is the biochemically weathered mantle on the Earth's surface that sustains life, functions as a vast reservoir for the collection and storage of water, and absorbs and neutralizes agricultural, domestic, and industrial wastes. As the sustenance for ecosystems, soils can be viewed as the most important part of the natural environment; yet of all parts of the environment, soils are probably the most abused. . . .
>
> The physical environment in deserts is harsh, vegetation is sparse, and life in general is precarious. Soil formation [the transformation of rock into soil] is slow and easily disrupted. Recuperative powers after disruption are weak because biological activity, which is the main force influencing the rate of soil formation, is low except when occasional rains induce a growth of ephemeral vegetation. It is this lack of resiliency to disruption that leads people to refer to desert soils as fragile. . . .

> Once the soil surface in the [desert] is disturbed, recovery is extremely slow. . . . It is futile to speak of recovery from disturbance of soils in those regions in any time frame related to human occupancy. . . . Once a dune or a gully has appeared or the soil stripped from a slope in the arid regions, a change will have occurred that is, to all intents and purposes, permanent, with no chance of a return to the original soil conditions. . . .
>
> There is no possibility of setting a realistic permissive level of vehicular use; any use will be destructive. If there is to be recreational vehicular use, it should be on an acceptable sacrifice area. It should be remembered, however, that there can be no acceptable sacrifice area unless the much greater runoff and sediment produced can be tolerated downslope of the sacrifice area.

Dunes, washes, and dry lakes were considered less vulnerable to damage than steep slopes or bajadas, but even there it was found that ORV activity had harmful consequences. Acutely sensitive dune-dwelling animals—kangaroo rats, for example—were especially intolerant of ORV disturbance. Agitation of dunes accelerated moisture loss and set sand artificially in motion, increasing air pollution and befouling, if not burying, nearby plant communities. In the washboard patterns that formed following vehicular disturbance, water collected and then evaporated instead of running into washes. Seeds that required abrasion to germinate—after tumbling downstream in a flood—thus failed to produce plants, and populations of animals that relied on such habitats (reptiles, small mammals, and coyotes) were slowly thinned out. Indeed, the chain of environmental consequences associated with ORVs prompted the Geological Society of America to observe that where vehicle use was heavy, almost all existing life was ultimately eradicated.

By February 1972, the problem had gained enough national attention for President Richard Nixon to issue executive order 11644. Recognizing that ORV use came into "frequent conflict with wise land and resource management practices, environmental values, and other types of recreational activity," it was intended to "ensure that the use of off-road vehicles on public lands will be controlled and directed so as to protect the resources of those lands, to promote the safety of all users of those lands, and to minimize conflicts among the various uses of those lands." Toward that end, heads of government agencies were ordered, within six months,

to establish rules and geographic zones for ORV use, along with corresponding penalties to be levied against offenders.

In other words, vehicles of human transportation and amusement
would no longer have free run of the desert. After barely more than a
decade of heady license, their wings were deemed to require clipping by
no less powerful an executive authority than the president of the United
States.

Not incidentally, the mounting dissension over ORVs coincided precisely
with the growth of the Barstow-to-Vegas race. To environmentalists, the
event provided an easy target—a big, fat symbol of the sort of thing that
shouldn't be allowed to go on in the desert. Protests began to be loudly
lodged as the number of entrants approached three thousand in the early
seventies, and over the next few years they grew steadily in pitch.
Meanwhile, though the Federal Land Policy and Management Act
hadn't yet been enacted, the handwriting was on the wall with regard to
the role of the BLM. In the wake of Nixon's executive order, in 1972 the
bureau began requiring permits for ORV events. Two years earlier, the
National Environmental Policy Act had demanded the development of
environmental impact statements for land-use activities affecting federal
property.

As a consequence of all the above, in 1974 the BLM performed an
environmental impact statement on the projected effects of that year's
Barstow-to-Vegas race. Released in October of that year—at two and a
half pounds and 450 pages, containing fifty charts and twenty-five
maps—the report found, among other things, that:

- About seventy-five hundred acres of wildlife habitat had
been, and would continue to be, damaged by the race. On more
than half of the affected area, habitat loss ranged from 80 to 100
percent. Seventy-seven "significant" species of animals were
affected.

- While the race would "produce only momentary intrusion
of noise, fumes, and dust," it nevertheless "would result in permanent loss of soil by wind and water erosion." Most of the
affected ground had high potential for soil compaction, and
recovery would require decades to centuries. Motorcycle tracks

across wet playas could be expected to remain visible for thirty years.

- As against the "short-term economic gains and psycho-social satisfaction of those associated with the race," the event would "result in loss or deterioration of natural, cultural, recreational, and aesthetic values which would otherwise be passed on to future generations" and "further marshal that trend which extends to the nation's wild lands—the habits, activities, commotion, and pollution of the urban world. Thus, the integrity of the desert itself will be further impaired."

- Mitigation of these effects was constrained by the BLM's limited manpower and funding, as well as by the nature of the race itself—"a 'thrill' event, pitting man against environment, with concomitant threats to human safety and environmental damage." But if the event were disallowed, people who had been planning to participate might try to hold an unsanctioned race anyway, which, in creating a confrontation with BLM and police, might result in violence.

Three weeks before the scheduled date, a permit for the race was granted.

The course had already been approved, following multiple flyovers by BLM officials and negotiations with private landowners, public utilities, and the Southern Pacific Railroad, which owned some of the property. The San Gabriel Valley Motorcycle Club, which had been handcuffed in its preparation by the lack of a permit, set about advertising the event, mailing entry blanks, ordering trophies, toilets, and ambulances. Four tons of lime and thirteen hundred black-and-yellow arrows were used to mark the course; to discourage riders from straying off the route, several undisclosed but mandatory checkpoints were set up, where referees marked cards on gas tanks, proving that the riders had stayed on the course. Every car entering the start area was handed a large plastic garbage bag and encouraged to use it. The organizers spent a total of $29,000, raised from the official entry fee of $11.25 per contestant. The number of riders who entered the race was 2,922; about 2,000 more rode without entering. Almost exactly half of the official starters—a total of 1,456 riders (their average age over thirty)—finished the race. Twenty-six riders were injured, mostly with broken bones.

According to Rick Sieman, the 1974 race—the largest Barstow-to-Vegas spectacle yet staged—was a "monumental, astonishing event. The ground shook; the adrenaline flowed." The shutters clicked; the calipers closed. That is to say, the race was monitored and measured more closely than any motorcycle event that had ever taken place. Soil readings were collected at twenty-six points along the course; at each site, a thirty-five-millimeter camera on a post took a 360-degree series of photographs. Thirty dustfall sample jars were placed at ten strategic spots. Small mammals in the vicinity of the start area—kangaroo rats, mainly—were trapped and retrapped for six days before the event and again afterward. Aerial photography supplemented the pictures taken at ground level. The resulting BLM report, released three months after the race, found that it had affected 25 percent more land than the previous year's event; as a result, it had damaged even more soil and vegetation than anticipated. Two-thirds of the earth samples showed evidence of compaction. Annual plants were eradicated from some segments of the course. Vegetation in pit and parking areas was heavily impacted. Two study sites located sixteen miles from the starting line lost half of their preexisting plants. A pair of previously undiscovered archaeological sites were destroyed. Near the start area, there was a 90 percent reduction in the number of small mammals. (A year later, some mammals' population densities were still 80 percent lower than similar but less disturbed habitats.) During the race, the concentration of dust in the air was found to be six to ninety times higher than normal for the area—a thousand times higher during the first fifteen minutes. In the dirt-bike documentary film *On Any Sunday*, the dust cloud generated by Barstow-to-Vegas was said to settle "three weeks later on London;" in fact, it fell right nearby, at a rate of one thousand to seventeen thousand tons per square mile—an increase of about a third in the area's normal *monthly* dustfall.

In January of 1975, before the BLM report was even released, the San Bernardino County Board of Supervisors unanimously recommended that the race be discontinued. The following September, the San Gabriel Valley Motorcycle Club offered to route the event around Soda Lake, place more pit toilets along the course, and start the race in three waves, each an hour apart. But the BLM, citing the damage documented in its report, wasn't having any. It authorized a scrambles ORV event in the Rand open area in the northwestern Mojave, but it denied the club's application for a 1975 Barstow-to-Vegas race. Symbolically speaking, the wide-open approach to the North American desert was over.

When Louis McKey received this news, he decided not to take it lying down.

McKey was a forty-three-year-old electrician from Fontana, a suburb of San Bernardino. Originally from Oregon, his family had moved to California during World War II; afterward, as a teenager, Louis lied about his age in order to join the army infantry, with which he served in Korea. After his discharge, he fell in love with a girl from Fontana and moved there soon afterward. He went to work for Kaiser Steel, which operated an enormous plant in the town, processing ore from the Eagle iron mine near Joshua Tree National Monument.

"In the fifties, people told me the desert was a hostile environment," McKey remembers. "But I liked solitude, so I went out there and did some amateur prospecting, and saw what a beautiful place it was. When people say there's nothing between L.A. and Las Vegas, I just laugh. They don't know what they're talking about."

McKey also liked to fish, hike, and backpack. Occasionally he volunteered to help the state fish and game department stock streams with trout or rebuild damaged watercourses. He knew that, even on private property, the public was entitled to use a stream if the landowner didn't have title to its source. Hence, when a man charged McKey's nephews twenty-five cents for fishing a creek that ran through his property, McKey went there himself and threw out a line. When the owner appeared on horseback and demanded a quarter, McKey read him the riot act and reported him to the state. The man was subsequently forced to build gates in the fences along his property.

"I've always stood up for our rights," explains McKey—the kind of guy who, when he saw people tampering with pumps in a gas station late at night, stopped and got out of his car to deter them. When his daughter proposed more discretion in such circumstances, McKey lectured her about the necessity of taking personal responsibility for the public welfare. "We're United States citizens," he said by way of explanation. "It's our obligation."

In 1949, McKey had briefly owned a Harley-Davidson motorcycle but decided that "it wasn't my bag." Nevertheless, he had a friend who owned a dirt bike and entered the first Barstow-to-Vegas race in 1967. McKey agreed to work in his pit crew, and as a result, he "saw the start. I felt the excitement. After that, I was so pumped I had to get involved."

McKey joined a motorcycle club. He bought a Suzuki 100, took it out in the desert, and practiced riding it up and down hills. "I tried to go up a dam and couldn't," he remembers. "I wasn't adept at riding fast in the desert; I couldn't read terrain. I enjoyed it, but I didn't feel capable of racing." More to his liking were trips where "four or five of us would go out and camp for a week. We'd ride every day and then hike. Motorcycles were the method of transportation to get us to a place where we could do something. Just to ride a motorcycle doesn't mean that much to me; even today, a lot of people in my own club don't understand that. When they ask me to go for a ride, I'll only say yes if there's a purpose—to go and see some palm trees, say. I like to take pictures of flowers and insects, and I can spend six hours without going a hundred yards. A lot of your off-roaders just like to go out and ride."

In time, McKey graduated to a competition-model trail bike. He began to enter races and eventually stepped up to a Yamaha 125 ("*That* was a motorcycle"). Finally he settled on a 250. "I never had any desire to race anything larger than that. You can go faster, but this requires skill. I only rode serious competition one year—1973. I started riding Barstow-to-Vegas in '68 or '69, but I was just taking part and having fun, trying to master the bike and the terrain. My family and I raced every week. Novice riders get no recognition at all, and they don't deserve to, because if they were good enough, they'd become intermediates. But I felt they should get *some*, even if they didn't deserve it."

McKey took to recording all the race results in his class. In one Mother's Day event, the first thirty-three novices received points, and the thirty-third finisher was named Wallis Weatherwax—a member, as it happened, of the Desert Ducks Motorcycle Club. McKey began buying ads in *Cycle News*, generally beginning with the words QUACK! QUACK! and singling out for recognition the valiant Wallis Weatherwax, whose name consequently became a symbol for upstart desert racers. But as the controversy over Barstow-to-Vegas intensified, the most enduring symbol to arise from the ads was another character—one that McKey conjured from Weatherwax and his aptly named club. A shadowy but stubborn champion of the rights of everyday citizens, this mysterious figure would wage a one-man war against the powers that be—specifically the BLM. In the tradition of superheros everywhere, he concealed his civilian identity but left his mark ("Quack! Quack!") wherever he struck. Leading out-of-breath authorities on a merry chase across the California desert, he might have been called Zorro. But in the mind of Louis McKey, he—that is, McKey himself—was the Phantom Duck of the Desert.

The way McKey remembers it, after the 1975 race was canceled, the Phantom Duck anonymously "invited a few of his friends" to ride their motorcycles through the desert between Barstow and Las Vegas on the Saturday after Thanksgiving. One of the two dozen or so bikers who showed up brought along a map and was therefore accused by the others—including McKey—of being the Phantom Duck. Gratified by the turnout, McKey continued to promote the protest incognito; for correspondence he used various general-delivery addresses, one of which was in Helendale, a desert town on Route 66 that at the time consisted only of a post office and gas station. "I liked that," he says.

Sometime in 1976, McKey made an appointment—under his real name—to discuss off-road-vehicle recreation with the director of the BLM's California Desert District, Gerry Hillier. Hillier told McKey that, in accordance with the new law, the BLM would be restricting ORV activity to specific areas and permitted events, but that Barstow-to-Vegas wouldn't be one of them because it had gotten out of control and was threatening the natural resources of the desert. The following fall, more "Quack! Quack!" letters and ads appeared in *Cycle News* inviting people to repeat the "memorial trail ride" of the year before. This time, about forty people did. A guy named Bernie Rice, who had lobbied independently to promote the ride, got his turn to be accused of being the Phantom Duck.

The following Monday, Hillier was in his office in Riverside when an aide came in and said that McKey was outside demanding to see him again immediately. "He had fire in his eye," Hillier remembers. "He pointed at me and said, 'I'm gonna get you, you son of a bitch! You won't let good motorcyclists use that course, but Colosseum Gorge has been destroyed by miners. They've done more damage up there than any motorcyclist has *ever* done.' Well. The Newmont Mining Company had wanted to drill for core samples on Clark Mountain. They'd come along, seen that Flipma hadn't passed yet, and asked us for guidance. My geologist advised them about the location of water bars and things like that, but there weren't any rules of operation in existence yet. So they bladed a road up there. And apparently they removed quite a bit of brush."

"The way it used to be, you could travel the side of the gorge with a horse or a motorcycle, but not even with a four-wheel-drive," McKey remembers. The mining company said they wanted to improve an 'existing road,' then they blasted it so much that you could drive a Cadillac through there." Thus, the moist, mossy interior of Colosseum Gorge— the place that Rick Sieman identified as the most beautiful and challenging section of the entire Barstow-to-Vegas course—had been bulldozed after being declared off-limits to bike racers for environmental reasons. Years later, when the miners built another road around and above the gorge, the BLM required boulders to be placed at the top and bottom of the lower route in order to block access to the canyon; but by then, McKey says, "the beauty of Colosseum Gorge was gone."

The following year, Hillier recalls, the Barstow-to-Vegas protest ride was "extremely emotional." A year after the passage of FLPMA, the California BLM still had no rangers on its desert staff and was thus powerless to police the event. The American Motorcyclists Association, complying with the new rules in an effort to foster the image of bikers as law-abiding citizens, announced that none of its members would take part in the Phantom Duck trail ride. Nonetheless, many riders in AMA colors were among the 150 who showed up.

Little by little, the real identity of the Phantom Duck was coming to light. This was helped along by Rick Sieman, who had given up art restoration (dealing with "little old blue-haired ladies and their foo-foo dogs," as he puts it) to become an off-road-racing writer. "One of the first things I wanted to do when I took over *Dirt Bike* Magazine in 1978 was find out who the Phantom Duck was," he remembers. "I put the word out through the underground—hard-core dirt bikers who went way back. Three days later, I got a call from the Duck himself. I went over and met him at his home in Fontana, and did the first story ever on the Phantom Duck of the Desert—this guy who was just an electrician, but who had enough nerve and backbone to try and do something that he believed should be done. I thought he was great."

McKey himself had been steadily assuming a higher profile. In 1978 he wrote letters—each backed by an advertisement for that year's protest ride—to every member of Congress, asking for help in reestablishing the Barstow-to-Vegas race. Gerry Hillier had suspected McKey of being the Phantom Duck ever since meeting him in his BLM office, and in September 1978 the bureau ran a check on one of the Duck's post-office boxes. It was found to be registered to one Phyllis Gould, the sister of Louis McKey. Two months later—one week before the date of that year's protest, and at a time when McKey himself happened to be serving jury duty—the agency summoned both brother and sister into federal court.

Hillier was seeking an injunction against McKey's promotion of the trail rides, which Hillier felt were acquiring qualities that—even if they didn't match the numbers—echoed the overtones and effects of the outlawed race itself. Under the law, groups of fifty or fewer were allowed to assemble in the desert without a permit, but Hillier maintained that McKey was encouraging much larger gatherings. By then the BLM desert district had seven rangers to enforce the law (on twelve million acres), but there were threats that they'd be run over or shot if they got in the way of the motorcyclists. Through his magazines and other means, Sieman set about creating a legal defense fund for McKey; to raise money, the two of them (plus a friend named Al Fols) started a corporation called Phantom Duck of the Desert, Inc. "We put our own homes on the line to keep Louis out of jail," Sieman says.

Hillier and McKey and their attorneys met in U.S. District Court in Los Angeles at 10:30 A.M. on a rainy Tuesday in late November, two days before Thanksgiving of 1978. Presiding over the hearing was Judge Warren Ferguson, a magistrate known—in Hillier's words—as "a champion of people whose voices aren't often heard." Ferguson had made his reputation defending battered Mexican wives for as little as a case of lemons; during the Vietnam War, he had gained notoriety as a judge by allowing an organized protest to take place—after the application had been denied by the Los Angeles Police Department—when President Richard Nixon appeared at the Century Plaza Hotel.

McKey's attorney—George Stephan of the Encino firm Flame, Sanger, Grayson, and Ginsburg—tried to make the case that the BLM was attempting to deprive McKey of his First Amendment rights by preventing him from protesting the government's actions by way of "a symbolic ride on unpaved, but established and open, roads." In lengthy testimony, Gerry Hillier acknowledged that, except for private mining roads around Clark Mountain and Colosseum Gorge, much of the planned protest route followed legal rights-of-way. But he maintained that the "event" (using the BLM's definition of a gathering of more than fifty) couldn't be controlled since it wasn't legally permitted—and considering the expected number of participants, it wasn't likely to confine itself to the public thoroughfares anyway.

At several points, Judge Ferguson questioned Hillier directly. To wit:

> JUDGE FERGUSON: Part of the civil protest of the defendants in this case—and this is the basis on which they make their First Amendment argument—is that the Bureau of Land Management, or the government, sees no problem in turning over public lands to multimillion-dollar corporations for the purpose of mining, but if one person who has a motorcycle wants to get out there and enjoy the beauty of the desert he is prohibited from doing that.
>
> GERALD HILLIER: Okay.
>
> FERGUSON: What is your answer to that argument?
>
> HILLIER: My answer is very simple that as your Honor probably well knows, the Bureau of Land Management is faced with administering a broad variety of laws, some of which Congress passed are really in conflict with one another. But the fact remains that most mining—and I speak now of hard rock mining, gold, lead, silver, zinc, those types of minerals—are still administered under the 1872 mining law, which, basically, exists to encourage mineral development in the western United States, in which a miner can go in and basically do whatever he has to do to explore and claim and develop his claim into a producing mine. The government does not turn over the land to that miner; the miner simply goes out and makes—does whatever he wants to do, exploration-wise. There have been repeated attempts in the Congress to amend, change, modify, the 1872 mining law, and all, including one in the last session of Congress, have failed.
>
> BLM is working very closely with San Bernardino County in terms of attempting to get some control on management of the surface resources to reduce environmental damage associated with mining. We voluntarily work with some of the larger mining

companies in terms of road location, but, basically, the Congress has said the lands shall be open for mining. And I have no approval or discretionary authority over people coming in under the 1872 mining law unless they file for a patent and then, of course, it gets into a question of do they have a valid discovery?

Now, in terms of preventing one man going out and riding his motorcycle, the President, through Executive Order 11644, and the Congress, through the recently passed Federal Land Policy and Management Act, has recognized that off-road vehicle use of the public lands is considered one of the legitimate uses of the public lands, where it can take place properly and can be administered. And the California Vehicle Management Plan that we have, that is attached to my affidavit, is in fact an interim attempt at identifying those areas where one man, or a hundred people, or five hundred people can ride their motorcycles, or ride their dune buggies, or their triwheelers, or go jeeping, or whatever they want to do, and it identifies those places where they can do it. And we have not precluded one man going out to the desert and enjoying the desert and enjoying its scenic beauty. . . . in fact, more power to him. But we do have some areas that we identified as very sensitive areas that the public use has to be restricted and they are so sensitive and so fragile, or they involve endangered species such as the tortoise.

And then we have a situation where one man attempts to gather a number of people around him and then that creates its associated and periphery problems in terms of camping, in terms of sanitation, in terms of crowd control, that is completely apart or it's something in addition to the impact of one person riding a motorcycle across public lands.

Ferguson decided to grant the BLM's request for a restraining order against McKey. He stated his position this way:

Well, last night, after watching the exciting Sunday night football game between Houston and Miami, I resumed my reading of Will Durant's *History of Civilization*. In the process of skipping around his volumes—but I was reading the volume on Greece last night—he makes a very interesting phrase. He says that men became civilized when they recognized that liberty exists when there is adherence to the law.

And it may be that I can effectively enforce what the Bureau of Land Management asks.

But primarily I have to appeal to the reason of Mr. McKey. I can only repeat and reiterate some of the things that I said earlier this morning, that it is absolutely necessary, in our form of government, that we have dissent. And dissent must be not only tolerated, but it has to be encouraged.

But dissent has to be verbal and nonviolent. It has to be exercised in an intelligent way. It is true that it does not necessarily have to be the spoken word; we place just as much value on symbolic dissent as we do on verbal dissent. The Supreme Court has clearly defined the difference between protected symbolic dissent versus nonprotected symbolic dissent. We have a right to wear black armbands to protest government conflict that we disapprove of. On the other hand, we can't burn our draft cards. And the difference is very dramatic. Dissent cannot be violent—even unintentional violence.

And as citizens, the government has a duty to permit you and encourage you to dissent over the policies of the Bureau of Land Management. The government must protect your right to criticize the law with reference to the use of that fragile desert by multimillion-dollar mining corporations because it's only with that dissent and only with that viewpoint expressed do we arrive at the truth, do we arrive at the right decision.

But the facts of this case indicate to me that I must grant the motion of the Bureau of Land Management to issue the injunction.

Now, you may say, "Judge, what's the difference between this and the march to Selma?" Both involve an aspect of the right to assemble, to petition for the redress of grievances. Fundamental differences. The march to Selma involved racial discrimination. It involved very fundamental, basic protest against the most fundamental of constitutional rights, that is, the right to be treated equally.

But nobody—nobody—has the right to ride a motorcycle over lands owned by somebody else.

You don't have to confine your protest to Congress. We hear the phrase, "Well, if you don't like it, protest to Congress." That type of protest is generally ineffectual because today—and it was admitted from the stand that the Bureau of Land Management has acted in getting the laws changed, and you have a right to make your protest to the Bureau of Land Management. Maybe you can get them to see the wisdom of getting Congress to change the law.

But if we are to have a civilization that Will Durant describes, that civilization began when man recognized that liberty exists only when there is adherence to the law, I have to grant this injunction. If I were the head of the Bureau of Land Management, an administrative official, I might say that there would be no harm in using the old road, the old highway, and I would maybe issue a permit. That is not my function. The law says that for the type of conduct that is going to take place, trying to take place, on November the 25th, that you just get a permit. And I can only find that that requirement of the law is reasonable, does not violate any of your constitutional rights. You have the right, with the forty-nine others, to go ahead because there is no requirement of a permit in that instance. And the permit requirement is sensible.

I explained to you this morning the impact of the destruction of the desert upon our grandchildren. You say, "Judge, but why do they let multimillion-dollar corporations engage in that same sensitivity?" And I probably would agree with you. It's so fragile, and whether or not we are going to leave an inheritance to our children of that desert is in doubt.

Now, I can either appeal to your reason or not. It does not make any difference whether you agree with me or do not agree with me. I am appealing to your reason, and reason and common sense says that that bike ride should not take place. You should not permit it. You should not encourage it. You should actively engage in stopping it because, like Mr. Stephan said this morning, you people are good people, and I told him that of course you are. And good people obey the law.

All right.

The defendants, Louis McKey and Phyllis L. Gould . . . are

hereby restrained from promoting, organizing, sponsoring or participating in any off-road motorcycle trail ride, or other similar event, such as the one scheduled by them for November 25, 1978, until they apply for and receive permission in writing . . . (and) are directed to assert all reasonable efforts to stop anyone from participating in the Phantom Duck of the Desert Fourth Annual Barstow-to-Las Vegas Unorganized Trail Ride. The injunction is effective immediately . . . (but) will not prohibit the defendants—there are two defendants—a total of fifty people, this one year, from using the old road and other roads which are ostensibly open to the public between Barstow and Las Vegas. . . .

All right. I have spoken as forcibly as I possibly can. With that I have to leave it with your sense as American citizens. . . .

Now, get me that order as soon as you can because it is raining out and I do not want to get stuck in the freeway traffic.

When court was adjourned, McKey approached Hillier and offered to help him prevent a mass gathering on the condition that the BLM designate a route for the fifty protestors to follow. Believing that "that would have been tantamount to endorsing the event," Hillier declined.

Five days later, on the Sunday after Thanksgiving, the following report appeared in the *Los Angeles Times*:

CYCLISTS DEFY COURT BAN ON RACE IN DESERT

The "Phantom Duck of the Desert Fourth Annual Barstow-to-Las Vegas Trail Ride" proved more powerful than a federal court order Saturday.

Approximately 580 motorcyclists roared away from the starting point 20 miles east of Barstow at 7:30 A.M. despite an injunction obtained last week by the Bureau of Land Management (BLM) aimed at halting the race.

But BLM inspectors, outnumbered by cyclists 60-to-1, were present along the route to count riders and take pictures, and an agency spokesman said it was considering pressing the legal action against the race organizer . . . [although] Ken Kleiber, chief ranger for the Barstow Resource Area . . . said "The Phantom Duck" apparently had not been sighted among the riders.

Some time later, Rick Sieman was at home "sitting at my breakfast table having coffee. There was a knock at the door, and a federal marshal was standing there. He said, 'Mr. Sieman? Sign here, please.' He had a stack of papers three inches thick. I was being indicted for conspiracy, for violation of land-use [laws]. . . . it went on and on, count after count after count. They wanted fines of hundreds of thousands of dollars; they wanted to put us in jail for years. I've never seen such heavy-handed shit in my life. The BLM had never been challenged by any group of off-roaders before, and they were gonna try and make an example of us. They tried to crush us."

In fact, Sieman, McKey, and their partner Al Fols were being indicted for contempt of court—i.e., for violating Ferguson's restraining order. They pled not guilty, and Ferguson again heard the case. However, after listening to testimony from Hillier, a BLM public-information officer, and a miner who was mad at the bikers for messing up his access road, Ferguson suddenly astounded everyone by calling a halt to the proceedings, apparently in disgust.

According to Sieman (and his attorney Stephan), the defendants had succeeded in proving that the federal government not only had been waging war against its own citizens, but "didn't have a clue" as to who had actually ridden where on the Saturday after Thanksgiving. The way Hillier remembers it, Ferguson acknowledged that the BLM probably had a case for criminal conspiracy, "but didn't think McKey deserved [to go to jail]. He considered Louis an honorable man, but wrongly guided. And he found that the government clearly hadn't listened to him or tried to work with him." Sieman's involvement was deemed to be protected by freedom of the press. Therefore, rather than declare anybody guilty or not guilty, Ferguson stopped the trial and commanded the estranged parties to work out their differences that same day.

"He left the building but ordered us to stay there until an agreement was signed," McKey remembers. "At one point, we'd already signed it but the BLM hadn't, so we held Rick Sieman back by the arms while he screamed and yelled and kicked at them." The agreement maintained, among other things, that the BLM had "a constitutional duty to act without prejudice" toward the defendants, but that the "trail ride should not have needed to have taken place; and in the absence of a Bureau of Land Management permit, it would be wrong for an event to happen in the future."

In the eyes of the defendants, they'd beaten the BLM in court. In the view of Gerry Hillier, "it was a wash."

In the afterglow of this "understanding," the influence of the Phantom Duck didn't exactly subside. Rather, the place in the BLM's ribs where McKey had lodged his thorn continued to swell, sending shooting pains through the agency's entire body. In 1980 McKey sued the Desert District for excluding him from its media mailing list despite the fact that, as president and "press director" of Phantom Duck, Inc., he'd published fifteen newsletters and several articles in *Dirt Bike* and *Cycle News*. U.S. district court judge A. Wallace Tashima agreed that the bureau had "arbitrarily denied [McKey] access to BLM information made available to others, in violation of his First Amendment rights." McKey was duly placed on the list.

That same year, the California Desert Plan was nearing completion. Having taken three years and six million dollars to prepare, it was the largest regional planning effort ever attempted in the United States. In accordance with its mandate for multiple use, the plan identified a dozen crucial factors requiring direct attention: cultural resources, Native American values, wildlife, vegetation, wilderness, wild horses and burros, livestock grazing, recreation, motorized-vehicle access, geology and minerals, energy production and utility corridors, and land tenure adjustment. To administer these "elements," the BLM divided the desert into zones termed Class C, L, M, or I, where it recommended controlled, limited, moderate, or intensive use. The largest category—comprising almost half the total—was Class L. Class C represented 2.1 million acres (out of 25 million in the California Desert Conservation Area, half of which were controlled by the BLM) to be studied with an eye toward wilderness designation. The other zones provided for a variety of uses including mining, grazing, oil and gas exploration, and ORVs.

With regard to the last, the plan noted: "The proliferation of roads and trails in the CDCA has resulted in a serious problem in many areas and provides the most difficult management issue for BLM and the public. Many of the Desert's loveliest and most fragile resources can only be enjoyed by use of vehicle access routes, but these resources are quickly destroyed if vehicles travel everywhere." The plan thus confined vehicles mainly to preestablished "routes of travel" including "roads, ways, trails, and washes" and limited off-road parking and camping to within one hundred feet of such routes. It did, however, designate thirteen open free-play (already heavily used) areas where ORVs could go wherever their drivers wanted. It also provided for three long-distance point-to-point races: Stoddard Valley to Johnson Valley; Johnson Valley to Parker; and the so-called Parker 400. Barstow-to-Vegas remained conspicuously absent.

Between the alternative avenues of sweeping protection and intensive use, the BLM was obviously trying to steer a middle course. Hence, as may have been predictable for a program that proposed to "manage, use, develop, and protect" the desert all at the same time, the plan was embraced by almost no one. As far as conservationists were concerned, it was far too lenient on livestock and didn't include nearly enough wilderness, thus leaving most of the desert vulnerable to continuing degradation. In the minds of ORV enthusiasts, the place was practically being locked up.

The BLM fielded the brunt of public dissatisfaction during the fall of 1980, when it invited comments on the proposed plan. In keeping with McKey's public status, the agency invited him to offer his comments at a hearing in San Bernardino on October 20. McKey surprised them by showing up with a .45 automatic military pistol displayed in a holster on his hip.

"The BLM had a new assistant state director moderating the meeting," McKey remembers. "His name was Ron Hofman. He was from the East and didn't know doodly-squat about what was going on out here, so I wanted to leave him with an impression. I practiced for a couple of weeks. I went to the San Bernardino Police Department and asked if there was any problem with me wearing a gun, and they said not if it wasn't loaded. At the meeting, I wore my combat infantrymen's badge and sat on the end of the aisle so this thing hung out with the flap open, totally exposed."

When McKey was called upon to speak, he stepped to the microphone and said:

"I would rather not make suggestions to you people because I know that you don't listen to them. . . . I think I would much rather talk to a toad. . . . Mr. Hofman . . . you have not performed the duties that Congress has asked you to. . . . You are making all these decisions based on an inventory of less than two percent [of the desert]. . . . It is ridiculous, utterly ridiculous. . . . [The plan states] that after twenty years . . . the public will have become a full participating partner in BLM management activities. That is a bunch of crap and you know it. You know you are not going to get public acceptance of this garbage. . . . If you believe this is true and honest . . . you will go where everybody else is going to go that is sitting there and I don't think it is a very nice place."

The parts of the plan that inspired McKey's costuming referred to the needs for "establishing a BLM presence within areas needing protection" and "close coordination with the Department of Defense and with local military bases . . . in managing public uses on public lands within the vicinity of the bases."

"When I was a young lad of nineteen," McKey said, "the United States Army Infantry gave me this little badge up here. They pinned that on me and said, 'Son, that is yours. You did your duty for your country.' That is the combat infantrymen's badge. They give you that for killing people. . . . I fought for my country and I was damn proud to do it. And I tell you what: I am going to fight for freedom and I am going to fight for human rights and I am going to fight you and you and you, and all the rest of you. . . . I will do anything necessary to eliminate those who will take away the freedom of the American people in regards to the multiple use of the public lands."

Turning to address the audience, McKey cautioned: "When you go out to the desert you had better arm yourself, because no matter where you are out there, you are subject to the Green Berets jumping you at any minute. And what is going to happen out there is the same thing that is happening in Alaska today. It may not be common knowledge, but you should know, Ron Hofman . . . that a BLM uniform disappears quickly in Alaska. They don't last long. They are never seen or heard from again. And if that is what this country has to come to to protect the rights of the citizens from people like you and your ideas, and from stuff like this, then that is what we are going to have."

When McKey was finished, he noticed two police officers standing behind him. As he returned to his seat, they asked him to step outside. McKey said, "After you." One of the cops said, "No—after *you*." At that point, the other officer reached for McKey's gun. McKey backed away and warned him, "Don't touch my body." The atmosphere in the room was electric.

Eventually the officers succeeded in peacefully escorting McKey outside, where they satisfied themselves that his gun wasn't loaded. Nevertheless, they took it into custody for "safekeeping." McKey picked it up at the police station the next day. A day later, however, a local newspaper published the false rumor (along with the actual facts) that McKey had been cited for carrying a loaded weapon. From then on, McKey says, "the story just kept getting bigger. I didn't attend any meetings for a while after that, because I wouldn't have been able to keep a straight face. If anybody questioned me, they'd see that the whole thing was a charade. But I wanted [the BLM] to keep the impression that I was a threat to them."

The strategy worked. A few weeks after the hearing, the BLM announced that it wouldn't assign any rangers to that year's Phantom Duck protest ride. The announced reason was that they were needed in more heavily used parts of the desert over the Thanksgiving weekend, but internal BLM memos—which were also circulated and published after McKey obtained copies—cited the "overt threat to BLM employees' lives as a result of the recent gun-toting episode" by the Phantom Duck, who had, the memos suggested, been elevated to "folk hero" status by the agency's feud with him.

On December 18, 1980, the California Desert Plan was approved and adopted by the U.S. Department of the Interior. The BLM was subsequently sued by the American Motorcyclists Association, the California Mining Association, and Inyo County, California, which claimed that the plan was unfairly weighted toward preservation. One month after its adoption, Ronald Reagan was inaugurated as president, and to the post of secretary of the interior he promptly appointed one James Watt. Soon afterward, it began to seem that the government intended to eliminate the BLM altogether. Under Watt's tenure, the agency's budget for wildlife habitat was reduced by 48 percent; for wilderness, 42 percent; for soil, air, and water management, 48 percent; for land-use planning, 25 percent. In 1982, Watt eliminated 1.4 million acres of wilderness-study areas from consideration, opening them to exploration and development. The Sierra Club sued and was upheld in federal court, which found that Watt had "failed to follow the law" in his attempt to overhaul programs implemented by Congress. But the BLM, whose status had been so recently enhanced and empowered under President Jimmy Carter and interior secretary Cecil Andrus, was now clearly on the run. In an effort to derail the lawsuit threatening the Desert Plan, the agency began rifling through its inventory for possible concessions.

In 1982 it found some. The BLM reduced its recommendations for wilderness in the desert from 2.1 to 1.9 million acres; it eliminated 47,500 acres from the East Mojave National Scenic Area, which the Desert Plan had created; it increased the legal off-road camping distance from one hundred to three hundred feet; it moved to open the Panamint Dunes wilderness study area, west of Death Valley, to ORVs. And lastly, but far from least, it offered to reinstate the Barstow-to-Vegas motorcycle race.

The resumption of Barstow-to-Vegas took the form of an amendment to the Desert Plan. The rationale given was that rules had recently been developed by desert racers allowing greater controls on such events; for example, crews had been consolidated so that one could work for several clubs, reducing the size of the pit areas, which did so much damage to soil and vegetation. Moreover, District 37 of the American Motorcyclists Association volunteered to reduce the number of entrants to twelve hundred, with no more than four hundred riders in each of three starting waves. The AMA worked with the BLM to determine an acceptable course, confining it to existing roads, trails, and washes. A new environmental impact statement indicated that less than 1 percent of the route would cross previously unaffected areas. "Although there would be unavoidable adverse effects on a number of resources directly on the race course," the bureau found, "the impacts would be lower than those that led to the canceling of the race in 1975." A raft of rules was outlined to define where the racers could and couldn't go and how they had to conduct themselves when they got there. The Sierra Club and other groups dutifully filed suit, claiming that the BLM hadn't implemented enough environmental safeguards to mitigate the effects of the race. But after driving the course with a gaggle of attorneys, Judge Tashima ruled that the event could go forward.

At 8:02 A.M. on November 26, 1983, the first Barstow-to-Vegas race in nine years took off for the bomb. As it turned out, only 1,056 riders signed up. One of them was Louis McKey, now sufficiently comfortable with celebrity to be wearing his name on the outside of his racing jumper, with the word *Duck* emblazoned on his pants. As McKey sped along, other riders came up behind him and—noticing who it was that they were passing—reached out to shake his hand or pat him on the back. "It was great," he remembers, "to get that recognition from my peers."

He wasn't quite so enthusiastic about the reincarnated race itself. "There were so many rules that they turned a great race into something mediocre," McKey says. "The BLM regulated the route so strictly that they took the creativity out of it. The AMA didn't have enough people manning the course, and they directed people wrong." At one point, ribbons tied to bushes by a mining company were mistaken for course markers, and several hundred racers followed them straight down a wash, ending up twelve miles off course. To get back on, some cut straight across the open desert. Elsewhere, in one of two wilderness-study areas traversed by the route, environmentalists claimed that riders left an eight-foot-wide road in terrain that had previously been untouched.

In subsequent years, Phantom Duck, Inc., would collaborate with the BLM in Nevada—"where it's easier," McKey says, "to make a real race course"—on the non-California part of the route. "Riders like variety, so we mixed up the terrain," he says. "It went through dry lakes, sand washes, rock washes, and crossgrain"—i.e., the stream courses, furrows, and flanks that etch the faces of bajadas. ("I *love* crossgrain," McKey says.) Despite its name and image, the race hadn't finished in Las Vegas for some time; the city's suburbs were expanding, making a motorcycle race through its outskirts increasingly impractical. As opposed to the general notion that Barstow-to-Vegas took place in the middle of nowhere, the fact of the matter was that it connected the two fastest-growing population centers in the United States.

Housing development in the Mojave Desert might be said to have started with the Small Tract Act of 1938, which authorized the government's sale of five-acre plots on eight million acres of public land between the Mexican border and Kern County, California. An individual parcel could be leased for three to five years, after which, if a home had been built, it could be bought for "not less than $1.25 an acre." When the act was passed, the Los Angeles land office was inundated with applications, three-quarters of which were for tracts near Twentynine Palms on the border of Joshua Tree National Monument. Hence, over a period of a dozen or so years following the war, 138,000 "jackrabbit homesteads"— many sporting small, cheap cabins quickly constructed for "home, health, recreational, or business" purposes, in accordance with the terms of the act—spread across the desert all the way to Victorville and Barstow. As the Twentynine Palms weekly newspaper, the *Desert Trail*, explained it:

> As Southern California became more congested, and many were forced to leave cities for health reasons, the small tract people started to make their year 'round homes here, even though they had no roads, electricity or water. Their need and desire to live in the desert were matched by their tenacity, with the result that all these modern necessities are gradually being added. . . . Several water hauling services allow "inside plumbing," while some have put down their own wells and have pressure pumps. Many miles of telephone lines have been extended. . . . As electricity became available, for cooking, heating and cooling, more and more people moved here, not only from Southern California, but from the Northwest and Eastern states. Others use their homes for vacations and for weekend entertaining. Families started moving into their enlarged desert homes, with the result that school buses are adding more miles to their routes. . . . Roads have been made and trees and shrubs planted. Many cabin owners . . . are permanent residents, participating in the business and social affairs of the community. They have enthusiastically told their friends about the wonders of desert living, and more and more people are becoming 5-acre plot owners as the result.

As time went on, however, more and more people found it difficult not only to make a living in the desert but to pay taxes on their property. The upshot was widespread abandonment of the buildings, which soon turned into eyesores. Today, scores of them continue to deteriorate as they stand forlornly amid the creosote bush like ramshackle clubhouses deserted by fickle kids, blasted by endless wind and sun, offering "places of business" only to clandestine drug manufacturers and "recreational homesites" only to their namesake jackrabbits and assorted other rodents.

Other, more powerful entities had designs on the Mojave, however. Stimulated by the military interest stemming from World War II, the aerospace industry focused its sights on twenty-five-hundred-square-mile Antelope Valley, seventy-five miles north across the San Gabriel Mountains from Los Angeles. The catalyst was Edwards Air Force Base, where Chuck Yeager broke the sound barrier in 1947. South of Edwards, a WPA-era facility called Plant 42 became the birthplace of every new air force fighter that appeared into the sixties, augmented in the seventies and eighties by the Stealth and B-1 bombers. Meanwhile, in the small town of Mojave, the local municipal airport became the nation's number-one test site for experimental civilian aircraft.

One outgrowth of all this was jobs: Antelope Valley was a magnet for every defense contractor and commercial aircraft manufacturer in the United States. In the eighties, however, as coastal California real estate departed the realm of affordability, the desert acquired another kind of allure: located little more than an hour's drive from the L.A. Basin, homes in Antelope Valley were as much as $100,000 cheaper. His-torically, the place had been deemed virtually unlivable because of its relative isolation and raw climate—biting winds in winter and daily sum-mer temperatures in excess of one hundred degrees. But freeways and air conditioning had changed all that, as had the California Aqueduct. Hence, as urban sprawl overflowed L.A., Antelope Valley—a place that had only recently seemed (to the fighter pilots in Tom Wolfe's *The Right Stuff*, for example) a "fossil landscape that had long since been left behind by the rest of terrestrial evolution," characterized only by "wind, sand, tumbleweeds, and Joshua trees"—suddenly found itself the hottest (in more ways than one) home-building area in California. In 1989 alone, eleven thousand new single-family homes were started in the area of Palmdale, a town whose population nearly tripled in ten years. Farther south and east, the established city/suburbs of Riverside and San Bernardino—onetime bedroom communities to L.A.—were now attract-ing commuters of their own. They came from the area around Palm Springs and from Victorville south of Barstow, where the population doubled in eight years and new housing starts were doubling *every* year.

The overall tone of construction and development harked back to the suburban subdivisions that overwhelmed southern California's more hospitable sections during the fifties and sixties. The spearhead of the modern thrust was the "planned community"—a self-contained (often to the point of being walled) minicivilization containing not only thousands of homes but shopping malls, industrial parks, maternity wards, schools, restaurants, golf courses, and often—in the desert—artificial lakes. Even if roads, water, power, telephone lines, and sewage systems had to be provided, in the eyes of developers—and several of the nation's largest now joined the ranks of defense contractors and aircraft manufacturers as local employers—the desert was a dream construction site: effectively flat, consummately cheap, uncoveted by competing interests. Brand-new civic districts, even towns, could be created from whole cloth (or, more accurately, from desert-tortoise and Joshua-tree habitat). Immediately beyond the ordered borders of the new housing developments, hardcore desert was starkly juxtaposed with lush, manicured lawns: Bermuda grass gave way to creosote bush, pavement suddenly turned to dirt, and bent, bedraggled Joshuas stood amid the construction rubble of rising shopping malls, looking far more desolate than they did in unpeopled "wastes." Even in places yet to be built up, nonsensically infinite road layouts foreshadowed a human flood. In the prologue to *City of Quartz*, his sociopolitical examination of Los Angeles, Mike Davis described Antelope Valley's "hundreds of square miles of vacant space engridded to accept the future millions, with strange, prophetic street signs marking phantom intersections like '250th Street and Avenue K':

> The pattern of urbanization here is what design critic Peter Plagens once called the "ecology of evil." Developers don't grow homes in the desert—this isn't Marrakesh or even Tucson—they just clear, grade and pave, hook up some pipes to the local artificial river (the federally subsidized California Aqueduct), build a security wall and plug in the "product." With generations of experience in uprooting the citrus gardens of Orange County and the San Fernando Valley, the developers—ten or twelve major firms, headquartered in places like Newport Beach and Beverly Hills—regard the desert as simply another abstraction of dirt and dollar signs. The region's major natural wonder, a Joshua tree forest containing individual specimens often thirty feet high and older than the Domesday Book, is being bulldozed into oblivion. Developers regard the magnificent Joshuas, unique to this

desert, as large noxious weeds unsuited to the illusion of verdant homesteads. As the head of Harris Homes explained: "It is a very bizarre tree. It is not a beautiful tree like the pine or something. Most people don't care about the Joshuas."

With such malice toward the landscape, it is not surprising that developers also refuse any nomenclatural concession to the desert. In promotional literature intended for homebuyers or Asian investors, they have started referring to the region euphemistically as "North Los Angeles County." Meanwhile they christen their little pastel pods of Chardonnay lifestyle, air-conditioned and over-watered, with scented brand-names like Fox Run, Mardi Gras, Bravo, Cambridge, Sunburst, New Horizons, and so on. The most hallucinatory are the gated communities manufactured by Kaufman and Broad, the homebuilders who were famous in the 1970s for exporting Hollywood ramblers to the suburbs of Paris. Now they have brought back France (or, rather, California homes in French drag) to the desert in fortified mini-*banlieus*, with lush lawns, Old World shrubs, fake mansard roofs and *nouveaux riches* titles like "Chateau."

But Kaufman and Broad only expose the underlying method in the apparent madness of L.A.'s urban desert. The discarded Joshua trees, the profligate wastage of water, the claustrophobic walls, and the ridiculous names are as much a polemic against incipient urbanism as they are an assault on an endangered wilderness. The *eutopic* (literally no-place) logic of their subdivisions, in sterilized sites stripped bare of nature and history, masterplanned only for privatized family consumption, evokes much of the past evolution of tract-home Southern California. But the developers are not just repackaging myth (the good life in the suburbs) for the next generation; they are also pandering to a new, burgeoning fear of the city. . . .

Stretching now from the country-club homes of Santa Barbara to the shanty *colonias* of Ensenada, to the edge of Llano in the high desert and of the Coachella Valley in the low, with a built-up surface area nearly the size of Ireland and a GNP bigger than India's—the urban galaxy dominated by Los Angeles is the fastest growing metropolis in the advanced industrial world. . . . [increasingly characterized by] an erosion of the quality of life for the middle classes in older suburbs as well as for the inner-city poor.

Ironically the Antelope Valley is both a sanctuary from this maelstrom of growth and crisis, and one of its fastest growing epicenters. In the desperate reassurance of their gated subdivisions, the new commuter population attempts to recover the lost Eden of 1950s-style suburbia. Older Valley residents, on the other hand, are frantically trying to raise the gangplanks against this ex-urban exodus sponsored by their own pro-growth business and political elites. In their increasingly angry view, the land-rush since 1984 has only brought traffic jams, smog, rising crime, job competition, noise, soil erosion, a water shortage and the attrition of a distinctively countrified lifestyle. . . . it is all too easy to envision Los Angeles reproducing itself endlessly across the desert with the assistance of pilfered water, cheap immigrant labor, Asian capital and desperate homebuyers willing to trade lifetimes on the freeway in exchange for $500,000 "dream homes" in the middle of Death Valley.

Actually, a few miles beyond Death Valley—280 miles from L.A.—an almost identical scenario was under way at Las Vegas. Single-family homes in Clark County were going up at a pace akin to that of Antelope or Victor Valley, but the population there was growing even more rapidly: During the 1980s, Las Vegas Valley added the equivalent of a small city each year. In 1980, Clark County had been home to five hundred thousand people; ten years later, it had gained three hundred thousand more—a rate of growth that was good for a number-one ranking in the United States. Nevada itself was growing more quickly than any other state in the union (49 percent during the eighties), and two out of every three Nevadans lived in Clark County. As the nineties opened, five thousand people were moving to Las Vegas Valley every month, and on each corresponding cycle of the moon, a thousand new homes rose up to receive them. More than thirty-one thousand construction permits were issued in 1989 alone.

The people occupying the new houses didn't fulfill the traditional stereotypes of Las Vegas society. Though the largest age group—about half the population—was between twenty-five and forty-five, the fastest-growing age group was over sixty-five. In this onetime capital of conjugal annulment, the number of divorces was now declining. Meanwhile, the number of marriages exploded: from fifty-nine thousand in 1985 to seventy-six thousand five years later. Sin City, it seemed, found itself in a family way—Las Vegas now had as many shopping malls as casinos, and the plastic-grid character of its civilization resembled that of any other mindlessly sprawling suburb in the country. As Stanley W. Paher had written as early as 1971: "Behind the mask of the Strip is an air-conditioned town made up of substantial citizens who seldom if ever gamble. . . . They enjoy boating and skiing. . . . They do anything that a family might in Seattle or Boston."

Las Vegans' aquatic enthusiasm would have been far more appropriate in those places. While the names of new communities in Antelope Valley aspired to evoke the outskirts of Paris or London, their counterparts in the Nevada desert—evincing an equivalent grounding in reality—suggested an ecosystem in imminent danger of drowning. Among Clark County's new housing projects were the Lakes, Green Valley, Silver Springs, Sunset Bay, Desert Shores, Bay Breeze, and Bermuda Springs. Developers matched these names with moisture-intensive landscaping, specifying sod lawns and shade trees for yards in a region with 20 percent relative humidity and four inches of annual rainfall. Combined with the legions of swimming pools, golf courses, and air conditioners that helped make such denial possible, Las Vegas had one of the highest per-capita levels of water use in the country: upward of 250 gallons per day.

Unfortunately, not even the fabled springs of "the meadows" could meet such demand. Wells had been drilled in Las Vegas Valley since the turn of the century, and as a result, its "inexhaustible supply of artesian water" was now drying up; springs and riparian vegetation were disappearing along with animals that depended on them. A desert fish, the Las Vegas dace (*Rhinichthys deaconi*), went extinct, and pupfish were endangered at Devil's Hole sixty miles to the northwest. In North Las Vegas, the earth cracked open underneath a housing subdivision, prompting an emergency request to the federal government for $14 million to relocate damaged homes.

This problem was even more advanced in Antelope Valley, where the water table had been sinking three feet per year for half a century. Ever since the Depression, water had been pumped out of the ground for agriculture, rendering the desert soil yet drier. As a result, the soil took up less space, and gravity inspired it to settle downward: between 1955 and 1981, a five-hundred-square-mile area around Lancaster sank four feet. By 1991, scores of huge fissures had appeared in areas earmarked for development, while dozens more had opened the surface of Rogers Dry Lake at Edwards Air Force Base. One such crack—half a mile long, twelve feet deep, and four feet wide—forced the closure of a runway, cramping the landing style of the space shuttle.

Even during the boom years of dam building and World War II, Las Vegas had had to pass emergency ordinances against water overuse, with mandated hours for lawn sprinkling and enforced recycling of water for air conditioners. Hoover Dam had provided a reprieve: ever since it had gone on line, Clark County had gotten most of its water—three hundred thousand acre-feet per year—from Lake Mead. At the rate Las Vegas was growing, however, its days of sufficiency from even this source were numbered, if not already past. Analyzing the projected numbers, the Las Vegas Valley Water District announced that no new water commitments would be made beyond 1995. It didn't take local authorities long to formulate a frightening equation: Ø Water = Ø Growth. The district was directed to go out and find some more.

It fulfilled this mission in desert basins hundreds of miles to the north. The way western water laws are traditionally structured (and Nevada is nothing if not traditionally western), any water source not in use can be claimed by anybody who wants it. In places like Nye County (population eighteen thousand), most of the natural runoff was going to "waste"—in other words, replenishing the underground aquifer upon which the local ecology was based. Thus, in 1989, the Las Vegas Valley Water District claimed all the unallocated perennial-yield water in twenty-six basins to the north. Thousands of protests were subsequently filed by everyone from ranchers to scientists to environmentalists to Native Americans to the United States government itself. Asserting that such a massive tap could disrupt springs even in Death Valley, ex–Arizona governor Bruce Babbitt—before being appointed secretary of the interior by President Bill Clinton—labeled Las Vegas's plan "the most environmentally destructive project in the history of the West." It called to mind the infamous Owens Valley water grab of the twenties, when the mushrooming population of Los Angeles—in laying claim to the eastern runoff from the Sierra Nevada—transformed Owens Lake into a dust bowl, which, when the wind came up, fouled the previously pristine air above none other than Antelope Valley a hundred miles to the south. As a direct result, the northwestern Mojave Desert now possesses the worst particulate air pollution in the United States.

Nevertheless, in the 1980s, the magnetism of Antelope and Victor Valleys was that they offered alternatives to the overpopulated and overpriced L.A. Basin. Las Vegas Valley carried this attraction a step further: it represented an escape from California altogether. In addition to relatively uncrowded freeways, comparatively clean air, a lower crime rate and cost of living (though all these advantages were, of course, quickly eroding as the population grew), Nevada—with hundreds of millions of dollars donated annually by tourists in the casinos, which themselves enjoyed profits, taxed at six percent by the state, of four billion dollars a year—could dispense almost entirely with taxes on its own residents. The state had no personal income tax, no inheritance tax, no corporate income tax, no franchise tax, no unitary tax, no admissions tax, no capital stock tax, and no business inventory tax. Indeed, compared with California, Nevada was a statutory Nirvana: the entire state was practically a free port, corporations were unfettered by financial reporting requirements, and that pesky bane of industrial ambition—environmental regulation—was minimal. In California, whose environmental laws were the strictest in the nation, it might take a factory two or three years to get an air-pollution permit. In Nevada it took two or three months. It wasn't really so surprising, then, that between 1985 and 1990, thirty-five hundred new companies established themselves in Clark County—among them a number of factories and firms specializing in garbage disposal and hazardous waste.

Still, the rock-solid base of the local economy—employing one Las Vegan out of every five—remained the tourist and gaming industry. It seemed that no matter how many hotels and casinos were built, people would come from around the country to fill them. In only two years at the end of the eighties, Las Vegas gambling receipts grew by 30 percent, stimulating yet another headlong rush into hotel construction. When it opened in 1990, the three-thousand-room Mirage Resort-Casino was the biggest hotel in the world—but as Governor Bob Miller giddily pointed out, within six months it would be only the third largest on the Strip. By the early nineties, the plan was that Las Vegas would boast nine of the ten biggest hotels in the world. Bearing out the beloved hotel room/employment formula, the city led the nation in job growth for several years running. With almost no legislative measures in place to control development, at the end of the eighties Las Vegas's potential for expansion seemed—except for that little water problem—unlimited.

Until, that is, the desert tortoise was declared a threatened species by the U.S. Fish and Wildlife Service.

During the buildup of Las Vegas and Antelope Valley, the passage of the Federal Land Policy and Management Act, the development of the California Desert Plan, the rise and fall and resurrection of the Barstow-to-Vegas motorcycle race—during, in other words, the presidential administrations of Richard Nixon, Gerald Ford, Jimmy Carter, Ronald Reagan, and George Bush—Kristin Berry had been going about her business: the study of *Gopherus agassizii*. After completing her doctoral work in biology at Berkeley, she'd returned to the desert and Ridgecrest, where she married a man who, like her father, worked at China Lake Naval Weapons Center. The base had a laudable natural-history program, but unfortunately for Berry, it also had a laudable naturalist. Like any other Ph.D., Berry had considered teaching, but she found that it didn't hold her interest.

"Academics engage in pure science that often doesn't get implemented," she explains. "I like to solve problems: How many sheep can you have in a place without disturbing tortoises? How many vehicles can tortoises tolerate per square mile? As opposed to: What's the function of some particular organ? I have a personal long-term goal of sound land management in the desert, which involves protecting representative portions of ecosystems so that they last into perpetuity. It's an important part of our national heritage; we have to have *some* development, but we don't have to damage whole ecosystems. To me, the tortoise is just an umbrella for doing good science and management and maintaining genetic diversity.

"Before I got involved with the tortoise, I didn't know anything about the Bureau [of Land Management]. But I'd learned about many land-use projects in the West Mojave that were disrupting ecosystems, and when I looked at who owned and managed the land I was interested in, it was the BLM. At that time, the bureau was setting up a team to conduct inventories and surveys and develop the Desert Plan. I decided I wanted that job."

True to her aim, Berry was hired to work on the "wildlife element" of the California Desert Plan. After this work was finished in 1980, she stayed on to help assemble a management strategy for the tortoise, which had recently been designated a sensitive species. In the era of Reagan/Watt, however, the BLM lacked the funds to employ her. For years, Berry had to raise her own salary from such sources as the state fish and game department, the University of California, and utility companies like Southern California Edison, which were required to perform environmental-impact studies under the terms of the California Environmental Quality Act. Hence, Berry could—to employ inappropriate terminology—kill two birds with one stone, advancing the environmental obligations of developers while continuing to carry out research on the tortoise.

By the time the Desert Plan was finished, Berry and her growing army of associates—biological researchers from various agencies and universities—had set up study plots throughout the desert. Each consisted of about a square mile, within which individual tortoises were marked and data assembled on population density, distribution, age, size, sex, and mortality. The plots were established in undisturbed areas where tortoise densities were relatively high and checked in the spring over a period of a half dozen years. By 1988, Berry was ready to argue that in the western Mojave, tortoise populations had declined between a tenth and two thirds from their 1980 levels. In some ostensibly protected spots—the Desert Tortoise Natural Area near Ridgecrest, and the Chuckwalla Bench east of Palm Springs (termed "best of the best" tortoise habitats eight years earlier)—numbers had crashed by 50 to 70 percent. Some parts of the western Mojave were losing tortoises at ten times the normal death rate for adults; juveniles also represented a shrinking proportion of the total population, portending even lower numbers for the future, when young tortoises failed to enter the breeding pool. In view of the animal's role as an indicator species, the outlook was unnerving.

Inevitably, Berry's findings were assailed by those who didn't want to believe that the tortoise, and by extension the desert, was in trouble. But her methods were also criticized by some "pure" scientists who doubted her objectivity—occasionally because she'd fired them for, in their view, amassing data that didn't show the tortoise to be threatened. To the extent that Berry's credibility is called into question, it stems from the fact that—in the words of Wes Chambers, who was the BLM's deputy director for development of the California Desert Plan—she's trying "to be both an advocate and a scientist. She has a paradigm of her own that things have to fit into." Moreover, because of her tenacity and combativeness, she has a knack for antagonizing others, sometimes through actions that are considered consummately unprofessional.

"She's so goddamned strong-willed," says Chambers. "She used to fly to Sacramento on her own and camp on the state director's doorstep with data. She was always coming into my office, tearing some study apart, and saying, 'We've got to do something about this!' The area managers got to hate her; she was criticizing them without going through the proper channels, and dealing with things tangential to her job. Most of us were bureaucrats looking toward our retirement, but here you had an individual who didn't care about any of that. She was willing to put her future, her credibility, and her position in the bureau in jeopardy."

"She's absolutely single-minded in her defense of the tortoise," says Gerry Hillier, ex-director of the BLM's California Desert District. "She's a single-use advocate in a multi-use organization."

"Things are either black or white with her," says another biologist. "Either you're for the tortoise, or you're against it."

"She has a good list and a bad list," says another, "and she keeps biologists from working if their data don't reflect her biases."

"I'm not objective about her, and neither is anybody else who's likely to be talking to you. The fact that I disapprove of her working methods might be sour grapes; after all, she shut my project down—and I'd been working on tortoises in the Mojave for thirteen years."

"She's a controlling, competitive personality. She sits on virtually every committee that awards government contracts for tortoise research, but she doesn't want funding for local entities that she can't control. Her approach is, 'You'll do it my way or not at all.'"

"She was out at the Eureka Dunes once with a BLM area manager. He told her, 'The problem with you is you don't see the whole ball of wax.' She said, 'Oh yes I do. I see your balls are wax.'"

"She's not very good at filtering her words. And she doesn't suffer fools."

"She's sort of prim, but she'll set her lips. We need a few rocks in the road like her."

"Her accomplishments are enormous, but she's had a tough time;

she's had to spend her life as a lone voice battling within this macho cow-boy agency. She's been very effective, but at great personal cost."

"She's led a stressful and difficult life."

"She's a hero to thousands."

"She's done something nobody else in the BLM has done—come up with hard data that shows a species to be in decline, and established the causes."

"She's more a politician than a biologist, but she considers herself a biologist."

"She's an extremely good naturalist without being a good scientist."

"She's a very good scientist, but in order to get results, she pushes the data and uses terms that other scientists wouldn't use. Where I might say, 'The data seem to indicate,' she would say, 'The data show.'"

Much of Berry's research has been presented in BLM reports, rather than published in scientific papers where it can be subjected to peer re-view. Considerable initiative—for example, a request under the Freedom of Information Act—can thus be required to read them. If other scien-tists want to go to that trouble (which they sometimes do, at the behest of organizations like the American Motorcyclists Association), they some-times discover interesting details. For example, a study plot upon which Berry reported a 50 percent population decline had originally contained only two tortoises; therefore the loss of half the population meant that only one animal had died. The 90 percent decline that Berry estimated for the western Mojave since the 1870s turned out to be based on remi-niscences of elderly desert dwellers, trying to recall their subjective impressions from the 1920s.

When Berry first publicized the decline in tortoise populations, the first suspect hauled in for questioning—by developers, ranchers, ORV users, and others whose aims were adversarial to those of wild animals—was drought. For several years at the end of the eighties, California received far below its normal amount of rainfall, with the Mojave getting even less than its meager average. Tortoises were becoming dehydrated and losing weight; some were even found to have starved. As Ken Nagy, a UCLA biology professor, pointed out, "It's quite a feat to starve an ani-mal whose energy metabolism is so low that it can go two or three years without eating." Indeed, as a "K-selected" species, the tortoise popula-tion was adapted to remain stable despite variation in its living condi-tions—a point driven vernacularly home by Dave Fisher, a West Mojave rancher (and chairman of the BLM Desert Advisory Council), in 1991. *"Drought!"* said Fisher. "What the hell—this is a *desert!* The tortoise has been living here for thousands of years. Even *I've* seen it drier than it is now."

Indeed, the most alarming problem was neither drought nor starvation in itself, but a related condition associated with stress: disease. A mysterious malady now plaguing tortoises—particularly on the devastated Chuckwalla Bench—was shell necrosis: the onset of lesions, peeling, and discoloration of the underside, or plastron. But another syndrome was even more widespread and disturbing. In 1988, in the northwestern Mojave, Berry discovered tortoises resembling kids with colds: their chin glands were swollen; their noses were runny; dirt was caked in the dried mucus around their nostrils. Moreover, they were undernourished—too weak even to retract their heads or forelegs. And as a result, they were dying.

The illness—eventually tagged "URDS," for upper respiratory disease syndrome—wasn't unheard of. For decades, its symptoms had been seen in captured tortoises in North America and abroad. It had recently been detected in the wilds of Utah, and soon after being discovered in California, also began to turn up in Nevada and Arizona. In California, it was at first thought to occur only near heavily developed regions (i.e., in the western Mojave), but then it began appearing in relatively undisturbed spots in the eastern desert as well. It was a certifiable plague: a contagious, rapidly spreading, and fatal epidemic.

Eventually, URDS was found to arise from a previously unidentified pathogen. Newly named *Micoplasma agassizii*, it was exceedingly noxious, midway in size between a bacterium and a virus. One theory explaining its spread indicted the release of sick pets: in Utah, even the state fish and game department had been known to turn ill tortoises loose. In addition to transmitting diseases to the wild, the random reintroduction of such animals, without regard for their geographic origins, was suspected of weakening local populations through genetic contamination—possibly producing weak offspring, upsetting local social systems, and exceeding the carrying capacity of regions that received them. Antelope Valley, so close to L.A., probably bore the brunt of this practice more heavily than any other single spot, though the burgeoning population of Las Vegas undoubtedly did its part.

Drought and disease notwithstanding, few would deny that the tortoise's main problem reflected the plight of so many other species: habitat loss due to development. Between 1980 and 1988, human numbers in the range of the tortoise increased by 20 percent, with fully two-thirds of that growth taking place in Antelope and Las Vegas Valleys. As habitat in other parts of the desert was eroded, individual populations grew increasingly fragmented, becoming—after the fashion of endangered species everywhere—isolated in islandlike clusters that could be extinguished by a single ill effect (e.g., disease).

The effects of human development in the desert extended far beyond the confines of housing subdivisions. As people moved in, so did new roads, power plants, water projects, gas pipelines, airstrips, and ORVs. On the outskirts of every housing development, the surrounding hills were crisscrossed by tire tracks: the patchwork insignia of out-of-school kids, who often brought BB guns with them. Not to imply that every animal was being driven out. The proliferation of people inspired an upsurge in waste and garbage, which had a salutary effect on at least one species—*Corvus corax*, the common raven, referred to by Kristin Berry as a "flying rat." Before World War II, ravens had been relatively rare in the desert, but according to some surveys, their numbers in the Mojave septupled between 1968 and 1988. Notorious predators of insects, small reptiles, and other birds, ravens like to nest and perch in power poles, which were increasing along with the other artifacts of civilization. Underneath one such nest in the western Mojave, Berry and her colleagues found 250 baby tortoise shells. Hence, in 1989 she launched a counterattack: in partnership with four other government agencies, the BLM began poisoning ravens near Needles, Ridgecrest, and Twentynine Palms. The program was aborted after one week, however, when the U.S. Humane Society filed a lawsuit and won a restraining order.*

Concern for *Gopherus agassizii* had been gradually escalating since the 1930s, when it was first declared illegal to purchase or sell tortoises in California. In 1961, the law was expanded to outlaw "needlessly harming, taking, or shooting any projectile" at them, and in 1972, the animal was officially installed as California's state reptile. In Nevada, the tortoise had been termed a "species of concern" since the late 1960s and classified as

---

*The BLM continued to experiment with raven control, however, under the supervision of a "technical review team" made up of representatives from the federal government, private industry, and conservation organizations including the Humane Society.

rare and protected since 1978. Still, while the animal (theoretically) enjoyed statutory safety, its habitat did not. It may have been against the law to "harm" a desert tortoise, but it was still perfectly legal to bulldoze thousands of acres of its range.

The only thing capable of changing this situation would be listing as a threatened species under the Endangered Species Act—a move proposed by environmental groups in 1984, following Berry's first status report. A year later, the U.S. Fish and Wildlife Service (FWS), the federal agency responsible for protecting endangered species, ruled that "the listing of the tortoise is warranted, but precluded by other pending proposals of higher priority." In 1989, however—in light of the recent population tailspin, especially as precipitated by URDS—environmentalists decided to take more drastic action. On May 31, the Defenders of Wildlife, the Environmental Defense Fund, and the Natural Resources Defense Council served the Fish and Wildlife Service with a sixty-day notice of intent to sue for protection of the tortoise. Exactly two months later, *Gopherus agassizii* was declared an endangered species on an emergency basis north and west of the Colorado River—in other words, throughout the Mojave Desert.

In many ways, protection of the tortoise under the Endangered Species Act didn't differ much from existing policies in the states concerned. Any attempt to "take"—i.e., harass, harm, pursue, hunt, shoot, wound, kill, trap, capture, or collect—tortoises was now punishable by a fine of up to $25,000 and a jail sentence of up to six months.* Public agencies, private businesses, and individual citizens were all equally subject to this law. The crucial difference in the federal statute was that it imparted a broader meaning to the term *harm*—encompassing not merely the "intentional" actions enumerated above but also "incidental" ones that altered an animal's habitat in such a way as to impair its normal behavior patterns, an interpretation with considerable portent for such wide-ranging species as the desert tortoise and the spotted owl. Moreover, when an animal is listed as threatened or endangered in an emergency, as was the tortoise, the rules of the act take effect immediately, bypassing the formal process of public hearing and review.

---

*The penalties have since been raised to $100,000 and one year.

It doesn't take much insight to divine the reaction of developers in the fastest-growing region in the country when an animal found throughout the area was suddenly declared endangered. As far as "growth" was concerned, if the spotted owl was perceived to be playing havoc with provision of raw materials, its plodding reptilian counterpart was now preventing use of products. It seemed that the specter of endangered species had flown from the forest, casting its dreaded shadow over a previously cloudless realm of opportunity.

When the tortoise was listed, the city of Las Vegas had just issued a request for proposals for housing projects on four thousand acres north of town. Several developers were negotiating to build master-planned communities nearby; one had already broken ground on a project covering one thousand acres. The Summa Corporation—holders of the leftover fortune of Howard Hughes—had recently sold off most of its properties in order to invest $60 million in planning, surveys, engineering, permits, access roads, consulting fees, and other infrastructure for a gargantuan development on twenty-five thousand acres—twenty-six square miles—northwest of Las Vegas. The entire project, called Summerlin, was in desert-tortoise habitat. Literally hundreds of new schools, roads, hospitals, sewer lines, flood control projects, and utility corridors in Clark County were either in progress or awaiting permits; the Las Vegas Valley Water District had ten projects under way, and a major freeway was in the process of being widened. When the tortoise was declared endangered, all this work came to a halt. So did the operation of several sand-and-gravel pits upon which local builders relied. Thirty thousand jobs in Las Vegas depended on construction; ninety-seven thousand more jobs were predicted to arise in the next four years, during which seventy-two thousand new homes would be needed for two hundred thousand new people moving in. In the face of such demand, developers now had to hire consultants to check each potential building site for *Gopherus agassizii*; if any tortoises were found, construction was forbidden. At the very least, a permit would have to be obtained and a certified biologist hired to remove the animals—a process that could take up to a year.

When the environmental groups announced their intention to sue, the crayon was on the sheetrock as far as Clark County developers were concerned. Some didn't even wait around to see what the Interior Department decided; they just went out and bulldozed their building sites, plowing under any tortoises that may have been present (and thereby ensuring that none would be discovered later on). This practice continued—often at night—even after the emergency listing, as the county continued issuing grading permits along with a directive to comply with the law. Responsibility for enforcement resided with the Fish and Wildlife Service, which employed only one agent to oversee the entire area. The sixty-day notice effectively enabled the locals to gird themselves for the inevitable—and seeing clearly what was at stake, fortify themselves they did. On the very same day that the desert tortoise was declared endangered, the city of Las Vegas, the Nevada Development Authority, the Southern Nevada Homebuilders Association, and seven development companies led by the Summa Corporation filed suit against the Department of the Interior, calling the listing "arbitrary, capricious, and unlawful," claiming that they deserved to be excluded from it, and asking that it be blocked by a federal restraining order.

The plaintiffs based their case on the claim—advanced by the Nevada Department of Wildlife, which itself took issue with the federal listing—that tortoises in southern Nevada weren't affected by URDS and that therefore no "emergency" existed. Moreover, in a world that had recently contained only fourteen black-footed ferrets, a couple of dozen California condors—even a few thousand northern spotted owls—they questioned the very notion that a species with tens of thousands of members scattered over hundreds of thousands of square miles could be called endangered. Considering the time and money that such a "capricious" classification would absorb, the plaintiffs argued, it "could bring the entire real estate development and construction industry in southern Nevada to a standstill." In one year, it would cost Las Vegas $11 million in uncollected tax revenues, unfiled building permits, and lost users' fees.

The belief that URDS existed in Las Vegas Valley had arisen with Nevada veterinarians, who had diagnosed the ailment in recently captured animals. The Nevada Department of Wildlife was found to have released tortoises in Las Vegas Valley after keeping them in pens with others that had shown symptoms of the disease. Within a year of the listing, researchers would find that one of every five tortoises in the area was in fact infected. The epidemic was perhaps a symptom of—but certainly a catastrophe on top of—myriad other environmental problems facing

Gopherus agassizii, all of which were inarguably at work in Clark County. Whether because of this or simply because the FWS had obviously acted within its authority, Washington, D.C., district court judge Stanley S. Harris found the tortoise's listing "manifestly defensible" and denied the plaintiffs' motion for an injunction. He added, however, that he'd arrived at his conclusion reluctantly—he said that he considered the listing "broader than necessary," opined that the FWS "could have limited the geographic scope of its rule with no detriment to the tortoise," and went so far as to observe "that relatively few recognize the extraordinary scope of the Endangered Species Act and the extent to which its provisions preclude the application of economic common sense."

Four months later, a U.S. Court of Appeals upheld the district court's decision, stating that the FWS was correct to act as if there were an emergency if one was strongly indicated. "Appellants face a heavy burden in establishing that the secretary [of the interior] acted irrationally by including Nevada but not including the Arizona Sonoran population in the listing," the eighteen-page decision read (in response to the plaintiffs' claim that it was unfair to single out the Mojave population for endangered status). "Since the agencies have great discretion to treat a problem partially, we would not strike down the listing if it were a first step toward a complete solution, even if we thought it 'should' have covered both the Mojave and Sonoran populations."

The plaintiffs, motivated as they were by intense economic emotions, were prepared to go on to the Supreme Court. But wilier voices began to be heard. Seven years earlier, an amendment to the Endangered Species Act had legalized the "incidental taking" of certain listed animals, providing that a plan were employed to further the survival of the species as a whole. "Mitigation" of lost animals and habitat was required under this law. Usually this amounted to land purchased elsewhere for the purpose of preservation, but it could also take the form of zoning ordinances, educational programs, or restrictions on vehicles or pesticides. Some forty species—including, in California alone, the Coachella Valley fringe-toed lizard, the San Mateo Mission blue butterfly, the Tipton kangaroo rat, the San Joaquin kit fox, and the Kern County blunt-nosed leopard lizard—had already come under the sway of such "habitat conservation plans." One was clearly in the cards for the tortoise. The developers' problem was that it was still too far away—they wanted to keep building *now*.

Even environmentalists agreed that "the meadows" of Las Vegas Valley—once Nevada's most densely populated tortoise range—had become unsuitable for the animal. Much of the so-called habitat under dispute, surrounded as it was by subdivisions, was only slightly more supportive to tortoises than the green-felt tables at Caesar's Palace. If it wasn't already, Las Vegas Valley was well on its way to becoming a natural "sacrifice area" like any other urban center. Bearing this in mind— and urging the environmentalists and feds to do likewise—the developers offered a deal. Let us continue, they suggested, with projects already under development when the tortoise was listed. We'll pay a prearranged "mitigation fee" for the privilege. You use that money—far more of it, incidentally, than you ever had coming from the public sector—for tortoise preservation. It might be land acquisition; it might be field studies; it might be research into URDS. It might even be a space colony where you and your animal friends can go live together on Mars. We'd support that idea enthusiastically, but we don't really care. Please just let us get back to building the next smog-choked clone of southern California in a desert basin that gets three times less rainfall than L.A.!

This was too attractive a deal for the tortoise people to pass up. They set about figuring how much they needed while the developers and the local authorities wrangled over what constituted "commencement of development," circa August 4, 1989. Certain criteria were established with regard to previous land disturbance, applications for permits, and so forth, though some landowners naturally claimed that they'd "commenced development" simply by purchasing their properties, even if they hadn't begun work. "Permits were given for some projects that had done very little grading," says Jean Mischel, an Environmental Defense Fund representative who went on to become a deputy attorney general for the state of Nevada. "Basically, anybody who wanted to pay the fee got in."

The amount that the tortoise advocates demanded—for research, land acquisition, and a conservation center to be constructed south of Las Vegas—was $2.3 million, $2 million of which would be paid by developers. In a heavyweight clean-and-jerk display of Clark County's political muscle, the other $300,000 was contributed by the state of Nevada. Development was allowed to continue on seven thousand acres, from which 841 tortoises were ultimately removed for studies on social structure, courtship behavior, nesting, combat, and the like. Research contracts were eventually awarded to the Smithsonian Institute, Drexel University, and the University of Florida, which was conducting research into URDS. A year and a half later, a short-term habitat conservation plan for the area was finalized. The steering committee that developed the plan included a vast consortium of representatives from Clark County, its cities, the U.S. Congress, the state congress, the governor's office, the Nevada department of wildlife and agriculture, the BLM, the National Park Service, the Desert Tortoise Council, the Nature Conservancy, the National Resources Defense Council, the Defenders of Wildlife, the University of Nevada, and various homebuilders', cattlemen's, and miners' associations. The plan expanded on the terms of the court settlement, okaying the development of twenty-two thousand acres in Clark County over the following three years, at a mitigation-fee rate of $250 per acre (later raised to $550) to continue funding research and land acquisition. By far the largest landholder in Clark County and Las Vegas Valley was the BLM; ever since the nineteenth century, local ranchers had been grazing cattle on that property, though in many cases their own children would no longer be continuing the tradition. Using the mitigation money, the Nature Conservancy convinced some of these aging ranchers to give up their grazing privileges on a "willing buyer/ willing seller" basis, enabling the old-timers to retire from an increasingly bitter and beleaguered business, and establishing four hundred thousand acres of newly preserved tortoise habitat where not only grazing but recreation, mining, landfills, and competitive and commercial events were restricted or prohibited.

In the end, Kristin Berry considered the Las Vegas solution an entirely effective way of implementing the Endangered Species Act. "It shows that where there's goodwill, there are all kinds of possibilities for compromise that won't compromise the long-term welfare of the animals," she said. "In Las Vegas, every effort was made to come up with something that would benefit tortoises *and* be workable for developers." Nick Niarchos, an attorney who handled the tortoise negotiations for the Summa Corporation, thinks that the Las Vegas settlement represented "a win-win situation for everybody. They [i.e., the environmentalists and the FWS] had us beat, but we had something to offer them. It was a uniquely cooperative agreement among a very diverse group of people.

"Especially," he adds, "when you compare it with the logging industry."

❖

In California, things didn't proceed with quite as much alacrity. Unlike in Nevada, much of its desert land was "checkerboarded" in private and public ownership—a legacy of the old-time practice of selling every other parcel to the railroads, but making it more difficult to preserve large chunks. Moreover, with the advent of an economic recession, the western Mojave building rush had fallen off the torrid pace set by southern Nevada. Hence, civic agencies and developers weren't quite as desperate to keep the runaway train on track. Perhaps most important, in California they were already well practiced at dancing through loopholes in environmental law if not ignoring it altogether. The fact that the Mojave ground squirrel had been classified as endangered in California since the 1970s had done approximately nothing to retard the paving of the western Mojave; a mitigation program for the squirrel was just taking effect when the tortoise was listed, but many developers continued work with no more response than a nod and a wink. Legions of biological consultants suddenly emerged from the woodwork to offer their "expert" surveying services when *Gopherus agassizii* was listed; some were more reliable than others, but all were being paid by people who desperately wanted them not to find tortoises on their property. While one regional water quality control board and one town (Adelanto) were disciplined for pursuing or permitting projects in desert-tortoise habitat, charges were seldom filed against lawbreakers, for the same reason as in Clark County: unless some local eco-gumshoe produced a tortoise carcass, local law enforcers had lots of other things to occupy their attention.

Gradually—proceeding through the requisite galaxy of core groups, steering committees, planning teams, conflict-resolution systems, management priorities, and data analysis—the BLM pieced together a plan for the western Mojave. Weighing such factors as tortoise density and how much future development a proposed project might inspire, the process was so slow and painstaking that many developers began work without knowing how much money they would ultimately be assessed in compensation—whether they would be required to purchase one, or three, or five acres of undisturbed habitat for each acre that they built up. Meanwhile, controversial moves were made to protect the species in specific regions. Basing its decision on a "jeopardy biological opinion," the FWS terminated sheep grazing in high-density tortoise habitat. The

Rand Mountains—site of the Desert Tortoise Natural Area, where URDS was first detected in California—were placed under a one-year quarantine with no human entry allowed. And to the delight of environmentalists, the BLM announced that permits for three cross-country desert motorcycle races were being canceled: the Parker 400; Johnson Valley, California, to Parker, Arizona; and, um, oh yes, Barstow-to-Vegas.

Ever since the event had been reinstated in 1983, Louis McKey and his cohort Rick Sieman had been keeping a low profile. "We'd made such a ruckus," Sieman remembers. "The Duck had been elected Man of the Year in *Cycle News* four years in a row. We'd done a hell of a job, even though we didn't really understand anything about how to manipulate PR at that point. In '83 I said: 'Louis, I'm putting in too many hours. I can't take it anymore.' He said, 'Me too.' I started off-road racing in trucks; consequently my riding of motorcycles was limited to play-riding, just to keep my skills sharp. And doing Barstow-to-Vegas every year, no matter what."

The race had proceeded without great incident through the mid-eighties. Though the field was now limited to twelve hundred riders, environmentalists continued to lobby annually for its cancellation as the BLM annually continued to permit it. In 1987, however, a new level of agitation began to materialize. A month before that year's race, Howard Wilshire, a geologist and anti-ORV activist (coeditor of a book entitled *The Environmental Effects of Off-Road Vehicles,* he was also the senior scientist on the hydrological report that temporarily derailed the Ward Valley nuclear dump), was doing fieldwork in the East Mojave when he came upon a brand-new, twelve-foot-wide graded road south of Baker. He learned that the bulldozing had been done by the American Motorcyclists Association (which was now cosponsoring the race) to smooth out bumps in that year's course. The action had occurred without the permission of the BLM—but within the boundaries of the East Mojave National Scenic Area, the agency's new management centerpiece, created by FLPMA and proposed for national-park status under the California Desert Protection Act. It took Wilshire approximately a nanosecond to blow the whistle on the AMA, which was subsequently fined eighteen hundred dollars. Moreover, a five-year Barstow-to-Vegas permit, which had been under consideration, was shelved.

On the morning of that year's race, BLM officials discovered that a tunnel through which the riders would be passing had been jammed full of wooden railroad ties. Cautionary yellow ribbon crisscrossed the entrance, before which was scattered a pound of roofing nails. More nails were hammered into the ties, spelling out a salutation to arriving bikers: FUCK THE DUCK. The lumber was wedged so tightly into the tunnel that a winch was required to remove it, delaying the start of the race. Responsibility for the impediment, the delay, and the aggravation was proudly claimed by members of the militant environmental group Earth First!, which had recently embarked on its notorious program of radical subversive action in defense of natural resources.

When the tortoise was declared endangered two years later, environmentalists demanded that Barstow-to-Vegas be halted on just that basis. However, despite the fact that the course ran through five densely populated tortoise areas, Fish and Wildlife biologists decided that the animals wouldn't be jeopardized if the race corridor were narrowed to twenty-five feet and the start moved north to the army's National Training Center at Fort Irwin, where tortoise populations had already been thoroughly decimated. Route markings were also improved, although—in an effort to decoy Earth First!—Louis McKey created a diversion with false markers. His stratagem succeeded: on race day, the Phantom Duck's phony route was found littered with four-pronged spikes.

Despite all the publicity about the tortoise and the apparent probationary status of the race, that year's riders strayed as much as sixty feet from the route—inevitable, it would seem, in a feverishly contested off-road event. Some of the racers also veered into a wilderness-study area near Silver Dry Lake. Hence, two weeks later—owing to an environmental assessment addressing all of the above plus the plight of the tortoise—the BLM announced that no Barstow-to-Vegas permit would be issued in 1990.

"There probably will never be a consensus about Barstow-to-Vegas," Gerry Hillier, then manager of the BLM's California Desert District, reflected. "It's one of those things fraught with so much emotion that it's difficult to draw rational conclusions. The AMA has created the illusion that the race is indicative of how open or closed the desert is, while the Sierra Club considers it symbolic of how protective the BLM is of desert resources. The course is *not* pristine desert. It's been a right-of-way into California for 150 years; it's full of roads, power lines, gas pipelines, and fiber-optic cables. If you're going to hold a race in the desert, it might be the best place to do it. But everything good that we do seems to get overlooked if we continue to permit the race. It probably wouldn't matter if we cut the number of entrants down to ten—the symbolism would still be there. It got to the point where it was playing very badly for the BLM, and it wasn't doing the AMA any good, either. In terms of cost to taxpayers, it had become a horse collar. It was no longer environmentally acceptable in a broad sense, even if it was in a narrow sense."

In September of 1990, having failed in its fight to win a permit for the event, the AMA announced to its members that, for the first time in eight years, Barstow-to-Vegas was being canceled. With the blessing of the BLM, the organization would instead sponsor a 120-mile hare-and-hounds race in the Johnson Valley ORV open area, called the "Battle to Victory" (i.e., B to V).

"In '89, Louis told me he knew Barstow-to-Vegas was going to be canceled again," remembers Rick Sieman. "He said we had to do it [protest the cancellation] one more time. At first I said, No way. I had a racing team by then; I was making my living half-and-half from writing and racing, doing eight races a year plus two world-championship closed-course events. It was a lot of work. I was the driver, and after every event the truck had to be torn down and rebuilt. But Louis badgered me until I said, Okay, let's do something.

"At first we just tried to get a small core group of people to keep the spirit of Barstow-to-Vegas alive. I came up with the name Sahara Club, which was chosen for the maximum possible irritation level. We were trying to talk to people about how to combat the irrational part of the environmental movement. I think you have to separate environmentalists from environmental wackos. I consider *myself* an environmentalist— I've got a vegetable garden, and I recycle cans and do some basic things that you should do. Anybody who says they're against environmentalism—who wants brown skies and dirty water—is an asshole. But anybody who goes to the environmental extreme of saying that an insect or a turtle's life is as valuable as a human life—the fringe, the wackos, militant vegetarians, and so forth—I'm going to fight. I have to trust my common sense, which tells me that a human being is more important than a mosquito or a spotted owl or a tortoise. It also tells me that eighty-five percent of Barstow-to-Vegas is on hard-packed power-line roads, plus a few interconnecting sand washes, crisscrossing underneath a freeway. If you make a case for not riding in other areas, I'll probably agree with you in many instances; but anybody who tells you the desert tortoise, or any wildlife, is on a hard-packed goddamn road that's used every day by Department of Water and Power people and miners and folks who live in the area is out of their skull.

"For Gerry Hillier to say that 'broad public opinion' is enough to have [Barstow-to-Vegas] cease . . . well, wasn't it twenty-five or thirty years ago that 'broad public opinion' held that black people couldn't go to certain restaurants? That they had to go to certain schools, or sit in the back of a bus? Yet the government said, 'Wait a minute—you're taking the rights away from a group of people.' By law, Gerry Hillier is not allowed to have an opinion. His job, as mandated by Congress, is simply to monitor the use of public land, and part of that law states clearly that public use of the land should include recreation, mining, cattle—multiple interests. I don't *care* if broad public opinion doesn't like or understand off-road racing; I have the *right*, under federal land-use laws, to have recreational activity in that desert."

Basing the "Sahara Club" on these principles, Sieman and McKey "printed up some cheap brochures and handed them out at Barstow-to-Vegas. The response was overwhelming. Then, after our newsletter came out, we started getting interest from the cattle industry, and I said, Wait a minute. Maybe this is bigger than we thought. Maybe a group is needed that isn't just hard-core off-road enthusiasts. Newsletter number two had a broader scope: it was oriented more toward multiple-use interests— the spotted owl, loggers, miners, ranchers. Sure enough, it struck a nerve ending. We started getting all kinds of people—the club just grew and grew and grew. We started out almost by accident with three hundred dollars' worth of printing out of our own pockets, and in a year we got four thousand members."

What did the three hundred dollars produce that was so inspiring? An early Sahara Club fund-raising flyer began like this:

> You know that the Sierra Club is trying to stop off-road use dead in the water. . . . Their ultimate goal is the elimination of all off-road vehicles . . . and that includes bicycles, campers and wheelchairs. . . . the SAHARA CLUB was formed to fight the Sierra Club head-on. . . . Lou and Rick have been battling for your right to use your land for a long time . . . and now they're ready to turn

pro and go for the throat full time. . . . Are you sick and tired of
making excuses for having honest fun off-road? Do your own
industry "leaders" make you feel guilty about disturbing a patch
of sand? What's more important . . . a kid sharing fun off-road
with his family, or closing off millions of acres so we don't disturb
a tortoise? Stand up to the wimps and to the enemy . . . join the
Sahara Club and put some pride back in your life!

In his first newsletter, Sieman established the club's tone and position
with off-the-cuff discourses on such subjects as the AMA ("Department
of Pure Bullshit") and Senator Alan Cranston ("the Cadaver"), who had
introduced the California Desert Protection Act in the U.S. Congress.
Surmising that Representative Mel Levine, who sponsored the same bill
in the House, might soon replace Cranston in the Senate, Sieman con-
jectured: "The Cadaver and Levine are real pals. Bedroom buddies?
Who knows? All we know is they both spend a lot of time supporting various gay functions and events." Of Tom Hayden (the "Scumbucket
Democrat from Santa Monica"), Sieman wrote that his "pock-marked
face . . . breaks into a smile when he gets a chance to do anything to
screw you out of public land," and closed with the interrogative non
sequitur: "Would you trust this man with a poodle in a Motel 6?" The
newsletter also went so far as to publish a private address—and name
and telephone number—of a home where Earth First! members
("Nature Nazis") met in L.A., as well as license-plate numbers and
descriptions of cars that had been seen there.

As a matter of fact, as time went on, Sieman began to evince an utter
obsession with Earth First! In Sahara Club newsletter number two, he
published an instructive illustration from an Earth First! booklet about
how to set exploding traps for dirt bikers. "[This] should wake you up
to the realities of what we're dealing with," he wrote. Wearing a dis-
guise and carrying a concealed tape recorder, he infiltrated Earth First!
meetings, eavesdropped on the group's plans, adopted its techniques for
gaining media attention, and—working with "people in the insurance
industry" as well as (according to him) the FBI—continued to publish
the names and addresses of Earth First! members, encouraging his readers to "track them down and perhaps 'reason' with them about the error
of their ways.'" Earth First! members across the country soon began
receiving anonymous threatening phone calls, hate mail, even unso-

licited bills for things like magazine subscriptions. When Earth First!
staged its "Redwood Summer" logging protest in northern California in
1990, Sieman conducted a "dirty tricks" workshop for antienvironmental
groups there, teaching them how to beat the protestors at their own
game. Shortly thereafter, a man wearing sunglasses and a hat fled after
delivering a box to an Earth First! office in Arcata; when the box was
opened by a bomb squad, it contained the Sahara Club newsletter.
Sieman offered a $100 prize for information leading to the arrest of any
Earth First! member, adding that "we were thinking of offering a $150
reward if the Earth Firster was delivered to the cops with a bloody nose
and a few broken bones, but our lawyer advised us against this, saying it
was illegal. Then there's the fact that so many of them are homos, that
you might get splashed with AIDS-tainted blood." He put out a call for
"big, tall, ugly" volunteers to be christened "Sahara Clubbers" and
"issued personalized walking sticks about the size of baseball bats" for
dealing with "Earth First scum." Sahara Club newsletter number three
included a drawing of a pig—the "official Scratch 'N Sniff Earth First
Mini Poster. Here's how it works: (1) Look at the picture of the Earth
First Piglet. (2) Take your right index finger and scratch your butt with it.
(3) Scratch the drawing of the Earth First Piglet. (4) Smell the finger. It
should smell just like a typical Earth First member." When Earth First!
leader Judi Bari was maimed by a bomb that exploded in her car, Sahara
Club newsletter number four rejoiced that "Bari, who had her crotch
blown off, will never be able to reproduce again," and added, "We're just
trying to figure out what would volunteer to inseminate her if she had all
her parts."

Sieman later admitted that "a lot of wine and beer" was required for
him to write such stuff; he explained that the Sahara Club newsletter was
trying to "come from the outrageous far-out end." With regard to Earth
First!, he admitted that "the major threat to my rights is the Sierra Club.
But it's real hard to fight them—they're probably the most effective and
powerful group around. So instead you attack what's most visible, and
that's Earth First! If you have a bunch of bullies around, don't you try to
expose the most vocal or visible of them, even though maybe there's a
whole group of punk kids running as a gang? Earth First! is the best
thing that ever happened to us; it's such a beautiful target. I'd *pay* to have
an enemy like that to write about. Then we just tie them in with the
mainstream environmental groups that are trying to do us damage—

which isn't too hard, since I've proven any number of times that the mainstream groups are supporting Earth First!

"There's an element in this society that's on a level right below moss and parasites," Sieman went on, elaborating on his feeling for Earth First! "Just absolute trash—bitching, carping, malcontent misfits who run around with this horrible, nasty, foul, vicious attitude creating chaos and hell wherever they go. Judi Bari and [her former lover and fellow bomb victim] Daryl Cherney are sick sons of bitches. They don't contribute anything to society; all they want to do is tear down. He brags about the fact that he's never worked a day in his life; she has three illegitimate kids and doesn't even know who the fathers are for two of them. What kind of chance do those kids stand to grow up in this world and become useful, productive people? People like Bari and Cherney seem to want to attack everything that I hold dear: that you earn your way and pay your own dues and bring your family up as good as you can. I'm from a Czechoslovakian background; my parents worked in steel mills and coal mines. I'm sort of old-fashioned, though I'm not religious because I don't like the word *belief*. But if I *know* something—if I can prove it under laboratory conditions—I'll base my way of life on it. The words *know, fact*— *those* things mean something to me. For example, people *believe* that we're destroying the desert between Barstow and Las Vegas, when in *fact* we're driving down goddamn fire roads. So when the BLM tells us that there's no path between Barstow and Las Vegas where we can ride that doesn't go over sensitive land, we know we're being lied to. And I will continue to protest that. One way or another—win, lose, or draw— I'm gonna go out on Thanksgiving weekend, and I'm gonna ride that thing."

PROTEST RIDE FOR B TO V? Rumors of thousands of teed-off riders holding a protest ride continue to flood into the Sahara Club offices. Now, we are certainly not allowed to organize any sort of a protest ride . . . why, that would be illegal . . . but we can say that the Phantom Duck, Rick Sieman and some friends will be there to protest ride legally on Thanksgiving weekend. We cannot encourage literally thousands of good citizens to join us. But be assured, we will ride our vehicles from Barstow to Las Vegas on Turkey Day. We will start our casual trail ride at 9:00 AM on Saturday and DO NOT ENCOURAGE

OTHERS TO JOIN US at the Harvard Road off ramp, east of Barstow. So if you're in the area at that time and see a Sahara Club banner, please disregard it.

If you feel that you must protest on your own, in some fashion, with 49 or less people, then that decision is up to you and your friends.

Naturally, we don't expect anyone else to show up, as off-roaders are wimpy people who will not stand up for their rights. After all, you people are do-nothing losers who don't mind having their rights dumped on. You will be far too busy to protest, or will figure it won't make any difference. Nope. Chance of anyone cluttering up the trail ride of Rick and the Duck are quite remote.

Whatever. We'll be there. You won't. That's OK. It's much safer that way. Let us put our balls in the fire again. We're used to it. Quite frankly, the "average" off-roader out there is not worth our concerns. Average. Try below average. If you're reading this newsletter, chances are that you're above average. But listen up, all you Sahara Clubbers. Forget about trying to reach the complacent do-nothing wimps. They don't care.

WHY IS THIS RACE SO IMPORTANT? Because it's a monumental battleground to the eco-freaks. If they can stop this recreational event, they can stop just about anything they want. . . . [it's] a highly visible event that says that people have the right to enjoy our public lands. People, if we lose here, it will be a downward slide from this point on.

The above message was published in the fall of 1990 in Sahara Club newsletter number six. At about the same time, an anonymous announcement appeared in the mailboxes of conservation groups that had opposed Barstow-to-Vegas:

NOTICE TO ALL
ENVIRONMENTAL GROUPS . . .

You succeeded in killing the Barstow to Vegas race with pressure on the Bureau of Land Management. They folded.

But now it's time to pay the piper!

Will you be ready for the largest ever BARSTOW TO VEGAS PROTEST RIDE? Better brace yourself for it! Rumors were floating that Rick Sieman and the Phantom Duck were considering a protest, but we realize they are under constant scrutiny from the Fed Heads.

We're going to take the load off their shoulders: the FREE-DOM RIDERS have taken over this job, and will be contacting over 50,000 riders. We expect at least half of them to respond.

You will be responsible for 25,000 (or more) infuriated riders on Thanksgiving weekend . . . riders with an attitude! BAR-STOW TO VEGAS is alive and well, thanks to you. . . .

B TO V 1990!
WHEN THE BANNER DROPS, FREEDOM RIDES!

As Thanksgiving weekend approached, the BLM made plans for dealing with the first Barstow-to-Vegas protest ride in eight years. As Gerry Hillier warned in a meeting of the Desert District Advisory Council: "This will be cast as a civil-rights event, but it really isn't. It would be if we didn't allow events anywhere else, but we do permit a hundred and thirty [off-road] events per year. There are two other alternatives for Thanksgiving weekend: a 'dual-sport' two-day family ride through Barstow to Trona into Inyo County, and a 'Battle to Victory' protest event on Saturday in Johnson Valley. Still, Rick Sieman and his band of yahoos and terrorists say they're going to be out there, and we'll have the Highway Patrol available for backup. Sieman also says that Earth First! will be onsite, disguised as BLM rangers. It looks like we're going to have a real picnic."

Hillier acknowledged that at the time of the first Phantom Duck protests, "the BLM was nervous about its law-enforcement authority. We were afraid it would be revoked." FLPMA had just passed, and the Desert District had hardly a single ranger on its staff. Now, however, the agency's authority was clearly defined and established—and it was prepared to take firm action in enforcing its decisions. To wit, in light of the "uncontrolled" nature of the protest rumored to be developing, the BLM announced that beginning the day before Thanksgiving and continuing for twelve days afterward, "all public lands used for previous Barstow-to-Vegas race course routes as well as starting and pitting areas" in California would be closed to public entry. The BLM explained that the action was being taken "to protect natural resource values," citing particular concern about "possible impacts to the desert tortoise and its habitat." Violation of the order by anyone, including environmentalists, was punishable by a fine of up to one thousand dollars and/or a year in jail.

One need hardly guess how Rick Sieman and his Sahara Clubbers reacted to this announcement. Two days before Thanksgiving, they sued the BLM, claiming that the agency was illegally blocking access to public land and attempting to deprive them of their right to protest under the First Amendment. However, in an emergency hearing late Wednesday afternoon, U.S. district judge Dickran Tevrizian rejected the group's petition for a restraining order against the BLM—whereupon Rick Sieman proclaimed that on Saturday morning, come hell or high water, he planned to ride his motorcycle through the closed area. "I told the BLM I was gonna be there and would go around them or through them or whatever was necessary," he said. "I didn't want any doubt in their mind as to who was doing it, or why."

Saturday morning dawned clear and cold. Driving into Barstow from the East Mojave on Friday night, I had stopped by the Harvard Road turnoff. Only a couple of mobile homes were parked there in the dark—a far cry from the days when thousands of dirt bikers and their families camped out on Thanksgiving weekend. Looking a few hundred yards off into the desert toward the traditional starting area for the race, I could see the dim lights of trailers containing rangers and officials from the BLM. The scene was quiet to the point of seeming almost sleepy.

By 8 A.M. the next morning, a much larger encampment had materialized. A crowd of people was being circled by four helicopters, which laid a loud thwack-thwacking soundtrack over the scene; several TV news cameras were working their way through the mob. Some of the milling people wore sheathed knives or handguns on their belts; one was walking around with a Rottweiler on a leash. I noticed several baseball caps displaying the outlaw nicknames popular with motorcycle clubs: the Mavericks, the Lost Coyotes, even Racers under Jesus. One guy wore a Sahara Club T-shirt that said PLANT A SIERRA CLUBBER; the picture showed a pair of feet with hiking boots protruding from the earth beside a Joshua tree.

A number of brown-uniformed BLM rangers were present, as well as San Bernardino County sheriffs' deputies and officers from the California Highway Patrol. At the boundary of the closed area, three BLM rangers—two male, one female—stood stone-faced in mirrored sunglasses with their arms crossed. A couple of protesters were dragging a heavy piece of iron machinery toward them through the dust. When they deposited it at the rangers' feet, the bikers identified it as a tank tread sprocket, discarded on public land nearby by the U.S. Army. The rangers didn't respond. In fact, aside from the cacophony of copters and filibustering bikers, there was hardly any noise at all.

One of the protestors was a trim, gray-haired guy in a red-and-black motorcycle jacket, underneath which was a white T-shirt with a red circle on the chest. Inside the circle, forming that universal symbol of disapproval, a diagonal slash bisected three letters: *BLM*.

"This is a tank staging area for Fort Irwin," the man was saying, referring to the army's nearby National Training Center. "I told the BLM that we wanted a peaceful protest on the same roads that the National Guard uses for training, but they said no. They told me in '89 that the '90 race would be canceled because they could no longer afford the manpower to fight the environmentalists. So you're just giving in to the damn environmentalists! The BLM manages the land for pressure groups like the Sierra Club and Earth First! They're the only terrorists we've ever had out here. Are you trying to encourage us to be violent?"

"We buy you all this stuff with our green [registration] stickers, and every year you take more of our land away," protested another.

"I've heard that 'Closed' signs out here were put up by Earth First!," continued the gray-haired man. "Well, I don't have to abide by the signs of Earth First! I was also told that Earth First! people were going to be here disguised as BLM rangers. So if I see anybody wearing a BLM uniform in a legal riding area, I'll assume it's an Earth First! person trying to hurt me—and I'll take whatever steps I need to in order to keep away from him."

"Definitely!" grinned another biker.

"This closure was made specifically to prevent me and my friends from exercising our First Amendment rights," the gray-haired guy went on. "This is the United States of America, and I fought for my country. I thought that obligation was over with, but I'll do it again if I have to."

Somebody asked the man his name.

"Louis McKey," he answered proudly. "The Phantom Duck of the Desert."

Suddenly I heard a roar of engines from the direction of the freeway. When I looked behind me, I saw four dirt bikes—a Honda 250, a Suzuki 350, and a Husqvarna 500 and 510—coming toward us in deafening fits and starts. The riders wore full racing gear: bright-colored leathers, chest and shoulder pads, knee-high boots, helmets with faceplates. They looked every inch like troopers from *Star Wars*.

At the front of the phalanx was a portly guy with a waxed mustache, a stuffed toy tortoise on his front fender, a wooden-grip pistol on his belt, a radio headset on his helmet, and a little girl on his gas tank. This was Rick Sieman—who would later divulge that the radio was hooked up to an NBC-TV crew, and that the girl was the daughter of someone who'd stayed at his motel the previous night. Apparently she had a trail bike, and when she heard what the Sahara Club was doing, paid twenty dollars to join up.

Sieman stopped his bike before the wall of BLM rangers and began lecturing them in front of the TV cameras. "Why are you blocking this public land?" he asked in a surprisingly high-pitched voice over the din of the helicopters.

One of the rangers said only that Sieman would be arrested if he went any farther.

"You're acting like little Nazis," said Sieman. "How can you go home and look yourselves in the mirror?"

The rangers continued to stand there, impassive and expressionless. Sieman handed the girl off to her father. Like someone trying to crack the facade of a mannequin impersonator, he finally made the rangers move by pushing his bike toward them; they pushed it back. Eventually, however, the four riders gave up, turning around and pointing their bikes back the way they'd come.

One of them was a good-looking guy with sharp cheekbones, an aquiline nose, and a long, square Dudley Dooright–like jaw. Later I would learn that this was Barry Van Dyke, son of the actor Dick. As he and the others got ready to ride away, I heard him say to a bystander: "It's open all the way, south of the freeway." Then the four men gunned their engines and sped off toward the interstate, rear wheels fishtailing in the dirt, the power of petroleum roaring between their legs.

Based on what Van Dyke had said, it seemed to me that Sieman and the others—like most people who still planned to protest the race closure—had decided to ride south of the freeway in an area that hadn't been declared off-limits. But then I heard another explosion of horsepower. When I looked up, all four motorcycles were speeding east through the open desert north of the freeway, trailing plumes of white dust; they'd skirted the flank of the BLM blockade and were heading straight for the prohibited area.

The first one to get there was Sieman. He thrust his fist dramatically skyward—an image that, the next day, would occupy the entire top half of a page in the *Los Angeles Times*. Whoops, hollers, cheers, and clapping rang out as the motorcycles disappeared, literally in a cloud of dust, the helicopters in hot pursuit. Looking altogether anemic in their wake, a lone BLM ranger went after them on a four-wheeled ATV.

I ran to my truck and got on the freeway. I thought I might catch up with the group farther east; after all, I could go seventy-five miles an hour while they were picking their way through the desert. Visibility in the adjoining countryside was unobstructed, and then the helicopters served as constant signals of the bikers' whereabouts.

The Saturday holiday-weekend highway was very busy. Scores of cars flew by me toward Las Vegas at speeds upward of eighty miles per hour, oblivious to the drama in the surrounding desert. As I pulled onto the freeway, a speeding white Volvo, rather than pulling over, swerved as if intending to hit me, then veered away. For a moment, I had four Cadillacs in view at the same time. The letters on one car's license plate were MYWAY. Another had a bumper sticker that read MURDER ISN'T A RIGHT, IT'S A WRONG—STOP ABORTION. In its rear window, three teenage boys were laughing, bouncing up and down in their seats, and rocking from side to side.

The terrain climbed gradually toward the Soda Range, the flanks of the etched brown mountains strewn with khaki-colored sand against the pure blue sky. Approaching Cat Mountain, I saw helicopters hovering north of the highway and, creeping along in the desert below, the tiny-looking motorcycles. I took the next exit and turned left, driving north into the desert, hoping to intercept them. But by the time I reached the crossroads, the bikes had already passed—they were just disappearing over a ridge to the east. I put my truck in four-wheel-drive and took out after them, bouncing and swimming over the sandy road. I felt just like somebody on TV, and for good reason: one of the helicopters was circling right above me. Not until that instant did I realize that I had entered the closed area. Having gotten caught up in the excitement, I'd become one of the outlaws.

The thrill of the chase goaded me to keep on. But knowing that I might be in trouble, I decided to turn around as soon as I reached a wide place in the road and drove resignedly back to the freeway. Continuing east in the conventional manner, I soon spotted the helicopters hovering over the next exit; as I pulled into the Chevron station at Rasor Road, I saw that the bikers had been caught. But even before I got out of my truck, a BLM ranger pulled up alongside and pointed at me.

I told him that I'd entered the closed area by accident, and that I'd turned around as soon as I'd realized it. I explained that I was a journalist, and that Gerry Hillier and Barbara Maxfield, the BLM public-affairs officer, knew who I was. As the ranger took my driver's license and went to use his radio, I strolled over to where the bikers were being held in handcuffs. One of them—a tall, tough-looking guy in red and black leathers—asked someone to call his mother and tell her he was finished riding so she wouldn't worry. Sieman was protesting that he'd been arrested without a charge; he seemed to be claiming that a sheriff didn't have the authority to detain him for a federal land-use offense. He said that his pistol wasn't loaded—its purpose was purely symbolic. Nearby, a middle-aged blond woman in sunglasses was fulminating that the Sierra Club was trying to eliminate all sports, and that our boys were in Kuwait because we couldn't drill for oil on our own land. This turned out to be Sieman's wife, Arlene.

Somebody asked Sieman if he'd enjoyed his ride. "It was beautiful," he said. "That's a pretty sensitive area, you know. I think I saw fifteen bighorns. About two hundred tortoises." Hands cuffed behind his back, he asked one of the sheriff's deputies to push his glasses up the bridge of his nose. The cop complied.

After a while, the deputies put Sieman in the back of a van where he couldn't talk to anybody. The BLM ranger returned my license and let me go. A month later, however, I received a citation and fine of fifty dollars in the mail. Later, like a fool, I told Sieman and his lawyer, Alan Ghaleb, about what had happened. In an attempt to prove that he and his mates had been treated prejudicially by the BLM, Sieman subsequently identified me in *Dirt Bike* as a Sierra Club member (which I'm not), implied that I'd been "arrested" in the closed area (which I hadn't), and claimed that I'd given the ranger a "bogus" story that I "had permission from BLM director Gerry Hillier" to be there. So much for his unswerving allegiance to "the words *know* and *fact*."

As for the Phantom Duck, he had stayed behind with the crowd near Harvard Road, where he managed to stop the U.S. Army in its tracks. Within a few minutes of the flight of the four, an armored convoy from Fort Irwin had come down the same road. McKey personally blocked its path, and when the convoy commander asked him what he was doing, he explained that he was helping the BLM enforce its closure of the area. He was consequently arrested for obstruction of transit over public lands.

It was all undeniably great theater—or, more pertinently for the 1990s, terrific TV. "Boy! I wish I was one of those guys!" I heard somebody exclaim when the four horsemen took off for the forbidden zone. The scene was rife with resonance from countless action movies; Sieman had seemed, for a shining moment, an outlaw cowboy hero in full gallop toward the horizon, with the feeble posse of society in pathetic pursuit. He was Steve McQueen in *The Great Escape*, Marlon Brando in *The Wild One*, Paul Newman in *Cool Hand Luke*, even the boy on his bike in *E.T.*, evading the clutches of the evil establishment. To put a literary spin on it, he might have even been Huck Finn lighting out for the territory— nobody could fence him in. He was hightailing it out of town! Listening to his own "common sense"! If that made him an outlaw, so be it! The pigs might catch him eventually, but at least he'd showed them he had balls! He wasn't taking any more crap from impotent tight-assed bureaucrats! He was an American! Dirty Harry! Rambo! Even if he *was* a pompous, ignorant, self-centered reactionary without the vaguest understanding of or regard for any life-form other than his own, by God, he was taking matters into his own hands!

In his own mind, anyway. In the real world, following a jury trial, Rick Sieman and his three companions were each fined $850 for violating a federal land closure. Within a month of their protest ride, the BLM announced that any application for a 1991 Barstow-to-Vegas permit would be denied; a year later, it again closed the historic routes of the race over the holiday weekend. Two days before Thanksgiving, however, U.S. district court judge Gary Taylor—the same magistrate who issued the sentences for the 1990 protest—granted a temporary restraining order against the BLM, ruling that Sieman, McKey, and eight others would be allowed to stage a symbolic trail ride through the closed area.

Prior to that, Sieman had announced that the 1991 Barstow-to-Vegas ride would be his last. In the future, he said, he would be running the Sahara Club from Mexico—"a place where some freedom still exists for the use of land. . . . where a man can fire up his dirt bike and ride down a dirt road without being pursued by the hounds of hell."

Epilogue

Eight years after its introduction by Senator Alan Cranston, the California Desert Protection Act was passed on October 8, 1994, the final day of the 103rd U.S. Congress. In the end, its adoption was the work of Senator Dianne Feinstein (D-California), who, having amended the bill sixty times to mollify its opponents, overcame a last-minute rearguard effort to kill the compromise altogether. Aiming to avert a Democratic triumph on the eve of the 1994 elections, Senator Malcolm Wallop (R-Wyoming) had succeeded in filibustering the bill until the closing day of Congress, but Feinstein won over enough Republicans to silence him and carry the vote.

Upon signing by President Bill Clinton, the act created sixty-nine wilderness areas totaling almost four million acres and expanded Death Valley and Joshua Tree National Monuments, converting them into national parks. In concession to such interests as the National Rifle Association, the East Mojave National Scenic Area was declared a national preserve rather than a park, allowing the continuation of hunting and grazing but transferring control from the Bureau of Land Management to the National Park Service. Mining in the preserve thus became subject to the terms of the relatively restrictive Mining in the Parks Act, as opposed to the General Mining Law of 1872.

While the Desert Protection Act left the Mojave Road open to four-wheeled travel, it closed many other routes in newly designated wilderness areas and forebade campfires at new sites within the Mojave National Preserve—prompting Dennis Casebier to observe that "the Park Service is going to do what's expected of it. A robin is always gonna lay the same kind of egg—you don't have to climb up into the nest to see if it's gonna be blue." On the other hand, rancher Gary Overson was pleasantly surprised by the yolk of the new agency, which he found "as good or better than the BLM. It might just be because they're new here, but they're willing to work with us."

As Overson spoke, however, the 104th Congress—swept into office on a Republican tide within a week of the desert bill's signing—was doing its best to negate the legislation. One year after the act was adopted, the House Interior Appropriations Committee—guided by Representative Jerry Lewis (R-San Bernardino), who had waged a long and bitter battle against the desert bill—voted to give the Park Service one dollar to manage the new Mojave National Preserve. Though this was touted as a cost-cutting measure, the requested funds were—in one of the most glorious displays of mulishness since the days of Borax Smith—in fact earmarked for the BLM, whose underfunding had inspired the Desert Act to begin with. As this book went to press, the Congress and President Clinton were still wrangling over the terms that would apply, with one presidential veto having already frustrated Lewis's effort to subvert the new law.

While Overson accurately characterized this state of affairs as "a merry-go-round," it was nothing compared to the seesawing status of the Joshua tree—which, Jim Cornett reported, was reclassified in 1993 as a lily, signifying the Mojave's eternal resistance to objective regulation.

Acknowledgments

The American desert commands a veritable army of acolytes, enthusiasts, and experts, many of whom helped me in the writing of this book.

Three people were especially resilient in fielding my repeated questions and steering me toward all manner of aid and information. Two of them, Jim Cornett and Dennis Casebier, are subjects of individual chapters in *The Mojave*. The third, Jim Dodson, labors behind the scenes as an activist and lobbyist for the Sierra Club. A tour of the northwestern Mojave that he gave me at the beginning of my study proved fruitful throughout the duration of the project.

Many others helped me repeatedly in various ways. Almost every topic covered in this book was originally suggested by ecologist extraordinaire Roger Luckenbach. Robert Stebbins and Howard Wilshire provided me with considerable scientific background, while Debbie Sease and Elden Hughes acted as weather vanes on the political front. Gerry Hillier and Barbara Maxfield of the Riverside BLM (California Desert District headquarters) briefed me on points of environmental policy, as did Philippe Cohen of the University of California Natural Reserve system. Pat Brown-Berry, Peter Burk, and Ken Norris discussed various desert issues with me, and Lois Clark outlined the movement to create

Mojave County. Steve Smith of the Ridgecrest BLM served as a perennial human guidepost; Blaine Heald of the Needles BLM took me along on a ranger patrol that opened my eyes to many problems in desert regulation. Ed Rothfuss, former superintendent of Death Valley National Park (then Monument), and John Bailey of the Needles BLM described the logistic and political challenges facing their agencies. Tom Ganner offered both his opinions and a roof in Ridgecrest, and Michael and Eileen Keener left their light on for me whenever I passed through Helendale.

I was educated on individual topics by many experts from different fields. Bob Reynolds and Jane Nielson valiantly strove to penetrate my skull on the subject of geology, while Doug Prose and Don Moore helped me with my research on the military. Kristin Berry, Betty Burge, Bruce Bury, Wes Chambers, Tom Clark of the Barstow BLM, Judy Hohman of the U.S. Fish and Wildlife Service, Claudia Luke, Ron Marlow, and Ken Nagy furnished me with information about the desert tortoise, while Jeff Harris of the Clark County Planning Department, Terry Murphy of the Southern Nevada Homebuilders Association, Jean Mischel, and Nick Niarchos shed light on the social politics of the Las Vegas valley. I learned much about motorcycles from Bob Perkins, Maynard Hershon, Dave Mensing of the Riverside BLM, Bob Doornbos of Honda, and Louis McKey—the Phantom Duck himself, who provided me with transcripts from his court trials and public hearings. I found out about the effects of grazing from the late Bob Ausmuss, Steve Johnson, Jim Andre of the Granite Mountain Reserve, and Larry Morgan, Mike Blymeyer, and Kevin Madsen of the Needles BLM. Gary Huff, Dave Baker, and Lou Perry of the San Bernardino County Sheriff's Department, Jerry Bronson and John Blashley of the Barstow and Palm Springs BLM, and Bob Moon and Paul Henry of Joshua Tree National Park (then Monument) all took the time to tell me about crime in the desert.

I was schooled on nuclear issues and hazardous waste by Chris Brown of Citizen Alert, Lynn Anspaugh of Lawrence Livermore Laboratory, Ward Young and Phil Klasky of the (BAN) Waste Coalition, and Curt Gunn and John Key of the Ridgecrest and Riverside BLM. Karl Lindblom, Betty Hadley, Dave Reynolds, Marty Schiffenbauer, Chris Rauber, Jim Billingsley of Glamis Gold, Chuck Christman of the Mine Safety Health Administration, Ray Painter of Local #30 of the

International Longshoremen and Warehousemen's Union, and Larry Vredenburgh, Ahmed Mohsen, George Deverse, and Greg Thompson of the Bakersfield and Ridgecrest BLM educated me on various aspects of mining and the history of Randsburg.

Among the institutions that have shed light on different subjects for me are the Mineral Policy Center in Washington, D.C., the Palm Springs Desert Museum, the University of California library at Berkeley, the museum of the University of Nevada at Las Vegas, the Twenty Mule Team Museum in Boron, California, the San Francisco Camerawork Gallery, the California Academy of Sciences, Jane Scantlebury of the Berkeley Public Library, Pat Guy of the Bay Area Library and Information System, and the libraries and clipping files of Joshua Tree National Park and the Las Vegas *Sun*.

John Taft of the Conservation Endowment Fund, Frank Wheat, and Catherine Fox helped in different ways with fund-raising. In this department I am especially indebted to the amazing Patty Schifferle, who served as a crucial advocate in arranging completion funding. My heartfelt thanks to her; Jim Compton of the Compton Foundation; my editor, Bill Strachan; my agent, Fred Hill; and all the other friends and contacts whose help, support, and generosity enabled me to research and write *The Mojave*.

SELECTED BIBLIOGRAPHY

"Aerospace Valley Takes Off." *Newsweek*, July 15, 1985.

Anderson, Gloria. *Disposing of Low-Level Radioactive Waste—A Guidebook for Citizen Participation*. League of Women Voters, Southern California Regional Task Force, June 1990.

Anderson, Harry, "L.A.'s Housing Finds an Oasis in Antelope Valley." *Los Angeles Times*, February 26, 1990.

Anspaugh, L. R., et al. "Historical Estimates of External Gamma Exposure and Collective External Exposure from Testing at the Nevada Site—II." *Health Physics* 59, no. 5 (November 1990).

———. "Radiation-Related Monitoring and Environmental Research at the Nevada Test Site." In Robert H. Gray, ed., *Environmental Monitoring, Restoration and Assessment: What Have We Learned?* 28th Hanford Symposium on Health and the Environment. Sponsored by U.S. Department of Energy and Battelle, Pacific Northwest Laboratories, Richard, Washington, 1990.

Bailey, H. P. *The Climate of Southern California*. Berkeley: University of California Press, 1966.

Banham, Reyner. *Scenes in America Deserta*. Layton: Peregrine Smith, 1982.

Berry, Kristin H. *Avian Predation on the Desert Tortoise*. Bureau of Land Management Report to the Southern California Edison Company, 1985.

———. "Incidence of Gunshot Deaths in Desert Tortoise Populations in California." *Wildlife Society Bulletin* 14 (1986): 127–32.

———. *Livestock Grazing and the Desert Tortoise.* Trans. 43rd North American Wildlife and Natural Resources Conference. Washington, D.C.: Wildlife Management Institute, 1978.

———. *The Status of the Desert Tortoise in the United States.* Report from the Desert Tortoise Council to the U.S. Fish and Wildlife Service, 1984.

Bury, R. Bruce. *North American Tortoises: Conservation and Ecology.* Wildlife Research Report No. 12, U.S. Department of the Interior, Fish and Wildlife Service, Washington, D.C., 1982.

Carr, J. N. "Randsburg—and Beyond." *High Desert and Southern Sierra Newsletter* 2, no. 1 (January 1995).

Casebier, Dennis. *The Mojave Road.* Norco: Tales of the Mojave Road Publishing Company, 1975.

———. *Mojave Road Guide.* Norco: Tales of the Mojave Road Publishing Company, 1986.

———. *Reopening the Mojave Road.* Norco: Tales of the Mojave Road Publishing Company, 1983.

Castleman, Deke. *Las Vegas.* Oakland: Compass American Guides, 1991.

Caufield, Catherine. *Multiple Exposures.* New York: Harper and Row, 1989.

Chandler, John. "Pumping Threatens to Sink High Desert's Future." *Los Angeles Times*, March 17, 1991.

Christensen, Jon. "Sin City's Lucky Tortoise." *Nature Conservancy* 42, no. 4 (July/August 1992).

Clifford, Frank. "Panel Tackles Desert Nuclear Waste Issue." *Los Angeles Times*, July 8, 1994.

Coues, Elliott, ed. and trans. *On the Trail of a Spanish Pioneer—The Diary and Itinerary of Francisco Fray Garcés.* New York: Francis P. Harper, 1900.

Daniels, J. I., et al. *Pilot Study Risk Assessment for Selected Programs at the Nevada Test Site.* Lawrence Livermore Laboratory, University of California UCRL-LR-113891, June 1993.

Davidson, Keay. "Beating Atom Bombs into Post-Cold War Plowshares." *San Francisco Examiner*, December 29, 1991.

Davis, Mike. *City of Quartz: Excavating the Future in Los Angeles.* New York: Verso, 1991.

Dohrenwend, John C. "Basin and Range." Geological Society of America's Centennial Special Volume, No. 2, Chapter 9, 1987.

Environmental Handbook for Cyanide Leaching Projects. Department of the Interior, National Park Service, Energy, Mining, and Minerals Division.

Erikson, Kai. *A New Species of Trouble.* New York: Norton, 1994.

Fischer, Kenneth E. "Illegal Labs Pose Cleanup Problems." *Pollution Engineering* (November 1990).

"Flying Saucers at Giant Rock Airport." *California Traveler* 23 (December 1967).

Fradkin, Philip. *Fallout: An American Nuclear Tragedy.* Tucson: University of Arizona Press, 1989.

Friesen, H. N. *Summary of the Nevada Applied Ecology Group and Correlative Programs.* U.S. Department of Energy (DOE/NV-357), October 1992.

Gallagher, Carole. *American Ground Zero: The Secret Nuclear War.* Cambridge: MIT Press, 1993.

Galvin, John, ed. *Record of Travels of Francisco Garcés.* San Francisco: Howell Books, 1967.

Gilbert, R. O., et al. "Radionuclide Transport on the Nevada Test Site." *Health Physics* 55, no. 6 (December 1988).

Goin, Peter. *Nuclear Landscapes.* Baltimore: Johns Hopkins University Press, 1991.

Graham, Frank. "Gambling on Water." *Audubon* (July/August 1992).

Greene, Bob. "Up on Two Wheels." *Hot Rod* (April 1970).

Hensher, Alan, and Larry Vredenburgh. *Ghost Towns of the Upper Mojave Desert—A Special Research Report.* Los Angeles, 1987.

Hogan, James T. *Ecology of the Joshua Tree in Joshua Tree National Monument, California.* Master's Thesis, University of Nevada at Las Vegas, May 1977.

Horning, John. *Grazing to Extinction: Endangered, Threatened and Candidate Species Imperiled by Livestock Grazing on Western Public Lands.* Report from the National Wildlife Federation, June 1994.

"How the Hermit of Giant Rock Sealed His Strange Secret." *The American Weekly*, November 8, 1942.

Howard, George W. "The Desert Training Center/California-Arizona Maneuver Area." *Journal of Arizona History* (Autumn 1985).

Jaeger, Edmund C. *The California Deserts* (3rd ed.). Stanford: Stanford University Press, 1955.

———. *Desert Wild Flowers.* Stanford: Stanford University Press, 1940.

———. *Desert Wildlife.* Stanford: Stanford University Press, 1950.

———. *The North American Deserts.* Stanford: Stanford University Press, 1957.

Jarvis, Elena. "Rambo's Racers." *Defenders* (January/February 1990).

Johnson, Hyrum B. "Vegetation and Plant Communities of Southern California Deserts." California Native Plant Society Special Publication No. 2, 1976.

Kelly, Susan Croce, and Quinta Scott. *Route 66—The Highway and Its People.* Norman: University of Oklahoma Press, 1988.

Koranda, J. J., et al. *Radioecological Studies Related to the Baneberry Event.* Lawrence Livermore National Laboratory, University of California (UCRL-51027), March 1, 1971.

Krzysick, Anthony J. *Ecological Assessment of the Effects of Army Training Activities on a Desert Ecosystem: National Training Center, Fort Irwin, California.* U.S. Army Corps of Engineers, Construction Engineering Research Laboratory, Technical Report N-85/13, June 1985.

Larson, Peggy. *The Deserts of the Southwest: A Sierra Club Naturalist's Guide.* San Francisco: Sierra Club Books, 1977.

LaRue, Steve. "More Testing Sought for Ground Water in Radioactive Dump Site." *San Diego Union-Tribune,* September 2, 1994.

Las Vegas Review-Journal, Nevada Development Authority, and First Interstate Bank of Nevada, N.A. *Las Vegas Perspective.* Las Vegas: University of Nevada, 1991.

Laudermilk, J. D., and Philip A. Munz. "Plants in the Dung of Nothrotherium from Gypsum Cave, Nevada." Carnegie Institute of Washington, Contributions to *Paleontology* 453 (1934): 29–37.

Limerick, Patricia Nelson. *Desert Passages: Encounters with the American Deserts.* Niwot: University Press of Colorado, 1989.

Lingenfelter, Richard E. *Death Valley and the Amargosa: A Land of Illusion.* Berkeley: University of California Press, 1986.

Lintz, Joseph, ed. "Quaternary Geology of the East Mojave Desert." *Western Geological Excursions* 1, Field Trip #14, 1984.

Luke, Claudia, Alice Karl, and Pam Garcia. *A Review of the Status of the Desert Tortoise.* Tiburon, Calif.: Biosystems Analysis, 1991.

McArthur, Richard D. "Radionuclides in Surface Soil at the Nevada Test Site." Water Resources Center Publication #45077 (DOE/NV 10845-02), Desert Research Institute, University of Nevada, August 1991.

MacMahon, James. *Deserts.* New York: Alfred A. Knopf, 1985.

McKelvey, Susan D. *Yuccas of the Southwestern United States.* Jamaica Plain, Mass.: Arnold Arboretum of Harvard University, 1938.

Marinacci, Mike. *Mysterious California: Strange Places and Eerie Phenomena in the Golden State.* Los Angeles: Panpipes Press, 1988.

Merriam, C. Hart. "The Death Valley Expedition: A Biological Survey of Parts of California, Nevada, Arizona, and Utah—Part 7: Notes on the Geographic and Vertical Distribution of Cactuses, Yuccas, and Agave." *North American Fauna* 7, no. 2 (1893): 345–59.

Miller, Alden H., and Robert C. Stebbins. *The Lives of Desert Animals in Joshua Tree National Monument.* Berkeley: University of California Press, 1964.

Miller, Richard L. *Under the Cloud: The Decades of Nuclear Testing.* New York: Free Press, 1986.

Moehring, Eugene P. *Resort City in the Sunbelt—Las Vegas 1930–1970.* Reno: University of Nevada Press, 1989.

Munz, Philip A. "Let's Save the Short-Leaved Joshua Tree." *National Parks* 22, no. 92 (January/February 1948): 8–12.

Murphy, Bob. *Desert Shadows: The Bizarre and Frightening True Story of Charles Manson.* Billings, Mont.: Falcon Press, 1986.

Mydans, Seth. "Urban Sprawl Has Plans for a Move to the Desert." *New York Times,* March 16, 1989.

Nagy, K., and P. A. Medica. "Physiological Ecology of Desert Tortoises in Southern Nevada." *Herpetologica* 42, no. 1 (1986): 73–92.

O'Farrell, Thomas P., and LaVerne A. Emery. *Ecology of the Nevada Test Site: A Narrative Summary and Annotated Bibliography* (NVO-157). Applied Ecology and Physiology Center, Desert Research Institute, Boulder City: University of Nevada, 1976 (prepared for U.S. Energy Research and Development Administration, Nevada Operations Office, under Contract AT [29-2]-1253, Modification 19).

Paher, Stanley W. *Las Vegas: As It Began, As It Grew.* Las Vegas: Nevada Publications, 1977.

Pearson, June. "This Is a True Story About Mr. Van Tassel Who Lives in a Rock and Has a Time Machine." *Desert Magazine* (March 1967).

Peterson, Peter Victor. *Native Trees of Southern California.* Berkeley: University of California Press, 1966.

Poirier, Richard. *A World Elsewhere: The Place of Style in American Literature.* New York: Oxford University Press, 1966.

Pope, Clifford H. *Turtles of the United States and Canada.* New York: Alfred A. Knopf, 1939.

Pratt, Helen. "The Mystery of Giant Rock." *Desert Spotlight* (September 1947).

Prose, Doug V. *Land Disturbances from Military Training Operations, Mojave Desert, California.* U.S. Department of the Interior, U.S. Geological Survey, Map MF-1855, 1986.

"Rand Mining Company." *Skillings Mining Review* (June 11, 1994).

Reisner, Marc. *Cadillac Desert: The American West and Its Disappearing Water.* New York: Viking Penguin, 1986.

Reith, Charles C., and Bruce M. Thomson, eds. *Deserts as Dumps: The Disposal of Hazardous Material in Arid Ecosystems.* Albuquerque: University of New Mexico Press, 1992.

Robbins, Jim. "A New Kind of Mining Disaster." *New York Times,* February 5, 1989.

Rowlands, Peter. *The Vegetation Dynamics of the Joshua Tree in the Southwestern United States of America,* doctoral dissertation, University of California at Riverside, June 1978.

Schine, Eric. "Has U.S. Ecology Cleaned Up Its Act?" *Business Week*, November 8, 1993.

Sharp, Robert P. *Geology Field Guide to Southern California*. Dubuque, Iowa: Kendall/Hunt Publishing Company, 1975.

Shore, Debra. "Badlands." *Outside* (July 1994).

Short-Term Habitat Conservation Plan for the Desert Tortoise in Las Vegas Valley, Clark County, Nevada. San Diego: Regional Environmental Consultants, 1991.

Shreve, Forrest, and Ira L. Wiggins. *Vegetation and Flora of the Sonoran Desert*. Stanford: Stanford University Press, 1964.

Solnit, Rebecca. *Savage Dreams: A Journey into the Hidden Wars of the American West*. San Francisco: Sierra Club Books, 1994.

Starry, Roberta Martin. *Exploring the Ghost Town Desert*. Pasadena: Ward Ritchie Press, 1973.

Steinbeck, John. *The Grapes of Wrath*. New York: Viking Press, 1939.

Steinhart, Peter. "Desert Folly, Desert Hopes." *Defenders* (January/February 1990).

The Story of Borax. Los Angeles: U.S. Borax and Chemical Corporation, 1979.

Story, Ronald D., ed. *Encyclopedia of UFOs*. Garden City, N.Y.: Doubleday, 1980.

Titus, A. Constandina. *Bombs in the Backyard: Atomic Testing and American Politics*. Reno: University of Nevada Press, 1986.

"U.S. Agents Investigating Critzer Mystery." *Desert Trail*, July 31, 1942.

U.S. Department of the Interior, Bureau of Reclamation. *Construction of Hoover Dam*. Las Vegas: K.C. Publications, 1976.

U.S. General Accounting Office. *Rangeland Management: BLM's Hot Desert Grazing Program Merits Reconsideration*. Report to the Chairman, Subcommittee on National Parks and Public Lands, Committee on Interior and Insular Affairs, House of Representatives, RCED 92-12.

Van Dyke, Dix. *A Modern Interpretation of the Garcés Route*. Los Angeles: Annual Publications of the Historical Society of Southern California 13, 1927.

Vredenburgh, Larry M. *A Brief Sketch of the Mining History of the Western Mojave Desert and Southeastern Sierra Nevada*, April 1993.

Vredenburgh, Larry M., Gary L. Shumway, and Russell D. Hartill. *Desert Fever: An Overview of Mining in the California Desert*. Canoga Park: Living West Press, 1981.

Wagner, Frederick H. "Livestock Grazing and the Livestock Industry." In H. P. Brokaw, ed., *Wildlife and America*. Washington, D.C.: U.S. Government Printing Office, 1978.

Wald, Johanna, and David Albersworth. *Our Ailing Public Rangelands*. Reports by the National Wildlife Federation and Natural Resources Defense Council, December 1985 and October 1989.

Wallis, Michael. *Route 66: The Mother Road*. New York: St. Martin's Press, 1990.

Webb, Robert H., and Howard Wilshire, eds. *Environmental Effects of Off-Road Vehicles*. New York: Springer-Verlag, 1983.

Webber, John Milton. *Yuccas of the Southwest*. U.S. Department of Agriculture Monograph No. 17, 1953.

Weight, Harold O. *Twenty Mule Team Days in Death Valley*. Twentynine Palms, Calif.: Calico Press, 1955.

Wells, Philip V. "Macrofossil Analysis of Wood Rat (Neotoma) Middens as Key to the Quaternary Vegetational History of Arid America." *Quaternary Research* 6 (1976): 223–48.

Wells, Philip V., and Rainer Berger. "Late Pleistocene History of Coniferous Woodland in the Mojave Desert." *Science* 155 (1967): 1640–47.

Wells, Philip V., and C. D. Jorgensen. "Pleistocene Wood Rat Middens and Climatic Change in the Mojave Desert." *Science* 143 (1964): 1171–74.

Wilshire, Howard G. *Waste Dumps on Public Lands: Theory and Practice of Environmental Impact Studies*. Unpublished manuscript.

Worman, Frederick C. *Anatomy of the Nevada Test Site*. Los Alamos Scientific Laboratory, University of California, 1963.

Wynn, Marcia Rittenhouse. *Desert Bonanza: The Story of Early Randsburg, Mojave Desert Mining Camp*. Glendale: A. H. Clark, 1963.

INDEX